Righting the Longstreet
Record at Gettysburg

Also by Cory M. Pfarr
and from McFarland

*Longstreet at Gettysburg:
A Critical Reassessment* (2019)

Righting the Longstreet Record at Gettysburg

Six Matters of Controversy and Confusion

CORY M. PFARR

Foreword by James A. Hessler

McFarland & Company, Inc., Publishers
Jefferson, North Carolina

This book has undergone peer review.

LIBRARY OF CONGRESS CATALOGUING-IN-PUBLICATION DATA

Names: Pfarr, Cory M., 1989– author.
Title: Righting the Longstreet record at Gettysburg :
six matters of controversy and confusion / Cory M. Pfarr.
Other titles: Six matters of controversy and confusion
Description: Jefferson, North Carolina : McFarland & Company, Inc., Publishers, 2023 |
Includes bibliographical references and index.
Identifiers: LCCN 2023008791 | ISBN 9781476685977 (paperback : acid free paper) ∞
ISBN 9781476648699 (ebook)
Subjects: LCSH: Gettysburg, Battle of, Gettysburg, Pa., 1863. |
Longstreet, James, 1821-1904—Military leadership. | Military art and science—
Confederate States of America. | BISAC: HISTORY / United States /
Civil War Period (1850-1877) | HISTORY / Military / United States
Classification: LCC E475.53 .P485 2023 | DDC 973.7/349—dc23
LC record available at https://lccn.loc.gov/2023008791

BRITISH LIBRARY CATALOGUING DATA ARE AVAILABLE

**ISBN (print) 978-1-4766-8597-7
ISBN (ebook) 978-1-4766-4869-9**

© 2023 Cory M. Pfarr. All rights reserved

*No part of this book may be reproduced or transmitted in any form
or by any means, electronic or mechanical, including photocopying
or recording, or by any information storage and retrieval system,
without permission in writing from the publisher.*

Front cover image: "James Longstreet, in the postwar years."
(HistoryInFullColor.com)

Printed in the United States of America

*McFarland & Company, Inc., Publishers
Box 611, Jefferson, North Carolina 28640
www.mcfarlandpub.com*

For Glenn Tucker,
a courageous historian

Acknowledgments

Writing a book is always a challenge. It is a long-term endeavor that takes commitment and perseverance. It is an even more formidable task when you are juggling a full-time job, a growing, active family, and a faith life that means you strive to always put God first. I could not have completed this four-year project without my wife, Michelle, who not only serves as a sounding board (in times of frustration) and a source of constant encouragement, but also happens to be an impeccable editor with a keen eye for detail and a discerning ear for proper tone. As always, this book would not have been possible without her. The same goes for my four wonderful children, Anita, David, Abigail, and Isabel. They not only demonstrated great patience when I was oftentimes working on this project after work in the evenings or on the weekends, but they also offered a constant source of love, inspiration, and support in ways they do not yet entirely understand. I would also like to thank my editor, Mike Valentino, who, in short, saw things I did not and fixed them. It was a great pleasure to work with Mike and I look forward to engaging with him again on future projects. Thank you also to the McFarland team for their professionalism throughout the entire publication process. And last but never least, thank you to God and His Son, Jesus Christ. I would not be able to do anything without Him. "With man it is impossible, but not with God. For all things are possible with God" (Mark 10:27 ESV).

Table of Contents

Acknowledgments — vi

Maps by Hal Jespersen — x

Foreword by James A. Hessler — 1

Introduction — 5

Essay 1. The Reverend Jones Pens an Essay: Examining the Roots of the Longstreet-Gettysburg Controversy — 7

Essay 2. A Letter to General Sickles: Longstreet's July 2 Attack — 27

Essay 3. The Force of Circumstances: Reconnaissance Activities on Longstreet's Front, July 2 — 66

Essay 4. A Severe Case: Diagnosing the Treatment of Longstreet's Countermarch — 94

Essay 5. Under Hill or Longstreet? Anderson's Division on July 2 — 121

Essay 6. Suppressed No More: Helen Longstreet's *Lee and Longstreet at High Tide* — 139

Chapter Notes — 173

Bibliography — 195

Index — 201

Maps

BY HAL JESPERSEN

Sickles' Positions, 2:30–3:30 p.m., July 2, 1863	35
Plans for July 2, 1863	43
Actual Attacks, July 2, 1863	45
Hood's Digression, 4:15 p.m., July 2, 1863	53
Peach Orchard and Cemetery Ridge, 6–7 p.m., July 2, 1863	56
End of McLaws' Attack, 7:30 p.m., July 2, 1863	62
Confederate Reconnaissance, July 1–2, 1863	87
Longstreet's March, 1–3 p.m., July 2, 1863	99
Anderson's Attack, July 2, 1863	124

The historian should be fearless and incorruptible; a man of independence, loving frankness and truth; one who, as the poet says, calls a fig a fig and a spade a spade.... He should never consider what this or that man will think, but should state the facts as they really occurred.
—Lucian (c. AD 125–180)

Foreword

BY JAMES A. HESSLER

My own introduction to Lieutenant General James Longstreet came from Michael Shaara's popular 1975 novel *The Killer Angels,* which it must be said is nearly 50 years old at the time of this writing. I liked the Longstreet that I met in those pages. He was cool-headed, all-knowing, and I was informed that he was a defensive genius. The novel encouraged me to read actual histories, however, and I learned intriguingly that Longstreet was blamed by many of his former colleagues after the war for losing the battle and dishonoring Robert E. Lee's memory. Some historical versions even presented Longstreet as a sulking, insubordinate malcontent. None of this prevented me from liking Longstreet even more when he appeared in the 1993 motion picture *Gettysburg*. The only sin committed by big-screen Longstreet, besides actor Tom Berenger's inhuman beard, was the fact that he could not stop a seemingly off-kilter General Lee from attacking "the high ground" repeatedly. That was my indoctrination to James Longstreet, and I know that *millions* more people received the same from the classic novel and cultishly popular movie.

Yet, the historical fact remains that Longstreet was blamed by several ex-Confederates for the Gettysburg outcome. As many readers are likely aware, a postwar smear campaign led by the likes of former Southern generals Jubal Early and William N. Pendleton attempted to deflect blame for the defeat in Pennsylvania away from the then-deceased Lee and toward his "Old Warhorse" instead. Longstreet was accused, among a host of other sins, of maneuvering his troops too slowly at Gettysburg, sulking when Lee reneged on a promise to fight defensively, and even outright disobedience of Lee's orders. The upshot of these allegations was that large portions of early Civil War historians were willing to blame Longstreet for the Confederate defeat at Gettysburg, and the historiography was severely impaired as a result. Pro-Longstreet assessments did appear in the literature, but generally much later, and by then the damage to Longstreet's reputation was done. It is not my intention to rehash the causes and outcomes of Longstreet's postwar troubles here. Readers should refer to William Garrett Piston's *Lee's Tarnished Lieutenant: James Longstreet and His Place in Southern History* (1987) and Cory Pfarr's *Longstreet at Gettysburg: A Critical Reassessment* (2019) for more details.

Despite the sheer volume of published Gettysburg material, it might surprise some readers that a thorough point-by-point assessment of every major allegation leveled against Longstreet regarding the Gettysburg campaign was not produced until Pfarr's aforementioned *Longstreet at Gettysburg* in 2019. The success of Pfarr's book proved that there was still an audience eager to openly evaluate Longstreet's Gettysburg actions. While promoting *Longstreet at Gettysburg* on the book-signing circuit, Pfarr found himself often directed to certain common topics during question-and-answer sessions or reader interactions. Pfarr believed that public confusion on these topics often stemmed from misleading assertions published in popular battle histories. To address these concerns, Pfarr has crafted six new Longstreet-related essays for this volume.

The first contribution sets the stage with "The Reverend Jones Pens an Essay: Examining the Roots of the Longstreet-Gettysburg Controversy." In this essay, Pfarr discusses the role played by the Reverend John W. Jones and others in assassinating Longstreet's character in the pages of the *Southern Historical Society Papers*. Pfarr adds an aspect of the debate that has long interested me: the extent to which Longstreet fueled the fire with his own contributions to William Swinton's 1866 book, *Campaigns of the Army of the Potomac*. Pfarr illustrates how the Reverend Jones and others shrewdly manipulated the record, including Longstreet's own actions, to present him as disloyal to Lee's memory.

As I am Union general Daniel E. Sickles' primary modern biographer, Pfarr's second essay, "A Letter to General Sickles: Longstreet's July 2 Attack," is of obvious interest. In addition to having written about Sickles, I speak frequently about him to groups across the country. I attest to the fact that Gettysburg enthusiasts continue to debate the merits or demerits of Sickles' Gettysburg actions and will always do so. During my own encounters, audiences are frequently surprised to learn of the friendship that existed between Longstreet and Sickles during their twilight years. Both men readily supported each other when called upon. "I believe it is now conceded that the advanced position at the Peach-Orchard," Longstreet wrote to Sickles near the end of his life, "taken by your corps and under your orders saved that battle-field to the Union cause." In this essay, Pfarr examines the arguments that both generals made in favor of the other's performance, Longstreet's belief that Sickles' controversial advance from Cemetery Ridge aided the Union cause, and Pfarr's own assessment of the impacts. Gettysburg enthusiasts will continue to debate this topic, and that's a good thing, but read Pfarr's reflections to see where the historical evidence leads him.

Although the so-called "sunrise attack order" (a false allegation that Lee expected Longstreet to attack near sunrise on July 2) has long been discredited by serious historians, the perception that Longstreet moved his troops too slowly on July 2 was perhaps the hardest criticism for him to dodge. To briefly recap the traditional interpretation of events on July 2: General Lee ordered reconnaissance of the Army of the Potomac's left flank. The results helped convince Lee that the enemy's position was vulnerable and accessible. Longstreet was assigned to attack the Union's left, but his two divisions had to "countermarch" (i.e., turn around) to avoid Northern signalmen on Little Round Top and took several hours to reach their jumping-off point. When they arrived, the Union Army's position differed significantly from when the reconnaissance occurred several hours earlier.

The events leading to and resulting in "Longstreet's countermarch" have long been steeped in controversy. Longstreet's postwar critics blamed him for the fiasco. Pfarr's third essay, "The Force of Circumstances: Reconnaissance Activities on Longstreet's Front, July 2," may become the most controversial in this volume. Pfarr takes numerous academic and popular historians to task for what he considers to be misinterpretations of postwar accounts, the actual timing of the reconnaissance, and unwarranted criticism of Longstreet's own alleged inactivity.

The countermarch itself is considered in the next reflection, "A Severe Case: Diagnosing the Treatment of Longstreet's Countermarch." I have led many tours over the ground that comprised Longstreet's countermarch. I can attest that it remains an area of interest to Gettysburg enthusiasts, and varying theories abound. In this essay, Pfarr addresses factors such as the lack of historical source material, Longstreet's need for concealment, and what he considers "the prevalent modern allegation that Longstreet blundered in allowing McLaws to lead the countermarch instead of just about-facing the column and letting Hood take the lead."

Academic and professional historians sometimes forget that battle interpretations can be influenced by public misconceptions that exist in social media forums or at gatherings such as Civil War roundtables. Pfarr addresses this in "Under Hill or Longstreet? Anderson's Division on July 2." Pfarr tackles confusion over whether General Richard H. Anderson's Third Corps division was under Longstreet's direct supervision during the second day. He provocatively proposes that historians have used this uncertainty to knowingly perpetuate an agenda that blamed Longstreet for any mismanagement of Anderson's men.

Pfarr closes his reflections with "Suppressed No More: Helen Longstreet's *Lee and Longstreet at High Tide*." In this essay, Pfarr reintroduces readers to Helen Dortch Longstreet, Longstreet's second wife and widow, who fought to protect her husband's memory following his death. The focus of this essay is an examination of her published defense of General Longstreet's military career and his performance at Gettysburg. Historians have dismissed or deemphasized Helen's work as an unreliable "defense" of her husband due to her obvious bias. Pfarr challenges readers and historians to compare Helen's pro–Longstreet bias with the obvious anti–Longstreet bias of other memoirs written during this period. Pfarr asks, "Who are we to believe?" Regardless of where one lands with her historical work, Pfarr successfully demonstrates the loyalty that this remarkable woman retained for her husband long after his death.

As I stated at the outset, my introduction to Longstreet was a favorable one from popular literature. I subsequently became a public historian, the author of three Gettysburg-related books (all of which included Longstreet in my central theses), and a licensed battlefield guide at Gettysburg National Military Park (GNMP). While touring the Gettysburg battlefield with hundreds of visitors annually, I can attest that more modern visitors arrive with the positive perception of Shaara's Longstreet rather than Jubal Early's traitorous version. I remain a firm believer, however, that Gettysburg students should familiarize themselves with all aspects of the historiography. Those who do so will encounter the biased musings of the *Southern Historical Society Papers* and certain anti–Longstreet historians. To balance the historiography, we now have Pfarr's two volumes to assess the criticism of Lee's "Old Warhorse" and the motives behind them. In my opinion, Longstreet has finally achieved some level of victory at Gettysburg thanks to books such as this one.

James A. Hessler is a licensed battlefield guide at Gettysburg National Military Park (GNMP) and co-author of *Gettysburg's Peach Orchard: Longstreet, Sickles, and the Bloody Fight for the "Commanding Ground" Along the Emmitsburg Road* (with Savas Beatie, 2019).

Introduction

I'll be the first to admit that it was somewhat difficult for me to write an introduction for this volume of essays. The difficulty was not for lack of ideas or topics to cover. I could have easily gone on at some length about topics such as my reasons for writing two books about Longstreet at Gettysburg, or what initially precipitated my interest in James Longstreet, or for that matter the American Civil War in general. However, as with anything I set out to write, I want to offer the reader something fresh, something relatively impactful that might bear fruit for future history and historians.

The principal reason for not wanting to include an introduction to this book, to just lead with the foreword and go right into the first essay, was because I think the less of me that is in the book, the better. With this particular topic, and in fact with all topics I research and write about, my intention is always that the work speak for itself. Like Helen Longstreet, the general's second wife, intended for her book, *Lee and Longstreet at High Tide: Gettysburg in the Light of the Official Records*, my focus was to simply produce a "carefully sifted story of the records."

Too often in historical works, and especially American Civil War studies covering a battle at the tactical level, historians have woven a lot of themselves into their work. We can see this in rather blatant ways, as when historians take on the roles of the "Monday morning quarterback" or the "armchair general"—sliding down the slippery slope of imposing "if only" and "should have" judgments on historical figures who were acting in the moment and with the information available to them at the time, not decades later, or in the case of the Civil War, well over a century and a half later. Another way I think some historians have—unfortunately for the historical record—left their personal mark on this topic and similar topics is by filling in blanks in the historical record without a firm rooting in the text by advancing a personal judgment despite not having enough primary source material to make a judgment either way on a controversial issue. Yet another tendency, which even surprised me when I was examining some of the most influential Gettysburg secondary source material for this book, is when some historians actually alter the primary source material so it better suits their narrative. In certain other cases, historians have even gone so far as to use evidence from one day of the battle to support a claim from a different day of the battle.

We must not engage in any of these imprudent practices when handling historical topics. We owe it to our historical subjects and to contemporary and future students of the war to try our best to always stick to the primary text, cross-reference sources, and be okay with saying "I don't know" whenever the source record is simply too scant to advance a definitive conclusion. And absolutely, under no circumstance, should we ever be altering sources to fit a narrative.

So, as to keep this brief, I will end with a recommendation I have given (when asked) to many who aspire to study the Battle of Gettysburg more deeply, or really any historical topic, Civil War or otherwise. If you are an avid student of something, do your own careful research. If you are passionate about a topic and think it matters, immerse yourself in it. Do not settle for the secondary sources that have come before. If you are seeing something different in the primary source record that consistently or significantly differs with past scholarship, pursue it and see where it leads. Depend on primary source research, not just on a reading, however careful, of secondary source commentary. Indeed, part of the reason why the Longstreet at Gettysburg topic has been in the state it has been for well over a century is because most have simply accepted the status quo traditional narrative that has solidified over time through secondary source publications. The congealed plotline remained largely unchallenged, and a rebuttal was left unarticulated in comprehensive book form.

My experience with writing this book and *Longstreet at Gettysburg: A Critical Reassessment* was really quite as simple and challenging as that—identifying a consequential knowledge gap and pursuing it to its core. Had I not found a significant knowledge gap, I simply would have never pursued it or written these books, no matter how interesting I personally found James Longstreet or his actions at Gettysburg.

My ultimate hope is that you find this work rewarding for your continual efforts to better understand the Battle of Gettysburg and James Longstreet's substantial role in it.

Essay 1

The Reverend Jones Pens an Essay

Examining the Roots of the Longstreet-Gettysburg Controversy

Lee was never really beaten. Lee could not be beaten! Overpowered, foiled in his efforts, he might be, but never defeated.—John B. Gordon

"It is all my fault," meant just what it said.—James Longstreet

"The laurel crown of the brave leader," "the indomitable fighter," "the courageous soldier," "our grand old chief," "the peerless soldier of the centuries"—such were the myriad ways in which the Reverend John William Jones described Robert E. Lee, the former commander of the Confederate Army of Northern Virginia during the American Civil War, in a February 14, 1896, letter to the Richmond, Virginia, *Dispatch*. Jones' lavish epithets were customary. Well before 1896, it became almost mandatory for many ex-Confederates, particularly those who had served in some capacity under Lee, to describe their former leader in this fashion. The coterie of postwar Lee admirers, whose long-standing credo was that Lee had neither made a wrong decision nor committed any blunder during the war, used these epithets almost as codewords to distinguish between those who, in their eyes, remained loyal to Lee and those whose loyalty had wavered. In advancing such pandering language, Jones wanted readers to know he was a loyalist; one of them; a zealous Lee defender.

As he sat down to write his letter to the *Dispatch*, dawn broke on yet another mid-winter morning in Virginia. Jones was then busy serving as campus minister at the Miller School in Crozet. He had been putting the finishing touches on a new textbook, *School History of the United States*, but today the Baptist minister would put pen to paper to pick a familiar bone with Lee's former senior lieutenant general, James Longstreet.

Jones had served as secretary for the Southern Historical Society from 1875 to 1887, and was one of the founding members of the *Southern Historical Society Papers* (*SHSP*) in 1877. It would not be an exaggeration to say that the impetus behind the publication of those papers *was* the Longstreet-Gettysburg Controversy, which then involved debate over a cacophony of contentious issues, most prominently Lee's tactical vision for the summer 1863 campaign; Lee's alleged order for Longstreet to attack the Federals at sunrise or "early in the morning" on July 2; Longstreet's attitude and generalship, in light of Lee's non-adoption of his tactical suggestions; and Lee's supposed order for Longstreet to attack simultaneously with Confederate Second Corps commander, Richard S. Ewell, on the early morning of July 3.[1]

Many of the initial *SHSP* volumes focused almost entirely on Longstreet's controversial Gettysburg performance, especially Volumes 4 and 5. In Volume 4, Jones published several responses to an inquiry from French historian Comte de Paris, who had asked for insight as to why the South lost at Gettysburg from Confederates who had participated in the battle. In March and April 1877, several Confederate officers wrote Jones, to include Jubal Early, Fitzhugh Lee, William Allan, Walter Taylor, and others, who collectively ascribed the loss at Gettysburg mainly to Longstreet's actions. Jones also apparently wrote Longstreet, asking for his views; however, Lee's "Old Warhorse" went on to publish his first lengthy, public accounts of Gettysburg elsewhere, in the *Philadelphia Weekly Times* in November 1877 and February 1878. Ultimately, though, Jones did not take "no" for an answer, and subsequently published Longstreet's two *Times* articles in Volume 5 of the *SHSP* in 1878, along with several fiery replies from others, most notably Jubal Early. As the specific arguments made in these articles have been amply covered elsewhere and are outside the scope of this essay, it suffices to say that antagonistic barbs were traded. Demonstrative of the belligerent charges Jones and others brought to bear against Longstreet's actions at Gettysburg was the minister's encouragement of another anti–Longstreet group member, "I am anxious for you to slice up what is left of Longstreet." On yet another occasion, Jones wrote, "I suspect that Longstreet is very sick of Gettysburg before this. Certainly there has not been left 'a grease spot' of him."[2]

And so, in mid–February 1896, when Jones read an article in the Richmond *Dispatch* that he quickly judged left out "some very important points in the history of the controversy," the minister could not just idly sit by. He was provoked to action. Jones was concerned that the recently published article did not sufficiently describe the origins of the postwar

The Reverend John William Jones in the postwar years (Wikimedia Commons).

"Longstreet-Gettysburg Controversy," especially in its narrative regarding "who commenced it." Jones sought to set the record straight.

To begin, Jones first addressed General Lee's infamous statement following the repulse of the Pickett-Pettigrew-Trimble Charge on the third day of the battle: "This is all my fault; I have lost this battle, and you must help me out of it as best you can." Like many Lee admirers in the postwar years, Jones dismissed Lee's statement, characterizing it as a mere representation of the general's sublime humility and nobility, not as an unvarnished truth. To Jones, and many other ex-Confederates, Lee's statement originated with his supreme virtue and out of concern that divisiveness would envelop the Confederate High Command after the July 3 repulse and the loss of the battle more generally. Lee was purposefully putting everything on his shoulders, they claimed. Jones went even further, alleging Lee "had shown the same superb magnanimity as when at Chancellorsville he had *given* [emphasis added] the glory of the victory to Stonewall Jackson." In Jones' estimation, even when it came to Jackson's flank attack at the April–May 1863 Battle of Chancellorsville, the triumph actually belonged to Lee, and in an act of admirable humility, Lee had "given the glory" to Jackson.

In notable contrast to Jones' grandiose approach in describing the alleged motivation undergirding Lee's statement, Longstreet's postwar comments on Lee's statement would characteristically prove blunter and more resolute. "This remark, made just after the battle, 'It is all my fault,' meant just what it said," Longstreet asserted. It was these kinds of comments that most rankled the postwar Lee admirers, especially since they contrasted so sharply with their own. To them, Longstreet's matter-of-fact commentary only demonstrated he was not one of them, and refused to be. They also equated his remarks with disrespect and disloyalty to Lee. As an ex-Confederate, the expectation was one was either all-in on Lee, or conversely, a pariah. Neglecting to heap lavish praise on Lee or defend his every action and decision, led to classification as an arrogant egotist. Realistically, Longstreet clearly meant no disrespect toward Lee in holding this and other similar opinions of Lee's Gettysburg performance. Adding to his analysis of Lee's post–July 3 attack statement, Longstreet observed it only reinforced "the nobility and magnanimity of that remark, when we reflect that it was the utterance of a deep-felt truth, rather than a mere sentiment."[3]

Jones explained to the *Dispatch* that Lee's "it is all my fault" remark directly prevented other Confederate participants at Gettysburg from laying blame elsewhere immediately after the battle, and more generally, in the years leading up to Lee's death in October 1870. "There was in army circles after the battle of Gettysburg a good deal of talk as to the causes of our failure, and it seemed to be very generally understood that the fault was not Lee's, but that his orders had been disobeyed," Jones contended, while alleging that "no one was disposed to publish any criticisms of his [Lee's] subordinates … to preserve among themselves the harmony and good-will counselled by their great commander." To Jones, Longstreet shattered that "harmony and good-will" in the spring of 1866 when *New York Times* correspondent William Swinton published his book, *Campaigns of the Army of the Potomac*. As part of Swinton's research for the book's Gettysburg section, the journalist sought out Longstreet, who ultimately provided commentary on the Confederate side of the battle throughout a series of interviews. Jones held that Longstreet's contributions to Swinton's book, and most specifically, the character of those contributions, gave life to the Longstreet-Gettysburg controversy. The minister described Longstreet's contributions to Swinton's *Campaigns* as "the first publication made in reference to the cause of our defeat at Gettysburg by any Confederate who participated in the battle, so far as I have been able to ascertain," while alleging "it will thus be clearly seen that General Longstreet first began this controversy by his criticisms of General Lee." It was these "criticisms of General Lee," which Jones otherwise described as "severe" criticisms against "the idolized commander of the Army of Northern Virginia," that most upset the minister and, according to Jones, many officers who fought at Gettysburg. Jones, who served as a Baptist minister in Lexington, Virginia, and campus minister at Washington College (where Lee served as president from 1865 to 1870), claimed Lee possessed a copy of Swinton's book and had even read some of it, but never said or wrote anything about it. Likewise, Jones contended, "none of Lee's subordinates thought proper to make answer" to Longstreet.[4]

To my knowledge and research, Jones was correct that in providing commentary on the causes of the Confederate defeat at Gettysburg in Swinton's book, Longstreet was the first Southern officer at the battle to have his opinion published on the matter. Longstreet was clearly a contributor to the controversy. A footnote in Swinton's Gettysburg section read, "This, and subsequent revelations of the purposes and sentiments of Lee, I derive from General Longstreet, who, in full and free conversation with the writer, after the close of the war, threw much light on the motives and conduct of Lee during this campaign." Additionally, though Swinton was the author and perhaps tweaked Longstreet's contributions—just how much, we will never know—it is clear "Lee's Old Warhorse" was the originator of the remarks, for as Jones underscored, "the language ... bears a remarkable resemblance to what General Longstreet has since printed over his own signature."[5]

What did Longstreet actually contribute to Swinton's book? Did Longstreet criticize Lee? Was it "severe" criticism? Some of these questions can be addressed; others would only render subjective commentary, providing varied judgments subject to the eye of the beholder.

Longstreet's first main point was one he consistently repeated both in private letters and postwar publications until his death; namely, that the Confederates' summer 1863 campaign was supposed to be guided by the strategic offensive, but tactical defensive. Swinton wrote that Lee "was willing to" risk a "general battle" "only in case he should, by maneuvring [sic], secure the advantage of the defensive, or some special opening for a blow, should his opponent make a false move. Indeed, in entering upon the campaign, General Lee expressly promised his corps-commanders that he would not assume a tactical offensive, but force his antagonist to attack him." Beyond regularly discounting Longstreet's argument as a fabrication, Lee's postwar admirers typically characterized this particular claim as arrogant, believing it demonstrated Lee's senior lieutenant thought he knew better than Lee which tactical approach was best for the army. For Jones' part, he characterized Longstreet's allegation as a "claim that we lost Gettysburg because the Napoleonic genius of General James Longstreet could not overcome the obstinate stupidity of Robert Edward Lee."

Swinton's next sentence, to which Longstreet lent insight, struck at the core of Jones' and others' postwar idolization of Lee, an unforgiveable act. Swinton wrote that Lee, "Having, however, gotten a taste of blood in the considerable success of the first day … seems to have lost that equipoise in which his faculties commonly moved, and he determined to give battle." Swinton followed-up this assertion with the near-equally as blunt, "In adopting this course he committed a grave error, as the event proved, and judging from a merely military point of view." The language that very likely stung Lee admirers was "a taste of blood," "lost that equipoise," and "grave error." Swinton's writing and Longstreet's insight here track closely with subsequent Longstreet publications. Indeed, shortly before Jones wrote the *Dispatch* in February 1896, Longstreet published his memoirs, which included a similar statement: "That he [Lee] was excited and off his balance was evident on the afternoon of the 1st, and he labored under that oppression until enough blood was shed to appease him." In this version, separated by 30 years from Swinton's work, Longstreet substituted "taste of blood" for "enough blood" and, likewise, "lost that equipoise" for "off his balance."[6]

Did this language show Longstreet was disloyal to Lee and harbored a dislike for his former commander during and after the war, or did it merely show the extent to which Longstreet disagreed with Lee's operational decisions at Gettysburg and the passion he clearly felt for the topic? One thing is clear: Longstreet wrote and spoke bluntly about Gettysburg and many of his other wartime experiences, and it was perhaps this mode of expression that most divided Longstreet and his detractors in the postwar years. Having said that, was Longstreet alone in writing candidly about Lee in the postwar years? He was clearly not. Other Confederate officers who served under Lee, in some capacity, during the war wrote similarly on Lee's actions at Gettysburg, to include First Corps Artillery Officer Edward Porter (E.P.) Alexander, First Corps Staff Officer Gilbert Moxley Sorrel, and once-Army of Northern Virginia Division Commander Daniel Harvey (D.H.) Hill. As the most glaring example, Sorrel wrote, "To succeed, he [Lee] knew battles were to be won, and battles cost blood, and blood he did not mind in his general's work…. He would pour out their blood when necessary or when strategically advisable." Furthermore, and perhaps more importantly, Longstreet typically prefaced his criticisms of Lee's approach at Gettysburg with deference to his former boss, as he did in his November 1877 article: "Before discussing the weak points of the campaign of Gettysburg, it is proper that I should say that I do so with the greatest affection for General Lee, and the greatest reverence for his memory."[7]

The last assertion in Swinton's book that Jones and others took issue with was Longstreet's insight into an alternate tactical suggestion he afforded Lee during the battle. Through Swinton, Longstreet emphasized that on the evening of July 1 and morning of July 2 he had suggested Lee redeploy the army further south to a strong defensive position between Washington and the Federal army and invite the Federals to attack them in place. Swinton narrated:

> Besides, there was open another and still bolder move. Longstreet, holding the right of the Confederate line, had one flank securely posted on the Emmettsburg [sic] road, so that he was really between the Army of the Potomac and Washington; and by marching towards

> Frederick could undoubtedly have maneuvred [sic] Meade out of the Gettysburg position. This operation General Longstreet, who foreboded the worst from an attack on the army in position, and was anxious to hold General Lee to his promise, begged in vain to be allowed to execute.

Like his reaction to Longstreet's claims about the campaign's guiding tactical principle, Jones believed Longstreet's commentary here reeked of egotism and an apparent belief that Lee's "Old Warhorse" thought his tactical ability and judgment superior to Lee's. It further portended to Jones and other Lee admirers that Longstreet was alleging Lee largely lost the battle because he neglected to take his senior subordinates' advice, which as Longstreet clearly alleged through Swinton, would have "undoubtedly" forced "Meade out of the Gettysburg position."[8]

What did Longstreet actually allege in Swinton's book? His contentions were threefold: Firstly, entering the campaign, Lee had planned to pursue the strategic offensive and tactical defensive; secondly, Lee got carried away with the apparent success of the first day's battle and subsequently abandoned the tactical defensive on July 2–3; and thirdly, he had attempted to steer Lee back to the tactical defensive by suggesting the army redeploy to a strong defensive position and await a Federal attack. In all actuality, Longstreet's assertions in Swinton's book, especially his second one, were rather commonplace in the immediate postwar years. They certainly were not radical. James D. McCabe, Jr.'s, popular *Life and Campaigns of General Robert E. Lee*, published the same year as Swinton's work, was demonstrative of how many authors of that period were analyzing and covering the Confederate side at Gettysburg. Like Longstreet's commentary in Swinton's work, McCabe questioned Lee's decision to pursue the tactical offensive after the first day, "It was not General Lee's original intention to fight a general battle so far from his base of operations, and indeed, judging merely by the positions held by the two armies, it is strange that he allowed himself to be drawn into one. His army had before it the task of storming a rocky fortress stronger than that against which Burnside had dashed his army so madly at Fredericksburg, and every chance of success lay with the Federals." McCabe further described the Federals' Cemetery Ridge position as "the strongest … ever assailed by the Army of Northern Virginia" and, on Lee's decision to continue attacking it on the last two days of the battle, he remarked, "There are those who assert that General Lee himself was not free from the contempt entertained by his men for the [Federal] army they had so frequently vanquished, and that he was influenced by it in his decision upon this occasion. This may or may not be true. It is certain that the decision was an error."[9]

Temporarily moving away from Swinton, Jones also charged Longstreet with firing the first shot *after* Lee's death in 1870. Jones alleged that "a short time after General Lee's death General Longstreet gave out for publication the private letter which he wrote his uncle from Culpepper Courthouse, on July 24, 1863, and in which he distinctly claimed that we lost Gettysburg because Lee refused to take his advice, and fought the battle against his judgment." It was curious that Jones could only recall Longstreet releasing this letter "a short time after" Lee's death, especially upon noting that in every other instance in the article when a publication is introduced, Jones demonstrated he could readily identify the month and year of the publication. In the end, Jones misrepresented when Longstreet's July 1863 letter to his Uncle Augustus was released to the public. The letter was, in fact, first published on January 25, 1876, in the *New Orleans Republican*, and then again, more visibly, in Longstreet's November 1877 *Philadelphia Weekly Times* article, "Lee in Pennsylvania." Therefore, Longstreet did not publish this letter "a short time after" Lee's death; rather, over five years passed before the public had access to the letter. In the meantime, it was actually the postwar Lee admirers and defenders who fired the first shots after Lee's death on January 19, 1872, and 1873. It was on these consecutive anniversaries of Lee's birth that former Confederate officers Jubal Early, a division commander in the Second Corps at Gettysburg, and William Pendleton, Lee's Chief of Artillery, not only attempted to defend Lee's actions and decisions at the battle, but also went on the offensive against Longstreet's performance. Of greatest consequence was the way Early and Pendleton chose to attack Longstreet, since their allegations significantly broadened the controversy well beyond its heretofore scope.[10]

Indeed, when it came to their commentary on Gettysburg, Early and Pendleton both spent their January 1872 and 1873 speeches, respectively, not merely addressing the ways in which they disagreed with Longstreet's contributions to Swinton's 1866 book, but by advancing fabrication and speculation. Although Jones characterized Early's remarks on Gettysburg in a limited fashion as a "defense [of] General Lee from the charge that he failed by his own blunders or mistakes," even the most cursory reading of the speech portends otherwise. Early contended that during a conference Lee had held with Second Corps leadership on the evening of July 1, 1863, "General Lee ... determined to make the attack from our right on the enemy's left, and left us for the purpose of ordering up Longstreet's corps in time to begin *the attack at dawn the next morning* [emphasis added]." Two sentences later, Early tacked on, "Had the attack been made at daylight, as contemplated, it must have resulted in a brilliant and decisive victory." In short, Early proved himself to be the originator of the infamous "Sunrise Attack" theory, which alleged Lee ordered Longstreet to attack the Federals as soon as dawn broke on July 2. Early also clearly remained miffed at Longstreet's contributions to Swinton's book, using his displeasure to advance speculation about the former First Corps Commander's supposed attitude at Gettysburg. "If Mr. Swinton has told the truth in repeating in his book what he alleged to have been said to him by General Longstreet, [then] there was at least one of General Lee's corps commanders at Gettysburg who did not enter upon the execution of his plans with that confidence and faith necessary to success, and hence, perhaps, it was that it was not achieved." Thus, we find that along with inventing the "Sunrise Attack" charge, Early instigated the now-familiar speculation that Longstreet did not enter into the spirit of his orders on July 2 and 3 because Lee did not adopt his tactical suggestions, a charge which has consistently reared its head in almost every narrative of the battle over the last century-plus. Looking back on Early's speech, Jones could not help but compare "Old Jube's" assertions with Longstreet's "provocation" in Swinton's book, ultimately judging the former to be "very mild for General Early."[11]

Jones also drew attention to William Pendleton's January 1873 speech, which doubled down on the allegation that Lee had ordered Longstreet to attack at sunrise on July 2. Pendleton claimed that on the evening of July 1, Lee had "informed me that he had ordered Longstreet to attack on that front," referring to the "ground southwest of town," "at sunrise the next morning." Pendleton further alleged that he "learned from officers who saw General Lee"—in other words, through hearsay—that when the commanding general noticed Longstreet had not commenced the attack at sunrise or early in the morning, "he manifested extreme displeasure with the tardy corps commander." Most historians and students of the war rightly dismiss Early's and Pendleton's "Sunrise Attack" charge nowadays; however, the allegation's main and lasting consequence was not the claim itself. Rather, the main repercussion was the doubt cast on Longstreet's actions at Gettysburg, which the anti–Longstreet group employed easily and progressively to transition from the sunrise allegation to the more fluid and opportunistic follow-on contention that Lee *intended* for Longstreet to attack "early in the morning." Then, as the postwar decades progressed into the twentieth century and beyond, others would shorten "early in the morning" to "morning." In short, Early and Pendleton broadened the controversy and reframed it around Longstreet, ultimately opening a can of worms against Lee's "Old Warhorse" that may never be completely closed.[12]

The content of Jones' 1896 article demonstrated the pervasive utility and seductive quality inherent in all things "sunrise" and "early morning" attack. Here was Jones in the last years of the nineteenth century quoting from and repeating Early's and Pendleton's 1872–1873 arguments without mention or allusion that the duo's claims were wholly unsubstantiated, while, even more significantly, the allegations had actually been fully debunked as early as April–May 1875. It was then, in mid–1875, when Longstreet sought and received letters from four officers who served on Lee's staff at Gettysburg: Walter Taylor, Charles Venable, Charles Marshall, and Armistead Lindsay (A.L.) Long. Each of these men denied any recollection whatsoever of a "Sunrise Attack" order. To be fair, Jones would not be alone in continuing to perpetuate these misleading claims in the late 1870s, 1880s, 1890s, and beyond. Former Confederate president Jefferson Davis endorsed Pendleton's "sunrise order" claim in his 1881 work, *The Rise and Fall of the Confederate*

William N. Pendleton in the postwar years (Wikimedia Commons).

Government. Likewise, in his 1877 article on Gettysburg in the *SHSP*, Cadmus Wilcox, a Third Corps brigadier general at the battle, indicated that while he had "no knowledge personally" of whether "General Longstreet was ordered to attack at daylight or early the next morning," nevertheless he was "inclined to believe that he was so ordered." Many other ex-Confederate officers wrote similarly on this July 2 topic in the postwar years, while historians continued the trend into the twentieth century. Longstreet believed these allegations quickly spread like a virulent cancer on the understanding of the Confederate side of the battle. "Most Virginia writers on this subject have taken up and followed the false scent announced by General Pendleton," Longstreet observed in the late 1880s. More broadly and consequentially, Longstreet reflected, "Facts connected with this battle have been so distorted and misrepresented." In clear frustration, Longstreet could only then muster a rather curious solution, namely, "that a volume of distinct maps ... be written in order to make a demonstration, to the letter, of all its features."[13]

The remainder of Jones' article covered the slate of publications on the Longstreet-Gettysburg Controversy that followed Early's and Pendleton's 1872–1873 speeches, along with what was, by then, a stock summation of charges against Longstreet's performance and a defense of Lee's. Longstreet finally broke his public silence and entered the debate in earnest in 1876, publishing some hitherto private correspondence on Gettysburg in the *New Orleans Republican*, to include his July 1863 letter to his Uncle Augustus. Publication of the *SHSP* began in 1877 and the aforementioned Comte de Paris inquiry article followed soon thereafter. In late 1877 and early 1878, Longstreet published his first full-length essays on the battle in the *Philadelphia Weekly Times*, "Lee in Pennsylvania" and "The Mistakes of Gettysburg," respectively. Jones reprinted Longstreet's articles in the *SHSP* in 1878, which precipitated a steady stream of contentious words from Early. Rounding out the 1870s, Longstreet's *Times* articles were also reprinted in the 800-page *Annals of the War* compendium in 1879. Additional articles, letters, and memoirs that touched on the controversy followed in the 1880s, 1890s, and into the twentieth century. Detailed analysis of the merits and shortcomings of these additional postwar publications has already been advanced in other works covering the Longstreet-Gettysburg topic.

That said, did Longstreet, Early, or others further discuss the *origins* of the controversy in any of these publications that followed "Old Jube's" and Pendleton's speeches? Yes, for one, in Early's March 1877 letter responding to the *SHSP* Comte de Paris inquiry, the ex-Confederate once again contended that Swinton's book sparked the controversy, while parroting his earlier and ever since oft-repeated claim about Longstreet's attitude at Gettysburg. "From some communications made to Mr. Swinton by Gen. Longstreet after the war, and contained in the book of the former, you will find that Gen. Longstreet was strongly opposed to the attack and on the enemy's position at Gettysburg, and foreboded the worst results from it. He did not, therefore, enter into those attacks with that spirit of confidence so necessary to success." A few months later, writing in response to Longstreet's recently-published "Lee in Pennsylvania" article, Early credited Longstreet's contributions to Swinton's book as the impetus for his January 1872 response, stating: "I was prompted to make the remarks I did make in my address at the Washington and Lee University from the fact that I had read Mr. Swinton's 'Campaigns of the Army of the Potomac.'" Early exclaimed that Longstreet had been the one to "throw down the gauntlet" and "had no right to complain that a friend of General Lee took it up." Lee's "Bad Old Man," Early, also charged that Longstreet "had begun to muddy the stream … twenty days after the battle … by his letter to his uncle, and when he resumed the work then begun immediately after the war by his communications to Mr. Swinton." Early neglected to mention that, the contents of the letter notwithstanding, Longstreet's July 24, 1863, correspondence with his uncle remained private until 1876. That said, his mentioning of Longstreet's 1866 contributions to *Campaigns*, characterizing them as the first public writings (albeit via Swinton) from an ex-Confederate on the controversy, was accurate.[14]

In 1878, former Confederate cavalry officer and Lee's nephew, Fitzhugh Lee, also characterized Longstreet's Swinton interviews as the catalyst for the controversy, while also expressing support for Early and Pendleton's sunrise or "early in the morning" attack theories.

> His [Longstreet's] communications *just after the war* to Mr. Swinton, the historian, were in substance the same attack upon General Lee which he has repeated in this paper. It was therefore, in him, and came out before any of the utterances now complained of were made. The official reports of General Ewell, Early, and Pendleton, written soon after the battle, clearly stated it was well understood and expected that General Longstreet would make the main attack early in the morning of the 2nd of July.

In fact, Ewell's, Early's, and Pendleton's official reports *did not* confirm the anti-Longstreet group's postwar claim about supposed early morning understandings and expectations whatsoever. Nevertheless, a few sentences later, Fitzhugh Lee went all-in on Lee's alleged intentions. "I propose to show, first, it was General Lee's intention to attack at sunrise," he declared, before advancing the typical fallback argument, "or as soon as possible thereafter." A page later, Fitzhugh Lee reiterated his false claim, yet again, that the reports of Ewell, Early, and Pendleton's "all confirm this testimony."[15]

Cadmus Wilcox also touched on Longstreet's contributions to Swinton in his lengthy Gettysburg article in Volume 6 of the *SHSP*. The former Confederate major general contended Longstreet "not only freely gave his opinions about the battle to this historian, but he let it be known he opposed it." To Wilcox, Longstreet had been "quite free in his criticisms of General Lee" in Swinton's book. For these reasons, Wilcox also rejected Longstreet's claim that he had been disinclined to ever say anything about Gettysburg: "It is difficult to see why he should plead reluctance at this late date when he was so prompt, and in advance of all others by several years, in making public his opposition to this battle."[16]

For Longstreet's part, Lee's senior subordinate never directly addressed his critics' charge that he precipitated the controversy with his contributions to Swinton's work. That said, in his postwar writings, Longstreet did go into some detail about why he chose to begin writing about Gettysburg in the first place, even hinting he had intended to write about it earlier but was "delayed by reason of a press of personal business, and by reason of a genuine reluctance that I have felt against anything that might, even by implication, impugn the wisdom of my late comrades in arms." Significantly, Longstreet suggested that immediately following the Battle of Gettysburg, there existed in the army "a sly undercurrent of misrepresentation of my course." Perhaps there was some truth to this intuition, as evidenced by the postwar account of one of Longstreet's couriers during the campaign, Private William Youngblood. In his "Unwritten History of the Gettysburg Campaign," Youngblood alleged that during the army's retreat from Pennsylvania "a man whom I did not know rode up and relayed to Lee, 'General, there is a rumor throughout the army that General Longstreet failed in his duty is the cause of our disaster at Gettysburg.' The courier recollected that "General Lee, with firmness and fire, replied: 'It is unjust. Longstreet did his duty. Our failure is to be charged to me. My shoulders are broad and can bear it.'" Longstreet confirmed in his November 1877 article that it was, in fact, because of this perceived, post-battle whisper campaign from "accusers" that he proceeded to write a private letter to his Uncle Augustus on July 24, 1863, explaining some of the suggestions he afforded Lee at the battle and the extent to which he shared responsibility for the loss. Longstreet also explained why he started writing publicly about Gettysburg, declaring that since the early 1870s, "I have been so repeatedly and rancorously assailed ... that I feel impelled by a sense of duty to give to the public a full and comprehensive narration of the campaign from its beginning to its end." He expanded on this reasoning in his second article in 1878:

> What I have written about [Gettysburg] has been compelled from me by a desire on the one hand to have future historians properly informed upon the most important movement of the war, and a necessity on the other hand of correcting important mis-statements made ignorantly or maliciously concerning it.... I should probably have never written a line concerning the battle, had it not been for the attempt of the wordy soldiers to specifically fix upon me the whole burden of that battle—their rashness carrying them so far as to lead them to put false orders in the mouth of our great captain, and charge me with having broken them.[17]

Longstreet's neglect here, and elsewhere, to mention his contributions to Swinton's work is a rather glaring omission in his general argument, which held that he only began engaging in any discussion on Gettysburg because of what Early, Pendleton, and others said in the early 1870s. Perhaps Longstreet did not consider what Swinton wrote in *Campaigns* as part of *his* public writings; however, there is little question it was Longstreet's direct commentary that made it into the book. Even if Longstreet had not publicly "written a line concerning the battle" before Early's and Pendleton's attacks, he had certainly spoken a few lines with Swinton. That said, it was Swinton who, in his capacity as a historian, sought out Longstreet for insight regarding the Confederate side of the battle. Longstreet's candidness when speaking about anything to do with the battle (and the war more generally) are now well-known and recognized. Thus, it would have been out of character and even *more* surprising had Longstreet *failed* to mention anything to the historian about his and Lee's tactical differences at Gettysburg.

Equally clear was that Longstreet thought the postwar group had unnecessarily broadened the controversy to outlandish and fanciful proportions, as evidenced by his claim that "false orders" were being attributed to Lee by "wordy soldiers." Longstreet, in this instance, was undoubtedly referring to the sunrise and "early morning" attack order claims for July 2, along with some other allegations associated with orders he supposedly received for July 3; namely, that he had been ordered to attack at daylight on the third day, simultaneously with Ewell's corps, and that Lee had expected him to use his entire corps during the Pickett-Pettigrew-Trimble Charge. As events turned out, these matters proved to be the main, overarching issues (with several offshoots) that consumed postwar participants in the Longstreet-Gettysburg Controversy for the next 30 years.[18]

Did Early, Fitzhugh Lee, and later, Jones, in his 1896 article, tell the whole story though? Did Longstreet truly "start it" in 1866, when he agreed to be interviewed about Gettysburg for Swinton's *Campaigns*? One can almost hear the cacophony of voices from the anti–Longstreet group in the postwar years, crying, "Well, he started it!" Perhaps this topic would be better served if, instead of focusing on who started it after the war, we reframed the conversation around an examination of the *roots* of and unspoken *motivations* associated with the controversy. Indeed, the roots of the Longstreet-Gettysburg Controversy took hold well *before* the war's conclusion, while its postwar participants' underlying motivations were very much tied to things beyond simply getting down to the base truth of what happened on the Confederate side at Gettysburg. On the contrary, and as with most "causes," assuaging guilt, boosting ego, advancing sycophancy, or perhaps most of all, pursuing financial gain, were at the forefront.

Despite firing the first shot against Longstreet's actions at Gettysburg in 1872, Jubal Early's Gettysburg performance, and wartime record more generally—especially from late 1864 to early 1865—were not above question. Early's hesitation to move against Culp's Hill (and to a lesser extent, Cemetery Hill) on the evening of July 1 may have squandered the Confederates' best opportunity at Gettysburg to oust the Federals from their strong Cemetery Ridge line. John Bachelder, the foremost historian on the Battle of Gettysburg in the immediate postwar years, certainly thought so, and some historians have echoed variations of this charge since. Perhaps it was actually *those* minutes on the evening of July 1 that were the wasted "golden moments" for the Army of Northern Virginia at Gettysburg, not the morning hours of July 2 to which many historians have so frequently and misleadingly drawn attention. Additionally, on multiple occasions from the overnight hours of July 1 into the morning of July 2, Early proved to be the foremost officer whispering advice into the ears of both Second Corps Commander, Richard Ewell, and the commanding general. Early was one of the most, if not the most vocal of officers who suggested that the Confederates initiate their main attack on July 2 from their right, not their left (where he was), without having ever seen the right. Early also repeatedly petitioned against Lee's clear inclination that the Second Corps and the army would be better served if it were moved around to the Confederate right to support and provide for an in-depth attack against the Federal left. Indeed, other officers would go on to quite bluntly advance their belief that the Confederate Second Corps' position at Gettysburg was not only less than optimal, but absurd from an operational perspective.[19]

Furthermore, during the second day's battle, Early—and Ewell's corps more generally—had been ordered to take sufficient simultaneous action with Longstreet's assault to, at the very least, hold Federal units on that sector of the field in place, precluding them from being shifted to reinforce their left. Despite these orders,

Ewell did not send Major General Edward Johnson's division forward against Culp's Hill until sometime between 7 and 7:30 p.m. Early did not launch his attack until even later, near 8 p.m., hours after Longstreet's assault began, and with only two of his four brigades. Brigadier General John B. Gordon's six-regiment Georgia brigade was held in reserve, while Brigadier General William Smith's Virginia brigade was stationed on the extreme Confederate left looking out for the long and much-anticipated arrival of James Ewell Brown (J.E.B.) Stuart's cavalry command. As a result, even though Brigadier General Harry Hays' Louisiana Brigade and Colonel Isaac Avery's (Hoke's) North Carolina Brigade achieved some success against the Federal position at twilight—with pockets of infantry from both brigades gaining a brief foothold on East Cemetery Hill—no reinforcements ultimately came to their support. That Early withheld Gordon's entire brigade did not go unnoticed. It would not take long for many Confederates who participated in the attack to voice their disappointment regarding what they believed to be a missed opportunity and bungled attack at the division and corps command levels. "No one who has ever been in a similar position can understand how anxiously we looked for reinforcements. None came, however …," said one. Another penned, "It was soon so dark that we couldent [sic] see what we was doing. And the enemy got to geather [sic] again and we had no reinforcement and we had to fall back to our old position." Captain William Seymour, Harry Hays' adjutant, wrote, "The charge was a daring and desperate one, and, although unsuccessful on account of the failure of our supports to come up, we gained great credit for it…. This want of concert of action on the part of our Generals was the chief cause of the loss of the great battle of Gettysburg."[20]

It is also worth mentioning that, contrary to the apparently disgraceful, sulking, insubordinate Longstreet at Gettysburg, Early's career as a Confederate officer in the Army of Northern Virginia did not last until its surrender on April 9, 1865. Rather, after Early's three successive defeats in the Shenandoah Valley at the Battles of Third Winchester, Fisher's Hill, and Cedar Creek in September and October 1864 and his decisive defeat at the Battle of Waynesboro on March 2, 1865, Lee ultimately relieved him of his Army of the Valley command on March 30, 1865. In a letter to Early, Lee admitted that he "felt…. I could not oppose what seems to be the current of opinion" and "felt constrained to endeavor to find a commander who would be more likely to develop the strength and resources of the country, and inspire the soldiers with confidence." Lee had read in the press and heard from other officers that Early no longer held the confidence of his men. Major General William "Extra Billy" Smith even went so far as to inform Lee that Early was no longer considered "a safe commander." Lee was also apparently satisfied with the way Major General John B. Gordon, Early's former subordinate, was handling the Second Corps.

To boot was the way in which Early conducted himself after he learned of Lee's surrender. As opposed to Longstreet, who following the surrender, proceeded to Lynchburg, Virginia, and then traveled through the Carolinas to Cleveland, Georgia (where his brother, William lived); Canton, Mississippi (where his sister, Sarah Jane lived); and Mobile, Alabama, before seeking business opportunities in New Orleans, Louisiana, in the immediate postwar years, Early skipped the country on April 9. Lee's former "Bad Old Man" initially rode to Texas, then entered Mexico,

Early attacked this location, East Cemetery Hill, around 8 p.m. on July 2, several hours after Longstreet initiated his offensive against the Federal left (Author's Collection).

before traveling to Cuba and Canada. Early remained outside the United States until President Andrew Johnson granted him a pardon in 1869, when he finally returned to Lynchburg to resume his legal practice. While Longstreet publicly pronounced his support for North-South reconciliation and suffrage for blacks shortly after the war and went on to serve the Union in multiple Republican administrations until his death, Early forever characterized himself as an "unreconstructed rebel." Longstreet's actions led to his being largely labeled a pariah in the South in the postwar years, while Early was largely respected, if not admired, by the Southern people. However, this postwar trend begs the question: if Early was such a fighter and "unreconstructed rebel," why did he flee the country and not "face the music," so to speak, like Longstreet and several other former Confederate officers did after Lee's surrender? Why did it take a pardon for Early to return to his beloved South? Indeed, while many former Confederate officers, at the very least, stayed in the country, Early opted to run.[21]

Brigadier General William Nelson Pendleton's Gettysburg performance, late-war record, and postwar actions warrant a similar level of attention and inspection. Lee's chief of artillery's great failures at Gettysburg were undoubtedly two critical measures he took on the third day of the battle. For one, Pendleton had moved the artillery reserve too far to the rear to be readily available to replenish the main artillery line's ammunition in support of the Pickett-Pettigrew-Trimble Charge. Pendleton also, perhaps unknowingly, scrapped E.P. Alexander's, Longstreet's principal artillery commander at Gettysburg, advance artillery plan for the charge.

Alexander had intended to use some mobile howitzers and send them forward with Pickett's column; however, he never informed Pendleton of his intended use for them. Unfortunately for Alexander and the Confederates, Pendleton moved them before the attack commenced. As a result of these two actions, not only would the main artillery line be hampered by ammunition concerns and limitations, but there would be no advance artillery support for the assaulting column, as Lee and Longstreet had clearly intended and ordered. Along with Pendleton's July 3 mishaps, we would be remiss if we did not mention Pendleton's postwar claim that Lee ordered Longstreet to attack at sunrise on July 2, and simply point other historians and students of the war to the artillery chief's official report, which described a frenzy of ongoing Confederate reconnaissance activity up until the midday hours of the second day. It is almost astounding to note that all Pendleton had to do to refute his own postwar claim about orders for a sunrise, early morning, or even morning attack, for that matter, was to consult his own official battle report.[22]

Jubal Early, Longstreet's principal foe in the postwar war of words over the Battle of Gettysburg. This photograph was likely taken in the early 1890s, late in Early's life (Library of Congress).

While Early was relieved of his command in late March 1865, Pendleton and some other subordinate officers in the Army of Northern Virginia were busy on April 7, 1865, just two days before the army's surrender at Appomattox, Virginia, petitioning none other than Lee's senior subordinate, James Longstreet, to support their aim to persuade the commanding general to capitulate. Speaking about this affair in January 1873, Pendleton remembered that the group of officers sought him out to be their spokesman of sorts and "announced their joint wish that, if my views agreed with theirs, I should convey to General Longstreet, as second in command, and then, if he agreed, to General Lee our united judgment that the cause had become so hopeless we thought it wrong longer to be having men killed on either side." John B. Gordon, who also went on to join the anti-Longstreet group in the postwar years, also became associated with Pendleton's group, or at the very least, was made aware of their intentions. Gordon narrated in 1903 that "two days before the surrender, a number of officers held a council as to what was best to be done." He claimed he was "not present" at that council, but "learned through orders that three propositions were discussed," the third of which was "to surrender at once." The Georgian officer recollected "it was decided that this last course would be the wisest, and these devoted officers felt that they should do all in their power to relieve General Lee by giving him their moral support in taking the step." Longstreet did not want to surrender; so, when Pendleton approached him and said that he and some junior officers supported surrender and sought his consent in petitioning Lee to pursue that course, Longstreet apparently exploded with anger: "Don't you know that the Articles of War provide that officers or soldiers asking commanders to surrender should be shot?"[23]

In the postwar years, Pendleton pursued an intense devotion to Lee until his death in January 1883. Some would characterize it as an obsession. One historian has since held that Pendleton's attempts to memorialize and shape Lee's historical memory "transcended normal affection, and suggested unusual psychological motivations," boiling his purposes down to "a search for relief from his own inner turmoil" while using Lee "as a balm to soothe defeat." After the war, Pendleton returned to Lexington, Virginia, and continued his rectorship of Grace Church. He apparently also played a significant role in persuading Lee to relocate to Lexington and take up the Presidency of then-Washington College (now Washington and Lee University). Pendleton would be at Lee's bedside when his former Confederate commander died on October 12, 1870, reading the prayers for the dead, and would also deliver Lee's Episcopal burial service three days later. Furthermore, on the very day of Lee's death, the Lee Memorial Association was formed and launched, to which the Reverend William Nelson Pendleton would hold the position of Executive Director. In that position, Pendleton would actively mold Lee's post-death image into messianic proportions, often advancing comparisons between Jesus and Lee. Indeed, Pendleton would often describe Lee's character in religious terms, as he did once when claiming that, for Lee, there was never "a more sacred lustre [sic], the halo that will forever encircle his name."[24]

Since Lee's death and well before making his "Sunrise Attack" allegation in January 1873, Pendleton had been busy using the General to make a name for himself, speaking all over the South of Lee's eminence both as a general and a man. Pendleton's usual lecture was called, "Personal Recollections of General Lee," whereby he would make such fawning statements as, "Lee's character was stainless and his generalship invincible." Pendleton would tirelessly dedicate himself to this speaking tour until 1875—an ambitious, five-year endeavor in total.[25]

Sycophancy perhaps rose to its greatest height in the character of the Reverend John William Jones, who as you will recall, wrote the 1896 article about "who commenced" the Longstreet-Gettysburg Controversy. Whereas Longstreet was Lee's senior corps commander from the post–Seven Days Campaign until the end of the war, Jones was speaking in the postwar years as a former chaplain in Lee's army. Say what you will about Early and Pendleton, at least one of them was the army's artillery chief and the other rose to corps command. Jones had no such wartime credential to stand on, even while he attempted or encouraged others to "slice up" Lee's senior subordinate. Jones entered the story in earnest when the "Lee Memorial Volume" project was failing in the years immediately following Lee's death. The volume was intended to be a compendium of recollections of Lee from ex-Confederates who served under the general or from friends. Initially this project was put under the poor stewardship of Colonel Charles Marshall, one of Lee's former aides, where it was left languishing in idleness. Jones ultimately inherited the project when he began work on a biography of Lee in the mid–1870s. The former chaplain was afforded close access to the unfinished Marshall manuscript and the Lee family papers, publishing the project in 1875 as the *Personal Reminiscences, Anecdotes, and Letters of General Robert E. Lee*.

Jones used the publication of his Lee biography to catapult himself into the front ranks of the postwar Lee admirers and defenders. Jones was made the secretary of the *Southern Historical Society* and the editor of the *SHSP*, a position he held for over a decade, from 1876 to 1887. One modern historian has gone on to describe Jones as an unvarnished "sycophant" and "habitual name dropper," and a "cunning, ambitious man who rose to power among the cult of Lee writers at the expense of others." Demonstrative of Jones' sycophancy was how he often introduced contributors to the *SHSP*. For example, when Fitzhugh Lee, General Lee's nephew and former major general of cavalry in the Army of Northern Virginia, wrote on Gettysburg in Volume 5 of the *SHSP*, Jones gushed, "Even if his gallant service and military reputation did not entitle him to speak, we are sure that our readers will be glad to have the following paper from one so closely allied to our great Commander-in-Chief." In his 1896 article on the Longstreet-Gettysburg Controversy, Jones titled his last section "Points Established," apparently confident those points were interconvertible fact, before going on to include the verbiage, "General Lee made no mistake," in several sentences therein. Jones fashioned himself as a motiveless cog, wholly without ambition, who simply could not "stand idly by and see him [Longstreet] or his partisans criticice [sic] and belittle" Lee, "without raising my humble voice or using my feeble pen in indignant burning protest." Jones was also a regular attendee of meetings of the United Confederate Veterans, the predecessor organization to the Sons of Confederate Veterans, apparently leading off the gathering each year with the modest prayer: "God of Israel, God of Abraham, Isaac, and Jacob.... God of Stonewall Jackson, Robert E. Lee, and Jefferson Davis." Like Pendleton's predilection to compare Lee to Jesus, here was Jones equating the religious triumvirate of Abraham, Isaac, and Jacob to the late-nineteenth century Confederate heroes of Jackson, Lee, and Davis.[26]

In the end, as with most things in public life, it comes down to money. Many associations and groups rose in the wake of Lee's death and all were looking to advance and shape the postwar historical memory of Lee. To accomplish their goals, they needed money. The Longstreet-Gettysburg Controversy was aptly dubbed a controversy because it was just that—controversial. It was a perfect storm since controversy naturally stirs interest as battle lines are drawn. Interest draws crowds and subscriptions. People were interested in seeing how Early, Pendleton, and others in the group of Lee writers would defend their hero from the "scalawag" Republican,

Longstreet. Ultimately, crowds and subscribers equated to financial gain—money that would bolster these associations' and groups' attempts to fashion their postwar creation of Robert E. Lee.

When William Pendleton was the Lee Memorial Association's Executive Director and engaged in his speaking tour on Lee from 1870 to 1875, his motivations were as much financial as anything else. During the last two years of that speaking tour, Pendleton would grab the dais with one hand, advancing his "Sunrise Attack" theory, and with the other snatch money from his audience to fund various Lexington-based projects: the sculptor Edward Valentine's statue of a recumbent Lee (1875); the Lee Mausoleum (1883); and the rebuilding of Grace Church, which eventually would be renamed R.E. Lee Memorial Church in 1903. Money also swirled around and was sought after for the completion of the aforementioned "Lee Memorial Volume." Other former Confederates who served under Lee, like former lieutenant general Wade Hampton, also participated in these speaking tours. Pendleton, Hampton, and others would speak and then petition the audience for funds. When in 1875, Jones published his Lee biography, which apparently became a mainstay in nearly every Southern household, part of the profits went right into Pendleton's Lee Memorial Association.

Additional associations focused on all-things-Lee abounded in the years following the general's death. These groups amassed large sums of money too and the familiar characters involved in the Longstreet-Gettysburg Controversy were nearly always present. Along with the Lee Memorial Association, there was the Richmond-based Lee Monument Association, formed on November 3, 1870, two weeks after Lee's death. Unsurprisingly, the first president of the Monument Association was none other than the prime mover of the Longstreet-Gettysburg Controversy, Jubal Early. There was also the wealthy Ladies' Lee Monument Association, which combined with Early's Monument Association in 1886, and who passionately wanted Lee to be buried in Richmond's Hollywood Cemetery with a huge, bronze equestrian statue adorning his grave. Then there was the Association of the Army of Northern Virginia, whose architect, former Confederate brigadier general Bradley Johnson, originally attempted to form in early 1870 with Robert E. Lee himself at its head. Lee apparently opposed the whole venture, which says something about what he might have thought about the plethora of associations and groups who used his name after his death. Even so, after Lee died, Johnson's association was established anyway, with former Lee staffers, Walter Taylor and Charles Marshall, and of course, Early, leading the way. To round things out, there was also the Virginia Division, another sizable postwar group tied to Lee's name, literally, in this case, through his bloodline, via his son, W.H.F. "Rooney" Lee, and nephew, Fitzhugh Lee, another vocal critic of Longstreet in the postwar years.[27]

So, while the postwar anti-Longstreet group, particularly the originators of Early, Pendleton, and Jones, were likely motivated by a combination of guilt, ego, and financial gain in advancing the postwar Longstreet-Gettysburg Controversy, what motivations might Longstreet have had as a participant? Indeed, if the roots of the controversy were likely first established during the war and then nurtured in the years following Lee's death, when Lee worshippers attempted to fashion themselves *true* friends of Lee and attain a position in the Confederate pantheon they

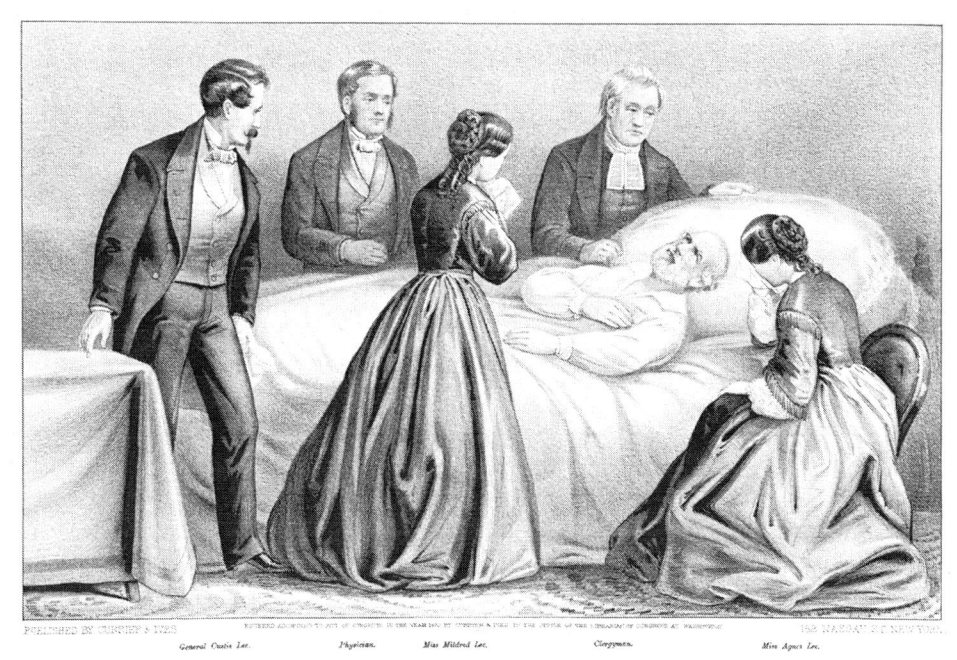

DEATH OF GENERAL ROBERT E. LEE,
AT LEXINGTON, VA., OCTOBER 12TH, 1870.

Robert E. Lee's death in October 1870 was like the drop of a hat in precipitating the formation of numerous memorial and monument associations, and other initiatives by some ex-Confederates who served under him during the war. Collectively, these associations and initiatives attempted to mold and shape how Lee would be remembered for posterity (Library of Congress).

were unable to accomplish during the war, where did that leave Longstreet's post–Gettysburg actions and motives?

On the face of it, Jones was correct in 1896 when he explored "who started" the controversy and pinned the tail on Longstreet. Lee's "Old Warhorse's" contributions to William Swinton's 1866 book clearly touched a nerve. His comments made several ex-Confederates who had served under Lee in varying capacities upset, though they would say little to nothing about it until after Lee's death. It is equally clear that the publication was Swinton's, not Longstreet's, and the general only participated because the historian had asked for his insight. Furthermore, the thoughts Longstreet offered on Gettysburg were, at the time, really nothing out of the ordinary. In the immediate postwar years, other historians and writers advanced similar interpretations on what they believed happened to the Confederates at Gettysburg. Longstreet was just the first, high-profile, ex-Confederate who opened his mouth. Perhaps most significant when judging Longstreet's motivations was the fact he did not publish his own work on Gettysburg for public consumption until a decade after Swinton's book. If Longstreet was so eager to make a name for himself, whether as the Confederate officer who was "right" at Gettysburg or the brains behind Robert E. Lee, as his critics would later charge him with insinuating, then why did it take him ten years after Swinton to put his own name on a Gettysburg-related publication, and still further, four years after Early broadened the controversy with his January 1872 speech in Lexington?

If Longstreet's motivation in contributing to Swinton was indeed calculated to boost his image in the eyes of the Southern people and solidify himself as the man who could have led the South to victory at Gettysburg if only *his* advice had been taken, then he had odd timing. Indeed, in the same year and the year to follow, Longstreet wrote his now-notorious series of letters to the *New Orleans Times* newspaper, where he expressed support for North-South Reconciliation and recommended cooperation with the Party of Lincoln, the Republicans. Of course, Longstreet suggested the South pursue this course to benefit the South, believing cooperation would make for a quicker and less painful postwar experience; however, that is not how the published letters were ultimately interpreted by most Southern readers, who, along with several of Longstreet's former friends and comrades, pilloried him. Jones briefly mentioned Longstreet's politics in his 1896 article, contending that "the only thing 'politics' has had to do with the [Longstreet-Gettysburg] controversy has been that ever since Longstreet became a Republican, a partisan Republican press has labored to make him the great general on the Confederate side, and to exalt him at Lee's expense."[28] Jones was stretching here. Of course Longstreet's Republican stripe did not help him in the postwar South, while common sense dictates that when people disagree with your politics, they are more easily prone to disagree with and distrust what you say about other topics, to include, in Longstreet's case, the Battle of Gettysburg. But even more importantly for the purposes of this essay, Longstreet's politics, and most particularly *when* he threw his hat in the political ring in 1866–1867, says quite a bit about any alleged motivations he had in contributing to Swinton's book around the same time. In short, how could Longstreet have sought admiration and fame from the South with his Swinton contributions, while concurrently sabotaging those aspirations with his letters to the *New Orleans Times*, which he knew and had been told beforehand would "ruin" him?[29]

The most likely explanation for Longstreet's "first shot" in Swinton was that, though it may have been a shot, it was a blank, or at least, it was meant to be. It certainly was not intended to precipitate a decades-long controversy. No, Longstreet's main sin was his blunt, resolute, and often deeply principled attitude. It was this attitude that permitted Longstreet to be one of the last officers in the Army of Northern Virginia to advocate for surrender and to love and respect the Southern people, while also telling them soon thereafter that accepting the war's result and cooperating with the North's leading political party was in their best interest. In the same way, it was this attitude that allowed him to love and respect Robert E. Lee, while concurrently not worshipping him and claiming he never made a mistake. Indeed, it was this attitude that was at the heart of the Longstreet-Gettysburg Controversy, since the anti–Longstreet, Lee defenders could never accept what or how Longstreet spoke about their hero, or as Jones admitted in his 1896 article, "His [Longstreet's] attacks upon General Lee have been as unjust as they have been unseemly and ungrateful."[30]

Essay 2

A Letter to General Sickles
Longstreet's July 2 Attack

I believe it is now conceded that the advanced position at the Peach-Orchard, taken by your corps and under your orders saved that battle-field to the Union cause.—James Longstreet to Daniel Sickles

Uncomfortably reclining in his Washington, D.C., residence, James Longstreet, now serving out his sixth year as the United States Commissioner of Railroads, grimaced as he shifted his weight to pen a letter to his former foe at the Battle of Gettysburg and now dear friend, Daniel Sickles. The 81-year-old Longstreet, increasingly plagued by poor health and a severe case of rheumatism in his foot, had but a little over a year left to live. This letter was important though and needed to be attended to, especially given its recipient. Beginning with "My Dear General Sickles," Longstreet proceeded to inform his friend that he very much wished to be in Gettysburg on that day, September 19, 1902, for the unveiling of a new monument—a bronze equestrian statue—dedicated to the commander of the Federal Twelfth Corps at the battle, Henry Slocum.[1]

Former Confederate Longstreet and former Federal Sickles had formed a close bond in the post–Civil War years. Both generals jointly participated in multiple anniversaries of the Gettysburg battle, perhaps most notably the 25th Anniversary in 1888, and special battlefield visits, as in the early 1890s with author and diplomat John Russell Young, where the former foes rode together in the same carriage and Sickles apparently helped Longstreet ascend Little Round Top. Additional meetings ensued throughout the remaining years of the century. On St. Patrick's Day in 1892, Sickles and Longstreet met in Atlanta, Georgia, for a Knights of St. Patrick banquet, and shared a joyous evening of "hot Irish whiskey punch," with Sickles toasting Longstreet and the latter singing the Star-Spangled Banner before both men alternated escorting each other to their separate hotels well into the night. In 1901 and 1902, Longstreet and Sickles met again on three separate occasions, namely: President William McKinley's second inauguration ceremony, the United States Military Academy Centennial at West Point, and then, for the last time, on Memorial Day 1902 in Washington, D.C., where Longstreet was cordially welcomed into a tentful of over one thousand Federal Third Corps veterans.[2]

On the surface, it was a friendship that seemed unlikely, seeing as Longstreet and Sickles found themselves on opposing sides during the war, and most significantly, at Gettysburg, during the battle's most calamitous day, July 2, 1863, which cost the latter a leg. However, in the postwar years, both men seemed to find common ground as firm and vocal supporters of North-South reconciliation. In his September 1902 letter to Sickles, Longstreet reaffirmed his dedication to reconciliation in writing about how his perspective on the outcome of the Battle of Gettysburg had drastically changed over time: "It was the sorest and saddest reflection of my life for many years; but, to-day, I can say, with sincerest emotion, that it was and is the best that could have come to us all, North and South; and I hope that the nation, reunited, may always enjoy the honor and glory brought to it by the grand work." Likewise, shortly after Longstreet's death in January 1904, Sickles wrote the introduction to *Lee and Longstreet at High Tide*, a book written by Longstreet's second wife, Helen Dortch Longstreet, where Sickles celebrated Longstreet's call for a peaceful North-South reunion—dubbing him "a rainbow of reconciliation"—while clearly pronouncing his own fervent support for unity: "If it be thought strange that I should write a preface to a memoir of a conspicuous adversary, I reply that the Civil War is only a memory, its asperities are forgotten, both armies were American, old army friendships have been renewed and new army friendships have been formed among the combatants."[3]

James Longstreet in 1901, a year before he wrote his famous letter to Daniel Sickles (The Longstreet Society).

Additionally, even a momentary glance at the all-consuming, Gettysburg-related controversies that engulfed both Longstreet and Sickles in the postwar years leaves no doubt as to why they probably came to understand one another better than anyone else did then or since. In Longstreet's case, shortly after Robert E. Lee's death in 1870, several ex-Confederate officers began publicly raising doubts about Longstreet's performance at Gettysburg. These men, to include Jubal Early, William Pendleton, and others, recognized that Longstreet, as a postwar Southern Republican and Catholic, was especially vulnerable to criticism, no matter how untethered to fact their accusations became. They also knew Longstreet was interviewed for an immediate postwar publication, where the general made known he had disagreed with a number of Lee's tactical decisions at Gettysburg. In the postwar South, Lee was the supreme marble man, and questioning *any* of Lee's wartime decisions, especially those made at what was considered by many to be the most important battle of the war (and a Southern loss to boot), was simply unforgiveable. If Lee *could not* be blamed, Longstreet, an easy target given his unpopular postwar political decisions, *had to* be blamed. The anti–Longstreet group initially concocted a completely unfounded tall tale about an alleged "Sunrise Attack" plan for the second day of the battle. Once that tale was debunked by the mid–1870s, they turned to broadening their accusations against Longstreet, claiming that at different points along the course of the three-day battle, he exhibited a combination of slowness, sulkiness, and even insubordination. Over 30 years later, at the time of Longstreet's death, the group was still repeating these charges successfully, creating a lengthy paper trail with long-standing, negative effects on the coverage of the general's performance in most Gettysburg battle studies published since.[4]

In Sickles' case, the controversy involved his decision to move the Federal Third Corps to the Peach Orchard during the mid-afternoon hours of July 2. The debate over Sickles' decision and comparisons between his original position on lower Cemetery Ridge and the ground at the Peach Orchard began even before the Third Corps made its move. The Army of the Potomac Chief of Artillery Henry Hunt had discussed the merits and disadvantages of the ground along the Emmitsburg Road in detail with Sickles during the late morning hours. Since that discussion, the Sickles-Peach Orchard controversy has raged on from the Joint Congressional Committee on the Conduct of the War in 1864,[5] throughout the postwar years, past Sickles' death in May 1914, and in historians' Gettysburg battle studies into the modern era. Over the decades, Sickles consistently claimed he made the move because his corps' original position—with its left flank located just north of Little Round Top—was on low-lying ground, and thought to be unfit for effective use of artillery.[6] He believed the ground approximately 1,500 yards to the west along the Emmitsburg Road (and 60 feet higher in elevation) afforded superior visibility and proved a better location for artillery.[7] Not only did Sickles think this position along the Emmitsburg Road might prove more advantageous for his own corps' efforts, but he was also worried about how the Confederates might be able to leverage the ground against him, if seized. Furthermore, Sickles claimed he was confused by Federal Army of the Potomac Commander George Meade's orders during the morning and early afternoon hours of July 2. Specifically, his chief's directive to extend his line to the ground that had been occupied by Brigadier General John Geary's Twelfth Corps division on the northern face of Little Round Top until approximately 5 a.m.[8] In fact, Sickles' confusion was somewhat justified when Meade testified to the Joint Committee on the Conduct of the War and held that Sickles' "left was to extend to Round Top mountain, plainly visible, *if it was practicable* [emphasis added] to occupy it." That said, instead of stressing this point, Sickles frequently advanced other less credible justifications for his move in the postwar years. Despite Sickles' advanced position being 1,100 yards longer than his original position, the Third Corps commander consistently claimed he had lacked the manpower to extend his line to cover Little Round Top. At other times, Sickles would falsely claim he had recognized the importance of Little Round Top and posted Third Corps troops there.[9]

Sickles advanced other reasons over the decades for the move, which proved to be a mixed bag of truth, semi-truth, and falsehood. One truthful allegation was Meade ordering Major General John Buford's First Division of the Cavalry Corps, stationed near the Peach Orchard and protecting the army's left flank, to Westminster. No force ultimately replaced Buford at the Peach Orchard; a blunder that surely must have sharpened Sickles' uncertainty. Sickles' impression that Meade was insufficiently concerned about the army's left flank and that there was a growing threat against it was compounded when he sent out a probing reconnaissance consisting of the 1st U.S. Sharpshooters and the 3rd Maine regiment around noon.[10] These units clashed with Confederate brigadier general Cadmus Wilcox's men in Pitzer's Woods. Even though Wilcox was not part of what would be the Confederates' main flanking force under Longstreet—whose two divisions were then still located near Herr Ridge—Sickles would not have known that at the time. In Sickles' estimation, the enemy was clearly concentrated in his front, further raising his suspicions the Confederates intended to seize the higher "commanding ground" along the Emmitsburg Road and use it against what he deemed to be his inferior position. Another reason Sickles frequently advanced with much less intrinsic truth was his belief Meade planned to retreat from Gettysburg on July 2 and how he had moved his corps forward to prevent the army's redeployment to Pipe Creek.[11]

Of course, criticisms against Sickles' move are, by now, exceedingly well-known. First and foremost, critics argue Sickles flagrantly disobeyed orders in moving his corps out to the Emmitsburg Road.[12] They assert Sickles created an unnecessary salient in the Federal line, attempted to occupy too broad a position for his corps' strength, and left both his flanks hanging in the air—his left on Houck's Ridge and his right on the Emmitsburg Road.[13] They further contend that Sickles essentially threatened the integrity of the Federal army's strong interior ("fishhook") line from Culp's Hill around to the northern base of Little Round Top, and that it was only through the determined efforts of Meade, army engineer Gouverneur K. Warren, Federal Second Corps commander Winfield Scott Hancock, and a few others to provide artillery and infantry support from other corps that saved the Federal left on July 2. Simply put, Sickles blundered badly and others were left to mop up the mess.[14]

And so, yes, by the 1880s, Longstreet and Sickles shared a close friendship, perhaps kindled by dueling controversies that, at least at times, seemed to match the intensity of their July 2, 1863, fight. Gettysburg Licensed Battlefield Guide and Historian James Hessler has dubbed the generals' postwar relationship a "public alliance," with "each man ... ready to defend the other's war-record when called upon." Indeed, whether public, private, or both, the warmth between the former enemies was apparent in the introductory remarks Longstreet included in his September 19, 1902, letter to his former adversary—"My Dear General Sickles." Though, as events turned out, Robert E. Lee's former senior lieutenant had things of an even more momentous nature to say to his friend on this particular day. Significantly, Longstreet apparently felt compelled to tell Sickles exactly what he thought about the former Federal Third Corps commander's controversial actions at Gettysburg. "On that field you made your mark that will place you prominently before the world as one of the leading figures of the most important battle of the Civil War," Longstreet candidly reflected, only to follow up with an even more praiseworthy and forthright statement about

Sickles' July 2 performance, penning, "I believe it is now conceded that the advanced position at the Peach-Orchard, taken by your corps and under your orders saved that battle-field to the Union cause." Though only a private letter at the time, it was still a controversial statement; yet perhaps unsurprising when coming from a man who by 1902 was accustomed to being controversial; a man who made bold assertions others might have thought, but never dared express in a postwar environment where accepted interpretations and narratives about the Gettysburg battle were already rapidly congealing.[15]

Over the decades-worth of Gettysburg historiography produced since Longstreet's 1902 letter, scholars have regularly offered up heroes and causes on the Union side that contributed to saving the day for the Federal Army of the Potomac on July 2; however, two suggestions that come up much less, or at least two that almost always serve to furrow the brow of those with whom you discuss the topic is Daniel Sickles and his decision to move the Federal Third Corps from lower Cemetery Ridge to the Peach Orchard on the afternoon of July 2.[16] What would have induced Longstreet to write such a thing? Was he just stroking a friend's ego or is there evidence that suggests Longstreet had actually thought seriously on the topic in the years since the battle? Additionally, can an assessment be made about the overall validity of Longstreet's 1902 statement while simultaneously, and most importantly, avoiding the murky waters of what-if discussion?[17] All of these topics collectively require methodical analysis of some key circumstances, events, happenings, and non-happenings involving Longstreet's and Sickles' command on July 2.

Maj. Gen. Daniel Sickles, USA, commander of the Federal Third Corps at Gettysburg, pictured here in 1902. Despite facing one another on the field of battle on July 2, 1863, a fast friendship blossomed between Longstreet and Sickles in the postwar years (Library of Congress).

*

A detailed examination of all Longstreet's post-battle writings on the July 2 battle, from his official report to his articles in the 1870s and 1880s to his 1896 memoirs, *From Manassas to Appomattox*, reveals it was not until rather late in life that the general *specifically* called out Sickles' move to the Peach Orchard as a decisive, positive event for the Federals at Gettysburg. Just a few weeks after the battle, Longstreet penned his official report, where he compared Sickles' Emmitsburg Road position with his own two divisions' initial position along Warfield Ridge, clearly expressing how underwhelmed he was with the former: "The enemy's first position along the Emmitsburg road was but little better, in point of strength, than the first position taken by these two divisions [Hood and McLaws]."[18] That said, throughout all his written accounts in the postwar years, he clearly alluded to the adverse effect the move had on his attack. Indeed, even while Longstreet made no explicit comment about the consequences of Sickles' advanced position anchored at the Peach Orchard until his memoirs, the prototype for his 1902 statement was present as early as his two *Philadelphia Weekly Times* articles, published in the 1870s. Perhaps Longstreet's neglect to draw specific attention to Sickles' move until his memoirs was not wholly coincidental, given that particular volume was written during the time period when Longstreet and Sickles were most in each other's company at Gettysburg anniversaries and other events.

Indeed, the overarching themes to which Longstreet consistently drew attention in the postwar years explained the reasons his July 2 attack was only partially successful and most often centered on actions the Confederate army failed to take; however, he also signaled consequential actions taken by the Federals. Above all else, Longstreet frequently mentioned the lack of support afforded his two divisions on the second day from the other two Confederate corps. He reiterated this point many times in all his postwar accounts, but never as clearly and extensively as in his 1877 article, "Lee in Pennsylvania," where he emphasized:

> If General [Richard] Ewell had engaged the army in his front at that time (say four o' clock) he would have prevented their massing their whole army in my front, and while he and I kept their two wings engaged, [A.P.] Hill would have found their centre weak, and should have threatened it while I broke through their left and dislodged them. Having failed to move at four o'clock, while the enemy was in his front, it was still more surprising that he did not advance at five o'clock with vigor and promptness, when the trenches in front of him were vacated, or rather held by one single brigade (as General Meade's testimony before the Committee on the Conduct of the War states). Had he taken these trenches and scattered the brigade that held them, he would have found himself in the Federals' flank and rear. His attack in the rear must have dislodged the Federals, as it would have been totally unexpected—it being believed that he was in front with me. Hill, charging upon the centre at the same time, would have increased their disorder and we should have won the field. But Ewell did not advance until I had withdrawn my troops.... General Early says that my failure to attack at sunrise was the cause of Ewell's line being broken at the time I did attack. This is not only absurd, but impossible. After sunrise that morning, Colonel Venable and General Lee were at Ewell's headquarters discussing the policy of opening the attack with Ewell's Corps. They left Ewell with this definite order: that he was to hold himself in readiness to support my attack when it was made. It is silly to say that he was ready at sunrise, when he was not ready at four o'clock when the attack was really made. His orders were to hold himself in readiness to co-operate with my attack when it was made.[19]

Longstreet was reasonable in his analysis. Lee's orders on July 2 to Richard Ewell, the Confederate Second Corps commander, were to make a simultaneous demonstration with Longstreet's attack—listening for the sound of the First Corps' guns to commence that demonstration—while looking for an opportunity to convert that demonstration into a full-on attack. Likewise, Ambrose Powell (A.P.) Hill, the Confederate Third Corps commander, was ordered to support Longstreet's attack with Richard Anderson's division and to take advantage of any further opportunities to threaten the Federal center. Both orders to Ewell and Hill were issued with the intention to achieve concert of action across all three Confederate Corps and to hold Federal units in place, precluding Meade from shifting units from one part of his interior line to another to meet a specific threat.[20] Ultimately, both Ewell and Hill failed to meet Lee's expectations on July 2. Edward Porter (E.P.) Alexander, Longstreet's principal artillery commander at Gettysburg, drew sharp attention to Ewell's shortcomings on July 2 in particular, while also alluding to an overall lack of oversight that rested at the feet of Lee, writing, "The official reports are a painful record of insufficient comprehension of orders and inefficient attempts at execution, by officers each able to shift the blame of failure upon other shoulders than his own. Between the lines the apparent absence of supervision excites constant wonder."[21] Indeed, Ewell largely engaged in an ineffective and short-lived cannonade and only commenced his own attack once Longstreet's assault had all but concluded, while Hill managed to only launch three of Anderson's five brigades in support of Longstreet and afforded no additional support from his corps. Lastly, Lee took no action during Longstreet's attack to remediate the half-actions or inaction of his two new corps commanders.[22]

In stressing the lack of concert of action across the Confederate corps, the focus of Longstreet's analysis seemed to naturally insinuate that Sickles' Federal Third Corps received continuous support almost immediately after the Confederate assault began. Longstreet referred to George Meade's own statements to support his claim that the Federals drew upon numerous reinforcements from other parts of their line to blunt Longstreet's attack against their left. Indeed, Meade stated in his official battle report, "Perceiving the great exertions of the enemy, the Sixth Corps, Major General Sedgwick, and part of the First Corps to the command of which I had assigned Major General Newton, particularly Lockwood's Maryland Brigade, with detachments from the Second Corps, were all brought up at different periods, and succeeded, together with a gallant resistance of the Fifth Corps, in checking and finally repulsing the assault of the enemy."[23] Longstreet cited Meade's testimony from the Joint Committee on the Conduct of the War, where the Federal commander described the extent to which he stripped parts of his line to meet Longstreet's two-division attack: "My extreme right flank held by one single brigade of the Twelfth Corps, commanded by General [George] Greene."[24]

In all his postwar accounts, Longstreet minced no words in stressing the negative impact the steady flow of Federal reinforcements had on his attack. In one account from the 1870s, he maintained, "We felt at every step the heavy stroke of fresh troops—the sturdy regular blow that tells a soldier instantly that he has encountered reserves or reinforcements," while, very similarly in his later memoirs, he declared, "While Meade's lines were growing my men were dropping; we had no others to call to their aid, and the weight against us was too heavy to carry.... Nothing was heard or felt but the clear ring of the enemy's fresh metal as he came against us." Joseph Kershaw, a brigade commander in McLaws' division, perhaps summed up the odds facing Longstreet best when writing, "These mighty shocks of contending armies were sustained, on our part, by two divisions of infantry numbering, with the artillery, not more than 10,000, or at the highest estimate 13,000 men." In "The Mistakes of Gettysburg," Longstreet accurately acknowledged that not all reinforcements sent to the Federal left engaged his men; however, he described how their simple presence had a palpable effect on his attack:

> It has never been claimed that we met this immense force of sixty-five thousand men at one time; nor has it been claimed that each and every one of them burnt powder in our faces. But they were drawn off from other parts of the field to meet us, and were hurried to our front and massed there, meaning to do all the mischief they could. If some of them did not shoot us, or stick us with their bayonets, it was simply because they could not shoot through the solid blocks of their own troops, or reach us with their bayonets over the heads of their comrades. But they were in position and eager for battle—ready to rush down upon us the moment the line next in front of them was broken. The *morale* of their presence in reinforcing the position and threatening our flanks as we pressed on, was about as effective as their actual bloody work could have been.[25]

E.P. Alexander echoed Longstreet's comments about the effect of the seemingly continual flow of Federal reinforcement to the Union left: "The mere sight of the long lines and solid blue masses which appeared to the Confederates as they cleared the woods and scanned the opposite slopes, was calculated to paralyze the advance. Ten fresh brigades were in position before them, besides the remnants of the 13 brigades which had been driven back. About 75 guns were in action supporting this huge force. To this day there survive stories showing how the Confederates were impressed by this tremendous display."

While noting the lack of support from his own army and the effect extensive Federal reinforcements had on his attack, Longstreet also either alluded to or directly called-out the consequences of Sickles' move to the Peach Orchard throughout the postwar years. As early as the 1870s, Longstreet clearly contended that the intermediary fight against Sickles' corps on the ground between the armies' principal Seminary and Cemetery Ridge positions weakened his attack force for the succeeding combat east of the Peach Orchard. Despite pushing the Federals out of the Peach Orchard and back from the Emmitsburg Road, Longstreet noted, "they fought stubbornly," and during the follow-on combat along Plum Run, forced the Confederates to claw "their way over every foot of ground and against overwhelming odds. At every step we found that reinforcements were pouring into the Federals from every side." In essence, Longstreet held that Sickles' presence and resistance at the Peach Orchard not only drew blood, but created a temporary buffer that served to buy the Federals critical time for reinforcements to arrive.[26]

It is equally apparent that Longstreet further realized the effect Sickles' move had on Hood's division and his assaulting column's right flank, particularly the presence of Brigadier General John Henry Hobart Ward's 1,650-man brigade[27] and James E. Smith's 4th New York battery on Houck's Ridge.[28] Lee's "Old Warhorse" expressed that as a result of Sickles' salient extending well back from the Emmitsburg Road and running further south near Little Round Top, the Confederates struggled to

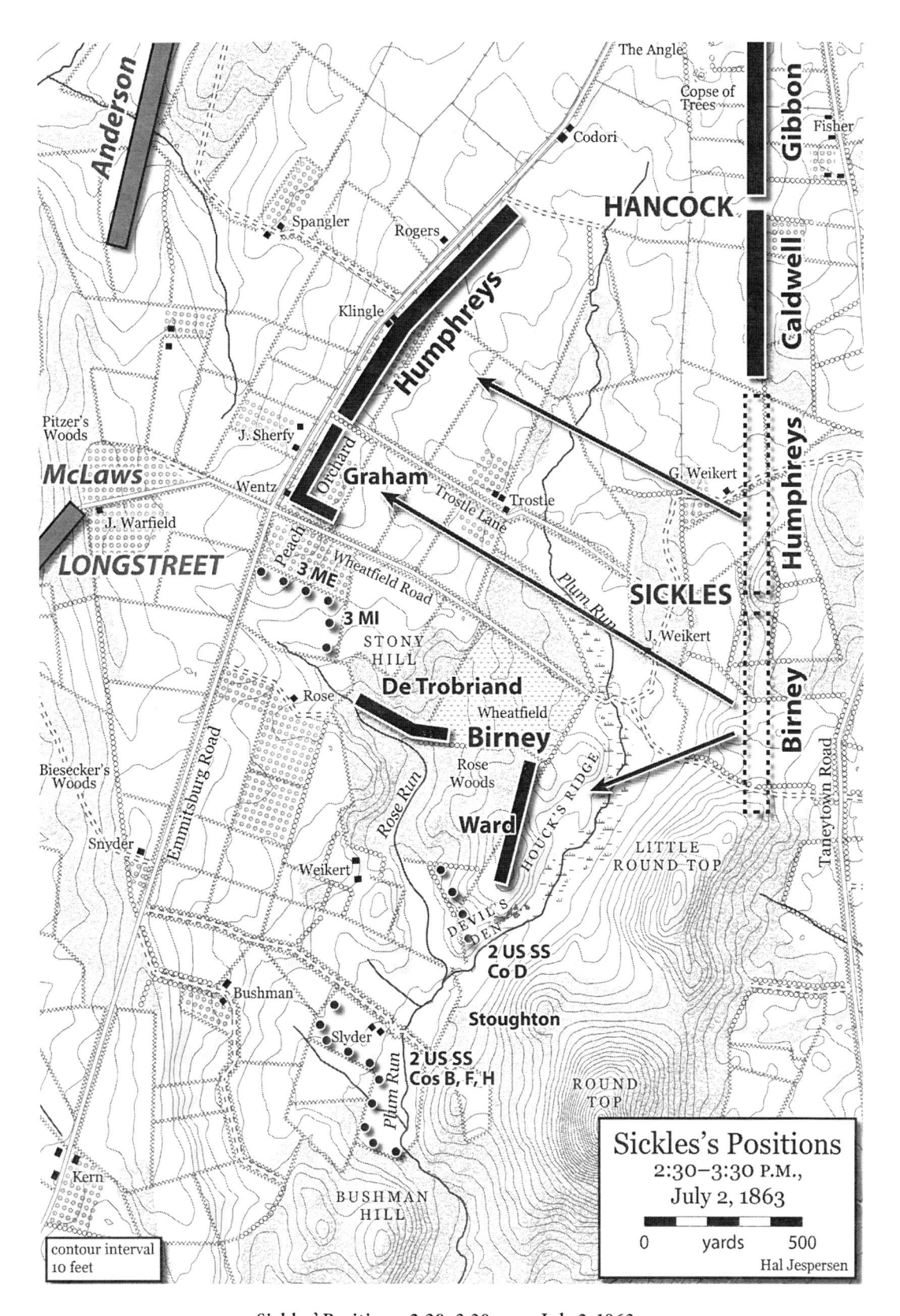

Sickles' Positions, 2:30–3:30 p.m., July 2, 1863.

maintain their intended attack orientation up the Emmitsburg Road. In short, Sickles' move forced Longstreet's two divisions to make impromptu alterations that collectively drew out his force over a much broader front than initially anticipated, diluting the assault's overall potency. Longstreet would go on to accurately and succinctly describe the cumulative effects of these developments on his attack, especially in pulling some of Hood's division to engage the Federals in unanticipated areas, like Little Round Top: "The defensive advantages of the ground enabled the Federals to delay our purposes until they could occupy Little Round Top, which they just then discovered was the key to their position. The force thrown upon this point was so strong as to seize our right, as it were, in a vice." Evander Law, a brigade commander in Longstreet's corps,[29] confirmed the effect Ward's brigade and Smith's battery had on the orientation and progression of the division's attack and the magnetic severity of the fighting on Houck's Ridge: "We soon came upon their first line of battle, running along the lower slopes of the hills known as Devil's Den.... The fighting soon became close and severe. Exposed to the artillery fire from the heights in front and on our left, as well as to the musketry of the infantry, it required all the courage and steadiness of the veterans who composed the Army of Northern Virginia."[30]

Between the publication of these earlier articles and his memoirs, Longstreet made additional comments on Sickles' move while at Gettysburg anniversary events and during other visits to the battlefield. At the 25th anniversary of the battle in 1888, Sickles explicitly asked Longstreet what he thought about the July 2, 1863, decision to move the Federal Third Corps to the Peach Orchard and which position he

When Longstreet's attack began around 4:30 p.m., the extreme left flank of the Federal army's main infantry line ended with Ward's brigade on Houck's Ridge. This modern-day photograph looks northeast toward that location from Slyder Farm Lane (Author's Collection).

would have preferred attacking—the lower Cemetery Ridge or Emmitsburg Road line. Longstreet immediately declared, "Why, on the continuation of Hancock's lines, by all means," only to add, "It would have enabled me to obtain a much better view of your line and give me more open field in which to work. I was thoroughly acquainted with Hancock's position, but had to go at you in the Peach Orchard without exactly knowing what I was meeting." Longstreet's claim that he was "thoroughly acquainted" with the Federal Second Corps position on July 2 was probably more than a slight exaggeration since in the entire lead-up to his July 2 attack, the Confederate High Command possessed a mistaken understanding of the Federal position. That said, Longstreet's stated rationale for preferring to attack Sickles' original position was reasonable. Not only did he draw attention to some of the confusion plaguing the Confederate High Command in the lead-up to the attack resulting, at least in part, from Sickles' move ("without exactly knowing what I was meeting"), but he also clearly alluded to his belief that had Sickles remained on or returned to Cemetery Ridge, "more open field" would have benefited his two divisions' preparation for and execution of the attack.[31]

In a May 1893 trip to the battlefield, Longstreet expanded upon his justification for preferring an attack on Sickles' original position, explaining how if Sickles had not moved out to the Emmitsburg Road, "We would have taken the Round Tops without firing a shot, and shelled the Union Army out of its position along Cemetery Hill [sic]." Of course, since Lee and Longstreet intended to direct the July 2 assault up the Emmitsburg Road toward Cemetery Hill and not against the Round Tops, the Confederate attack plan would have required substantial modification. In addressing the common claim that the Federals would have been better off had Sickles just adhered to Meade's alleged orders to, at least, partially cover Little Round Top, Longstreet believed "his [Sickles'] left flank would not have been heavy enough to resist an attack," while further declaring, "We would have had no problem whatever in working in his rear and outflanking him." In characteristically blunt fashion, Longstreet concluded, "The only thing left for Sickles was to do as he did."[32]

By the time his memoirs were published in 1896, Longstreet readily proclaimed his July 2 assault might have been more successful had he waited "thirty or forty minutes" longer to attack. Longstreet reasoned that if Meade and Sickles had been given that extra time, the Federal commander would have ordered Sickles to return his corps to its original position between Winfield Scott Hancock's Second Corps and the area just north of Little Round Top. With that retroactive move completed, the former First Corps commander contended that "my first deployment would have enveloped Little Round Top and carried it before it could have been strongly manned, and General Meade would have drawn off to his line selected behind Pipe Creek."[33] Writing just after Longstreet's death, Sickles echoed Longstreet's argument: "If Lee had waited an hour later, I would have been on Cemetery Ridge, in compliance with General Meade's orders, and Longstreet could have marched, unresisted, from Seminary Ridge to the foot of Round Top, and might, perhaps, have unlimbered his guns on the summit." Lafayette McLaws, one of Longstreet's division commanders at Gettysburg, also agreed with the additional delay argument, writing, "I therefore only assert my belief that if the attack had been delayed much better results would have followed." McLaws essentially argued that once the Confederate High Command found the Federals concentrated in their front in much greater force than expected, rear reinforcement to Longstreet's two divisions became even more essential, with additional delay until the arrival of Pickett's division a sound course forward. Of course, all three generals could not have known how such a scenario might have ultimately played out; however, Longstreet's base contention that he would have sought out, threatened, and potentially struck Sickles' left flank, which would have rested just north of Little Round Top, is a reasonable assumption. In making this statement, Longstreet inherently admitted he believed his divisions would have had a better chance of success on July 2 had Sickles returned to lower Cemetery Ridge in the mid-afternoon hours, as opposed to continuing his occupation of the Peach Orchard and its surrounding environs. Perhaps it was this overarching claim Longstreet made in 1896, coupled with his consistent analysis over the years of how Sickles' move negatively affected the inner-workings of his July 2 attack, that led Lee's "Old Warhorse" to outright tell Sickles in 1902 that his position "saved that battle-field to the Union cause."[34]

*

Thus far we have established that Longstreet thought a great deal in the post-war years about whether Sickles' move to the Peach Orchard proved both beneficial to the Federal army and detrimental to his own attack. It is now imperative to explore the validity of Longstreet's 1902 claim, while making every attempt to avoid the ever-present landmines of speculative discussion.

Before fully moving on to this analysis, two key facts need to be established and reiterated. First, a fundamental understanding of the Confederate High Command's attack plan against the Federal left on July 2 is vital. With all the ample attention given over the decades to the fight for Little Round Top, a false misunderstanding of sorts seems to have crept into the collective consciousness of many who study and discuss the battle. Simply put, neither Lee nor Longstreet designated Little Round Top as a Confederate attack objective on July 2. To the contrary, because of a misleading early morning reconnaissance report, Lee was led to believe there was no significant Federal force south of Cemetery Hill and the Confederate army had an opportunity to attack up the Emmitsburg Road—first to seize the Peach Orchard, then to use that higher ground between the two armies to gain Cemetery Ridge, and finally, Cemetery Hill. Lee made these objectives explicitly clear in his first official report on the battle, asserting, "In front of General Longstreet the enemy held a position from which, if he could be driven, it was thought our artillery could be used to advantage in assailing the more elevated ground beyond, and thus enable us to reach the crest of the ridge. That officer was directed to endeavor to carry this position…. After a severe struggle, Longstreet succeeded in getting possession of and holding the desired ground." In his second report, he again reiterated, "It was determined to make the principal attack upon the enemy's left, and endeavor to gain a position from which it was thought that our artillery could be brought to bear with effect. Longstreet was directed to place the divisions of McLaws and Hood on the right of Hill, partially enveloping the enemy's left, which he was to drive in." Based on these reports, it is clear that when Lee began formulating the Confederate battle plan on the second day, he had his sights set on where reconnaissance indicated the Federal left rested—near Cemetery Hill, not Little Round Top.[35]

The second key fact to address is perhaps an even more pervasive misstep in the mainstream understanding of the July 2 battle—namely that Longstreet could have attacked in the morning. To the contrary, it was an impossibility that Longstreet could have initiated his assault in the morning hours. I realize this statement strikes hard at a massive amount of postwar commentary and many twentieth century and modern narratives of the battle; however, upon closely examining the various events and circumstances that hamstrung the rapidity of the Confederate High Command's decision-making ability on the morning of July 2, it is an entirely reasonable assertion. Perhaps the most important detail to take note of is the time at which Lee first issued orders to Longstreet on July 2: 11 a.m. Understanding this reality leaves but one hour of morning left for scholars and students of the war to wrangle over, and that hour quickly vanishes once recognizing Longstreet was without one-eighth of his two divisions' attack force at 11 a.m.: Evander Law's brigade of Hood's division. Longstreet then asked Lee if his command could postpone its march to the right until the arrival of Law's brigade. Lee gave his permission, and with that consent went the morning.[36]

Unsatisfied with this answer, Longstreet critics have often then pivoted to not only blaming Longstreet for any delay up to the 11 a.m. hour, but also any delay occurring between approximately 12 p.m. and 3:30 p.m., when the divisions finally reached the general location of their attack jump-off points near Pitzer's Schoolhouse. The pre–11 a.m. argument is quite easily addressed when underscoring that until the 10 to 11 a.m. hour, Lee remained undecided as to where and with whom he wanted to initiate the day's attack and was uncertain as to what to do with Richard Ewell's Second Corps. Regarding the early afternoon hours, it is crucial to remember Lee explicitly ordered Longstreet's column to march *concealed* from Federal view, and therefore had ordered an additional reconnaissance to be conducted for the purpose of finding a hidden route. This reconnaissance was apparently not completed until the late morning or early afternoon hours. The remaining delay before 3:30 p.m. was consumed by the march and unforeseen countermarch ordeal.[37]

The importance of these two facts in analyzing Longstreet's 1902 claim concerning the positive value of Sickles' move to the Peach Orchard cannot be overstated. Significantly, they immediately squelch the need to discuss the potential benefits of Longstreet attacking earlier than he ultimately did in the mid-afternoon hours, and especially, the need to entertain arguments about Longstreet potentially seizing Little Round Top in the morning hours.[38] The short answer to these, ultimately non-productive, discussions is that events and circumstances on the Confederate side, along with Lee's honest misunderstanding (based on poor intelligence) about the nature of the Federal position precluded any chance for those speculative scenarios to ever play out. As a result, we are able to focus our full attention on assessing the validity of Longstreet's argument upon the historical timetable with Sickles moving out to the Peach Orchard around 3 p.m. and Longstreet ultimately initiating his attack around 4:30 p.m.[39] With these parameters established and upon weighing the evidence, did Sickles' decision actually disrupt the Confederate attack plan and boost the Army of the Potomac's chances for victory on July 2?

Perhaps one of the most important and least understood subtopics to comprehend about the July 2 fight on the southern end of the battlefield was the Confederates' initial battle plan against the Federal left. It has already been established that the Confederates' ultimate objective on July 2 was Cemetery Hill due to poor, but critical, intelligence leading Lee to formulate his battle plan to gain and attack up the Emmitsburg Road. Even discounting several post-battle and postwar writings from those who were present that morning and privy to this battle plan, the mid-morning exchange between Lee, Longstreet, and the First Corps division commander, Lafayette McLaws, alone confirms Lee's focus was up the Emmitsburg Road toward Cemetery Hill. Once McLaws reported to the front, he met with Lee and Longstreet, whereby the former informed McLaws that once his division reached the Confederate extreme right, his men should form perpendicular to the Emmitsburg Road. When Longstreet expressed concern and suggested McLaws' men form *parallel* to the Emmitsburg Road, Lee overruled the corps commander and reiterated the division should be placed perpendicular to the road. A quick glance at a map of the southern portion of the battlefield, with a focus on the Emmitsburg Road, will clearly outline the severity of Lee's instructions, especially when taking into account the actual position of the Federal army at any time up until the 3 p.m. hour. A point not nearly stressed enough when discussing the initial Confederate battle plan for Longstreet's July 2 attack is that his two divisions' original instructions would have looked very little like what ultimately transpired in the late afternoon hours. What ultimately transpired (because of Sickles' move) looked more like Longstreet's rejected proposal to have McLaws form parallel to the Emmitsburg Road, as opposed to Lee's original, perpendicular plan. In short, under Lee's intended attack orientation, both divisions would essentially have been moving northeastward toward Cemetery Hill at a right angle to the road, with one division opening the assault and another in support. A quick glance at A.P. Hill's official report confirms the accuracy of this observation when the Third Corps commander wrote erroneously about what he thought transpired on July 2, "The corps of General Longstreet was on my right and in a line, being nearly at right angles to mine." Lafayette McLaws pointed out the reasoning behind Hill's mistaken statement, writing, "I have no doubt he [Hill] reports Longstreet's position not from what he saw, but from what he knew were the orders of General Lee." McLaws corrected Hill's misconception, further explaining how his own division's line "was but an extension of his [Hill's] on the right, and even Hood, away to my right, never got positions at right angles." In sum, McLaws keenly recollected that Hood "tried to get that way, but did not succeed."[40]

With this reality in mind, what conclusions can be made about a Confederate attack forming perpendicular to the Emmitsburg Road and advancing northeasterly toward the assumed location of the Federal left near Cemetery Hill, if Sickles' corps had remained on or returned to lower Cemetery Ridge in the mid-afternoon hours? Dipping as shallowly as possible into speculative territory, we can make a few observations. With the Federal line in place just north of Little Round Top—Sickles holding the army's left flank—it is reasonable to assume that any Confederate attack executed in the way Lee had directed would have grievously progressed in front of several Federal corps, with the attacking column's right flank in the air and dangerously exposed. Before fully committing themselves to such a perilous attack, it is probably a fair assumption the Confederate High Command would have recognized at some point that the Federal position actually extended along Cemetery Ridge and much further south than expected. Very likely some delay would have ensued as the Confederates fashioned a revised plan; however, once altered and the assault launched, the battle in all likelihood would have been waged directly against Cemetery Ridge, with little to no significant intermediary obstacle for Longstreet's two divisions to overcome. Sickles himself made this point clearly and effectively in the postwar years, contending that remaining on or returning to lower Cemetery Ridge would not only "have surrendered to Lee the positions for his artillery which he states in his official report it was the object of his movement to gain," but also "abandoned to the enemy all the vantage-ground he sought and had to fight for all the afternoon."[41] E.P. Alexander signaled support for Sickles' argument, writing, "It was no harm to Meade to have our charge expend its first fury upon an advanced line in front; where the shank line in the rear gave such fine opportunity for artillery to cover the retreat of troops from the front.... Sickles claims that his advanced position is what gave Meade the victory, and in my opinion he has reasonable ground for thinking so."[42] With Longstreet able to seize the Peach Orchard, as Lee had intended, for use as an artillery platform and infantry launching pad without a significant fight, the Confederates might have found themselves in a better scenario than what ultimately transpired when Sickles moved west and forced a bloody engagement at the Peach Orchard, along Houck's Ridge, and in all areas between.[43] In essence, with Sickles on lower Cemetery Ridge, Longstreet might have been able to better unleash the full weight of his two divisions directly against Cemetery Ridge as opposed to expending a substantial portion of his attack's potency on the ground between Seminary and Cemetery Ridge.[44]

Although Longstreet's two divisions shattered Sickles' corps and ultimately seized that so-called middle ground, the Federal Third Corps' move to the Peach Orchard nonetheless had a significant negative impact on the Confederate assault. First of all, Sickles' advance position forced the Confederates to quickly fashion an impromptu attack plan. First Corps division commander Lafayette McLaws later underscored that the Confederates were "presented a state of affairs which was certainly not contemplated when the original plan or order of battle was given, and certainly was not known to General Longstreet a half hour previous." McLaws also described how the Federals were "massed in my front, and extended to my right and left as far as I could see." Soon after the First Corps divisions finished their countermarch and prepared to attack, Lee and Longstreet recognized the changed battlescape and the need to modify the attack plan.[45] Fitzgerald Ross, a Captain of Hussars in the Imperial Austrian Service and observer of the Gettysburg battle from the Confederate perspective, spent most of Longstreet's July 2 attack with or around Lee's senior lieutenant and noticed Longstreet had "a long consultation with the Commander-in-Chief" and then proceeded to "[ride] up the line and down again, occasionally dismounting, and going forward to get a better view of the enemy's position." While holding firm to attacking up the Emmitsburg Road with the Peach Orchard, Cemetery Ridge, and Cemetery Hill as the principal objectives (in that order), Sickles' move largely forced Lee to give up his *perpendicular* to the Emmitsburg Road plan and have the divisions form more parallel to the road; shift Hood's division to the right of McLaws; and commence the attack with Hood's, instead of McLaws', division. Under this revised plan, save for Evander Law's and part of Jerome Robertson's brigade, the entirety of Longstreet's two divisions now occupied attack jump-off points to the west of the road. It is also well-worth noting that the formulation of this revised plan and its execution needed to be done quickly because of the advanced state of the day. In this vein, historian Harry Pfanz fittingly described the altered attack plan as "hastily modified" due to it being "too late to make any major changes in it." Indeed, within about an hour, between 3:30 and 4:30 p.m., these actions were completed—no small feat—however, the execution of the actual attack would largely be implemented on the fly and against a Federal line that unexpectedly extended further south to Houck's Ridge, Devil's Den, and ultimately, Little Round Top with the arrival of Federal reinforcements.[46]

Speaking of the Federal Third Corps' left flank on Houck's Ridge, this reality ultimately had significant negative effects on Longstreet's attack. One must seriously wonder why Lee's altered attack plan—formulated *after* recognizing Sickles' advance position—stubbornly clung to the early morning intention to "attack up the Emmitsburg Road." Harry Pfanz aptly dubbed this persistent directive as one "that did not comport with reality." Did the Confederate High Command fail to recognize that Sickles' left did not end at the Peach Orchard, but extended well east and south along Houck's Ridge?[47] Confederate cavalry officer and Lee's nephew, Fitzhugh Lee, seemed to think so and expressed as much, writing in the postwar years, "Lee was deceived by it [Sickles' move] and gave orders to attack up the Emmitsburg road, partially enveloping the enemy's left; there was much behind Sickles." It is uncertain if Fitzhugh Lee was referring to additional Federal corps behind Sickles, the portion of Sickles' line east of the Emmitsburg Road, or both. Either way, part of Sickles' corps was certainly located well behind the road. Even so, for whatever reason, Lee's altered attack plan remained focused up the Emmitsburg Road—not only with McLaws', but also Hood's division. Lafayette McLaws made a similar argument to that of Fitzhugh Lee's, writing, "General Lee did not think the enemy's left was occupied so strongly as it was," while also dropping the bombshell statement that the commanding general "gave his orders for the movement of Longstreet's assault based on information obtained very early in the morning." In other words, Lee continued to wed himself to Captain Samuel Johnston's altogether-misleading early morning reconnaissance report to the very end, even when formulating the Confederates' revised attack plan in the late afternoon hours. Confirming this assertion, McLaws emphasized "that General Lee must have given his orders for the attack based upon false information, or perhaps it would be better to say wrong information." Dubbing the entire inaccurate grasp of the Federal position an "erroneous opinion," McLaws held that "if ... a different state of affairs was known by anybody to exist, it had not been reported to either General Lee or General Longstreet; at least it appears so," and even more significantly, that it "was never corrected." Indeed, one need only look at the number

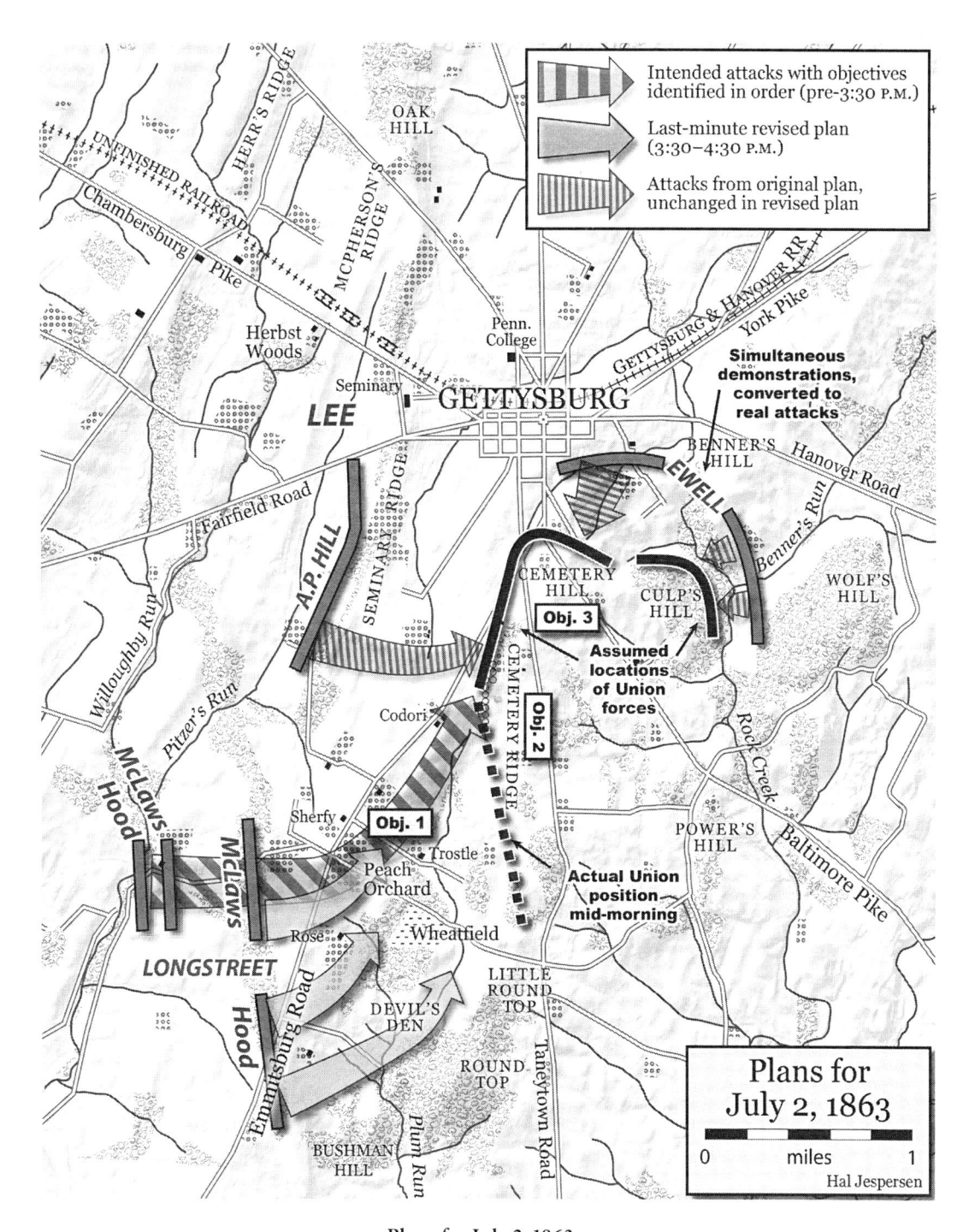

Plans for July 2, 1863.

of times Longstreet confirmed to Hood that they must obey Lee's orders to attack up the Emmitsburg Road—when the division commander made his last-minute plea to attack around Big Round Top—to understand Hood remained bound to an impractical attack plan based on stale (and faulty from inception) intelligence which discounted the portion of Sickles' line located east of the Emmitsburg Road. Sickles himself would effectively stress this point in the postwar years, declaring, "The only order of battle announced by General Lee on July 2 of which there is any record was to assail my position on the Emmitsburg road, turn my left flank (which he erroneously supposed to rest on the Peach-Orchard), and sweep the attack 'up the Emmitsburg road.'" In yet another account, Sickles accurately held that "In the afternoon … in view of the advance of my corps, General Lee was obliged to form a new plan of battle. As he believed that both of my flanks rested on the Emmitsburg road, Lee directed Longstreet to envelop my left at the Peach-Orchard, and press the attack northward 'up the Emmitsburg road.'" Perhaps Sickles' best description of the Confederate High Command's mistake or unintentional oversight when devising their mid-afternoon, altered attack plan is as follows, and worth quoting in full:

> The situation on the left flank of the Union army was entirely changed by my advance to the Emmitsburg road…. Fortunately for me, General Lee believed that my line from the Peach-Orchard north—about a division front—was all Longstreet would have to deal with. Longstreet soon discovered that my left rested beyond Devil's Den, about twelve hundred yards easterly from the Emmitsburg road, and at a right angle to it. Of course, Longstreet could not push forward to Lee's objective,—the Emmitsburg road ridge,—leaving this force on his flank and rear, to take him in reverse. An obstinate conflict followed, which detained Longstreet until the Fifth Corps, which had been in reserve on the Union right, moved to the left and got into position on the Round Tops.[48]

In being forced to ultimately address a Federal line that bent well back from the Federal salient's center of gravity at the Peach Orchard, Longstreet's July 2 assault was increasingly subjected to severe attenuation. E.P. Alexander succinctly described the effect the Federal line's extension to Devil's Den had on the Confederate attack, writing, "In reading the reports by the subordinate officers one cannot but be struck by the manner in which during this fighting the continuity of the lines was broken & regiments & brigades were separated & stretched out, & often found their flanks exposed." Likewise, Prussian Army officer Captain Justus Scheibert, who observed Longstreet's attack with British Lieutenant Colonel Arthur J. L. Fremantle from atop a large oak tree in A.P. Hill's sector, characterized all the Confederate assaults on July 2, to include Longstreet's, as having "no lasting success, since they had no concentration as a result of the spreading of the attacking troops and were also incoherent." In also writing on this topic, Lafayette McLaws maintained that although Hood was forced to reorient his division "towards the enemy's left, … he never did go far enough to envelop the left, not even partially." The combination of attempting to abide by Lee's continued instructions to attack up the Emmitsburg Road and the need to address the Federals' extended line to Devil's Den stretched Longstreet's attack force over a much broader front than had ever been anticipated. This reality led to a diluted power of assault, an inability to concentrate force at any one point, and a diminished potential to fully exploit a breakthrough (as at the Peach Orchard).[49]

In a postwar letter to Longstreet, Hood highlighted how Sickles' extended line along Houck's Ridge inhibited Hood's ability to carry out orders to attack up the Emmitsburg Road and ultimately led to the thinning of his division. Hood wrote, "His [Sickles'] left rested on or near Round Top, with line bending back and again forward, forming, as it were, a concave line, as approached by the Emmetsburg

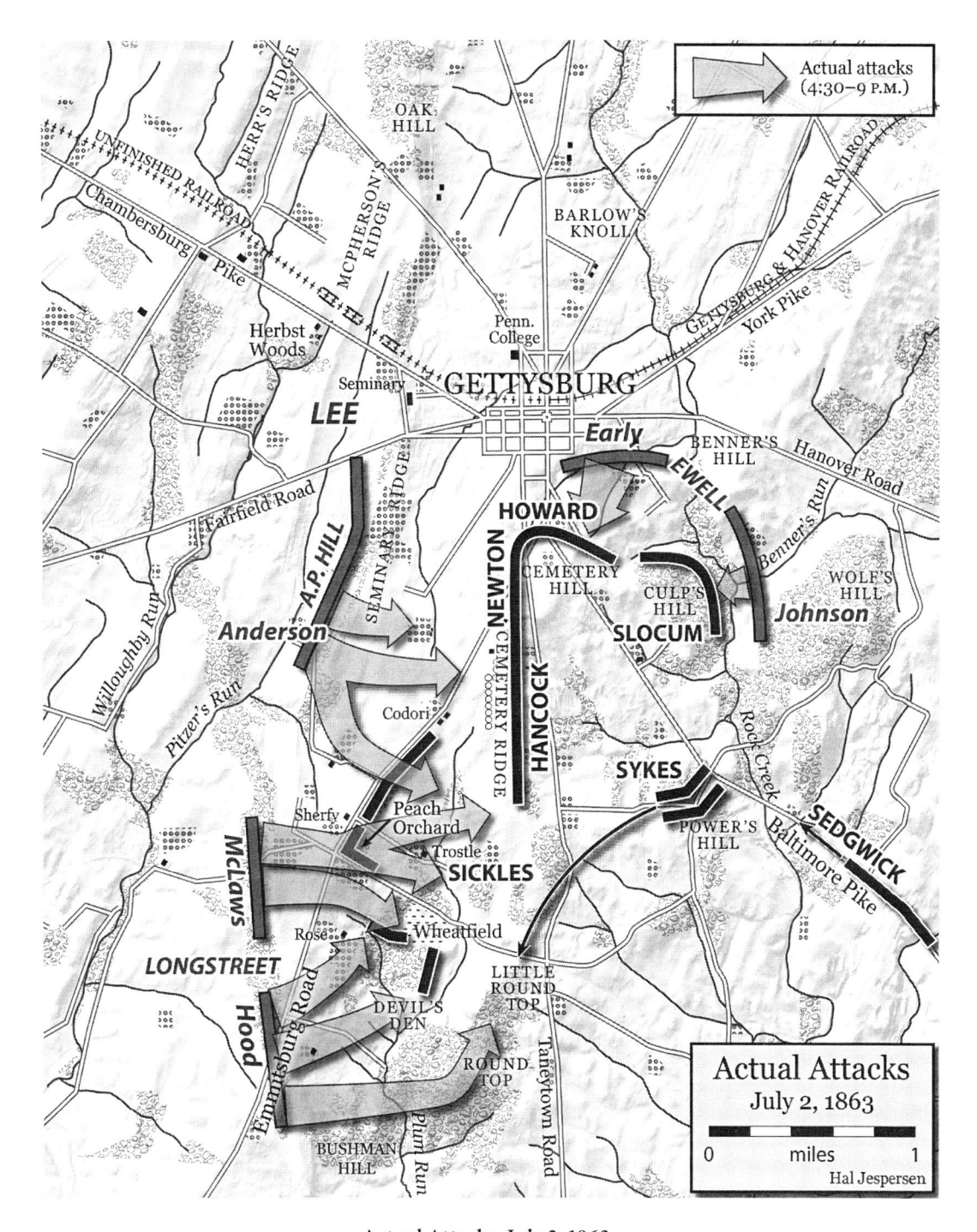

Actual Attacks, July 2, 1863.

[sic] road. A considerable body of troops was posted in front of their main line, between the Emmetsburg [sic] road and Round Top Mountain." Hood alleged that—going into the attack, not afterwards—he understood a significant Federal force was located between the Emmitsburg Road and Little Round Top, and that Sickles' left was actually located "on or near" the rocky eminence. The division commander also acknowledged "that in making the attack according to orders, viz.:

up the Emmetsburg [sic] road, I should have first to encounter and drive off" Sickles' extended line along Houck's Ridge. Likewise, Lafayette McLaws, commanding Longstreet's other attacking division on July 2, later recalled how had Hood "made the attack according to orders ... his division would be exposed to heavy fire from the main line of the enemy ... [and] subjected to a destructive fire in flank and rear, as well as in front." McLaws also believed that the Federal line's extension "far away" to the Confederate right proved the principal reason for Longstreet being "disconcerted and annoyed" in the minutes leading up to the attack, since "it was evident at a glance that the plan of battle, so far as his forces were concerned, could not be carried out."[50] Indeed, in describing the attenuation of his right division, Longstreet echoed Hood's and McLaws' recollections, describing how "our attack was to progress in the general direction of the Emmetsburg [sic] road, but the Federal troops, as they were forced from point to point, availing themselves of the stone fences and boulders near the mountain as rallying points, so annoyed our right flank that General Hood's Division was obliged to make a partial change of front so as to relieve itself of this galling flank fire." In another account, Longstreet recounted how Hood's brigades, especially his right-most brigade under Evander Law, were pulled further and further to the right, contending, "His [Hood's] right brigade was drawn towards Round Top by the heavy fire pouring from that quarter, [Henry] Benning's brigade was pressed to the thickening line at the angle, and G. T. Anderson's was put in support of the battle growing against Hood's right." Likewise, in one of E.P. Alexander's postwar accounts, the former artillery officer drew attention to Hood's "long & desperate fight upon Sickles left flank," which he stressed was found not along the Emmitsburg Road, but in "some broken ground in front of the foot of Little Round Top." Alexander's calling attention to "Sickles left flank" is significant as it lends credence to the argument that it was the location of Sickles' left flank that initially drew the First Corps' attack away from up the Emmitsburg Road and almost entirely toward all things south of the Wheatfield Road. Hood, reasonably, deemed it necessary to protect his flank and rear by addressing Sickles' left on Houck's Ridge; however, that move ultimately pulled at the seams of the First Corps' attack with consequential effect. Of additional consequence to the Confederate attack was how Hood's rightward drift did not stop at Houck's Ridge but proceeded yet further right and east toward the Round Tops, at least in part because of the presence of another Federal Third Corps unit—but more on that shortly.[51]

At this juncture, it would be irresponsible not to mention that all this action on the extreme right flank of Longstreet's July 2 assault proved so noteworthy that it actually influenced the Confederate High Command's attack on July 3. Significantly, Lee's initial plan on the third day was not the Pickett-Pettigrew-Trimble venture against the Federal center, but essentially a resumption of the July 2 fight over much of the same ground, with Hood's (by then under Law) and McLaws' spent divisions leading the attack and George Pickett's fresh division in support. Lee dashed this first plan upon meeting with Longstreet around 4:30 a.m., where the First Corps commander pointed out that Hood's and McLaws' divisions represented the army's right flank. Longstreet cautioned that if a significant Federal force threatened the attacking column's right (as it had on July 2; first at Devil's Den and then on Little Round Top), repulsed and counterattacked it, the Federals could gain access to the entire Confederate army's rear. Lee agreed with his senior lieutenant and later penned as much in his official report: "General Longstreet was delayed by a force occupying the high, rocky hills on the enemy's extreme left, from which his troops could be attacked in reverse as they advanced. *His operations had been embarrassed the day previous by the same cause* [emphasis added], and he now deemed it necessary to defend his flank and rear with the divisions of Hood and McLaws." In the postwar years, Lafayette McLaws acknowledged the severe threat his and Hood's division faced on their flanks on July 2, writing, "Both Hood and myself had as much as we could attend to prevent our flanks being turned." Indeed, Sickles' July 2 move to the Peach Orchard and the extension of his line onto Houck's Ridge, coupled with the eventual arrival of Strong Vincent's Fifth Corps brigade on Little Round Top, essentially forced battle at these locations and drew Confederate forces away from Lee's principal objectives. The rightward-shift effect on July 2 was so powerful that on the third day Lee agreed to withhold Hood's and McLaws' divisions to protect the army's right flank. At some point, Sickles himself must have realized this particular consequence of his July 2 move, since he drew some attention to it in the postwar years. Obviously referencing the aforementioned quotation from Lee's official report, he argued, "Lee points out that the same danger to Longstreet's flank, which required the protection of two divisions on July 3, existed on July 2, when his flank was unsupported."[52]

Returning entirely to our focus on July 2, it is altogether worth noting that unlike on the Federal side where George Meade effectively shifted troops from other parts of his line to meet the threat against his left, Longstreet did not have the benefit of additional reinforcements from other parts of the Confederate line to add further depth and weight to his assault.[53] In Sickles' case, despite his exposed position and having both flanks in the air, Meade successfully funneled troops from his center and right to increasingly blunt Longstreet's attack.[54] Near-astounding is the fact that Longstreet's two divisions and Richard Anderson's Third Corps division ultimately faced soldiers from six Federal corps on July 2: the First, Second, Third, Fifth, Sixth, and Twelfth. E.P. Alexander wrote extensively about the significant effect seemingly wholesale Federal reinforcements had on Longstreet's assault, emphasizing how "successive corps, divisions, brigades, & batteries concentrated on these two lone divisions," while stressing that "there was no possibility of help or reinforcement" available to Hood and McLaws; indeed no "reinforcement to the Confederates, to offset the great list on the other side." Alexander claimed to have heard Confederate infantrymen exclaim during the fight, "Have we got the Universe to whip?" In another account, Alexander held that there was not "a finer example of efficient command" than Meade's generalship on July 2, specifically citing the Federal commander's forwarding "to the scene reinforcements, both of infantry and artillery, from every corps and from every part of his line." The former artilleryman maintained that Meade "had engaged, or in hand on the field, fully 40,000 men by the time that Longstreet's assault was repulsed," while efficiently summarizing his thoughts on the topic of Federal reinforcement, and Confederate lack thereof, in one blunt statement: "One is tempted to pause for a moment to contemplate the really hopeless situation of the Confederate battle." Buttressing Alexander on this topic was Lafayette McLaws, who just as bluntly contended, "Longstreet's two divisions were not strong enough to cover the front of the attack, much less envelop the flank, and he should have been reinforced before making the assault he did."[55] Certainly, it is beyond dispute additional Federal reinforcements were critical in reinforcing Sickles' increasingly tenuous position; however, it is equally beyond dispute that the Confederates' July 2 attack plan included no provision for providing direct infantry reinforcement to Hood's and McLaws' divisions.[56] Instead, Lee seems to have entirely banked on simultaneous action across corps preventing the Federals from making successful use of their interior line and overwhelming them at one or more points along it.

Furthermore, though the center of Sickles' line was quickly pierced and overrun by William Barksdale's brigade of McLaws' division around 6 p.m., the simple fact that there was a significant Federal force located at the Peach Orchard (Longstreet's first objective for the day) meant that the attacking force would naturally be weakened for any follow-on action eastward against Cemetery Ridge.[57] In fact, this is essentially what transpired with Barksdale's brigade, along with the Confederate Third Corps brigades of Cadmus Wilcox and David Lang. Once achieving initial success along the Emmitsburg Road and advancing toward Cemetery Ridge beyond, these brigades met renewed resistance and were ultimately thrown back by: remnants of the Federal Third Corps; John Bigelow's 9th Massachusetts Battery; Freeman McGilvery's patchwork artillery line; George Willard's Second Corps brigade; the 19th Massachusetts and 42nd New York of Norman Hall's brigade (Second Corps); and the 19th Maine and 1st Minnesota regiments of William Harrow's brigade (Second Corps). Historians Glenn Tucker and Harry Pfanz have accurately described the state of Barksdale's brigade as it reached Plum Run just west of Cemetery Ridge, with Tucker asserting the Mississippians were "ragged and disorganized by the long advance over rough, broken ground," while Pfanz contended they were "fatigued and in some disorder." On the nature of the resistance Barksdale faced at Plum Run, Tucker turned one of his famously effectual phrases—"Here Barksdale hit something solid." Likewise, E.P. Alexander described how the Confederates' sense of elation upon clearing the Peach Orchard quickly turned to disappointment, writing, "when I got to take in all the topography I was very much disappointed. It was not the enemy's main line we had broken. That loomed up near 1,000 yards beyond us, a ridge giving good cover behind it & endless fine positions for batteries." In yet another account, Alexander held, "We only had a moderately good time with Sickles' retreating corps after all. They fell back upon fresh troops in what seemed a strong position extending along the ridge north of Round Top." Indeed, despite the rapid disintegration of Sickles' line at the Peach Orchard, the intermediary resistance the Confederates experienced there and afterwards along Plum Run knocked the collective wind out of Longstreet's attack north of the Wheatfield Road before it could reach its second objective, Cemetery Ridge. In other words, the Confederate wave peaked too soon, crashing down with heavy force at the Peach Orchard, while leaving only white water to contend with stiff Federal resistance east of the Emmitsburg Road.[58]

Though Longstreet's two-division attack was, for all intents and purposes, extremely successful in severely mauling several Federal corps on July 2, things could have very well gone much worse for the Federals. As already established, Sickles' move to the Peach Orchard forced the Confederate High Command to quickly formulate and execute an altered plan—perhaps over the course of just one hour. The implications of that abbreviated timetable on the tactical handling of the attack will never be fully understood; however, it is safe to say that it probably served to cause certain brigades to advance in semi-inopportune ways or towards unpropitious (for the Confederates) sectors of the field. Indeed, battle plans are rarely executed as intended, quickly-formed ones even less so, and quickly-formed ones against a misunderstood enemy position almost never. It is not an exaggeration to contend that the Confederate High Command never possessed an accurate understanding of the Federal position south of Cemetery Hill leading up to the July 2 attack, to include an understanding of both Sickles' original and advance positions.

As a result of that ongoing misunderstanding, once the attack began, Hood was still under orders to direct his division's attack up the Emmitsburg Road. This was undoubtedly an impractical directive, but it was still an order. Not nearly pointed out enough is the fact that Hood defied those orders, allowing a portion of his division, particularly Evander Law's right-most regiments to wander toward Big Round Top early in the assault, further exacerbating the division's collective rightward movement resulting from the location of Sickles' left flank at Devil's Den.[59] The refusal of Sickles' line at the intersection of the Emmitsburg and Wheatfield Roads certainly precluded Hood from literally adhering to his orders to attack up the Emmitsburg Road; however, it would not have impeded his ability to abide by the spirit of those orders in guiding his division's attack in that general direction. Ward's Federals on Houck's Ridge would certainly have prohibited the Confederates from attacking up the road itself, but its presence would not have stopped Hood from attacking in the general direction of the road by utilizing the 500-yard-wide Plum Run Valley between Little Round Top and Houck's Ridge to get at Ward's flank and rear. Of course, Hood was wounded early in the fight, certainly before Henry L. Benning and George T. Anderson entered the fight; however, not before the early stages of Law's and Robertson's advance. Hood later recollected being wounded "about twenty minutes" into the battle. Why did Hood allow part of Law's brigade to drift so far right toward Big Round Top, particularly the 15th and 47th Alabama regiments, at a time when the division commander neither had orders to seize Big or Little Round Top, nor would have been aware of ongoing Federal efforts to place troops there? Historian Edwin Coddington candidly called out the proverbial elephant in the room in answering this question, declaring, "Contrary to orders, Hood had moved his division away from the Emmitsburg Road for the purpose of taking Little Round Top." Indeed, perhaps Hood never fully relented on his immediate pre-attack suggestion to maneuver near or around the Round Tops after all. In response to Longstreet's repeated orders to carry out Lee's orders to attack up the Emmitsburg Road, Hood allegedly said to Colonel Philip Work of the 1st Texas just before the assault commenced, "Very well; when we get under fire, I will have a digression."[60] Indeed, many histories of the battle over the decades have muddied the waters when discussing the early stages of Hood's July 2 attack, misleadingly alleging that it was understood from inception Hood would swing part of Law's brigade toward the Round Tops, when in fact he had apparently allowed or even directed a portion of it to move in that direction—unbeknownst to Longstreet and contrary to orders.[61]

Indeed, as Colonel William Oates, commander of the 15th Alabama on Hood's extreme right, explained in one of his postwar accounts, Law rode up to him early in the regiment's advance—before crossing Plum Run—and ordered him to "hug the base of Great Round Top and go up the valley between the two mountains, until I found the left of the Union line, to turn it," which was certainly not in accordance with the division's orders to maintain at least a semblance of contact with the Emmitsburg Road.[62] Instead, here was Law ordering Oates to advance toward the ravine between the Round Tops. At the time of the division's initial advance, Hood and Law must have recognized that the main Federal force was anchored at Devil's Den, ending with Smith's battery and the 4th Maine regiment, and yet here was Law instructing Oates to "[find] the left of the Union line."[63] Additionally, neither Hood nor Law would have known of the then-ongoing Federal effort to hoist men onto Little Round Top.

Maj. Gen. John Bell Hood, CSA (National Archives).

Along with Law's alleged order for Oates to progress toward the ravine between the Round Tops, we must also address the issue of Oates, seemingly on his own initiative, advancing increasingly rightward toward Big Round Top. As events turned out, Oates' 15th Alabama, and the 47th Alabama (which was to guide on the 15th's left), were essentially given a free hand to follow Federal skirmishers located in their front toward Big Round Top. Speaking of Oates' own initiative, a close reading of his aforementioned postwar account reveals that the former colonel took matters into his own hands and even ignored Law's already-defiant order to direct the regiment toward the Round Tops' ravine, admitting that as his men approached Big Round Top he "gave the command direction to change direction *to the right* [emphasis added]." Furthermore, Oates' official battle report, written on August 8, 1863, even more clearly reveals his decision to act independently of orders. Oates held that upon crossing a stone fence at the southern face of Big Round Top "I received an order from Brig.-Gen. Law *to left-wheel my regiment* [emphasis added] and move in the direction of the heights upon my left, *which order I failed to obey,* [emphasis added] for the reason that when I received it I was rapidly advancing up the mountain, and in my front I discovered a heavy force of the enemy." Oates further alleged he could not obey Law's order because the 47th Alabama to his left "was crowding me ... and running into my regiment," while his right flank would have been exposed to flanking fire.[64]

It now being established that Hood, Law, and Oates, to one degree or another, either allowed or encouraged the extreme right of the division's attack to move toward the Round Tops, what exactly pulled it in that direction? The answer may surprise you. Once Oates crossed Plum Run and entered the woods in front of Big Round Top, his men fully engaged none other than a Federal *Third Corps* unit, Major Homer Stoughton's 2nd U.S. Sharpshooters, which were positioned behind a stone wall on the southwest face of Big Round Top.[65] It was this Federal force that ultimately resulted in Oates finding himself on the summit of that hill shortly thereafter, and completely out of touch with the rest of his brigade.[66] Cementing this wild diversion, unintended by the Confederate High Command and expedited by Stoughton's sharpshooters, was Oates' follow-on instructions from Law (now in command of the division) via his assistant adjutant, Captain L.R. Terrell. While Oates tried to make the argument his men should hold this position on Big Round Top while artillery was brought up to, in his opinion, make Little Round Top untenable, the Captain informed Oates that Law's orders were to continue north, turn the Federal left flank, and seize the smaller hill. Hence, Longstreet's attack was spreading into places untethered from orders and never imagined at the outset as a result of: Hood's subtle encouragement of moving the extreme right of his division toward the Round Tops; Law's instructions to Oates, in the first instance to advance toward the Round Tops' ravine, and then, secondly, after Oates disregarded those orders and found himself on Big Round Top, to seize Little Round Top; and, perhaps most importantly, the magnetism of the 2nd U.S.

Brig. Gen. Evander Law, CSA (Library of Congress).

Sharpshooters in leading Oates up Big Round Top. To boot was Oates' ensuing decision to detach the 15th Alabama's Company A under Captain Francis K. Shaaff—first to protect his flank from the retreating Third Corps sharpshooters, and then on a sideshow foray to capture Federal wagons behind the Round Tops. It is curious Oates thought a company sufficient to protect his flank against the sharpshooters once *on* the Round Tops, but apparently believed an entire regiment was necessary to address the same Federal force when making his move *toward* the hills.[67]

In the postwar years, Oates alleged that during the battle Longstreet had no idea two First Corps regiments reached the summit of and swung across Big Round Top. Oates also claimed that once his direct superior

Col. William C. Oates, CSA (Alabama Department of Archives and History, Wikimedia Commons).

took over divisional command from the wounded Hood, Law was personally located "along the line somewhere to the left."[68] And yet, Anderson never claimed to have seen Law and neither one of the other two brigade commanders in Hood's division—Benning and Robertson—recalled the receipt of any orders from Law during the attack. Furthermore, Robertson directly requested Benning and Anderson's help against the Federals along Houck's Ridge via written notes. Anderson received his note; Benning did not, while the latter recalled advancing to Robertson's assistance on his own initiative. Benning's consequential support, in particular, led to the Confederates' capture of Devil's Den around 6 p.m.[69]; however, where was Law? And even more importantly, how do we square Oates' claim that Law was located on the division's left with his assertion Longstreet was in the dark about the existence of First Corps units on Big Round Top? It being well-known that Longstreet was on the right of McLaws' division in the leadup to Kershaw's advance, realistically Law would have been located close to the corps commander. In fact, in the postwar years, Law stated that after Hood's wounding and the entire division becoming engaged, he became worried about Anderson's brigade on his left flank and ordered the entire division to halt for a time.[70] Seeking some support to his left from McLaws' division, which had yet to advance, Law described how he "hurried back to the ridge from which we had originally advanced"

Essay 2. A Letter to General Sickles 53

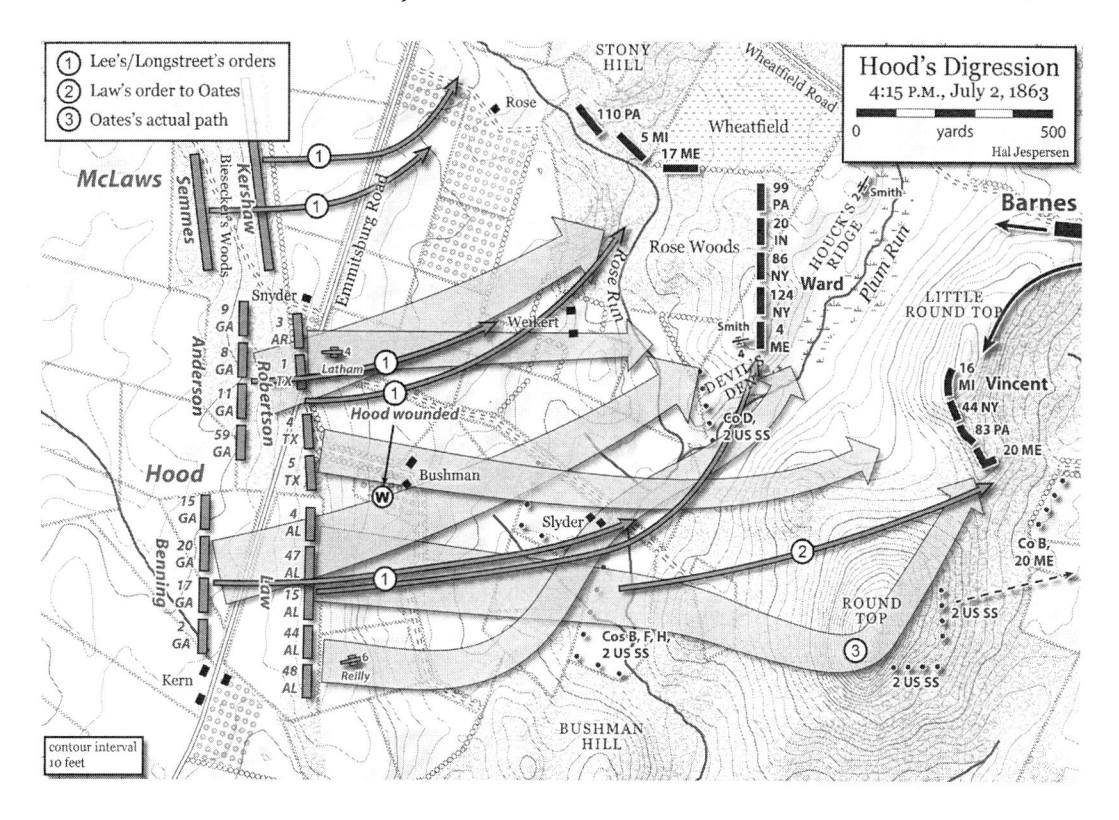

Hood's Digression, 4:15 p.m., July 2, 1863.

and actually spoke to Joseph Kershaw. In the ensuing conversation, Kershaw even asked Law to designate where he would prefer his South Carolinian brigade advance in support of Law's left flank. Soon thereafter, Kershaw "promptly moved to the attack, the movement being taken up by the whole division." Hence, according to Law's own testimony, he was physically located with Kershaw just prior to that brigade's attack—the very place we know Longstreet was located near at the time.[71] Before unilaterally committing Oates' 15th Alabama and Michael Bulger's 47th Alabama to an attack on Little Round Top (ultimately in combination with three additional regiments, the 4th and 5th Texas, and 4th Alabama) with the attendant consequence of forcing more units further to the right (and away from the Emmitsburg Road), perhaps some consultation with Longstreet around this time might have been prudent—either personally or by staff officer. To be fair to Law, who was just thrust into division command in the middle of a significant battle, perhaps it would have been equally judicious for Longstreet to have at least sent a staff officer to his right division to more closely examine and advise on the state of the attack in that sector. In his memoirs, Longstreet only offered his belief that Hood's "well-seasoned troops were not in need of a close guiding hand. The battle was on, and they knew how to press its hottest contention."[72]

With the Confederates' first attack objective—the Peach Orchard—located right in McLaws' front, it is altogether unsurprising that Longstreet focused most of his personal attention there on July 2. Especially considering Lee specifically requested Longstreet keep an eye on McLaws.[73] That said, the expenditure of the majority of the

Top: Monument to the 2nd U.S. Sharpshooters (USS), Companies E and H, on the Slyder Farm. The 2nd USS played a critical role during Longstreet's July 2 attack, pulling a significant portion of Evander Law's Alabama brigade much farther to the right than the Confederate High Command ever intended. *Bottom:* The western face of Big Round Top, looking eastward toward the hill's summit—a view not unlike the one the 15th and 47th Alabama would have had during their ascent on July 2. Note the daunting terrain challenges (Author's Collection).

A modern-day photograph from the summit of Big Round Top, looking westward. The 15th Alabama and 47th Alabama advanced to this position between 4:30 and 5 p.m. on July 2. In the distance, one can see (1) Evander Law's brigade's initial jump-off point along Warfield Ridge and just how far this portion of his command had to advance to reach this location and (2) the Bushman Farm, where their division commander, John Bell Hood, was wounded about 20 to 30 minutes into the fight (Author's Collection).

Confederates' increasingly-diluted force south of the Peach Orchard and how, where, or when certain units like Joseph Kershaw's, William Barksdale's, and William Wofford's brigades were sent in, casts some doubt on how good a handle the Confederate High Command, and Longstreet in particular as attack commander, ever truly had in executing their quickly-revised attack plan against a largely unanticipated situation.[74]

One need look no further than the experiences and testimonies of some First Corps brigade commanders who fought on July 2 to find evidence of this reality. Joseph Kershaw's command, the first brigade from McLaws' division to enter the fight, advanced from its position in Beisecker's Woods sometime between 5 and 5:30 p.m., ultimately engaging the Federals south of the Peach Orchard in the Stony Hill, Rose Woods, and Wheatfield sectors of the field. Compare this—what actually transpired—with the nature of Longstreet's and McLaws' repeated instructions to Kershaw in the minutes leading up to his brigade's advance. Kershaw stated in his official report that Longstreet initially directed Kershaw to attack the Federals at the Peach Orchard (where Barksdale ultimately attacked), "turn his [the Federals'] flank, and extend along the cross-road, with my left resting toward the Emmitsburg Road." In a March 1876 letter to Gettysburg historian John Bachelder, Kershaw

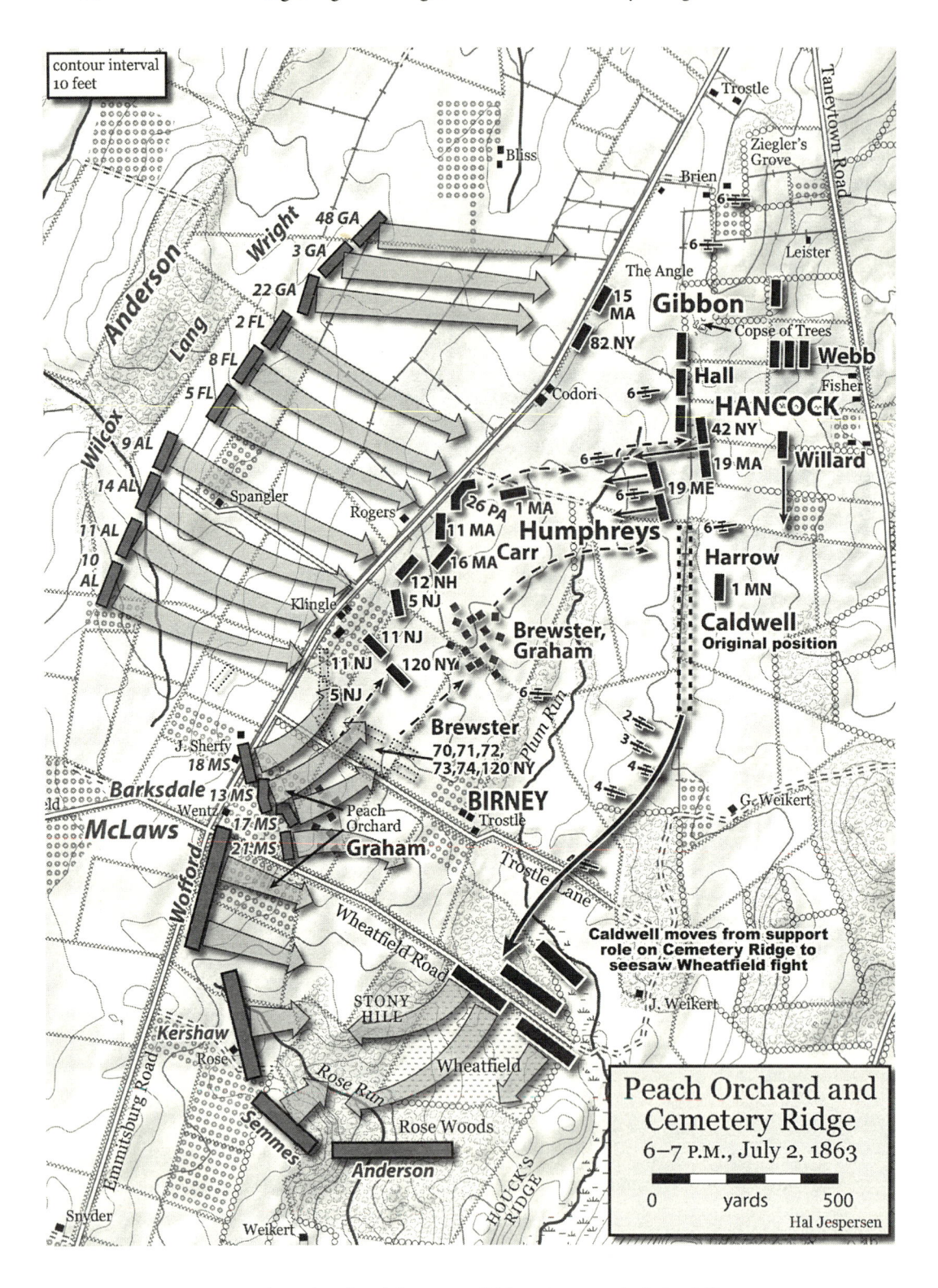

Peach Orchard and Cemetery Ridge, 6–7 p.m., July 2, 1863.

further clarified these initial orders to mean his brigade was "to dress to the right and wheel to the left"; in other words, he was to advance easterly to a point south of the Peach Orchard, then wheel left to an alignment nearly parallel with the Wheatfield Road, and finally, attack the Federals at the Peach Orchard from the south and push the assault up the Emmitsburg Road. It is clear these orders were provided before the Confederate High Command recognized the Federal left extended well south of the Peach Orchard. Kershaw also discussed his modified orders once Hood was directed to move his division to the right or south of McLaws' position, writing, "I was directed to commence the attack so soon as General Hood became engaged, swinging around toward the peach orchard, and at the same time establishing connection with Hood, on my right, and co-operating with him. It was understood he was to sweep down the enemy's line in a direction perpendicular to our then line of battle. I was told that Barksdale would move with me and conform to my movement."[75] Notice how even these modified orders differed almost completely from how Kershaw's brigade ultimately attacked. McLaws' attack was: held back for about 30 to 45 minutes after Hood's men stepped off; Kershaw's attack progressed south of the Peach Orchard; the South Carolinians had a tenuous connection at best in the Rose Woods with Hood's left (specifically G.T. Anderson's 9th Georgia regiment) via the 7th and 15th South Carolina regiments[76]; Hood's attack never swept up the Emmitsburg Road, but generally advanced eastward toward the Round Tops; and Barksdale's brigade did not attack simultaneously with Kershaw. In sum, it is clear both attack plans, neither the original nor the quickly-devised revision, wound up comporting with the reality of the situation—namely, the totality of Sickles' position—and certainly could not have foreseen the severe digressions from the "attack up the Emmitsburg Road" plan that occurred on Hood's front.

Additional unforeseen issues with Kershaw's attack popped up as his brigade advanced. The artillery and infantry-lined underbelly of Sickles' Peach Orchard position, extending east along the Wheatfield Road, caused Kershaw's brigade particular trouble, especially by way of firing into the South Carolinians' then-unsupported left flank.[77] Though Paul Semmes' brigade was advanced near-simultaneously in support of Kershaw, the commands of Barksdale and Wofford were temporarily held back. Kershaw described the immediate result of this decision, writing, "When we were about the Emmitsburg road, I heard Barksdale's drums beat the assembly, and knew *then* that I should have no immediate support on my left, about to be squarely presented to the heavy force of infantry and artillery at and in rear of the Peach Orchard." Kershaw further maintained that even when Barksdale's Mississippi brigade ultimately advanced, it "passed too far to my left to afford me any relief except in silencing the batteries that had so cruelly punished my left." Essentially, Kershaw seemed to portend that the distance separating his and Barksdale's brigade, along with the Mississippians' delayed advance not only left his flank extremely vulnerable, but also zapped the overall potency of his brigade's attack. That said, as with many Gettysburg topics, there are caveats. Kershaw also pointed out how his brigade committed a critical, self-inflicted error during its attack that served to further expose his left flank. The plan was for Kershaw's three leftmost regiments—the 2nd, 3rd, and 8th South Carolina—to wheel left during their advance to address the

A northward-looking view from the modern-day "Longstreet Tower" of the ground over which much of McLaws' and Anderson's divisions attacked on July 2 (Author's Collection).

An eastward-looking view from the modern-day "Longstreet Tower," showing much of the ground over which McLaws' division advanced and attacked on July 2 (Author's Collection).

Federal batteries positioned along the Wheatfield Road. Unfortunately for Kershaw's men, when the moment came, someone shouted to wheel right instead of left, which emboldened the Federal artillerymen along the road—allowing them to return to their guns and rake Kershaw's flank.[78]

The other caveat to criticism of how and when Barksdale attacked involves the Federal High Command's use of John C. Caldwell's Second Corps division. Meade had initially instructed Caldwell's men to take up position behind Humphrey's Third Corps division to provide the Federals support at the Peach Orchard and along the Emmitsburg Road.[79] However, the immediacy and veracity of the fight south of the Wheatfield Road and the relative inaction north of the road early in the assault precipitated Meade's decision to send Caldwell south to Federal Fifth Corps commander George Sykes' assistance. Caldwell never found Sykes, but he was snatched up by Major Henry E. Tremain, Sickles' senior aide, who directed the division toward the see-saw fight in the Wheatfield. The major consequence of moving Caldwell from behind Humphrey's position to the Wheatfield sector was that it left Federal forces north of the Wheatfield Road without any immediate infantry support and primed that front for a Confederate reaping. Barksdale's brigade was ultimately launched and its time of advance, perhaps by some degree of chance, was ultimately impeccable for the Confederates once Caldwell's four brigades shifted and became fully engaged in the Wheatfield. Indeed, in one of the most well-known and impressive attacks of the war, the Mississippians crushed Sickles' advanced position at the Peach Orchard, or as Kershaw later described the attack, "Barksdale ... advanced upon the Peach Orchard after I had become engaged; ... cleared that position with the assistance of my 8th South Carolina regiment, driving all before him, and, ... advanced far beyond that point, until enveloped by superior forces." More succinctly, one of McLaws' aides, G.B. Lamar, Jr., wrote, "I have witnessed many charges marked in every way by unflinching gallantry ... but I never saw anything to equal the dash and heroism of the Mississippians."[80]

Along with Kershaw's and Barksdale's brigade, perhaps the other brigade most often mentioned when discussing the execution of Longstreet's attack is Wofford's command. Over the decades, studies of the battle have increasingly questioned why Wofford, like Kershaw and Semmes, was sent south of the Wheatfield Road into the cauldron of death in the Stony Hill, Rose Woods, and Wheatfield sectors of the field instead of supporting Barksdale's brigade as it made its push from the Peach Orchard toward Plum Run and Cemetery Ridge.[81] Resultantly, three of McLaws' four brigades were expended south of the Peach Orchard, while the division's left only managed to maintain a tenuous connection with the right of Richard Anderson's Third Corps division as the attack spread northward. Wofford's advance has often been described as almost haphazard, with the rationale for how it was sent in never sufficiently explained; however, Longstreet actually provided a detailed explanation for the move in the postwar years, writing:

> We had carried Devil's Den, were at the Round Tops and the Wheat-Field, but [Romeyn] Ayres's division of regulars and [James] Barnes's division were holding us in equal battle. The struggle throughout the field seemed at its tension. The brigades of R. H. Anderson's division could hold off other troops of Hancock's, but were not strong enough to step to the enemy's

lines. When [John] Caldwell's division was pushed away, Ayres's flank and the gorge at Little Round Top were only covered by a sharp line of picket men behind the boulders. If we could drive in the sharp-shooters and strike Ayres's flank to advantage, we could dislodge his and Barnes's divisions, occupy the gorge behind [George] Sykes's brigades on Round Top, force them to retreat, and lift our desperate fighters to the summit. I had one brigade—Wofford's—that had not been engaged in the hottest battle. To urge the troops to their reserve power in the precious moments, I rode with Wofford.[82]

Longstreet's explicit naming of far-right locations, like Devil's Den and the Round Tops, clearly exposes just how Sickles' extended line along Houck's Ridge and subsequent Federal reinforcements sent to that part of the field were ultimately effective in sucking the majority of the First Corps' attack force further and further to the Confederate right. It appears the First Corps commander made a conscious mid-battle decision to divorce himself from what he clearly viewed as an increasingly-unfeasible attack alignment up the Emmitsburg Road and reasoned that his divisions' then-best opportunity to crack the Federal Cemetery Ridge line was at "Ayres's flank and the gorge at Little Round Top." Before reaching this principal objective, Wofford's line of attack would be aimed at the vulnerable right of Caldwell's Second Corps division, Philippe R. De Trobriand's and Ward's Third Corps brigades, and the remnants of Jacob Sweitzer's and William Tilton's Fifth Corps brigades, their collective flank exposed as a result of Barksdale clearing Charles Graham's Third Corps brigade from the Peach Orchard. Coupled with Longstreet's belief there existed an opportunity on lower Cemetery Ridge ("the gorge at Little Round Top"), he also stressed in all his postwar accounts that he had been under the impression that, at the very least, the full weight of Richard Anderson's five-brigade division would be thrown against Cemetery Ridge as the attack progressed north of McLaws' division—a portion of the attack not under Longstreet's, but A.P. Hill's purview. "My corps, with Pickett's Division absent, numbered hardly thirteen thousand men. I realized that the fight was to be a fearful one," Longstreet emphasized, while noting that he had been "assured ... my flank would be protected by the brigades of

Brig. Gen. William T. Wofford, CSA (Library of Congress).

Wilcox, [Edward] Perry, [Ambrose] Wright, [Carnot] Posey, and [William] Mahone, moving en echelon." At the time of the battle, Longstreet certainly could not have known Anderson, Hill, and ultimately, Lee, who was physically located with the Third Corps during the attack, would only fully commit the three brigades of Cadmus Wilcox, David Lang, and Ambrose Wright to the fight.[83]

Acting on his understanding at the time, Longstreet directed Wofford's brigade to advance southeast, below and parallel to the Wheatfield Road, personally leading the brigade into battle as he had done earlier with Kershaw's command. Wofford's Georgians ultimately attacked with great effect, serving to finally clear the Stony Hill, Rose Woods, and Wheatfield of Federal forces before merging with the remnants of other brigades in the area to make a final push against the Federal line just north of Little Round Top. In the end, Longstreet's attempt to strike "the gorge at Little Round Top," pierce the Federals' Cemetery Ridge line there, and cut off and

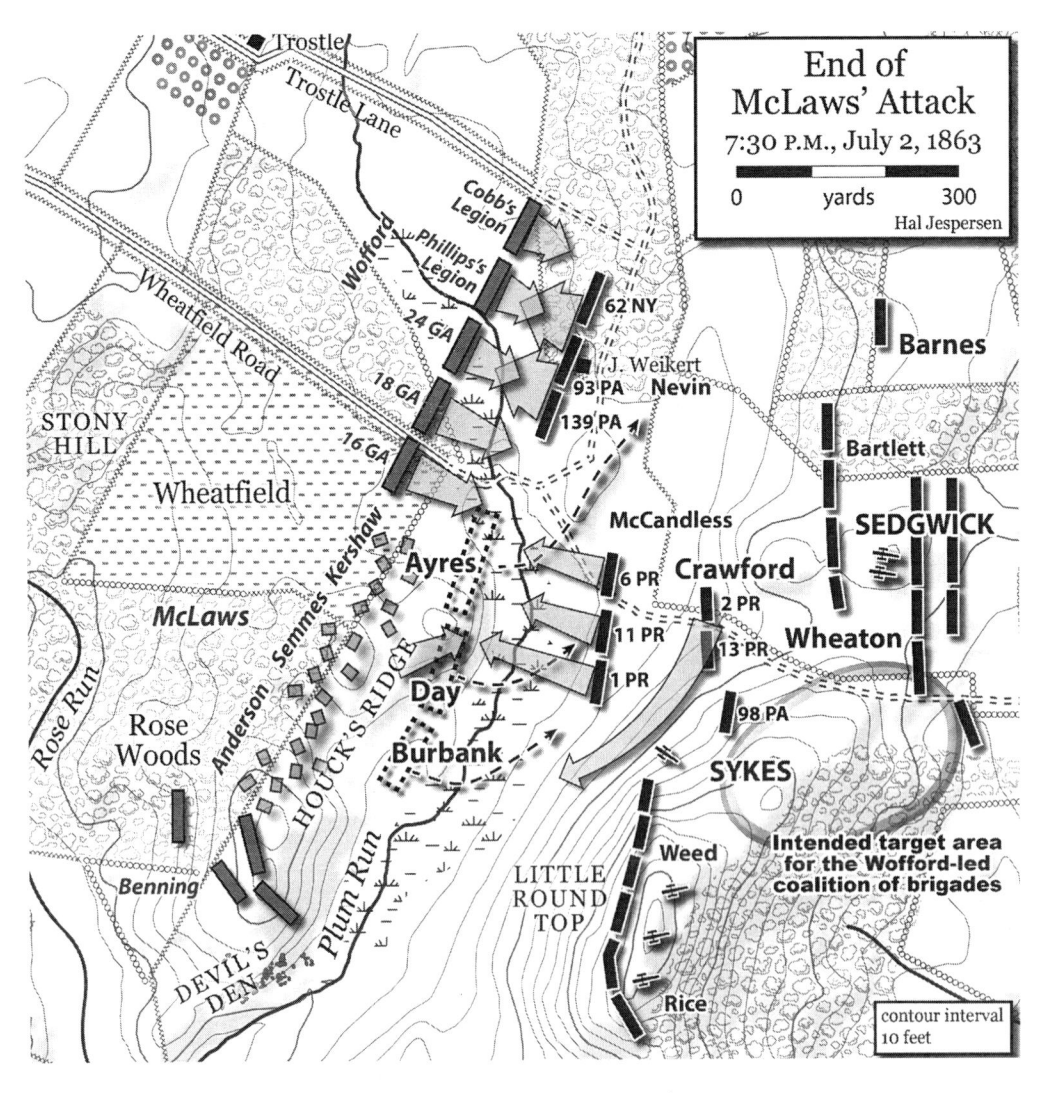

End of McLaws' Attack, 7:30 p.m., July 2, 1863.

The scene of Longstreet's final attack on July 2. Wofford's brigade advanced toward the camera position roughly between just left (south) of the Wheatfield Road and the Trostle Farm Lane. South of Wofford was the Anderson-Kershaw-Semmes coalition, which briefly attacked eastward off the northern end of Houck's Ridge (Author's Collection).

force back the Union Fifth Corps elements located on Little Round Top was unsuccessful; however, his rationale had merit. Of course, looking back on the battle from the comforts of one's armchair, certainly the case could be made that more favorable options potentially existed for the Confederates in the waning minutes of Longstreet's attack, but we will not be descending into armchair generalship here. Suffice to say, it is abundantly clear Sickles' advanced position, particularly the placement of his left flank along Houck's Ridge and the presence of the 2nd U.S. Sharpshooters still further left, served as a powerful, magnetic force in pulling the majority of Longstreet's brigades much further to the right than ever intended. Indeed, Longstreet's personal designation of a point along Cemetery Ridge just north of Little Round Top as Wofford's objective—a location nowhere near the originally-specified, primary objective of Cemetery Hill—plainly shows the consequential effect Federal forces between the Peach Orchard and Little Round Top had in disrupting Confederate attack plans on July 2.[84]

Put mildly, Dan Sickles had a colorful personality and a healthy ego. Some postwar statements he made about his July 2, 1863, move to the Peach Orchard beg to be repeated, not only for their historical value, albeit sometimes tainted, but perhaps simply because they are quintessential Sickles' repartee. In 1907, upon being asked if he was surprised there was, as of yet, no Sickles monument on the Gettysburg Battlefield, Sickles allegedly replied with something to the effect of "the whole damn battlefield is my monument." A bit less bombastically, in 1886, Sickles told a Boston audience, "If you discover a piece of commanding ground that the enemy evidently wants, and intends to make effective use of against you ... don't you think it is pretty good tactics not to let him keep it, but to take it yourself? Now, I do not profess to be a great tactician, but I think there is not a soldier here that is not tactician enough to know that." With picture-perfect imagery, Sickles also added, "I simply advanced out on to the battlefield and seized Longstreet by the throat and held him there." Asked on numerous occasions in the postwar years if, looking back, he would have changed his actions on July 2 in any way, Sickles consistently and resolutely replied, "I see nothing that I would change either in it or in any of the operations of that day."[85] The commander of Sickles' First Division at Gettysburg, David B. Birney, was just as resolute in his belief that the Third Corps' forward movement was the right one to make, writing in March 1864, "Gettysburg has glory enough for all, and the Third Corps is proud that its 'misapprehension of order' carried it into and brought on the battle instead of taking its rest [on lower Cemetery Ridge]."[86]

For Longstreet's part, Lee's "Old Warhorse" never challenged Sickles' belief in the propriety of his July 2 decision. Smattered throughout Longstreet's postwar writings, even before he kindled a personal and professional relationship with Sickles, were allusions to his own ardent belief that Sickles' move hurt the Confederates and helped the Federals on July 2. Indeed, according to Longstreet's second wife, Helen, by the last few remaining years of the general's life, he "always spoke of Gen. Sickles as the hero of Gettysburg." Helen frequently drew attention to Longstreet's 1902 letter to Sickles, "the last autograph letter he ever wrote," reiterating that in it he had "told [Sickles] that the taking of the Peach Orchard by Sickles' corps won the battle for the Union forces." Further underscoring Sickles' high regard for Longstreet's opinion on the matter, the former Federal Third Corps commander published the letter in a collection of correspondence in 1911, seven years after Longstreet's death and three years before his own.[87]

Like the debate over Longstreet's actions at Gettysburg, it appears the controversy over Sickles' move will be eternal. That said, when boiling it all down, the argument over whether the Federals would have fared better or worse had Sickles remained on or returned to lower Cemetery Ridge truly is a moot historical exercise. Perhaps Longstreet would have recognized the Federal line actually did not rest further north and near the Emmitsburg Road and actually extended along Cemetery Ridge to the northern base of Little Round Top. Perhaps he and Lee would have scrapped their plan to attack up the Emmitsburg Road, changed front, and used the additional ground between Seminary and Cemetery Ridge (with no Sickles at the Peach Orchard) to turn the Federal line by getting over or behind the Round Tops. Perhaps not. How would the Federal Fifth Corps have been employed in that situation? How would the Federal Sixth Corps, arriving and concentrating between 2 and 5 p.m., have been utilized to counter such an attack? We will never know, and in all actuality, a focus on these speculative scenarios is altogether unnecessary to address the crux of the matter, which consists of two fundamental questions, all other factors aside—did Sickles' move serve to significantly disrupt Longstreet's July 2 attack? If so, how?

Upon examining and weighing all of the evidence, the first question must be answered in the affirmative. Even without getting into the absence of direct infantry support behind Longstreet's two divisions, the lack of intended concert of action between Confederate corps, Meade and other officers' remarkable work in shifting reinforcements to the Federal left throughout Longstreet's attack, and other lesser factors that hampered the potential for Confederate success on July 2, Sickles' move coupled with the initially-misinformed and then quickly-revised Confederate attack plan was enough to throw the Confederates off balance and significantly hinder their chances for victory. In summarizing, influenced by faulty intelligence, the Confederate First Corps divisions arrived near Pitzer's Schoolhouse ready to execute an attack plan ("attack up the Emmitsburg Road") that never comported with the realities of the Federal position. Soon thereafter, Lee and Longstreet ultimately recognized there was indeed a significant Federal force located south of Cemetery Hill, with a substantial portion of it located right in their front along the Emmitsburg Road. Even after working quickly to modify the attack plan by shifting Hood's division further to the right, Lee inexplicably continued to insist (through Longstreet) that the Confederates attack up the Emmitsburg Road. This directive persisted even though Sickles' line did not end at the intersection of the Emmitsburg and Wheatfield Roads, but was refused at the intersection, ending much further to the east on Houck's Ridge. The extension of Sickles' line to Devil's Den alone meant Longstreet's attacking force would be subjected to severe attenuation and increasingly lack concentration of force and depth of attack at any one point. To compound this developing issue, Lee's continued issuance of stale (and never realistic) orders to attack up the Emmitsburg Road apparently emboldened Hood to allow several regiments on his division's right to drift way off track toward Big Round Top. The apparent magnetism of Sickles' 2nd U.S. Sharpshooters near Big Round Top coupled with Evander Law's and William Oates' disregard of orders was the last straw in precipitating a major shift of Hood's forces away from any semblance of contact with the Emmitsburg Road. These factors collectively diluted Hood's forces over a much broader front than was ever intended, effectively splitting the division in two, with the right portion engaging in an unintended fight for Little Round Top—and perhaps most importantly, precipitating tactical repercussions all the way up Longstreet's assault. The attenuation and drawing out of Longstreet's forces together with Sickles' "speedbump" between Seminary and Cemetery Ridge not only produced bloody combat and substantial casualties, but perhaps most importantly spelled serious trouble for Longstreet once he tried to push his weakened brigades toward Cemetery Ridge as the sun set on July 2.

Indeed, it has often and rightfully been argued that the casualties sustained in Birney's and Humphrey's Federal Third Corps divisions alone are enough to confirm the weakness of Sickles' advanced position on July 2. That said, it must also be conceded that the fact that *only one* of Longstreet's eight brigades fought north of the Wheatfield Road and anywhere near Confederate objectives for the day highlights just how effective Sickles' move ultimately turned out to be—if not *for* the Federals, then at least *against* the Confederates.

Essay 3

The Force of Circumstances

Reconnaissance Activities on Longstreet's Front, July 2

Genrl Lee then remarked that he had ordered a reconnaissance for the purpose of finding out a way to go into position without being seen by the enemy and I must hold myself in readiness to move. —Lafayette McLaws

The topic of Confederate reconnaissance in the leadup to Longstreet's July 2 attack is one that never fails to cause consternation among historians and students of the battle. And naturally, since much of the second day's battle involved James Longstreet and his two divisions of John Bell Hood and Lafayette McLaws, discussion of the topic predictably descends into a cacophony of charges against Lee's senior subordinate. Indeed, in what has become one of the mainstay criticisms of Longstreet's Gettysburg performance—originating just four days after the conclusion of the battle—critics have regularly accused the general of not conducting enough reconnaissance or scouting activities in the leadup to his July 2 attack. This allegation then leads into the attendant follow-on charges that, on the morning of July 2, Longstreet was essentially not himself (he has usually been characterized as a meticulous planner); was acting up because of tactical disagreements with Robert E. Lee; and his generalship was imprecise. The customary words historians have used are that Longstreet was not "careful" or "energetic" enough in the morning hours. Of course, the obvious destination of this trail of argument is to discredit any contrary explanation that Longstreet could not have attacked sometime in the morning hours of July 2; 10 a.m. to 12 p.m. seems to be the settled upon sweet spot on which most critics have set their hopes.[1]

This entire mode of argument is nothing more than a teetering house of cards built on a precarious foundation of hindsight, skewed analysis, and in many cases, an absence of critical primary source evidence. The real issue with reconnaissance activities on the Confederate center to right on the morning of July 2 was not that there was not enough of it; rather, the problem was that the numerous reconnaissance conducted ultimately turned out to be inadequate or inaccurate. Over a century's worth of Gettysburg studies have afforded us the opportunity to make some judgments on the accuracy of Confederate reconnaissance activities on the morning of July 2 and to more or less deem them lacking; however, the principal actors that morning with but minutes or hours, at most, to make decisions on the ground—and, in some cases, in the moment—would not have been privy to much of the insight we now possess. It is imperative to keep that crucial fact in mind while conducting analysis of various controversial topics, to include those that involve Longstreet, so as not to fall into the trap of armchair generalship.

Unfortunately for our collective understanding of the Gettysburg battle, discussion of Confederate reconnaissance activities on July 2, and particularly Longstreet's responsibility with respect to them, has been clouded with seductive, but ultimately misleading, hindsight narratives. A careful study of many of the most popular and influential books on the battle reveals that regarding this topic, historians have often ventured too far down the path of "if only Longstreet would have," or the similar but even more direct, "Longstreet should have." Additionally, as we will see, Longstreet's actions and movements on the morning of July 2 are actually not very well documented. Regrettably, this reality has not deterred many historians from filling in blanks in the historical record or advancing conjecture about what they believe Longstreet was or was not doing. In the absence of source information about specific time periods on the morning of July 2 and what Longstreet may or may not have been doing during them, historians should not assume that absence necessarily translates into inactivity, talking to no one, or examining nothing. It is hard to ignore the feeling that such default presumptions have been influenced by the near-bottomless repository of anti–Longstreet commentary that has, with limited exception, dominated the historiography of the Gettysburg battle for the last century and a half.

A different perspective, firmly rooted in the primary source record, is necessary to shed new light on this topic. Therefore, throughout the course of this essay, we will examine the origins of the charge that Longstreet did not engage in enough reconnaissance activities on the morning of July 2 and how this argument was deficient from the outset; historians' lack of attention to the quantity of Confederate reconnaissance missions on the morning and early afternoon of July 2, with a particular emphasis on the ignorance or inattentiveness given to one reconnaissance that stretched into the early afternoon hours and its rather wide-ranging implications on the Confederate timeline to attack; and the rather curious and revealing commentary from one of Longstreet's division commanders at Gettysburg, Lafayette McLaws, on all things reconnaissance. Additionally, we analyze and focus on any instances in the primary source record where reconnaissance participants indicated the possession (but apparently non-transmission) of intelligence that might have better informed the Confederate High Command, which will be imperative when advancing new conclusions about who might have blundered most in the lead-up to Longstreet's July 2 attack.

The first primary source that mentioned Longstreet and his alleged role in Confederate reconnaissance deficiencies on July 2 was a letter sent from Lafayette McLaws to his wife, Emily, on July 7, 1863. In fact, much of historians' criticism of Longstreet on this topic still springs from McLaws' comments in this particular letter. McLaws' critique began with his general belief that "the attack was unnecessary and the whole plan of battle a very bad one," before launching into a more pointed claim: "Genl Longstreet is to blame for not reconnoitering the ground and for persisting in ordering the assault when his errors were discovered."

Over the decades, Longstreet critics have employed these and other quotes from McLaws' July 7 letter very frequently, citing them as absolute and indispensable proof Lee's "Old Warhorse" was off his game and acting up at Gettysburg. Robert Krick, a former chief historian for the Fredericksburg and Spotsylvania National Military Park and zealous Longstreet critic, has postulated that McLaws was "among the most pointed detractors Longstreet ever earned" and "provides key testimony about his chief at Gettysburg." Of course, in making these and similar comments, Krick and many others consistently draw on the most-quoted assertion in McLaws' letter, which held that "during the engagement he [Longstreet] was very excited, giving contrary orders to every one, and was exceedingly overbearing. I consider him a humbug." Many historians employ this quote as surefire proof Longstreet performed poorly at Gettysburg, believing it speaks for itself and stands on its own merits. Never mind Lee had instructed Longstreet to keep an especially close eye on McLaws' division at Gettysburg. Never mind that McLaws was almost certainly unaware of that fact just four days after the battle; he was likely piqued about what he considered to be the micromanagement of his division's attack on July 2 and felt unconstrained to express some of that boiling frustration to his wife. Additionally, and most importantly, never mind that in McLaws' postwar writings, his thoughts on Gettysburg and Longstreet's performance in particular were almost entirely at variance with what he expressed in his July 7, 1863, letter. Indeed, McLaws does provide key testimony about Longstreet at Gettysburg; however, the extent of his testimony was not limited to the July 7 letter. We must consider McLaws' postwar commentary as well, since it reflects a man who had obviously thought quite deeply on matters.[2]

Maj. Gen. Lafayette McLaws, CSA (Wikimedia Commons).

McLaws' two-sentence commentary in his post-battle letter on Longstreet vis-à-vis Confederate reconnaissance activities on July 2 are not only rather ham-fisted, but also largely off-target. For ease of analysis, these two sentences can be split up into four parts: (1) "the attack was unnecessary," (2) "the whole plan of battle was a bad one," (3) "Genl Longstreet is to blame for not reconnoitering the ground," and (4) "Genl Longstreet is to blame … for persisting in ordering the assault when his errors were discovered." Three of these four parts—1, 2, and 4—can be quickly and concisely addressed. In saying the attack was unnecessary, the battle plan was bad, and Longstreet insisted the attack be made despite the existence of unforeseen realities, McLaws must have known and recognized Robert E. Lee, as commanding general, was first and foremost in control of all these factors. The attack was Lee's idea, the battle plan was Lee's, and unquestionably, Lee continued to expect Longstreet to attack even after it was discovered their understanding of the Federal position did not conform to reality. McLaws' charge that Longstreet unilaterally "persist[ed] in ordering the assault" was especially unfair. Lee was, in fact, the one who insisted the attack be made, while Longstreet, as Lee's direct subordinate, not only demonstrated his cognizance of that fact, but would have recognized it as his duty to carry out that order. After emotions had cooled in the postwar years, McLaws demonstrated his complete understanding of this reality, noting how if "Longstreet had not engaged" on the afternoon of July 2, "some … in the army … would have ascribed his conduct to the worst of motives," while adding that Longstreet's "orders were positive" and it was "imperative … upon an officer's honor to do his best to carry it out."

The third part of McLaws' two sentences referencing his post-battle belief Longstreet was to "blame for not reconnoitering the ground" in the lead-up to the July 2 attack—more or less the focus of this essay—is unsurprisingly what many historians have latched onto to make more general allegations against Longstreet's performance that day, and more specifically, the degree to which he engaged in attack preparations. McLaws' critique is not only broad and vague, but again, unfair and misdirected. First, McLaws *assumed* Longstreet spent no time attempting to examine the ground on July 2. McLaws was not with Longstreet the entire morning, so how would he have known how much personal reconnaissance his chief actually engaged in? Second, McLaws was mistaken in supposing it was Longstreet's responsibility, and his alone, to reconnoiter the ground. Generals of armies and corps commanders primarily relied on cavalry, scouts, staff officers, or a combination thereof to reconnoiter enemy positions for intelligence purposes and that was exactly how the Confederates engaged in reconnaissance of the Federal left flank on July 2. In the morning and early afternoon hours, Lee and Longstreet employed several officers to gather intelligence on the Federal position. Third, in the postwar years, McLaws made a critical observation that completely upended his post-battle claim. Referring to the scene around 3:30 p.m. when he and the Confederate High Command recognized the presence of Federal Major General Daniel Sickles' Third Corps at the Joseph Sherfy Peach Orchard and its extension to Devil's Den, McLaws maintained, "Thus was presented a state of affairs which was certainly not contemplated when the original plan or order of battle was given, and certainly was not known to

General Longstreet a half hour previous." McLaws' observation was key because it essentially meant all Confederate reconnaissance activities (and there were many, as we will see) occurring before Longstreet's lead division reached its attack jump-off point on Warfield Ridge were entirely moot by 3:30 p.m. Truth be told, nearly all the intelligence reconnaissance officers afforded Lee and Longstreet up to that point was seriously flawed; however, the critical point McLaws made here was that none of the reconnaissance conducted earlier in the day mattered once Sickles moved his corps forward to the Peach Orchard. Sickles forced the Confederate High Command into a situation where, despite their recognition that the Federal left was not where they expected it to be, it was too late in the day to significantly alter the attack plan. Spending an inordinate amount of time yet again "reconnoitering the ground" was not an option by 3:30–4:30 p.m. By that advanced state of the day, Lee's paramount goal was not to gather additional intelligence, but clearly to commence the assault and make any necessary adjustments as the attack progressed.[3]

Like McLaws, Longstreet's Chief of Staff, Gilbert Moxley Sorrel, showed keen awareness of the significance of the Confederates' intelligence failures in the lead-up to the July 2 attack. That said, Sorrel's postwar writings, published posthumously in 1905, captured the reconnaissance issue more accurately than McLaws had done in his immediate post-battle letter. Recollecting the state of events when Longstreet's two divisions were executing their infamous countermarch in the afternoon hours, Sorrel noted how "much valuable time was lost by this trial, which with better knowledge of the ground by *Lee's engineers* [emphasis added] would not have been attempted." Sorrel placed the onus for the Confederates' deficient intelligence gathering efforts where it belonged: on the officers Lee and Longstreet had tasked, since the early morning hours, with determining the location of the Federal left flank and examining the ground on and locating a concealed route to the extreme Confederate right.

Ultimately, McLaws came around to sharing Sorrel's viewpoint in the postwar years. Contrary to how most historians have misleadingly framed McLaws' perspective on the battle—that his emotive July 1863 outlook remained unchanged for the rest of his life—the division commander's postwar comments reflect a deep and more rational reflection on many of the controversial topics involving Longstreet at Gettysburg, to include the reconnaissance issue. McLaws described how once the Confederates reached their attack jump-off points on Warfield Ridge, their surprise at seeing a major Federal force at the Peach Orchard "can be ascribed but to the want of *proper reconnaissance* [emphasis added] having been made before the general plan of attack ... and it was assumed then, from hasty reports, *made probably by persons not skilled in such matters* [emphasis added], that there was not much to overcome, and this erroneous opinion was never corrected." "Hasty reports" by unskilled persons and the need for a "proper reconnaissance." Notice McLaws did not say, "the want of more reconnaissance." Though McLaws' characterization of at least some of these persons as unskilled or lacking experience in conducting reconnaissance activities was arguably misleading (as we will soon highlight), his reference to officers tasked with gathering intelligence in the pre-attack hours was unmistakable. Indeed, McLaws was no longer solely ascribing "blame for not reconnoitering the ground" to Longstreet; in fact, he made no mention of Longstreet at all in this passage. Rather, McLaws had noticeably shifted his attention to the officers who produced "hasty" intelligence reports for the Confederate High Command in the lead-up to the attack and his belief that the assault was ultimately hamstrung by the absence of a "proper reconnaissance."[4]

So, who were these reconnaissance officers and what did they examine in the morning and early afternoon hours of July 2? The list of officers who we know for certain took an active role in conducting reconnaissance on the Confederate right is actually quite extensive, and includes Captain Samuel Johnston, an engineer on Lee's staff; Captain John J. Clarke, one of Longstreet's engineers; Brigadier General William Pendleton, Lee's chief of artillery; Colonel R. Lindsay Walker, Ambrose Powell (A.P.) Hill's Third Corps artillery chief; Colonel Armistead Lindsay (A.L.) Long of Lee's staff; Colonel William P. Smith, Lee's chief engineer; Colonel Edward Porter (E.P.) Alexander, Longstreet's principal artillery officer at Gettysburg; Colonel John L. Black and Lieutenants Fred Horsey and J. Wilson Marshall of the 1st South Carolina Cavalry; Brigadier General Cadmus Wilcox, commanding a brigade in A.P. Hill's corps; Major General Lafayette McLaws, one of Longstreet's division commanders; and even Lee and Longstreet themselves.

For most serious students of the war, Captain Samuel Johnston's role as a reconnaissance officer on July 2 is now well known. By July 1863, Johnston was neither a stranger to Lee's staff coterie, nor to conducting reconnaissance activities. Prior to the war, Johnston was educated in Virginia as a civil engineer and in the immediate lead-up to his time at Lee's headquarters had served on the staff of James Ewell Brown (J.E.B.) Stuart, the most recognized cavalry commander in the Army of Northern Virginia and well known for his mastery of reconnaissance. During the Battle of Chancellorsville in April–May 1863, Lee had tasked Johnston with similar reconnaissance duties to what was expected of him at Gettysburg. Johnston provided Lee with intelligence about Federal activity around General Joseph Hooker's headquarters at the Chancellor House. Johnston would remain on Lee's staff until the army's surrender in April 1865, would rise to the rank of colonel in the engineering service, and by war's end, would describe himself as a "Reconnoitering officer."

Sections of books on the battle and a number of articles have gone into great detail examining Johnston's early morning reconnaissance, which was conducted sometime between the hours of 4 a.m. and 9 a.m. We need not go into specific detail on this reconnaissance as it has already been amply covered elsewhere; however, suffice it to say, that in the early morning hours, Lee ordered Johnston to gather fundamental intelligence on the location of the Federal left flank and the ground on the Confederate extreme right in preparation for a potential attack from that quarter. It is disputed whether Johnston made it to Little Round Top or Big Round Top; however, for our purposes here, it is adequate to note that Johnston made his observations from at least one of the Round Tops. Of greater importance were the results of this reconnaissance, as reported to Lee, and which are now equally well known. Once reporting back to the Confederate High Command, Johnston proceeded to inform Lee he only observed four Federal cavalrymen riding along the Emmitsburg Road toward Gettysburg and no major Federal force south of Cemetery

Hill. The repercussions of Johnston's assurance that he made it to the Round Tops unobstructed and observed no significant body of Federal troops near that position was monumental in shaping Lee's July 2 assault plan to "attack up the Emmitsburg Road."

Much less frequently pointed out is that, during his early morning reconnaissance, Johnston was not alone, but was actually accompanied by three or four additional officers, one of which was Captain John J. Clarke, an engineering officer on Longstreet's staff. Like Johnston, Clarke's background was in civil engineering. He was obviously respected, since a year earlier, in 1862, he had been entrusted with the significant task of helping to engineer the Richmond defenses. Unfortunately, Clarke neither wrote nor said anything in the post-battle or postwar years about what he observed during the early morning reconnaissance on July 2, 1863. Since no one ever suggested there was any disagreement between Johnston and any of the other reconnoitering officers as to what they heard or saw, including Clarke, it is likely that Clarke told Lee and Longstreet little that differed from Johnston's claims. If that had not been the case, as Longstreet's engineer and man-on-the-spot, surely Lee's "Old Warhorse" would have mentioned any significant discrepancies between Johnston's and Clarke's reported observations in one or more of his postwar publications. To the contrary, Longstreet made no mention of Clarke. Nevertheless, the key thing to remember when it comes to Clarke is that he was acting as Longstreet's representative on the early morning reconnaissance mission. Unfortunately, many past histories of the battle have only called attention to Johnston, while making no mention of Clarke. It is vital to note Clarke's presence since, as a member of Longstreet's staff, he would have been accountable to him and would certainly have directly reported his findings and observations to his chief.[5]

Clarke's attendance of the early morning reconnaissance also lends some insight into the controversy concerning Longstreet not permitting McLaws or one of his division's engineer officers to accompany Johnston's party. In the postwar years, McLaws recounted how Longstreet, upon "hearing my proposition or request to reconnoiter, spoke quickly and said: 'No, sir, I do not wish you to leave your division.'" Undeterred, McLaws returned to his division and attempted then to send his own engineer, Lieutenant Thomas Jefferson Montcure, "to go and join Major [sic] Johnston, and gave him instructions what to observe particularly, as he was an officer in whom I had confidence, but [he] was ordered back." Much has been made of McLaws' commentary on this issue over the years, likely because, on the surface, it is low-hanging fruit for Longstreet critics. A cursory analysis of surrounding events affords one the convenient opportunity to force Longstreet's denial under the traditional narrative; namely, he was so upset about how events were progressing that he was apparently willing to sacrifice operational undertakings to placate a sour mood. This interpretation is built upon assumption and pre-conceived bias; much like the assumption many historians have made about an oft-quoted statement Longstreet made to Major General John Bell Hood probably around the same time in the morning hours. To Hood, Longstreet divulged: "The General is a little nervous this morning; he wishes me to attack. I do not wish to do so without [George] Pickett. I never like to go into battle with one boot off."[6] Was Longstreet confiding here that he was going to do everything in his power to delay operations until Pickett arrived, as the predominant narrative has suggested? Or was Longstreet merely stating his understandable preference his entire corps be on hand for the day's attack? How often do people unburden themselves to others when it comes to carrying out a task, saying they wish this or they wish that, but then they go on to do what is asked of them anyway under existing circumstances and limitations?

The same rule against assumption and preconceived bias applies to McLaws not being allowed to join Johnston on a reconnaissance. First of all, how common would it have been for a major general to accompany two captains on a reconnaissance mission to examine an exceedingly advance position, potentially putting that division commander in danger well ahead of friendly lines? Secondly, considering McLaws made this request sometime between 8:30 and 9:30 a.m., how would the division commander have joined a reconnaissance mission that had already concluded by that point? Johnston had already reported his findings to Lee and the commanding general had already discussed tactical particulars with McLaws about where he wanted his division placed, i.e., perpendicular to the Emmitsburg Road, so why would Longstreet allow McLaws to accompany a reconnaissance that was already finished? Furthermore, the fact that Captain Clarke, a member of Longstreet's staff, had accompanied Johnston cannot be overlooked. Clarke represented Longstreet on this scouting mission and certainly the engineer, upon his return, would have reported his intelligence findings to the First Corps commander. There would have been little reason for Longstreet to want a major general, being one of his three division commanders, scouting way out in front of Confederate lines.

Lastly, on this particular subtopic, historians have often been remiss to make it explicitly clear to students of the battle that McLaws conducted his own reconnaissance anyway, contrary to Longstreet's instructions. We know this to be a fact because McLaws stated as much in the postwar years. After Lieutenant Montcure was ordered back, McLaws maintained, "I then reconnoitered myself for my own information, and was soon convinced that by crossing the ridge where I then was, my command could reach the point indicated by General Lee, in a half hour, without being seen." Further along in his narrative, McLaws also divulged that during a later conversation with Longstreet near Black Horse Tavern—where, during the march, his division was halted for fear of being seen by Federal signalmen on Little Round Top—he suggested they countermarch based on that personal reconnaissance he had conducted earlier. "I then told him of my reconnaissance in the morning," McLaws recalled informing Longstreet.[7]

McLaws' postwar accounts also provide insight into, perhaps, the most consequential Confederate reconnaissance issue historians have consistently overlooked over the decades—that being, Captain Samuel Johnston's concealed route reconnaissance activities,[8] conducted sometime between 9:30 a.m. and 1 p.m. In short, Lee ordered Johnston to examine the roads and locate a concealed marching route for Longstreet's divisions to their attack jump-off points on the extreme Confederate right. In Gettysburg historiography, very little mention has been made of Johnston's additional reconnaissance responsibilities on July 2 following his early morning mission. This oversight has had vast, negative repercussions on past analyses of

Longstreet's July 2 actions. The absence of this critical piece of the narrative has consistently led historians astray in making some misleading assertions about Longstreet's performance during the late morning hours, namely that he: was inactive, uncharacteristically skimped on preparations, and essentially just sulked around looking for any opportunity to delay his divisions' movement to the extreme Confederate right.

To begin, first recall our discussion in the previous section about McLaws' request to either personally or have Lieutenant Montcure join Johnston's reconnaissance. Remember that McLaws' request would have defied all logic if he had been asking to join Johnston's early morning reconnaissance, which had likely commenced soon after daylight and finished at or before 9 a.m. Now, consider part of the dialogue that transpired between Lee and McLaws that morning. After instructing McLaws to place his division perpendicular to the Emmitsburg Road, Lee expressed his wish McLaws "get there if possible without being seen by the enemy." Lee then asked the division commander, "Can you get there?" or "Can you do it?" to which McLaws replied he "knew of nothing to prevent me, but would take a party of skirmishers and go in advance and reconnoitre." So far, we see Lee asking McLaws if he can get to a specific position unseen, and McLaws suggesting sending a few men forward to reconnoiter for a viable, concealed route. Lee's follow-on response to McLaws is the most critical piece of this conversation. According to the division commander, Lee stated, "Major [sic] Johnston, of my staff, has been ordered to reconnoiter the ground, and I expect he is about ready." Lee was not referring to Johnston's first reconnaissance; this was clearly a different scouting mission. Further, since Lee's reply referenced Johnston and came in response to McLaws' offer to reconnoiter ahead for a concealed route, it is clear Lee intended for this Johnston-led reconnaissance to locate a hidden course to the right. In yet another postwar account, McLaws succinctly confirmed this analysis: "Genrl Lee then remarked that he had ordered a reconnaissance for the purpose of finding out a way to go into position without being seen by the enemy and I must hold myself in readiness to move."

Another portion of McLaws' postwar narrative is also relevant to our examination of Johnston's additional reconnaissance activities on July 2. Specifically, the division commander unveiled that "when I had the brief interview with General Lee before mentioned, he did not appear to be particularly anxious that Longstreet should occupy the left. He certainly was in no hurry for it.... My information at the time was that he was not decided positively as to the main point of attack, but was waiting for information." How often have we heard historians describe the emotional state of the Confederate High Command on Longstreet's front in the morning hours of July 2 in the way McLaws framed it here? Lee was not "particularly anxious," "was in no hurry," "was not decided ... [on] the main point of attack," and "was waiting for information." This last point on awaiting information very likely referred to the two sources Lee had on the ground around the time he spoke with McLaws, one being Colonel Charles Venable of his staff, whom Lee had sent to the Second Corps in the early morning hours to determine if the day's main attack might better be initiated from the Confederate left; and the other, the new, Johnston-led reconnaissance mission Lee had just ordered.[9]

Additional details in McLaws' postwar accounts and in testimonies from William Pendleton, Longstreet, and even Johnston himself further corroborate the existence of this concealed route reconnaissance, while providing insight into exactly what the captain reconnoitered from the late morning to early afternoon hours. McLaws maintained that after he spoke with Lee and made his personal reconnaissance, he proceeded to "the head of my column and sat on my horse" for a few hours until "about 1 p.m.," when "Major [sic] Johnston, of General Lee's staff, came to me and said he was ordered to conduct me on the march. My command was at once put in motion—Major [sic] Johnston and myself riding some distance ahead."[10] In another postwar account, McLaws maintained that Johnston's concealed route reconnaissance was one of the principal factors that precluded Longstreet from beginning his rightward movement earlier in the day. To McLaws, Longstreet had been "resting under the eye of General Lee, and under his orders to remain, until Major [sic] Johnson's [sic] return." Coupled with this testimony is the critical piece of postwar evidence from Johnston, when he recalled having examined "the roads over which our troops would have to move in the event of a movement on the enemy's left." Another applicable piece of evidence is a statement Longstreet made in his memoirs: "About ten o' clock General Lee returned to his head-quarters, but his engineer who had been sent to reconnoitre on his right had not come back." Furthermore, the Confederate army's artillery chief, William Pendleton, alleged in his after-battle report that sometime after he observed Federal cavalry "in considerable force" and Federal infantry, artillery, and trains "moving up along" the Emmitsburg Road "toward the enemy's main position," "this front ... was examined" by Johnston and Colonel Lee's chief engineer, Colonel William P. Smith. Pendleton provided no additional clarity as to the purpose of this Johnson-Smith reconnaissance; however, the timing of the examination, based on contextual details in Pendleton's report, are curious. The cavalry force Pendleton observed was almost certainly Brigadier General John Buford's Federal cavalry division, which was stationed near the Peach Orchard until the late morning hours. The Federal infantry, artillery, and trains to which Pendleton referred were very likely the remaining forces from Sickles' Third Corps, which began arriving on the field from Emmitsburg around 9 a.m. Bookending this commentary, Pendleton also tacked on his recollection that "about midday General Longstreet arrived and viewed the ground." In sum, Pendleton's post-battle commentary suggests Johnston and Smith engaged in a reconnaissance of the southern end of the field sometime between 9 a.m. and midday, likely closer to the late morning, midday hours, upon considering the artillery chief's recollection the engineers examined this front "some time" *after he had observed it* full of Federal cavalry, infantry, artillery, and trains.[11]

Joining all these pieces together, a reasonably clear picture emerges as to the time frame and purpose of Johnston's later reconnaissance. From McLaws, we discover Johnston did not return from, as Lee put it, "reconnoitering the ground," until as late as 1 p.m.; McLaws was waiting idly until Johnston's arrival; and Lee ordered Johnston to conduct the First Corps marching column unseen to its attack jump-off points. This last piece begs the question: If Johnston *had not* examined the roads to the right, why would Lee have seen fit to entrust the captain with conducting

McLaws on the march? From Johnston himself, we ascertain that he did indeed scout the roads leading to the Federal left. From Longstreet we find that when Lee returned from his final pre-attack visit to Ewell's front some time during the 10 a.m. hour, Johnston had yet to return from his reconnaissance. And from Pendleton, we discover Johnston and Smith examined the southern end of the field sometime between 9 a.m. and midday. Furthermore, recall McLaws' dialogue with Lee around the 8:30 to 9:30 a.m. time frame, when the commanding general expressed his desire for McLaws to get into position "without being seen by the enemy" and disclosed Johnston had just been sent out to reconnoiter. The sum total of all these accounts suggests, just before speaking with McLaws, Lee had ordered Johnston to conduct additional reconnaissance activities with the express purpose, at least in part, of scouting a concealed route for Longstreet's marching column, and those activities were not fully completed until some time in the early afternoon.

In their battle narratives, nearly all historians have solely drawn attention to Johnston's early morning reconnaissance, not his late-morning-to-early-afternoon assignment to locate a concealed route. Other than myself, I believe only mid-twentieth-century popular historian Glenn Tucker showed an awareness of Johnston's later reconnaissance activities, noting in his 1968 work, *Lee and Longstreet at Gettysburg*, "But the key element in the delay was Captain Johnston's reconnaissance. Lee told McLaws to wait until it had been made. Johnston was gone until early afternoon." In the same chapter, Tucker further specified that "Johnston could not possibly have found a route until after 11 a.m." As a result of this trend, students of the battle have long been deprived of a key piece of the July 2 story that sheds light on an additional outstanding issue the Confederate High Command was waiting for before commencing the movement to the right. Nowadays, more attention is rightfully given to the fact that, well into the morning hours, Lee was undecided as to where he wanted to initiate the day's main attack, his right or left. Additionally, more notice is being correctly allotted to the reality that, around 11 a.m., Lee permitted Longstreet to await the arrival of Evander Law's brigade of Hood's division before moving. However, very little attention has been afforded to either Lee's order that Longstreet's column march unseen to the right or to the Johnston-led reconnaissance to ensure those orders were fulfilled.[12]

As a result, many historians have advanced some rather wild allegations about Longstreet's performance on the morning of July 2. Popular historian and Longstreet biographer Jeffry Wert has frequently stressed his belief that Longstreet was inactive during the mid- to late morning hours. Referring to the time period when Lee was over on Ewell's front around 10 a.m., Wert alleged Longstreet merely "stayed at the observation post and waited for Lee's return," claimed he showed no interest in knowing if a "concealed route had been found," and contended that "Lee ... undoubtedly expected Longstreet to begin preparations, if not to begin the march, while he conferred with Ewell." Wert went even further and plainly asserted Longstreet did not "scout a route of march." Addressing these allegations, first, how do we know Longstreet only stayed "at the observation post and waited for Lee's return"? The historical record affords very little information as to Longstreet's specific movements on the morning of July 2; therefore, it would be speculative to assume he was entirely idle for a period of nearly two hours. Second, alleging Longstreet showed no concern for knowing if a "concealed route had been found" entirely discounts the fact that Lee had already sent Johnston out to scout for a concealed marching route. We also know from the postwar accounts of McLaws and Longstreet that, even upon Lee's return from the left, Johnston had yet to finish this reconnaissance. Third, how would Lee have expected "Longstreet to begin preparations, if not ... begin the march," when not only had Lee issued Longstreet no orders by that point, but Law's brigade was still miles away, and as already stated, Johnston had not returned from the very reconnaissance that was to facilitate that march? Wert's argument that Longstreet did not "scout a route of march" is equally misleading, since not only was scouting ahead to identify a marching route not part of a corps commander's job description, but as stated, that was the exact job Lee had assigned Captain Johnston.

Summing up his assessment of Longstreet's pre-attack performance on July 2, Wert again alluded to his belief the First Corps commander was too inactive, demonstrated an uncharacteristic lack of attention to detail, and continued in a bout of sulkiness over the dismissal of his tactical suggestions. "Had [Longstreet]," Wert wrote, "attended to the details that were his responsibility and not allowed his disagreement with Lee to affect his judgment and effort, the afternoon assault would have begun much sooner, but not several hours earlier." Wert clearly advanced this conclusion seemingly ignorant of Johnston's later reconnaissance activities, which stretched into the early afternoon hours. Additionally, the sweeping claim that Longstreet failed to attend "to the details that were his responsibility" in the morning hours is ambiguous. Lee's back-and-forth with Longstreet's and Ewell's corps, Law's absence until the noon hour, Johnston's concealed route reconnaissance until the early afternoon, and the additional ongoing scouting activities we will explore shortly, make it hard to determine what specific, consequential responsibilities Wert referred to that would have, one, been in a corps commander's wheelhouse and, two, assured an earlier attack. Furthermore, supposition is introduced whenever a historian jumps to the conclusion Longstreet was allegedly acting up because Lee had not taken Longstreet's tactical suggestion (turning movement off the Confederate right flank) in the early morning hours. There is just as much evidence to suggest Longstreet may have been frustrated by the dragging day, Stuart's and Pickett's absence, or Lee overriding his tactical suggestion regarding the deployment of McLaws' division (perpendicular versus parallel to the Emmitsburg Road), as there is that he may have been upset over the non-adoption of his tactical proposal made hours earlier. Lastly, in advancing the conjecture that if Longstreet had only taken this or that specific action "the afternoon assault would have begun much sooner," we descend into the quagmire of armchair generalship. Interestingly, Wert followed up this thought with his belief that Sickles' mid-afternoon move "increased the likelihood of a Confederate victory." The core concern here is the logical inconsistency in contending Longstreet's alleged inaction apparently upset the supposed imperativeness of an earlier assault, while also claiming the delay in attack actually increased the probability of Confederate success.[13]

Similar comments to Wert's have been published in other popular Civil War histories over the decades. Assessing Longstreet's performance on the morning of

July 2 in his widely read book *Battle Cry of Freedom*, academic historian James M. McPherson alleged, "Yet Longstreet may have been piqued by Lee's rejection of his flanking suggestion, and he did not believe in the attack he was ordered to make. He therefore may not have put as much energy and speed into its preparations as the situation required." McPherson's use of "may have" and "may not have" for this speculative discussion is appropriate; however, his raising of the same old charges in the same way reinforces the general, long-standing belief that something was clearly amiss with Longstreet on the morning of July 2. Volume 2 of journalist Shelby Foote's immensely popular *The Civil War: A Narrative* reiterated the same storyline, while also explicitly bringing reconnaissance into the discussion. "Renewing his [Longstreet's] plea for a withdrawal this morning," Foote asserted, "the burly Georgian had been rebuffed again: whereupon he turned sulky. Though he had of course obeyed all orders given him, he had not anticipated them in the best tradition of the Army of Northern Virginia, with the result that he was partly to blame for the delays encountered in the course of the *unreconnoitered* [emphasis added] flank march." Foote repeated the speculative claims that Lee's dismissal of Longstreet's early morning tactical proposal consequentially affected the corps commander's temper and reduced his operational approach to merely going through the motions; however, in the last sentence, he tacked on an additional claim that the march route was "unreconnoitered." Foote had clearly overlooked or was entirely unaware of Captain Johnston's later reconnaissance activities conducted, at least in part, for just that purpose—to identify a concealed marching route. Popular historian Noah Trudeau's *Gettysburg: A Testing of* Courage, published in 2002, echoed McPherson and Foote's contentions on this topic. Trudeau maintained that no one was sent to reconnoiter for a concealed route: "In an omission that would never be explained, neither Longstreet nor McLaws had detailed any officer of [E.P] Alexander's caliber to scout the way." Yet, in fact, Trudeau would go on to explain this omission, surmising, like McPherson and Foote, that Longstreet had lost all motivation to effectively or efficiently carry out his orders: "A partial explanation for Longstreet was that his failure to persuade Lee to attempt a much wider flanking move had left him visibly agitated and not sufficiently focused on the myriad of small details that a corps commander had to handle."[14]

Rather surprisingly, Glenn Tucker fell into some of the same common traps in his earlier book *High Tide at Gettysburg*, published in 1958. Tucker argued, "But with conditions as they were—without Stuart and without adequate knowledge—the fault in the main undoubtedly was Longstreet's. *He should have investigated the routes in the wasted morning hours* [emphasis added] *while Law was hastening to join him. He should have* [emphasis added] checked just how much Johnston knew before the column reached Black Horse Tavern and was about to be exposed." Not only did Tucker commit the error of armchair generalship, twice advancing claims about what he believed Longstreet "should have" done, but he also intimated that the roads to the extreme right were not "investigated." In making such a claim, Tucker exposed a clear unawareness of Johnston's reconnaissance activities following his early morning mission. Furthermore, the claim that Lee and Longstreet lacked "adequate knowledge" is almost assuredly true from the vantage point of hindsight;

however, Lee and Longstreet would not necessarily have known that to be the case on the morning of July 2. Indeed, the Confederate High Command received intelligence from a number of sources in the pre-attack hours, not only from Johnston's missions, but also from other scouting activities we will explore momentarily. Simply put, how can we judge what Lee and Longstreet considered "adequate knowledge" on July 2? They were not afforded the comfort of years of study and reflection on the battle to determine if they possessed the most accurate and reliable information. Rather, Lee and Longstreet moved and acted on the intelligence presented to them in the moment by their several reconnoitering officers.[15]

Wert, McPherson, Foote, and Tucker (in *High Tide*) are not alone. A number of other historians whose books likely occupy most students of the battle's bookshelves have made the same oversight regarding Johnston's late-morning-to-early-afternoon reconnaissance, to include Douglas Southall Freeman, Clifford Dowdey, Edwin Coddington, Harry Pfanz, Stephen Sears, and Allen Guelzo. In each of these historians' works on the battle, mention is only made of Johnston's early morning reconnaissance. No reference whatsoever is made of Johnston's subsequent role in scouting a concealed route for Longstreet's marching column.

In his one-volume history of the battle, *Gettysburg*, popular historian Stephen Sears appears to have modified key content of Lee's and McLaws' mid-morning conversation, as presented in McLaws' postwar writings. Consequently, Sears made no reference whatsoever to the Johnston-led concealed route reconnaissance to which McLaws clearly alluded in his accounts. Recall that, in McLaws' recollection, Lee expressed his desire for the division commander to place his brigades perpendicular to the Emmitsburg Road and to get there "without being seen by the enemy." Recall also that McLaws said he could get there but requested to first advance some men to reconnoiter. The direct quote of Lee's reply was as follows: "Major [sic] Johnston, of my staff, has been ordered to reconnoitre the ground, and *I expect he is about ready* [emphasis added]." McLaws then said, "I will go with him," and later, after Longstreet denied that first request, he recalled attempting to have Lieutenant Montcure "go and join Major [sic] Johnston." Thus, the situation as presented by McLaws was that Lee had *then* ordered a reconnaissance and Johnston was about ready to go. McLaws did not say he would consult Johnston and seek insight; rather, he tried, on two occasions, to either tag along with Johnston himself or have his engineer officer join the reconnaissance mission. Sears and I are reading from the same account, but Sears' paraphrase of Lee's and McLaws' dialogue is misleading to readers and changes its meaning. Sears represented Lee's reply as follows: "Lee told him that Captain Johnston of his staff had already reconnoitered the area, to which McLaws said, in that case he would go with Johnston to see for himself." McLaws' account, which is what Sears solely referenced to recreate this scene, never represented Lee as saying Johnston "already reconnoitered." To the contrary, McLaws alleged Lee said Johnston was preparing to reconnoiter, or "he is about ready." As a result of the alteration of Lee's reply, the remainder of Sears' paraphrase becomes skewed as well. McLaws never alleged he would seek Johnston's insight from a reconnaissance that had already been completed; rather, he stated he would "go with him" on a *new* reconnaissance Lee had just ordered.[16]

Like Sears, academic historian Allen Guelzo also altered McLaws' recounting of his conversation with Lee. In Guelzo's paraphrase of the dialogue, "Lafayette McLaws wondered out loud whether it wouldn't be a good idea to send someone out along that path to scout the field, and Lee replied that not only had he done so, but that his scout [Johnston] was at that moment just arriving back." Again, this mischaracterization of Lee's reply is entirely misleading for readers. McLaws never alleged Lee said Johnston was "just arriving back." Just the opposite. McLaws alleged Lee said Johnston was just setting out.[17]

Other modes of mischaracterization have dominated this topic over the decades. Virginia historian Douglas Southall Freeman made the typical Longstreet-did-nothing-in-the-morning argument in his extremely influential *Lee's Lieutenants*, published in three volumes in the 1940s. When Lee rode over to Ewell's front around 10 a.m., Freeman believed "Longstreet was expected to make his preparations during Lee's absence, but the lieutenant general was less disposed than ever to deliver his attack." Referencing Captain Johnston, Freeman further claimed Longstreet "had no reason to doubt" Johnston's early morning reconnaissance report "that the lower end of the ridge was unoccupied, but he felt that the attack should not be made. If he must assault, he would delay until the entire First Corps was at hand." Freeman's narrative, particularly his clear intimation that everything was waiting for Longstreet, was seductively misleading. First and foremost, Lee did not issue Longstreet any orders before he rode to the Confederate left; to the contrary, he only issued orders after his return from that front. Further, Freeman implied that while Lee visited Ewell's corps, he expected Longstreet to move his command to the right based on the reported findings of Johnston's early morning reconnaissance that there was no major Federal force south of Cemetery Hill; however, the Virginia historian made no reference whatsoever to the way in which Lee expected Longstreet to make that move. Indeed, Lee expected Longstreet to move along a concealed route, which as ordered by Lee, Johnston was then in the middle of scouting to locate.[18]

Like Freeman, another twentieth century Virginia historian, Clifford Dowdey, only mentioned Johnston's early morning reconnaissance. Of Longstreet's actions during the mid-morning hours, Dowdey also curiously claimed, "Except for getting his artillery out, ready to take positions, the burly corps commander had made no movement in the two and a half hours since Lee had given the order. Nobody knows how he passed the time." Dowdey, a fervent Longstreet critic, clearly intended these statements to be a critique of what he believed to be Longstreet's inactivity. That said, taken alone and literally, Dowdey's second statement is actually accurate, and an important one to grasp. Though historians have advanced much speculation on what Longstreet did in the morning hours, and more often, on what they believe he did not do, the source record is so scant on his operational decisions and movements during those hours that it is exceedingly hard to advance many specifics on "how he passed the time." We should be careful not to fill in the blanks with assumptions, hindsight, and speculation.

Freeman (in *Lee's Lieutenants*) and Dowdey's near-parallel commentary on Longstreet's alleged inactivity is not altogether surprising, given their shared common belief that Lee did, in fact, order Longstreet to move out sooner in the morning hours, specifically just after Johnston briefed Lee on his early morning reconnaissance and insinuated the Federal left flank rested near Cemetery Hill. Both historians leaned on a postwar account from Lee staffer A.L. Long, who claimed that after hearing Johnston's report, Lee told Longstreet ("quietly," according to Dowdey), "I think you had better move on." Freeman characterized Lee's alleged statement as his "suggesting movements" order, while Dowdey called it a "direct order" and "Lee's order 'to move on.'"[19]

Unfortunately for Gettysburg historiography and the treatment of Longstreet's July 2 performance in particular, this misleading contention that Lee's alleged statement was somehow an order instructing Longstreet to move to the right and attack has been one historians have clearly found hard to resist. Though they now may not go so far as to frame Lee's alleged statement as an order, historians since Freeman's and Dowdey's time have frequently advanced the argument Lee *expected* Longstreet to begin his march to the right in the mid- to late morning hours. Often this more whitewashed, but equally misleading assertion is advanced along with an apparent need to explain why Longstreet need not have waited for Law's brigade. In particular, historians have alleged Law could have easily caught up with the First Corps divisions during the march or even after they reached their attack jump-off points on Warfield Ridge. Characteristic of this watered-down Freeman-Dowdey creation, academic historian Edwin Coddington contended:

Regardless of whether Lee intended for a preliminary move of this sort, Longstreet *could have* [emphasis added] started shifting his infantry toward the Confederate right flank in the morning while Lee was conferring with Ewell. His excuse at first was that he was waiting for Pickett. When that was ruled out, he then insisted upon Law's appearance before starting to move his men to the right. He

Col. A.L. Long, CSA, Lee's military secretary (Library of Congress).

never explained why Law could not have found the rest of Hood's division just as easily near the Emmitsburg road as on the Chambersburg Pike.[20]

In this passage, Coddington led off with his belief Longstreet "could have" moved while Lee was over on Ewell's front. Besides being a clear instance of armchair generalship, this statement was, even more importantly, a strong indication of Coddington's unawareness of Johnston's concealed route reconnaissance. Following this recommendation, Coddington then made the baseless claim that, at some point in the morning, Longstreet said he was unable to move because he was waiting for Pickett. Coddington then turned to the issue of Law's brigade, questioning why Longstreet had to wait for Law's arrival before commencing the march.

In a similar vein, Robert Krick contended Longstreet "inexorably ticked off moments potentially golden for the south" in waiting for Law's arrival before commencing his rightward movement. Krick then promoted the speculative narrative of an idle Longstreet, claiming to know that it was while Longstreet waited for Law's brigade that he "lounged" and had a "relaxed encounter" with his division commander, John Bell Hood. Advancing additional speculation, Krick postulated:

> Had Longstreet insisted on awaiting Law's arrival at the line of departure before launching his attack, he might have been able to make a weak case; though under the circumstances that afternoon, a delay in attacking to augment the force by one-eighth would not have made good sense, especially given the en echelon arrangement that was used. He was not waiting to attack, however, but to *begin* a complicated march. Law of course would have arrived at the jump-off point for the march long before his turn came to fall in at the end of the column. Longstreet simply was dragging his feet.[21]

Likewise, in his study of the second day, Historian Harry Pfanz, a former superintendent of Gettysburg National Military Park (GNMP), pursued a comparable line of thought to Coddington's and Krick's. Pfanz alleged the "march began after Law's brigade arrived and probably after the fight in Pitzer's Woods; thus it must not have begun before noon at the earliest. Why it was necessary for Longstreet to hold both McLaws's and Hood's divisions on Herr Ridge awaiting Law's arrival instead of moving to the assigned positions at once, Longstreet and others did not explain." Putting aside that Lee gave Longstreet his express permission to wait for Law's arrival, in all actuality, Law's brigade was not the entire story. Coddington, Krick, Pfanz, and many other historians have left out the other consequential outstanding issue the Confederates were waiting for in the late morning to early afternoon hours—that is, the identification of a concealed route to the extreme right for Longstreet's column. Put simply, Longstreet's divisions were going to sit largely idle until a concealed route was located and fully developed. Recall McLaws' recollections that Lee instructed him to "hold myself in readiness to move," which is exactly what McLaws did until the early afternoon hours, when Johnston rode up and said he was ready to lead the column forward.[22]

From all things Johnston in the lead-up to Longstreet's attack, we now move into an enumeration of other Confederate officers' reconnaissance activities conducted between the evening of July 1 and the early afternoon hours of July 2. Pointing out these other reconnaissance activities draws into question the dominant reconnaissance-related criticism of Longstreet's July 2 performance, namely that he did not engage in enough pre-march "preparations" or reconnaissance of the ground on his sector of the battlefield. Over the course of this portion of our analysis, it will be made clear that a number of historians over the decades have insufficiently imparted the story of reconnaissance activities on Longstreet's front in the hours before his assault. In fact, many historians have regularly either skimped on details of other reconnaissance activities or left out certain scouting missions altogether.

In his official report published in September 1863, Lee's chief of artillery, William Pendleton, left us a lot of detail on what reconnaissance efforts he claimed to have taken part in from late July 1 until Longstreet made his attack on July 2. On the evening of July 1, he noted how he "sent members of my staff to reconnoiter the woods on the right, and explore, as well as they might be able, a road observed along a ravine back of those woods."[23] Pendleton was likely referring here to Pitzer's or Biesecker's Woods, while the "road … along a ravine" was almost certainly present-day Willoughby Run Road, which was ultimately employed by Longstreet's divisions on the afternoon of July 2 to get to the extreme Confederate right. Pendleton recalled how "soon after sunrise" on July 2, he went with colonels A.L. Long and R. Lindsay Walker and Captain Johnston,[24] to the "farthest occupied point on the right and front" and "surveyed the enemy's position toward some estimate of the ground and the best mode of attack." As a result of this particular examination, Pendleton judged that an "assault on the enemy's left by our extreme right might succeed, should the mountain [Big Round Top] there offer no insuperable obstacle." From there, Pendleton described how he returned to and "proceeded some distance along the ravine road noticed the previous evening," whereby "having satisfied myself of the course and character of this road, I returned to an elevated point on the Fairfield Road, which furnished a very extensive view, and dispatched messengers to General Longstreet and the commanding general." It was from this elevated point near the Fairfield Road that Pendleton alleged to have observed all the aforementioned Federal activity along the Emmitsburg Road and a considerable Federal cavalry force near the Peach Orchard. Pendleton also recalled seeing General Longstreet near this elevated point about midday to view the ground.

The artillery chief also wrote that, at an unspecified time in the morning, Longstreet indicated he wanted Colonel E.P. Alexander, his principal First Corps artillery officer at Gettysburg, "to obtain the best view he then could of the front." As a result, Pendleton "conducted the colonel" to an unspecified "advanced point of observation previously visited," likely referring back to "the farthest occupied point on the right and front." Pendleton noted how the route to this area was "now more hazardous, from the fire of the enemy's sharpshooters, so that special caution was necessary in making the desired observation." Shortly thereafter, the artillery chief remembered how "a sharp contest occurred in the woods to the right and rear of this forward point." Of course, Pendleton was referring to Colonel Hiram Berdan's 1st U.S. Sharpshooters and the 3rd Maine regiment's scuffle with Cadmus Wilcox's Confederate Third Corps brigade in Pitzer's Woods around the noon hour. More pointedly, Pendleton's description provides further insight into the general location of the "forward point" to which he referred. In saying the clash in Pitzer's Woods happened "to the right and rear of this forward point," Pendleton almost certainly meant from his advance perspective looking rearward toward Confederate lines. Naturally, that would imply "right" meant farther north up the Confederate line, suggesting Pendleton and Alexander were located south and east of Pitzer's Woods.

Once Pitzer's Woods was "cleared of the enemy," Pendleton apparently left Alexander and returned to Confederate lines to get "some view of the ground beyond them, and much further to the right than had yet been examined." Considering the action in Pitzer's Woods petered out after about 20 minutes and the 3rd Maine regiment returned to Cemetery Ridge before 2 p.m., Pendleton likely "rode in that direction," arriving at Pitzer's Woods sometime between 12:30 and 2 p.m. The artillery chief recalled how upon entering the woods, he then "met the commanding general, *en route* himself for a survey of the ground." Pendleton alleged that he stayed in the vicinity of Wilcox's brigade for some time, which he recalled being an area still beset by "a good deal of sharpshooting." Curiously, Pendleton noted how Cadmus Wilcox had already gone ahead for an observation of the ground in his front, "beyond the farther edge of the woods," and provided the artillery chief with "guidance" based on that observation. Armed with that "guidance," Pendleton alleged he then "accompanied Colonel [A.L.] Long to the farm-house at the summit, where the cross-road from Fairfield, &c., emerges." Considering the pre-attack location of Wilcox's brigade and Pendleton's references to a "farm-house at the summit" and "the cross-road from Fairfield," it is likely the advance location to which Pendleton referred was near the John and Mary Wentz Farm at the intersection of the Emmitsburg and Millerstown Roads (the only road in the area that could be credibly described as a "cross-road" from Fairfield), with the Joseph Sherfy and David Klingle Farms as secondary possibilities. From this advance point, Pendleton rather non-descriptively recalled "having noticed the field and the enemy's batteries, &c." Following this

Col. R. Lindsay Walker, CSA, commander of the Confederate Third Corps Artillery (Library of Congress).

reconnaissance, Pendleton recollected how he "returned to General Longstreet, for the purpose of conducting his column to this point." Soon thereafter, Pendleton discovered Longstreet's column on the "ravine road," the same road he had scouted on both the evening of July 1 and early morning of July 2. After instructing some of his staff to help the divisions along that narrow route, Pendleton's July 2 reconnaissance activities—as presented in his after-battle report—officially came to an end.[25]

Colonel A.L. Long of Lee's staff also carried out some reconnaissance duties on the morning of July 2, particularly on A.P. Hill's front along Seminary Ridge to the southern end of Spangler's Woods. In the postwar years, Long remembered Lee had asked him to assist Hill's artillery chief, Colonel R. Lindsay Walker, with the placement of the Third Corps guns and to "examine and correct, if necessary, the position of the artillery on other parts of the line." Long recollected drawing Walker's attention to Warfield Ridge to the right and south of Hill's corps, describing it as a "ridge springing obliquely from the right of Hill's position, and extending in a direct line towards Round Top mountain" and a position of "importance." Walker, and, for a time, Pendleton, accompanied Long while he examined the Third Corps artillery and observed the Federal position from Seminary Ridge. "On reaching Hill's position, about sunrise," Long recalled, "I discovered that there had been considerable accession to the enemy's force on Cemetery Hill during the night; but it was chiefly massed to his right, leaving much of his center and almost his entire left unoccupied." Returning later—Long alleged around 10 a.m.—he noticed how "the Federals had considerably increased in number and extended their left."[26]

As learned from Pendleton's account, First Corps artillery officer Colonel E.P. Alexander acted as yet another reconnoitering officer for the Confederate army on July 2. Arriving near the field around 9 a.m., Alexander was immediately summoned by Longstreet, who was then with Lee "on a hill in rear of our lines." Alexander recalled how "I found Longstreet with Gen. Lee on Seminary Ridge, from which we had a view of the town & of [the] enemy's line above it & toward our right.... In Gen. Lee's presence Longstreet pointed out the enemy's position & said that we would attack his left flank." According to Alexander, Longstreet ordered him to take command of all the First Corps artillery for the coming attack and to immediately proceed to the Confederate right and "get an idea of the ground." Longstreet pointed to the Federal signal station on Little Round Top and informed Alexander, under orders from Lee, he was to carry out these instructions while remaining unseen by the enemy. Having his orders within just ten minutes, the artillery officer recalled immediately riding off "to examine all the roads leading to the right & front, & to get an understanding of the enemy's position & how & where we could best get at it." He remembered, "I rode fast—having a courier or two with me, & I don't think it took me much over an hour to get a very fair idea of the ground & roads." In another postwar account, Alexander similarly held that his "instructions were to reconnoitre the flank to be attacked.... This duty occupied, according to the best of my recollection, one or two hours." In yet another postwar publication, Alexander clarified that he carried out Longstreet's orders "by noon," which were to "reconnoitre the enemy's left and to move some of the [artillery] battalions to that part of the field." Collectively, between all of these accounts, we learn that Alexander examined the ground and roads off to the extreme Confederate right, explored how best to get at the Federal left, and transferred some batteries down to that sector of the field sometime between the hours of 9 a.m. and noon.[27]

Also conducting and facilitating reconnaissance activities on Longstreet's front was Colonel John L. Black of the 1st South Carolina Cavalry. Black was a unique and significant case because, according to the colonel himself in his postwar memoirs, Lee "called [over] Gen. Longstreet and introduced me to Gen. L. & said, 'General, Col Black has an improvised command of cavalry and a Battery of artillery. I turn him over to you to explore your ground, watch your flanks and rear." In two March 1886 letters to Gettysburg historian John Bachelder, Black concisely summarized his July 2, 1863, role as being "turned over" to Longstreet "to explore his ground[,] watch his flank[,] and do whatever came to hand." Upon being assigned to Longstreet, Black recalled how he "accompanied Gen'l. Longstreet to the right & top of a hill on a pike leading out of Gettysburg," very likely referring to the Fairfield Road. "Here he made his headquarters," Black wrote, "& ordered me to take possession of a bridge in sight & supply him with two trusty cavalry subalterns." The bridge to which Black referred was the stone bridge on the Fairfield Road over Marsh Creek, located about 250 feet southwest of Black Horse Tavern. Captain J.F. Hart's South Carolina Battery, attached to the 1st South Carolina Cavalry, was subsequently ordered to take up position at this bridge. Responding to Longstreet's request for two cavalrymen, the colonel afforded the corps commander Lieutenants Fred Horsey and J. Wilson Marshall, who were then ordered to set off toward the Confederate right, gain a better understanding of the ground in that direction, note the presence of any Federal forces, and report back to Longstreet. Though, in his memoirs, Black contended that Horsey returned and reported his findings to Longstreet by 8 a.m., historian Harry Pfanz claimed this reconnaissance work was actually carried out and finished sometime after 11 a.m.., "before the fight in Pitzer's Woods, after Buford's brigades had pulled off and before the arrival of the Third corps brigades from Emmitsburg." Whatever the case, of the two lieutenants, Horsey had the longer ride, proceeding three or four miles toward the Confederate right and exploring "the ground Longstreet deployed on as his entire battle line of battle was to the right of where his corps was massed in Brigades." Black's tangled description here merely indicated that Horsey reached and scouted the ground near Warfield Ridge. Marshall, on the other hand, ultimately stayed near the Fairfield Road and was ordered to explore Black Horse Tavern. Curiously, once the two lieutenants returned and made their reports, Longstreet asked Black if "he could rely on" Horsey's "statements," in particular. "I answered if there was any officer in the army he could rely on he could on Horsey," Black recalled relaying to Longstreet.[28]

What do all of these additional accounts from Pendleton, Long, Alexander, and Black suggest about Confederate reconnaissance in the lead-up to the afternoon attack? In short, it suggests there was quite an extensive amount of reconnaissance activity on Longstreet's front throughout the morning hours, certainly more than just the Johnston-Clarke early morning reconnaissance. Pendleton's account suggests he carried out a substantial amount of observation between the Fairfield Road and points farther south and east of Pitzer's Woods, perhaps even as far east

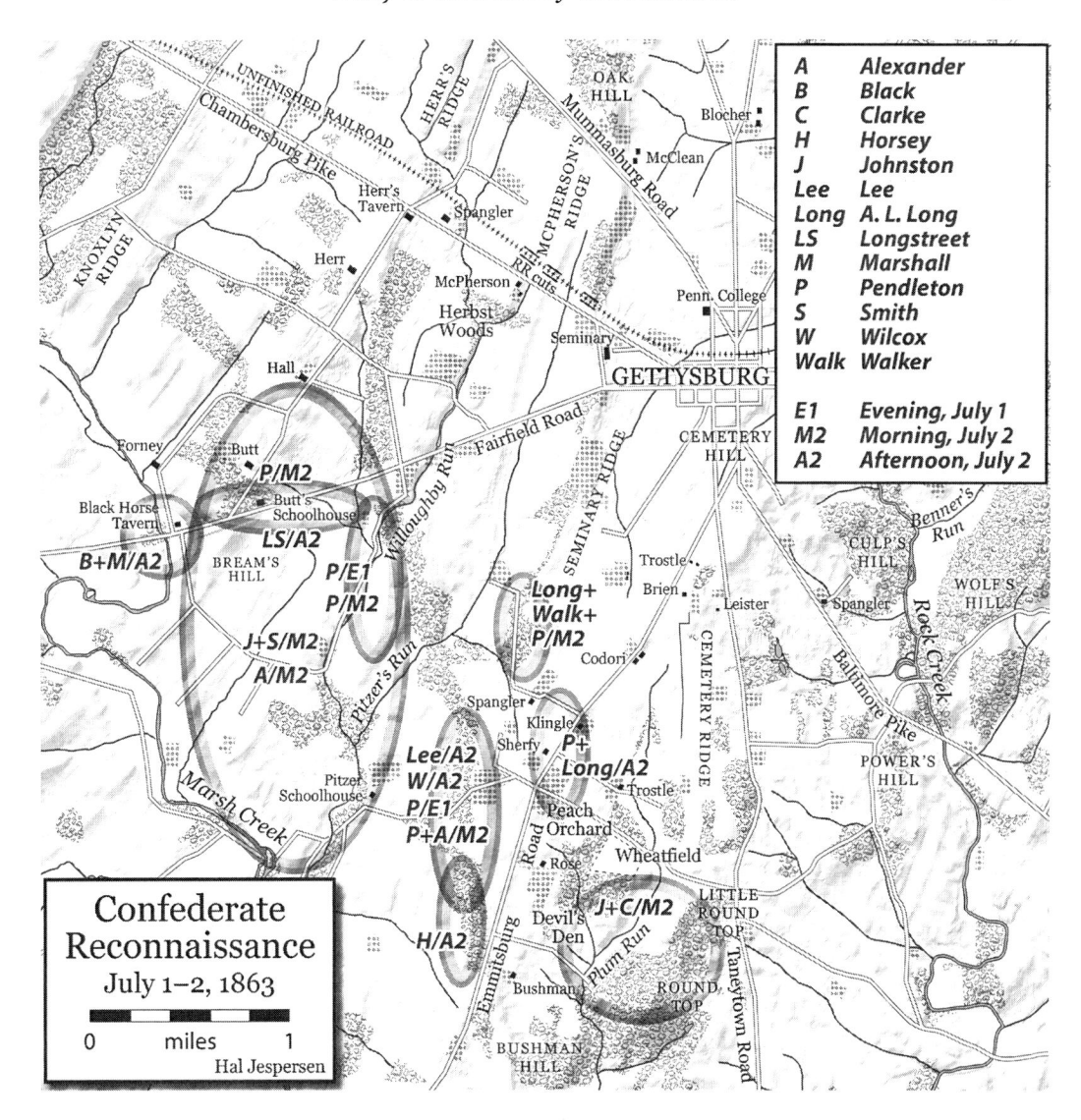

Confederate Reconnaissance, July 1-2, 1863.

as the Peach Orchard sector following the Berdan-Wilcox fight. Alexander's postwar recollections intimate he did much more in the lead-up to the attack than just bring some batteries down to the Confederate right. Indeed, the collective accounts further suggest several Confederate officers examined the extreme Confederate right and the Federal left. Along with Johnston, it appears Pendleton and Alexander gathered some understanding of the roads leading to the Confederate right: in the case of Pendleton, modern-day Willoughby Run Road, and for Alexander, a more non-specific, "all the roads leading to the right and front." Another important takeaway from these accounts is that many of these reconnaissance missions continued well into the late morning and early afternoon hours, yet another data point that calls into question the long-standing clarion call for a morning attack. Pendleton's activities extended perhaps until as late as 2 p.m.; Alexander's, Horsey's, and Marshall's until around noon; and according to Pendleton's report, even Lee and Longstreet were still actively viewing the ground into the early afternoon hours. We also learn of several instances, particularly by way of Pendleton's and Long's recollections, where Confederate reconnaissance officers observed significant Federal activity south of Cemetery Hill toward the late morning hours. For Longstreet's part specifically, we see that, on top of the Johnston-led reconnaissance activities (with his engineer Clarke's involvement in the early morning), he personally had Alexander and Black (Horsey and Marshall) out there on the Confederate right until the midday hours investigating the ground, gauging enemy activity in that sector of the field, and determining potential approaches to get at the Federal left.

So, with all this in mind, how have historians typically represented Confederate reconnaissance activities on Longstreet's front in the morning hours? Unfortunately, in many Longstreet-centric works and popular histories of the battle, historians have more or less only focused their attention on Johnston's early morning reconnaissance and how it ultimately misled Confederate attack efforts on July 2. Of course, Johnston's early morning reconnaissance did, in fact, do that; however, in just focusing on that scouting effort, some historians have missed the bigger picture, misleadingly promoting a narrative that suggests the Confederate High Command, and Longstreet in particular as attack commander, did very little in the morning hours to prepare for the attack and collect "current" or "timely" intelligence outside of Johnston's early morning mission. Additionally, as is the case with most commentary on this topic, historians' contributions have become mired in hindsight judgments on historical figures who were making decisions and acting in the moment. It is imperative to always remember that generals operated on the intelligence presented to them at the time, whether ultimately accurate or not. In the case of the Confederates' July 2 attack on Longstreet's front, the evidence suggests the High Command sent out a plethora of reconnaissance officers throughout the morning hours to gather intelligence. From that intelligence, they formulated a plan, based not on all the source evidence collected in the decades since the battle, but on the information they possessed at the moment.

In his biography of Longstreet, Jeffry Wert charged the general with "lacking in … energetic and careful preparation," a subjective allegation, which was only further clarified in a subsequently published essay on Longstreet's Gettysburg performance. "Longstreet … did little during the two hours of Lee's absence," Wert alleged, "except for order Colonel E. Porter Alexander to assume command of the corps artillery on the field and find a route the batteries could follow to get into position without detection from a Union signal station on Little Round Top." Again, do we know Longstreet "did little" over the course of a two-hour period in the morning when Lee was visiting Ewell's front, or do we lack a robust enough source record to make a judgment one way or the other? Either way, given (1) Lee went to Ewell's front specifically to determine if the day's main attack might better be initiated from there, (2) Law's brigade had yet to arrive, (3) Johnston was still out scouting for a concealed route for Longstreet's column (per Lee's orders), and (4) other reconnaissance activities were ongoing between 9 and 11 a.m., would it not have been reasonable for Longstreet to more or less wait for Lee's final decision, Law's arrival, and reconnaissance officers' forthcoming information? Perhaps more misleading and consequential was Wert's limited representation of Alexander's activities on the morning of July 2. In referencing what Alexander wrote about his activities in the postwar years, it is clear his duties extended well beyond simply locating "a route the batteries could follow" unseen by Federal signalmen.

Wert closed his assessment of Longstreet's actions in the lead-up to his attack by claiming "the hallmarks of" Longstreet's "generalship on previous battlefields … were lacking," namely, "careful planning, current intelligence, and attention to details." In sum, Wert wrote, Longstreet "neither ordered another, more timely reconnaissance, … spoke with McLaws and Hood, nor learned if Alexander had succeeded in locating a secure route for the artillery." Many of these charges are quite broad in nature. For instance, what exactly constitutes "careful planning"? The evidence suggests Lee and Longstreet planned for the attack as quickly as events and circumstances allowed and were guided by the information available to them at the time. The evidence further suggests "current intelligence" was sought by the Confederate High Command repeatedly throughout the morning and early afternoon hours. Under Longstreet's direction specifically were both Alexander's and Black's efforts, which were carried out roughly between 9:30 a.m. and noon. Additionally, in charging Longstreet with lacking "attention to detail," it is important to remember that a corps commander's personal observation was regularly limited by the safety precaution of physical distance. Realistically, their attention to detail largely depended on the accuracy and amount of detailed information provided by subordinates, and in this particular case, reconnaissance officers, who were out scouting the ground on the Confederate right and the approaches to the Federal left for several hours before the attack.

In his last point, Wert alluded to believing Longstreet failed to leverage some of the subordinates he had on hand like Hood and McLaws, or those he sent out to conduct reconnaissance duties, such as Alexander, to better understand the situation in his front. Though still hampered by the scant source record, Wert was correct in indicating there is currently no evidence suggesting Longstreet spoke with McLaws, Hood, or Alexander in the late-morning-to-early-afternoon hours. The curious part of this seeming lack of interaction is, in their post-battle or postwar recollections, several of these and other officers revealed they observed occurrences in the moment—developments on the Federal side—that, if reported, would very likely have proven helpful in giving the Confederate High Command a better understanding of the Federal position.[29]

We already know that, while observing the Federal position around 10 a.m., A.L. Long noticed an increase in the number of Federals and the extension of their left flank. How much of an increase and how far did the flank further extend? Did Long report this observation to Lee? Likewise, we have the aforementioned testimony from William Pendleton's official report in which, likely around the 9 a.m. hour, the artillery officer described how, from an elevated point on the Fairfield Road, he saw Federal cavalry in "considerable force" near the Emmitsburg Road, while Federal infantry, artillery, and trains moved northward along the road. Pendleton even reported Longstreet rode to that same observation point around midday. Did Pendleton speak with Longstreet and relay what he had seen? Recall also that Pendleton alleged he later moved out to a location in front of Cadmus Wilcox's brigade—"the farm-house at the summit"—accompanied by A.L. Long and saw "the enemy's batteries, &c." Pendleton claimed that just afterward he "returned to General Longstreet," ultimately finding him and his column advancing along Willoughby Run Road. Did Pendleton report his "farm-house" observations to Longstreet? Did Long report them to Lee? We also have McLaws in the postwar years alleging that, as he was sitting idle on his horse at the head of his division, until around 1 p.m., he observed, "in the distance the enemy coming, hour after hour, onto the battle ground."[30] Furthermore, the extent to which Alexander provided reconnaissance feedback to Longstreet remains a mystery. Alexander was ordered in part "to examine all the roads leading to the right & front, & to get an understanding of the enemy's position & how & where we could best get at it." Alexander claimed he carried out these orders within two hours, but what did he do with all the information he gathered? Did he report any of it to Longstreet? Did Longstreet ever seek him out after issuing orders?[31] Many of these questions unfortunately must remain unanswered because we simply do not possess the primary source evidence to lend further insight; however, it does seem rather implausible that, having observed significant Federal activity south of Cemetery Hill at different points in the hours preceding Longstreet's attack, several reconnoitering officers would have failed to report any of this information to Lee, Longstreet, or both generals.

A number of popular, bestselling histories of the battle over the decades have misled readers about the extent to which Confederate reconnaissance activities were conducted in the pre-attack hours on July 2. The Johnston-Clarke early morning reconnaissance has consistently received the bulk of the coverage, while oftentimes little to no information has been offered on most of the other scouting missions. As a result, most readers are left with the mistaken impression that after Johnston and Clarke returned around 7 to 8 a.m., the Confederate High Command did very little else from a reconnaissance perspective until Longstreet's attack was made in the afternoon. In Glenn Tucker's 1958 work, *High Tide at Gettysburg*, Black's, Long's, and Pendleton's scouting activities went undiscussed. Alexander's duties were only brought up in passing. On Alexander, Tucker wrote, he was to "reconnoiter the ground and co-operate with the infantry." Ten years later in his *Lee and Longstreet at Gettysburg*, Tucker did draw some attention to Pendleton's report, the artillery chief's collaborative reconnaissance activities with Alexander and Long, and his reference to Longstreet viewing the ground around midday. Likewise, Edwin Coddington's *The Gettysburg Campaign: A Study in Command* (1968) pointed out some of Alexander's, Long's, and Pendleton's reconnaissance efforts, but also left out any mention of Black's, Horsey's, and Marshall's scouting activities. Clifford Dowdey's *Lee and His Men at Gettysburg* (1958) also made no reference to Black, Horsey, and Marshall. Furthermore, the fact that Longstreet's engineer, Captain Clarke, accompanied Johnston on his early morning reconnaissance was omitted, while the full breadth of Alexander's reconnaissance-related activities was overlooked. Long's early-to-mid-morning observations from lower Seminary Ridge also went unmentioned and, of Pendleton, Dowdey only wrote, "Brigadier General Pendleton, in his anomalous position as chief of artillery, was at the southern end of Seminary Ridge at sunrise, tracing positions for guns across the Round Tops." Outside of Johnston's early morning reconnaissance, Stephen Sears' *Gettysburg* (2003) only mentioned Alexander, but included next to nothing reconnaissance-related in the description of his duties. Like many before him, no reference was made to Black, Horsey, and Marshall, or any other reconnaissance missions, except for a one-sentence description of Pendleton's and Long's observations: "Other reconnaissance missions, toward the Federal left, were undertaken by artillery chief William Pendleton and staff aide Armistead Long." Allen Guelzo's more recent *Gettysburg: The Last Invasion* (2013) called out some reconnaissance missions—Johnston's in the early morning, Walker's (with Long), Alexander's, and Pendleton's—though in very little detail. For instance, on Pendleton's activities, Guelzo wrote that he was "to scout another useful position." Additionally, as with Tucker, Coddington, Dowdey, and Sears, the reconnaissance roles of Black, Horsey, and Marshall are entirely absent. Of the well-known histories of the battle written in the last century, only Harry Pfanz's 1987 work, *Gettysburg: The Second Day*, spent an appropriate amount of time describing the reconnaissance conducted by Alexander, Black, Long, and Pendleton.[32]

In concluding this essay, it is only fitting that we return to Lafayette McLaws. Indeed, it was none other than McLaws, one of Longstreet's own division commanders, who quite likely initiated this reconnaissance controversy with his July 7, 1863, comment, "Genl Longstreet is to blame for not reconnoitering the ground." Particularly since the early twentieth century, many historians have run with this claim. What historians have drawn much less attention to are McLaws' postwar thoughts on the same topic, which though not always completely accurate, were certainly more keenly perceptive and reflective in addressing who was "to blame" when compared to his post-battle commentary. In some key postwar reflections, McLaws mused that since he and his engineer officer "had been forbidden to reconnoitre" (though McLaws did anyway) and "General Longstreet had not done it, and General Lee had not" (though, according to Pendleton, Lee and Longstreet at least viewed or surveyed the ground), "therefore it must have been that Major [sic] Johnston had gone there early in the morning." Of course, in this same account, McLaws had already described how in a dialogue with Lee sometime between 8:30 and 9:30 a.m. on July 2, the commanding general allegedly told him Johnston had just been sent to scout for a concealed route to the right. McLaws also neglected to mention all the other reconnaissance on the Confederate right throughout the morning to early afternoon hours, ranging from Clarke's and Smith's involvement with Johnston's reconnaissance activities, to the efforts of Pendleton, Long, Walker, Alexander, Black, Horsey, and Marshall.

Despite these missteps in commentary, probably committed out of ignorance more than anything else, McLaws moved on to his crucial main point. "If after that time [the early morning hours] a different state of affairs was known by anybody to exist, it had not been reported to either General Lee or General Longstreet; at least it appears so." Here, McLaws expressed his reasonable belief that even if someone had observed changes in the Federal position and to the location of the Federal left flank following Johnston's early morning reconnaissance, they seem to have never reported those changes to the Confederate High Command. What followed this speculation was McLaws' key statement: "All this resulted from defective and deficient organization of our staff corps; *not from anybody's fault, but from the force of circumstances* [emphasis added]." McLaws' analysis here was a far cry from his emotional outburst against his corps commander four days after the battle. Whereas in July 1863, McLaws solely and simply accused Longstreet of not reconnoitering the ground, upon years of reflection, McLaws had changed his mind, suggesting the real culprit was the dearth of "proper reconnaissance," reconnoitering officers' poor communication "up the chain," and a "deficient" staff corps. Indeed, McLaws' opinion on the reconnaissance controversy had clearly shifted from a singular focus on Longstreet to a less targeted and more accurate assertion that the issues resulting from Confederate reconnaissance efforts on July 2 were much more complicated, "not anybody's fault," and actually affected by "the force of circumstances."[33]

How true. Whereas many historians continue to frame the reconnaissance controversy exclusively around Longstreet—frequently advancing "if only he would have" (hindsight) and "he should have" (armchair general) arguments, while alleging he failed to conduct enough reconnaissance in the lead-up to his July 2 attack and neglected to prepare and demonstrate attention to detail (amongst other similar accusations)—this focus largely misses the mark. Rather, key primary source and postwar evidence suggests the real issue was that, for whatever reason, the *numerous* reconnaissance that were conducted turned out not to be of the best quality, while some reconnoitering officers appear not to have reported critical observations they made of the Federal position, which may have led to the modification of the Confederate High Command's decision calculus on July 2. The High Command was beholden to the information reconnoitering officers presented to them at that time, not to all the information we are now privy to as historians. In other words, Lee and Longstreet fashioned plans and directed events based on the intelligence they received in the moment. If the intelligence turned out to be poor or not forthcoming, both the plans and direction would consequently suffer through little fault of their own.

McLaws' follow-on claim that these reconnaissance issues resulted from "the force of circumstances"—adverse conditions the Confederates faced in the moment, uncontrollable by any one or two persons—was a prescient one. To be sure, one of the biggest, if not the biggest, "force of circumstance" confronting the Confederate High Command on July 2 was the unexpected advance of Sickles' Federal Third Corps to the Emmitsburg Road and the extension of its left flank to Devil's Den. Truth be told, the Confederate understanding of the Federal left on July 2 was always deficient; however, Sickles' move greatly flummoxed the existing, albeit flawed Confederate assault plan to attack "up the Emmitsburg Road." Actually, it would not be an exaggeration to say that once Sickles made his move, nearly all insight gleaned from Confederate reconnaissance efforts prior to that move was almost entirely moot. No one in the Confederate High Command had planned for or expected a significant Federal force stretching from the Emmitsburg Road to Devil's Den. With this reality in mind, it is important to remember that Sickles executed his move while Longstreet was already well into his march; so any Confederate opportunity to conduct new reconnaissance activities or significantly alter attack plans was constrained by an abbreviated timetable. By this point, not only was Lee itching to attack as the day advanced into the mid-afternoon hours, but the impending arrival of Longstreet's men to their attack jump-off points meant that to maintain some element of surprise, the attack needed to take place as quickly as possible before the Federals took full stock of the situation and flooded the attack zone with additional forces.

Coupled with many historians' hyper-focus on Longstreet, the lack of attention given to additional reconnaissance activities outside of Johnston's early morning mission, and the absence of a broader emphasis on the general "force of circumstances" affecting the Confederates in the pre-attack hours is the ever-important, but long-overlooked issue of Johnston's involvement with identifying a concealed route to the extreme Confederate right. Collective insight from McLaws, Johnston, Longstreet, and Pendleton lends credence to the argument Lee ordered Johnston to conduct additional reconnaissance activities for this express purpose sometime between 8:30 a.m. and midday. While overlooking the critical aspect of concealment in Lee's July 2 attack plans, historians have instead focused most of their attention on the absence of Law's brigade and their belief Longstreet need not have waited for its arrival to commence his divisions' rightward movement. Additionally, in comparing the Lee-McLaws morning dialogue as presented in McLaws' postwar account with how historians have regularly paraphrased the conversation, key parts of the conversation have, for whatever reason, been misleadingly altered. As a result, students of the battle have been presented with a skewed interpretation of when and how certain events developed on the morning of July 2, particularly regarding the extent to which ongoing Confederate reconnaissance efforts affected the timing of Longstreet's movement.

In sum, if there is just one general takeaway from this in-depth examination of Confederate reconnaissance activities on Longstreet's front in the pre-attack hours of July 2, it is that there was certainly much more going on than students of the battle have previously been led to believe. Indeed, the predominant, superficial narrative that "Longstreet was to blame" simply does not hold up upon close inspection of the source record.

Essay 4

A Severe Case

Diagnosing the Treatment of Longstreet's Countermarch

The odd divisions will face to the right, and the even to the left; the right and left guides of all the divisions will face about; the chiefs of odd divisions will hasten to their right and cause two files to break to the rear. The chiefs of even divisions will hasten to their left, and cause two files to break to the rear.—William Hardee

After book lectures, and of course during interviews, authors typically engage in a question-and-answer session. Not only does this part of the presentation often turn out to be the most entertaining and fun portion of the book event, but in some cases, the most revealing—whether through a question asked or an answer given. From my perspective, it turned out to be the former on a certain Longstreet-Gettysburg topic. After receiving the same question on three separate occasions, I knew something must be going on. The question, as you might expect, given the title of this essay, involved James Longstreet's countermarch on the afternoon of July 2. Specifically, the audiences and the interviewer essentially wanted to know why Longstreet seemingly created more unnecessary delay by doubling Lafayette McLaws' division back on itself during the countermarch, instead of simply about-facing the entire column and having John Bell Hood's division lead instead. The pervasiveness of this question piqued my curiosity about the source of this assertion and why it was seemingly such an important topic to students of the war. My first book, *Longstreet at Gettysburg: A Critical Reassessment*, went into significant detail about a topic I always thought to be much more controversial—namely, the initial portion of the First Corps march on the afternoon of July 2, which ended near Black Horse Tavern, and the decision to countermarch as opposed to taking the infamous "path across fields." I devoted an entire chapter to that particular topic[1]; however, I only spent a paragraph or two on the countermarch itself.[2] Besides describing the rationale behind the countermarch and how Hood's and McLaws' divisions actually went about executing it, I did not delve much further into the topic. I certainly was not aware of the extent to which students of the war seemingly considered McLaws' leading the countermarch another gaffe on Longstreet's part, or rather, had heard others make that argument. Perhaps I misjudged that critics might afford Longstreet a much-needed, hour-long reprieve when it comes to his July 2 performance. By now, I should have known better—no such reprieve granted!

In all seriousness, it is a great topic and I appreciate audience members and interviewers drawing attention to it. Much of the answer I afforded them is woven throughout this essay, but a careful analysis and examination of the topic has since revealed even more. Indeed, as is common with many subtopics of the Longstreet-Gettysburg Controversy over the decades, agenda, bias, myth, and misleading interpretations have regularly ruled the day when it comes to coverage of the countermarch. First of all, Longstreet's countermarch is typically introduced, framed, and presented as an exceedingly complicated topic. It is rather complicated at times, that is true; however, it does not mean we need to overly complicate or overstate the topic. Secondly, it bears mentioning that the lack of an extensive source record on this topic has likely contributed to the tendency to over-complicate or overstate, while perhaps leading some to indulge in excessive interpretation. Despite the rather limited primary source record and postwar commentary on this topic, there is certainly enough available to make some informed, well-supported observations, and dispel some of the misleading assertions that have been advanced on this topic since the postwar years.

Like many other contested issues regarding the Longstreet-Gettysburg Controversy, a few omnipresent attitudes seem to regularly hover like a dense mist over coverage of the countermarch topic. Foremost has been many historians' unmistakable tendency to approach the topic, like they have most Longstreet-Gettysburg topics, with the preconceived bias that Longstreet was sulking, dragging his feet, or intentionally trying to thwart Robert E. Lee's tactical plans because of the non-adoption of his own. For those who possess and project this bias, Longstreet at Gettysburg almost always winds up being couched in some descriptive combination of insubordination, duplicity, and stubbornness, or shaded by dramatic statements like "he was not his usual self" and "his heart was not in it." In other words, by holding this bias, analysis and coverage of the countermarch topic is to lesser and greater degrees veiled in the mode of a calculating, careless, lethargic, or pouting Longstreet. The second omnipresent attitude that has regularly intruded analysis of Longstreet's countermarch is the tendency to engage in so-called Monday morning quarterbacking or armchair generalship—meaning, passing judgment or criticizing someone after the event (without fully taking into account events and circumstances that person faced in the moment), or explaining what you think they should have done. The most persistent example of this tendency when it comes to Longstreet's countermarch is wrapped up in critics' broader, pervasive statement, "If only Longstreet had attacked earlier, he would have been able to…." Thus, to the armchair general holding this particular belief, Longstreet's decision to countermarch naturally becomes yet another source of nagging delay, drawing their speculative scenario further away from, in their view, a "better time" for the Confederates to get in position and attack the Federal army. Perhaps it was this prevalent tendency toward armchair generalship that Longstreet had in mind when he declared in a February 1897 letter to Harry Heth, a Third Corps division commander at Gettysburg: "It is quite absurd to attempt to figure out success for the Confederates at Gettysburg, by the plans of our chief, for the 2d and 3d days. He [Lee] has said so, events have showed it, and that is the verdict of all good military critiques."[3]

While making every attempt to avoid these and similar emotional and speculative pitfalls, new light can be shed on Longstreet's countermarch by cross-referencing numerous primary and postwar accounts present in the *Official Record*, *The Bachelder Papers*, *The Southern Historical Society Papers*, postwar essay compilations, personal letters and memoirs, and private collections. A careful analysis and examination of these records affords a clearer view of this topic's critical touch-points, namely a review of what kind of march Lee had in mind for Longstreet's two divisions on July 2, the amount of time it took Longstreet to decide a countermarch was necessary, the first instance when Longstreet's column was seen by Federal signalmen on Little Round Top, the reasoning behind why Longstreet allowed McLaws' division to continue leading the column during the countermarch, and if there is any merit to the allegation Longstreet prematurely gave up on concealment and ordered Hood forward by the "most direct route" during the latter stages of the march. Finally, all this collective analysis allows us to make some observations about the Confederates' shifting attack plans once Longstreet's two divisions finished their march to the extreme right.

To properly frame and contextualize much of the commentary and decisions during the countermarch, it is first necessary to understand the overarching fact that Lee always intended for Longstreet's march to the extreme Confederate right to be a concealed one—kept hidden away from the prying eyes of any Federal signal station. This is an important concept to fully internalize and understand because a number of misleading statements have been advanced over the years alleging all Longstreet really had to do in the morning hours (or the early afternoon hours, for that matter) was simply march his divisions to the right and attack. Setting aside the many other reasons why Longstreet did not begin his approach in the morning hours, this assertion ignores Lee's moderating order that the march proceed in a concealed manner. The evidence for Lee's concealed route order is overwhelming. A few examples will suffice. Of course, in Longstreet's own after-battle report, he uses the terminology, "concealed route." Gilbert Moxley Sorrel, a member of Longstreet's staff, noted in his postwar memoirs that "an attempt was made to move the troops to the right into position without discovery by the enemy." Lafayette McLaws described a conversation he had with Lee in the morning hours, in which the commanding general informed him, "I wish you to get there [his attack jump-off point] if possible without being seen by the enemy." Evander Law, a brigade commander in Hood's division, divulged it was "necessary to conceal our movements from the Federal signal station on Little Round Top." One of Law's regimental commanders, Colonel William C. Oates of the 15th Alabama, similarly expressed there existed a clear "purpose of covering the movement from the enemy." Likewise, Joseph Kershaw, a brigade commander in McLaws' division and whose 3rd South Carolina infantry regiment led the march, maintained: "We were then directed to move under cover of hills toward the right, with a view to flanking the enemy in that direction, if cover could be found to conceal the movement."[4]

Not only did Lee instruct Longstreet to proceed to the extreme Confederate right via a concealed route, as opposed to just any route to the right, but he also ordered that dedicated reconnaissance efforts be conducted in the late morning and early afternoon hours with the explicit purpose of locating one. Indeed, Lafayette McLaws unambiguously maintained that during the morning hours, "Genrl Lee then remarked that he had ordered a reconnaissance for the purpose of finding out a way to go into position without being seen by the enemy and I must hold myself in readiness to move." Captain Samuel Johnston, a prominent figure in Confederate attack planning and preparations on July 2, and of course was a consequential player during Longstreet's march, wrote to McLaws in the postwar years, admitting he had examined "the roads over which our troops would have to move in the event of a movement on the enemy's left."[5]

When did Johnston ultimately complete this concealed route reconnaissance work and inform McLaws, commanding Longstreet's leading division, that he was ready to direct the infantry column forward? McLaws said this event occurred as late as 1 p.m. on the afternoon of July 2. "Major [sic] Johnston, of General Lee's staff, came to me and said he was ordered to conduct me on the march. My command was at once put in motion—Major [sic] Johnston and myself riding some distance ahead." Even if McLaws potentially happened to be somewhat imprecise on his recollected time of 1 p.m.—perhaps, more accurately, it was sometime between noon and one o'clock—notice we are already beyond the so-often-talked-about, precious morning hours and into the afternoon. This begs the question: if it was so important to Lee that Hood's and McLaws' divisions quickly get to their attack positions to make an assault during the morning hours, then why did he put so much effort into locating and having the column march along a concealed route? In other words, if attacking early was so critical to Lee and he was repeatedly chafing and frustrated at Longstreet's alleged slowness and delay in the morning hours—as Longstreet critics over the decades would have us believe—why does the source record show a commanding general clearly not intent on enforcing speed, but actually concealment? Indeed, it is clear secrecy was paramount to Lee. McLaws shrewdly drew attention to this reality: "It is plain ... that, if General Lee had so ordered, General Longstreet's corps could have been on the flank of the enemy ... by half past 8 o'clock a.m." Rather, the division commander emphasized that Longstreet was "resting under the eye of General Lee, and under his orders to remain, until Major [sic] Johnson's [sic] return." Resultantly, Longstreet's leading division was not "at once put in motion," until Johnston—who had led, or at the very least been heavily involved in, scouting for a concealed route—came to McLaws and declared he was ready to conduct the column forward on the march. McLaws' recollections provide added clarity to Johnston's own postwar allegation that "we did not move off very promptly, nor was our march at all rapid. It did not strike me that Gen. Longstreet was in a hurry to get into position. It might have been that he thought hurry was unnecessary." Perhaps Longstreet was not "in a hurry" or gave the impression "hurry was unnecessary" because his foremost responsibility during the march was to abide by Lee's orders to march concealed. Indeed, the evidence suggests "hurry" was not the overriding priority. Put frankly, Lee's paramount desire for concealment not only served to delay the start of the Confederates' move to the right on July 2, but as we will see, also proved to have a significant delaying effect on the march itself. McLaws aptly described how Lee's concealed march order—to "go into position without being seen by the enemy"—quickly turned out to be a "millstone around his [Longstreet's] neck."[6]

We will not go into great detail here on Longstreet's initial march on the afternoon of July 2, as I have already covered that topic elsewhere.[7] That said, a brief summary of the march's early stages is contextually necessary to understand the who, what, when, where, and why of the countermarch. The story begins with a flurry of Confederate activity around 11 a.m. on July 2. It was at this approximate time Robert E. Lee (1) returned from Ewell's front, (2) decided the main Confederate attack on July 2 would be made from Longstreet's front on the army's right flank, (3) issued his "Old Warhorse" attack orders for the first time, (4) gave Longstreet permission to wait for the arrival of Law's brigade before commencing the First Corps march, and (5) awaited the completion of reconnaissance activities to locate a concealed route to the Confederates' extreme right. Likely, sometime between noon and 1 p.m., Captain Johnston returned from those reconnaissance duties, joined Lafayette McLaws, and informed him he was ready to conduct his division forward via a concealed route.[8] Indeed, Lee had tasked Johnston to guide McLaws' division to its attack jump-off points on Warfield Ridge, with Hood's division following. Once McLaws and Hood reached those attack jump-off points, they would then proceed to gain and align perpendicular to the Emmitsburg Road, before commencing their main attack up the road toward the presumed location of the Federal flank somewhere near Cemetery Hill. Richard Anderson's Third Corps brigade would join in the assault—his brigades attacking en echelon from right to left (Wilcox, Lang, Wright, Posey, Mahone, in that order)—as Longstreet's divisions progressed at right angles up the Emmitsburg Road toward the supposed Federal left flank.[9]

Throughout the mid-to-late morning hours, Hood's and McLaws' divisions were staged in the valley between Herr's and McPherson's Ridges (nearer the former); Hood located north of the Old Mill Road, with his right loosely anchored near Herr's Tavern (now the Inn at Herr Ridge Bed & Breakfast); and McLaws positioned south of the same road. Joseph Kershaw of McLaws' division recalled in the postwar years that his brigade was located "at the end of the lane leading to the Black Horse Tavern, situated some 500 yards to our right." In an 1876 letter to Gettysburg historian John Bachelder, Kershaw clarified his initial pre-march position, recalling that his brigade was situated near Dr. Samuel E. Hall's residence, which was located on the west side of Herr's Ridge Road and just south of the Old Mill Road intersection. As Johnston joined McLaws and began guiding the lead division forward, Longstreet rode near the middle of the column (perhaps close to the intersection of Hood's and McLaws' divisions), with Lee joining the First Corps commander on the march for some time. "General Lee rode with me a mile or more," Longstreet recalled in his memoirs. In another postwar account, Longstreet intimated, "I left General Lee only after the line had stretched out on the march, and rode along with Hood's division, which was in the rear." From near the intersection of Old Mill Road and Herr's Ridge Road, McLaws' division marched southwest until it reached the junction of Herr's Ridge Road and Red Oak Lane. Turning right onto the lane, the column passed the Adam Butt Farm and proceeded on a semi-circular route—initially northeast and then southwesterly—until it reached Black Horse Tavern Road.

Essay 4. A Severe Case 99

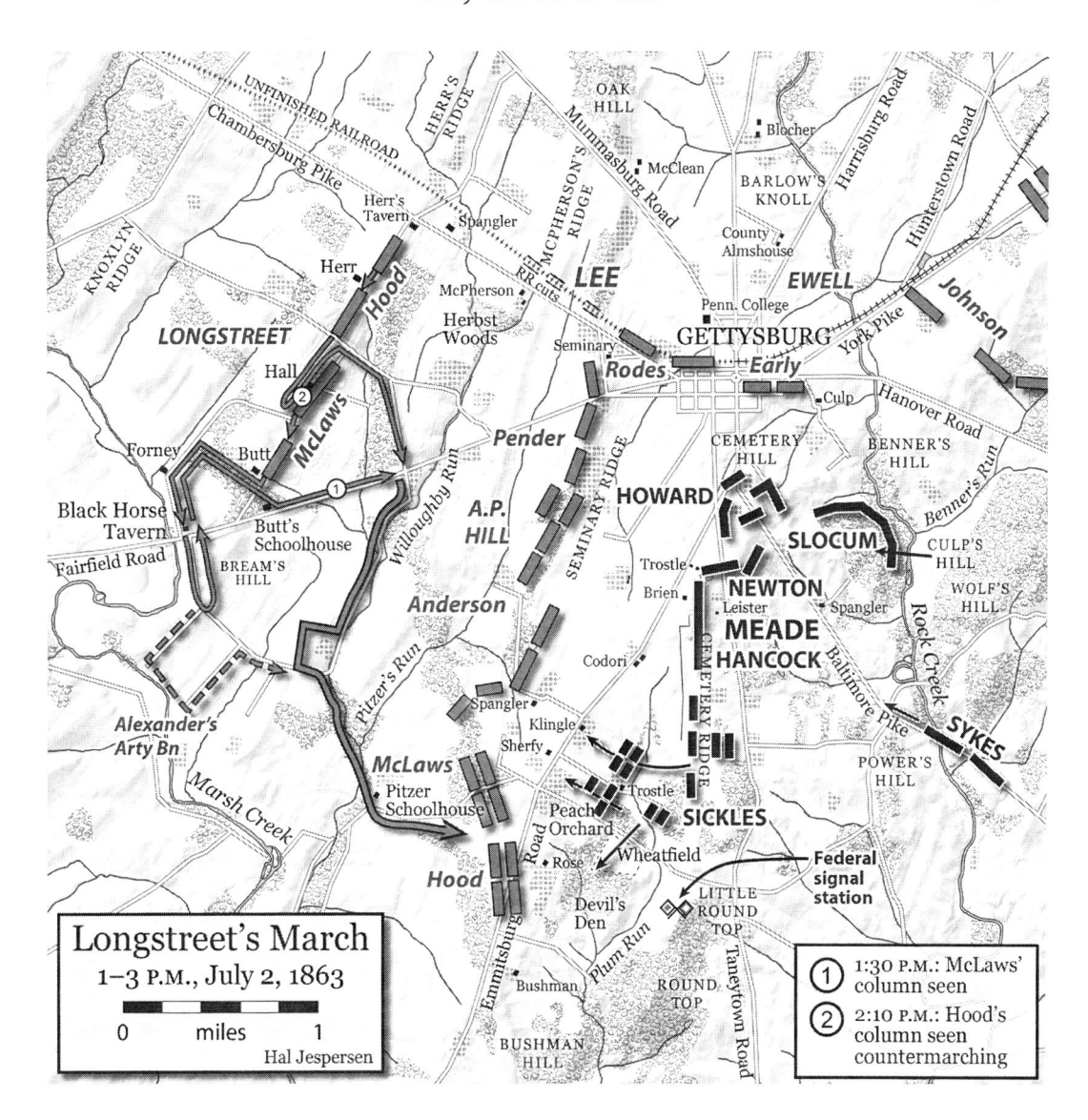

Longstreet's March, 1–3 p.m., July 2, 1863.

Passing the Mark Forney Farm on its right before turning left onto the Tavern Road, McLaws' division then moved southeasterly, passing between the bridge over Marsh Creek and Black Horse Tavern, crossing over the Fairfield Road, and ultimately halting about 400 yards south-southeast of the tavern near the present-day intersection with Plank Road. It was here Johnston and McLaws discovered that if the column continued, it would have to pass over an elevated point rising about 40 feet, known as Bream's Hill, exposing the Confederates to the prying eyes of Federal signalmen on Little Round Top, located about three miles to the southeast.[10]

Once halted, Johnston and McLaws proceeded to ride around the immediate vicinity to ascertain if there was a way around the elevated impasse. They apparently found no other option. In the meantime, several messages were sent to Longstreet,

Black Horse Tavern Road, leading to the Black Horse Tavern (left) and the intersection with the Fairfield Road. On the early afternoon of July 2, McLaws' division marched down this road, past the intersection, halted before the elevated and exposed "point of contention" near Bream's Hill, and then countermarched back toward the camera position in pursuit of a different route (Author's Collection).

who proceeded to the head of the column. Longstreet examined the situation with McLaws, who suggested the only remedy was a countermarch based on a personal reconnaissance he had conducted in the morning hours. Presented with no other viable option, Longstreet ordered the countermarch.[11]

At this juncture in our examination of Longstreet's countermarch, two important points need to be advanced and explained. The first critical point involves dispelling the dominating impression historians have given students of the war that Longstreet hemmed and hawed with McLaws for a rather extended period of time before making the decision to countermarch. Of course, this interpretation would fit rather conveniently into the traditional narrative of an inattentive, slow, or sulking

The Black Horse Tavern, located at the intersection of Black Horse Tavern and Fairfield Roads. In the context of the battle, the tavern has essentially become synonymous with Longstreet's July 2 march (Author's Collection).

Longstreet. If the First Corps commander was itching to delay his attack for as long as possible, as critics have long alleged, one would think this elevated point of contention near Black Horse Tavern and Bream's Hill would offer the perfect excuse for a dawdling commander who was dragging his feet (either on purpose or simply because "his heart was not in it"). So, following this line of interpretation, naturally Longstreet would have shown little urgency at this unexpected juncture, loitering away copious time to explore and evaluate any and all possible options, right?

No, on the contrary, not only did Joseph Kershaw, whose brigade was at the head of the First Corps column, describe how he believed Longstreet and McLaws were "both manifesting considerable irritation" upon returning from their examination of the elevated point on Bream's Hill, but he also shed critical commentary on how long it took Longstreet to make the decision to countermarch. Kershaw underscored that it only took McLaws and Longstreet "a few minutes (*not five*) [emphasis added]" to examine the unforeseen situation before McLaws "ordered 'Countermarch'" and the division began to execute the retrograde movement. For those predisposed to distrust any postwar account, Kershaw contended similarly in his after-battle report, "The column was halted while General Longstreet and McLaws reconnoitered the route. After some *little delay* [emphasis added], the major-general commanding returned, and directed a countermarch." In advancing this recollection in 1863 and years afterward, Kershaw was not describing a demurring general, but rather one who was acting as decisively as possible under the unanticipated circumstances, not

A view from Black Horse Tavern of Bream's Hill, rising from right to left in this view. McLaws' column crossed the Fairfield Road and advanced some distance down the southern extension of Black Horse Tavern Road, roughly to the Plank Road intersection. There, the column halted, lest it be seen by Federal signalmen three miles to the southeast on Little Round Top (Author's Collection).

one taking advantage of another opportunity for extended delay, but one who recognized the need to get the column moving again as quickly as possible.[12]

The second critical argument to be made at this juncture involves dispelling another pervasive interpretation that has repeatedly shown up in Gettysburg battle studies, namely the allegation that Longstreet's column was exposed and seen by Federal signalmen on Little Round Top at the elevated point near Black Horse Tavern. In his 1993 essay on Longstreet's July 2 actions, Robert Krick, former chief historian for the Fredericksburg and Spotsylvania National Military Park and fervent Longstreet critic, forcefully made this claim, maintaining that "at its top [the elevated point near Black Horse Tavern], the Confederates would come in clear view of Federals on Little Round Top." Employing Samuel Johnston's postwar allegation that he told Longstreet this elevated point would "discover your movements to the enemy," Krick fashioned a dumbfounded and indecisive Longstreet, who had "no comment" and "watched as the column went over the crest into view of the Federals and halted." Along with Johnston's recollection, Krick also relied on one of E.P. Alexander's postwar accounts, where the former artillery officer asserted, "Then I recall riding back for something, & finding the head of one of our divisions of infantry standing halted in sight of the signal station…. Finding that the road brought them into view they halted & sent back for orders or a guide." From this postwar recollection, Krick declared, "When he [Alexander] noticed the infantry not only failing to follow his example but also halted in clear view of Little Round Top—thus canceling *both* secrecy and speed—he was astonished."[13]

Curiously, this erroneous contention has even more unexpected origins than the ones Krick drew attention to, since none other than James Longstreet himself appears to have advanced this belief in his first major postwar account of the battle, "Lee in Pennsylvania," published in the *Philadelphia Weekly Times* in November 1877 (and later included in the *Annals of the War*, published in 1879). In this article, Longstreet alleged that when he went forward to examine the elevated point, he "look[ed] up toward Round Top [and] saw that the signal station was in full view, and, as we could plainly see the station, it was apparent that our heavy columns was seen from their position, and that further efforts to conceal ourselves would be a waste of time." Interestingly, in Longstreet's two other major accounts published in the 1880s and 1890s, respectively, the First Corps commander never repeated the claim of his earlier article that the column was seen at Black Horse Tavern. The other unexpected origin of this claim was Gilbert Moxley Sorrel, a member of Longstreet's staff, who bluntly wrote in his postwar memoirs, "We were seen from the start and signaled constantly."[14]

Contrary to Longstreet's claim in his 1877 account and Alexander's, Johnston's, and Sorrel's recollections, the column was neither seen at the point of contention near Black Horse Tavern, nor prior to the divisions' arrival and halt at that location. In fact, Longstreet's column went unseen by Federal signalmen on Little Round Top until it was well into its countermarch and proceeding in a northeasterly direction up the Fairfield Road (before turning right soon thereafter and resuming a southwesterly march along Willoughby Run). Indeed, it was not until 1:30 p.m. when Federal signalmen first reported a "heavy column of enemy's infantry, about 10,000 strong … moving from opposite our extreme left *toward our right* [emphasis added]." "Toward our right" described a Confederate movement in the direction of Cemetery Hill and Culp's Hill, not the Peach Orchard or lower Cemetery Ridge. Since the only time Longstreet's column moved in the direction of the Federal right was during its countermarch, the Federal signalmen could only have been making reference to that retrograde movement—not the initial march to Black Horse Tavern, the halt near the tavern, or the subsequent resumed march toward the Federal extreme left. Likewise, a little after 2 p.m., the signalmen again described how Confederate troops "were passing on a by-road from Dr. [Samuel E.] Hall's house to Herr's tavern…. A train of ambulances is following them." This latter report likely referred to Hood's division's brief countermarch up Herr Ridge Road to Old Mill Road before cutting southeast across woods and fields (modern-day Park Avenue) toward a rough country road parallel to Willoughby Run.[15]

Compounding this primary evidence that the Federals did not see Longstreet's column until the middle of the Confederates' countermarch are postwar accounts from both Joseph Kershaw and Lafayette McLaws. Kershaw, commanding the South Carolinian brigade at the head of the column, described how they "reached a point where the road passed over the top of a hill, from which our movement *would have been* [emphasis added] plainly visible from the Federal signal station on Little

Round Top. Here we were halted." Notice Kershaw's use of words. Never did he contend the column was at that moment "plainly visible" to the Federals on Little Round Top; rather, he clearly revealed that they "would have been" exposed if the forward movement had not ceased. Likewise, Lafayette McLaws, who was in command of Longstreet's leading division and riding with Johnston at the head of the column throughout the initial march, indicated that as he and the captain "rose a hill on the road we were taking, the Round Top ... plainly visible, with the flags of the signal men in rapid motion," McLaws then "*sent back and halted* [emphasis added] my division." Again observe what McLaws wrote. Never did he assert that the column continued up and over the hill, exposed to the signal station on Little Round Top; rather, he claimed he and Johnston discovered the problematic rise and immediately sent back orders to halt the division. Additionally, in recounting a conversation he alleged to have had with Longstreet once the First Corps commander arrived at the front to examine the situation, McLaws claimed he told his chief, "'Ride with me, and I will show you that we can't go on this route, according to instructions, *without being seen* [emphasis added] by the enemy.'" Note how in McLaws' dialogue with Longstreet, he asked the First Corps commander to ride forward with him from a location at or near the head of the column toward the exposed point, before explaining the column could not proceed any further "without being seen" by the signal station on Little Round Top, naturally implying the Federals had not yet observed them. Keeping all this collective evidence in mind, it is clear the Federals neither spotted Longstreet's marching column at the elevated point near Black Horse Tavern, nor at any other point prior to the First Corps' countermarch.[16]

While we are on the topic of Federal signalmen on Little Round Top spotting Longstreet's column twice during its countermarch, it is crucial to point out the consequential impact of those sightings on Federal High Command tactical planning on July 2. Indeed, the implications of these detections have typically been pointed out only in passing, if at all, in Gettysburg battle narratives, while in all actuality they ought to be fully highlighted and emphasized. It is clear that on the morning of July 2, Federal Major General George Meade, commander of the Army of the Potomac, was either anticipating a Confederate attack against his right flank, or seriously considering launching an attack of his own from that flank against the Confederate left. Around 10 a.m., Meade ordered Federal Twelfth Corps commander Major General Henry Slocum to conduct a reconnaissance and examine the ground in his front in preparation for initiating an attack. The Federal army commander continued to focus most of his attention on his right flank well into the afternoon hours. He directed the Federal Fifth Corps to take up position on that front and remain in readiness to support Slocum's corps either offensively or defensively. Likewise, Meade also initially intended for Major General John Sedgewick's Sixth Corps to be directed toward the Federal right when it arrived on the field in the afternoon hours. Collectively, Meade's mid-morning orders to Slocum and how he managed and intended to manage his major supporting infantry units, the Fifth and Sixth Corps—coupled with his rather lax approach in handling Daniel Sickles' Third Corps (until Sickles unilaterally moved his men out to the Emmitsburg

Road)—shows a commander who was mostly focused on his right flank, not his left for most of the day on July 2.[17]

What does any of this have to do with Longstreet's countermarch? Quite a bit, actually. If you review the Federal signalmen on Little Round Top's message from 1:30 p.m., they informed the Federal High Command that a "heavy column" was moving toward the Federal right flank. Then, just after 2 p.m., they reported Confederate infantry moving north toward Herr's tavern, which again would have suggested a general advance toward the Federal right. How would a Federal High Command, that up until that point in the day was most focused on its right flank, have interpreted these messages? How would they have played into the Federals' tactical decision calculus? Might they have validated Meade's dominating suspicion that the Confederates planned to initiate an attack from their left flank against Slocum's corps?

The point here is the Federals never reported Longstreet's column moving toward their extreme left throughout the entirety of the First Corps march and countermarch. Rather, the only messages sent to the Federal High Command reported the Confederates moving toward their right flank. Of course, Longstreet, and no one else in the Confederate High Command, intended for this occurrence; the actual intention was to remain concealed throughout the entirety of the march in accordance with Lee's orders. Nevertheless, this deception happened by chance and gave the Federals a false impression of where this "heavy column" was actually headed. Resultantly, Longstreet's countermarch inadvertently deceived the Federals, corroborating their already overt belief that the day's main action would be on their right flank, and amplifying the somewhat less-than-attentive consideration Meade gave to his left flank in the morning and early afternoon hours.

In closing out our analysis on this subtopic, it is also worthwhile to note how Longstreet's column remaining unseen until the countermarch and the timing of the column's discovery by the Federals creating a false impression of Confederate intentions on July 2 collectively strikes hard at some comments the anti–Longstreet group made in the postwar years. Cadmus Wilcox, a brigade commander in Richard Anderson's division of A.P. Hill's corps at Gettysburg and postwar anti–Longstreet group member, wrote of the situation near Black Horse Tavern, "He [Longstreet] saw Round Top, and then knew that further effort at concealment would be a waste of time," while further alleging, "Had he [Longstreet] been at the head of his column he would have seen the folly of further efforts at concealment hours before." In addressing these comments, it must be acknowledged that some of Longstreet's postwar writings on this topic, particularly his first major account in 1877, turned out to be their own worst enemy. As you will remember, Longstreet contended in his "Lee in Pennsylvania" that Federal signalmen spotted his column as it was halted near Black Horse Tavern and "further efforts to conceal ourselves would be a waste of time." Longstreet did not advance this claim in any of his other postwar accounts and we know from the Federal signalmen messages on July 2, along with the post-battle and postwar recollections of Joseph Kershaw and Lafayette McLaws, that Longstreet's allegation in this case was false and misleading. Wilcox seized on Longstreet's own statement that further concealment "would be a waste of time" and charged the First

Corps commander with being deliberately or naturally slow: "This responsibility for prompt movement was all the time on him [Longstreet]." Wilcox then went further and claimed Longstreet should have recognized that concealment efforts were "folly ... hours before." First of all, both Longstreet (in his 1877 account) and Wilcox were mistaken; the column was not seen at Black Horse Tavern. In fact, as proven, it was not seen until the countermarch. Secondly, as argued, the continued attempts at concealment via McLaws' suggested countermarch route unknowingly and unintentionally worked in the Confederates' favor (or at the very least, not to their detriment) by creating the impression they were moving toward the Federal right flank. Lastly, and most importantly, Wilcox puts the onus for concealment on Longstreet as if it were Longstreet's plan and orders for the First Corps column to march to its attack jump-off points via a concealed route. Concealment, as opposed to "prompt movement," was Lee's plan and orders, not Longstreet's, who as a professional soldier was merely attempting to fulfill them to the best of his ability, as events and circumstances allowed.[18]

Moving on from all things concealment, we now arrive at the main purpose of this essay: addressing the prevalent, modern allegation that Longstreet blundered in allowing McLaws to lead the countermarch instead of about-facing the column and letting Hood take the lead. This charge naturally suggests Longstreet's decision caused further needless delay. Despite being such a frequent accusation leveled at Longstreet in recent times, the argument is actually full of logic gaps and suffers greatly from a serious case of armchair generalship, which is not the job of an historian. Perhaps, first and foremost—and before delving into the particulars of this topic—historians and students of the war should seriously consider E.P. Alexander's postwar estimate about the extent to which the countermarch delay affected Confederate chances for success on Longstreet's front: "It hardly seems probable ... that in this instance the delay influenced the result of the battle."[19]

It would be impossible to determine where students of the war are deriving this "about-face" narrative in every instance, but perhaps the most prevalent sources are the ever-popular, one-volume histories of the battle—most notably, in this case, historian Stephen Sears' *Gettysburg* and Glenn Tucker's *High Tide at Gettysburg*. Indeed, in the countermarch section of his narrative, Sears advances the suggestion that "the quickest way to countermarch was simply to about-face the troops, but McLaws had been assigned specifically by General Lee to lead the column into attack position and he felt obliged to hold that place." Of course, the second part of Sears' quote is altogether accurate; however, why the need to suggest "the quickest way to countermarch"?[20] Making such a suggestion and then characterizing it as something simple that Longstreet should have considered and done plants a misleading and counterproductive seed in readers' minds, as opposed to simply discussing what happened and why. In his 1958 study, Glenn Tucker did not suggest Longstreet should have about-faced the column; instead, he mistakenly maintained that was exactly what Longstreet did. "He [Longstreet] ordered an about-face and a return toward the Cashtown road. This meant that Hood, who was in the rear of McLaws, now headed the column, and owing to the readjustment McLaws had to wait an hour before he could move at all."[21]

To begin our own analysis, let us briefly revisit where we are in Longstreet's march. Remember that while McLaws and Longstreet were together near Black Horse Tavern, they confirmed that if the column proceeded further on that route, it would be seen by Federal signalmen on Little Round Top. Therefore, Longstreet asked McLaws for suggestions and the division commander relayed that, based on a personal reconnaissance he had conducted in the morning hours, the only way to continue on a concealed route was by countermarching. Let us stop here for a moment. Longstreet was with McLaws. McLaws suggested, based on his earlier personal reconnaissance, the column needed to countermarch to maintain concealment. Note: McLaws' *personal* reconnaissance. It must be noted and recognized there is no record indicating Hood's presence with Longstreet and McLaws at this time. Further, there is no record of Hood ever making any suggestions as to how to handle the unforeseen situation near Black Horse Tavern. Longstreet consulted McLaws, who suggested they countermarch based on *his* reconnaissance. This begs the question: How would John Bell Hood have led the countermarch when it was McLaws' personal reconnaissance informing the countermarch route? It would not surprise me if armchair generals came up with a few scenarios whereby Hood could have been informed of McLaws' intended route; however, even so, how can we be certain that an about-face with Hood leading would have been executed any more rapidly or smoothly than what actually transpired with McLaws' division retaining the lead?

Point number two in response to this accusation revolves around the clear fact Lee intended for McLaws' division to initiate the attack on July 2, not Hood's division. We know this to be the case because of the content of a mid-morning conversation between Lee and McLaws, McLaws' leading place in the march, and also by what immediately transpired once McLaws reached his attack jump-off point on the afternoon of July 2. Once McLaws' division arrived on the field around 8:30 a.m., Lee immediately sent for the division commander and informed him he wished the division to march concealed to a "commanding" position and "the place I afterwards went to" (the Emmitsburg Road ridge at the Peach Orchard) and place it "across" and "perpendicular to" the Emmitsburg Road. Then, once Longstreet's two divisions eventually got moving toward the extreme Confederate right between noon and 1 p.m., it was McLaws' division that was tapped to take the lead. Additionally, once McLaws arrived on Warfield Ridge near Pitzer's Schoolhouse, it was his division that was immediately asked to initiate the attack toward and then up the Emmitsburg Road. Even though Hood was apparently given the exact same attack instructions in the morning hours—"to place my division across the Emmetsburg [sic] Road, form line of battle, and attack"—it was McLaws' division that was instructed to attack first, not Hood's. Thus, considering it was Lee's plan to have McLaws initiate the attack, it would make sense to have him lead the march, and therefore, also the countermarch and the resumed approach parallel to Willoughby Run.[22]

Furthermore, and perhaps most importantly in addressing this accusation, it is critical to emphasize that advancing hindsight speculation about what Longstreet should have done at this point or that point in the battle is ultimately unhelpful to understanding why Longstreet did what he did in the moment on July 1–3,

1863. Unfortunately this particular accusation—namely, that in countermarching, Longstreet could have saved time by simply about-facing his column and letting Hood lead instead of McLaws—is fraught with armchair general tendencies and completely ignores how Longstreet, McLaws, and most officers during the Civil War (especially West Pointers, like Longstreet and McLaws) were instructed in how to initiate and execute a countermarch. Indeed, the source of their knowledge on how to conduct countermarches did not derive from some spur-of-the-moment, vague notion about about-facing and flip-flopping the leading division; rather it would have originated with a process learned from a drill or tactical manual. During the Civil War, the most popularly used tactical manual was U.S. Army (Lt. Col.) and Confederate Army (Lt. Gen.) officer William Hardee's *Rifle and Light Infantry Tactics for the Exercise and Manoeuvres of Troops When Acting as Light Infantry or Riflemen*, more commonly known simply as *Hardee's Tactics*. Hardee, a tactics instructor at West Point from 1853 to 1856 and then commandant of cadets at the academy until 1860, published this tactical manual in 1855 at the behest of then-secretary of war and later Confederate president Jefferson Davis.[23]

In his manual, Hardee spent three pages on how to initiate and conduct a countermarch. Nowhere in his instructions does it say to about-face and have the trailing division now lead the countermarch. Rather it instructs the officer to order the following commands: "1. Countermarch. 2. Battalion, right and left—Face. 3. By file left and right. 4. March (or double-quick-March)." Hardee expanded on what he meant in the second and third commands, explaining how "the odd divisions will face to the right, and the even to the left; the right and left guides of all the divisions will face about; the chiefs of odd divisions will hasten to their right and cause two files to break to the rear, and each chief place himself on the left of the leading front rank man of his division; the chiefs of even divisions will hasten to their left, and cause two files to break to the rear, and each chief place himself on the right of his leading front rank man."

What can we glean from this lengthy, somewhat complex instruction about how to execute a right and left face, and left and right file? First, we can recognize that the initiation of a countermarch was not a simple "to the rear" marching maneuver, but actually a rather dense and tedious process, with the keyword here being "process." Upon recognizing that a countermarch was a defined tactical process, we can then understand how it was executed, which Hardee outlined in great detail. Essentially, the heads of the column are peeled back to the right and left and drawn off toward the rear unit by unit. Though the corps and division commander would take the lead in initiating the countermarch order, it was the brigade, and especially the regimental commanders, who supervised to ensure the process was properly executed and ran as smoothly as possible. With all of this in mind going forward, we need to reject the presentist tendency to try to impose our own speculative, "should have" suggestions on historical figures like Longstreet, for instance, who in this case not only lacked the benefit of hindsight, but more to the point, would have been relying on contemporaneous knowledge of how to execute a countermarch as outlined in drill manuals like *Hardee's Tactics*.[24]

To finish addressing this topic, we need to, yet again, return to Lafayette McLaws' instructive recollections of the countermarch. McLaws indicated that when the First Corps divisions were beginning to initiate and execute the countermarch, he noticed that Hood, "in his eagerness for the fray, ... had pressed on his division behind mine so that it lapped considerably, creating confusion in the countermarch." According to McLaws, Longstreet also observed this overlapping and disorder and even went so far as to ask the division commander, "General, there is so much confusion, owing to Hood's division being mixed up with yours, suppose you let him countermarch first and lead in the attack." McLaws replied, "General, as I started in the lead, let me continue so," to which Longstreet acquiesced and simply responded, "Then go on."

In analyzing this account, we can discern many important things that run contrary to the typical anti–Longstreet narrative of the countermarch (and Longstreet's Gettysburg performance, more generally). First, we see yet more proof the Confederate High Command intended for McLaws' division to lead the attack, considering McLaws quoted Longstreet as stating that "suppose you let him [Hood] countermarch first and lead in the attack." Since Longstreet considered making adjustments to allow Hood to "lead in the attack" due to the countermarch confusion, naturally that meant McLaws was originally slated to spearhead the assault. Moreover, McLaws does not present a checked-out, half-hearted, lackadaisical Longstreet during these moments on the afternoon of July 2; rather, the account indicates Longstreet was well-aware of the situation, attentive to the state of confusion near the confluence of his two divisions, and willing to apply an unconventional solution to attempt to move things along. Of course, McLaws declined the suggestion and insisted he continue to lead the march and assault (perhaps one could argue it might have been wise for Longstreet to overrule him and insist Hood take the lead), but the key takeaway here is that none of McLaws' recollections here corroborate the persistent anti–Longstreet narrative that the First Corps commander was careless, dragging his feet, sulking, uninspired, or actively trying to frustrate Lee's plans for the day by urging further delay.[25]

Lt. Gen. William Hardee, CSA (Library of Congress).

The exact route of Longstreet's countermarch is not altogether certain, though it is generally accepted that McLaws' division retraced its steps back along Black Horse Tavern Road and Red Oak Lane; again passing the Mark Forney and Adam Butt Farms, this time visible on their left. Though, once arriving at the intersection of Red Oak Lane and Herr's Ridge Road, McLaws did not proceed northeasterly toward his original starting point just south of the junction of Old Mill and Herr Ridge Roads. Instead, he led his division east (along near modern-day Paddock Drive and lower Fairplay Road) toward the Adam Butt Schoolhouse, which was visible on his division's right and located on the north side of the Fairfield Road. In the postwar years, McLaws recalled the countermarch to this point was effected with "considerable difficulty, owing to the rough character of the country in places and the fences and ditches we had to cross." Once reaching the Fairfield Road, McLaws turned his column left up the road until he reached a narrow country lane (modern-day Willoughby Run Road) on his right, referred to by Lee's chief of artillery, William Pendleton, as "the ravine road," which more or less ran parallel to Willoughby Run. It was at the intersection of this ravine road and the Fairfield Road that McLaws' and Hood's divisions reunited. As you will recall, Hood's division countermarched only briefly up Herr Ridge Road before cutting across fields and woods (roughly near modern-day Park Avenue) to arrive at the ravine road/Fairfield Road crossroads.[26]

View of the Fairfield Road entrance to the "ravine road," as it was called by some at the time. McLaws' division completed its countermarch to this intersection, then resumed its march in a southwestern direction along the ravine road toward Pitzer's Schoolhouse and Warfield Ridge beyond. Once McLaws' infantry cleared this intersection, Hood's division followed (Author's Collection).

When the divisions of Hood and McLaws arrived at this crossroads, the countermarch was effectively over and the march resumed along the new route parallel to Willoughby Run, which according to Joseph Kershaw—still at the head of the column—was then almost completely dry. Hood was forced for a time to wait at this intersection until McLaws' four brigades passed onto the ravine road, before following with his own four brigades of Evander Law, Henry Benning, Jerome Robertson, and George T. Anderson.[27] It is at this part of Longstreet's march, from the Fairfield Road to the Millerstown Road, that the historical record becomes a bit bereft of detail. The most descriptive account again originates with Lafayette McLaws, who emphasized how "my troops were moving easily forward along a road with fences on the side not giving room enough for a company front, making it necessary to break files to the rear," certainly implying this road was exceedingly narrow. In his after-battle report, William Pendleton clearly demonstrated, unlike in the postwar years, that he understood the unavoidable and unforeseen delay Longstreet ran into during his march and his acting under Lee's concealed march orders, writing, "He [Longstreet] was advancing by the ravine road (as most out of view), time having already been lost in attempting another, which proved objectionable, because exposed to observation." Pendleton further unveiled he was personally on the scene with "members of my staff," who "were also dispatched to remedy, as far as practicable, the delay." Joseph Kershaw, in his after-battle report and in several postwar accounts, mentioned this portion of the march, but afforded little additional detail. In his report, he noted the column moved "under cover of the woods, to the right of our line of battle," while in his *Battles and Leaders* account, he expressed how it moved "down" Willoughby Run "to the school-house beyond Pitzer's." Similarly, in a letter to postwar Gettysburg historian, John Bachelder, Kershaw held that the column "came to the bed of a stream [Willoughby Run] then nearly dry, moved along it, under cover of woods, to the right until we reached a small house, said to be a school house [Pitzer's Schoolhouse]."[28]

Ironically, Longstreet's own postwar writings mire this portion of the march in some befuddling recollections that have seemingly confounded and led many historians astray for decades. First, there is the rather ambiguous assertion in Longstreet's *Battles and Leaders* account that during the latter stages of the march, he ordered Hood "to move on and double with the division in front"; while likewise, in his memoirs, he contended, "To save time, I ordered the rear division to double on the front." A few sentences later in his memoirs, Longstreet even went on to describe his divisions' advance to their attack jump-off points as "the double line marched up the slope and deployed." That phraseology, "double with the division in front," ordering "the rear division to double on the front," and the reference to a "double line," is puzzling and problematic. It suggests that sometime during the portion of the resumed march from the Fairfield to Millerstown Roads, Longstreet ordered Hood's division to move up from its position in the marching column *behind* McLaws to a position *alongside* McLaws. In other words, it essentially implies both divisions were marching parallel and next to one another for a time. Perhaps this happened; perhaps it did not. There is no substantive, corroborating evidence available to confirm or deny Longstreet's claim.[29]

The "ravine road" along Willoughby Run. Unlike what is shown in this modern photograph, the streambed was described by Brig. Gen. Joseph Kershaw as "nearly dry" on July 2, 1863 (Author's Collection).

Longstreet advanced an even more perplexing assertion in "Lee in Pennsylvania," his first major account of the battle published in 1877. Unlike in his two later accounts that cover the countermarch, where as shown above, Longstreet alleged he doubled Hood's division to the front and to a marching position more or less alongside McLaws, in his earliest article, he claimed to have pushed Hood forward "by the most direct route, so as to take position on my right." Longstreet contended that this move "broke up the delay" the column was apparently experiencing along the marching route from Willoughby Run to the Millerstown Road. Explaining his motive in taking this action, Longstreet alleged that his observations near the elevated point at Black Horse Tavern convinced him that "further efforts to conceal ourselves would be a waste of time" and that he "became very impatient at this delay, and determined to take upon myself the responsibility of hurrying the troops forward." Curiously, Longstreet's remembrance here about advancing Hood "by the most direct route" during the march was very likely not his own, but actually inspired by a June 28, 1875, letter from Hood himself, in which the former First Corps division commander held: "In a short time I was ordered to quicken the march of my troops, and to pass to the front of McLaws. This movement was accomplished by throwing out an advanced force to tear down fences and clear the way."[30]

Despite some historians taking Hood's and Longstreet's claim at face value, there is no corroborating evidence to support the allegation that during the march Hood was pushed along a direct route in "front of McLaws." Perhaps Longstreet initially relied on Hood's 1875 account owing to his own inability to clearly recollect this part of the march and reasoned that the sound of pushing Hood forward by "the most direct route" to break up any further delay would silence any future censure about failing to operate proactively. Indeed, in the postwar years, not only did anti–Longstreet group members predictably criticize Lee's "Old Warhorse" for attempting to continue to march concealed—arguing he should have given up on that intention nearly from the beginning—but even someone as close to Longstreet as First Corps staffer Gilbert Moxley Sorrel alleged the concealed march plan was "abortive," and that the column was "seen from the start and signaled constantly."[31]

Of course, the anti–Longstreet group's and Sorrel's contentions were collectively false and speculative. As underscored earlier, Longstreet's column was not seen by Federal signalmen until sometime during the countermarch; however, truth mattered less than perception during the postwar battle over Longstreet's Gettysburg performance. Longstreet could have emphasized what he did do: that, as a loyal subordinate, he tried to faithfully abide by Lee's concealed march orders; he attempted to alleviate delay and address the lapping and confusion (in suggesting to McLaws that Hood take the lead); and he knew of no evidence the Federals observed his column before or near Black Horse Tavern. Instead, Longstreet pushed the inverse narrative, that: the column was actually seen near the tavern, any further attempt at concealment was a waste of time, and he was doing everything he could to rapidly advance the divisions (even unconcealed). Longstreet may have been proceeding on faulty memory, or simply no memory at all, on this topic (hence his obvious reliance on Hood's letter) and thought this narrative route would prove less damaging to his reputation and more palatable to his postwar critics. Whatever the explanation, it was ultimately a misleading narrative and one that has certainly deceived a number of historians over the decades.

Perhaps the most noticeable examples of when historians fell into this narrative trap was in Edwin B. Coddington's *The Gettysburg Campaign: A Study in Command* (1968), Glenn Tucker's *High Tide at Gettysburg* (1958), Volume 3 of Douglas Southall Freeman's *Lee's Lieutenants* (1944), and Shelby Foote's *The Civil War: A Narrative, Fredericksburg to Meridian* (1963). In Coddington's analysis of Longstreet's actions during the countermarch, he asserted: "Assuming the Federals had detected their movements, Longstreet concluded that further efforts to conceal them were a waste of time. Therefore he took over control of Hood's division, pushed it ahead of McLaws, and led it forward by the most direct route."[32] Likewise, Tucker wrote, "In the fields the two divisions doubled and moved abreast each other and at length Hood passed across the front of McLaws."[33] Upon introducing Longstreet's decision to countermarch, Freeman contended, "This was done, though it put Hood's division in advance."[34] Similarly, novelist Shelby Foote claimed in his popular three-volume narrative of the Civil War, "Some time was saved by giving the lead to Hood, who had followed McLaws till then."[35] In advancing this assertion, Coddington relied entirely on the misleading commentary in Hood's 1875 letter and Longstreet's similar claim in his 1877 article, while Freeman relied solely on Longstreet's article.

Tucker never explicitly identified his source[36] and Foote's book, though widely read and influential, contains no endnotes or footnotes. Despite Coddington's, Tucker's, Freeman's, and Foote's presentation of these allegations as established fact, there is no evidence to corroborate that during the march Longstreet advanced Hood "by the most direct route" and "ahead of McLaws." Of course, Hood *was eventually* pushed ahead of McLaws, but it most certainly did not occur during the march.

Unfortunately, over the decades, historians have used false story lines like this one to advance the usual narratives about Longstreet; that he was acting up, sulking, careless, unstable, or still smarting over his tactical disagreement with Lee. Coddington went on to conclude Longstreet's collective actions throughout the march "revealed a dark moment in Longstreet's career as a general." Likewise, even Harry Pfanz, a former chief historian for Gettysburg National Military Park (GNMP) and someone who was typically much more balanced in his handling of Longstreet's Gettysburg performance, stated after covering the First Corps march on July 2, "Longstreet's angry dissidence had resulted in further wasted time and delay." So, between Coddington and Pfanz, here we see Longstreet depicted as having a "dark moment" and consumed with "angry dissidence." Where is the evidence for these broad, but consequential allegations that have successfully tainted many perceptions of Longstreet's Gettysburg performance over the last century? Refraining from armchair generalship, hindsight, and speculation, while keeping in mind all the surrounding events and circumstances facing the Confederates during those moments on the afternoon of July 2, how exactly did Longstreet's actions and decisions during the march and countermarch result in "further wasted time and delay"?[37]

Realistically, Hood's recollection about being "ordered to quicken the march of my troops, and to pass to the front of McLaws" almost certainly refers to his move to the right of McLaws, once the Confederate High Command caught on to the need to alter the attack plan and extend their battle line farther to the right. In other words, in writing "to pass to the front of McLaws," Hood was more precisely referring to his passage to the right. This reasoning makes sense given the divisions' order of march up to that point, with McLaws leading the column and Hood trailing. Therefore, common sense dictates in passing to McLaws' right, Hood was naturally taking the lead and moving to McLaws' front; as a matter of fact, it also meant Hood would now initiate the attack, not McLaws, as had been the plan since at least the mid-morning hours. Furthermore, Hood's comment about "throwing out an advanced force to tear down fences and clear the way" did not refer to leveling fences along the marching route from Willoughby Run to the Millerstown Road; rather, it referred to the myriad fencing his division encountered when advancing from behind McLaws to the extreme right, across the Biesecker and Douglas Farms (both now part of the Eisenhower Farm).[38]

Just after introducing this order to move in front of McLaws in his letter, Hood then also followed up with some consequential contextual details: "The instructions I received were to place my division across the Emmetsburg [sic] road, form line of battle, and attack. Before reaching this road, however, I had sent forward some of my picked Texas scouts to ascertain the position of the enemy's extreme left flank. They soon reported to me that it rested upon Round Top Mountain." Hood's follow-on details here confirm he received his order "to pass to the front of McLaws" *after* the First Corps column had already reached Pitzer's Schoolhouse and Warfield Ridge, not earlier during the march. All of the events Hood described—moving toward the Emmitsburg Road, sending forward scouts to ascertain if there was an opportunity to attack around the Round Tops—occurred later, after his division arrived in the rear of McLaws' division and Warfield Ridge, after Lee and Longstreet decided to move him farther to McLaws' right, and therefore, certainly after the conclusion of the march. Similarly concluding on this topic, GNMP Historian Harry Pfanz astutely asserted, "It seems unlikely that Hood's division was rushed ahead before McLaws' division had reached its position and the location of Hood's left flank was thus defined."[39]

Many battle participants' accounts corroborate this conclusion. Conversely, no post-battle or postwar accounts mention anything about Hood's division moving by some unconcealed "most direct route" during the march to break up further delay. Brigadier General Evander Law only mentioned that "Hood's division was pushed forward until it uncovered McLaws, and soon reached the Emmitsburg road in front of Round Top. Here our line of battle was formed." Colonel William C. Oates, commanding the 15th Alabama regiment, Law's brigade, noted that the only significant movement he remembered was the shift from behind McLaws' division to its right. "We [Hood's division] turned to the right & passing through some open fields until we reached a position upon a ridge south of the mountain—Round Top I suppose—where we went into line," Oates informed historian John Bachelder, while tersely contending in another postwar account, "Finally, Hood marched across the rear of McLaws and went into line on the crest of a little ridge." Similarly, Joseph Kershaw of McLaws' division remembered "Hood's division was moving in our rear to the right, to gain the enemy's left flank." In his own postwar letter to John Bachelder, Kershaw recalled, "Hood's division passed altogether to the right," while never once describing anything about Hood taking some direct, exposed route during the march. Likewise, Lafayette McLaws only underscored Hood's movement in his division's rear and toward their right: "The head of his column was turned by General Longstreet's order to go on my right." Indeed, Longstreet himself in his after-battle report only drew attention to the decision to move Hood's division "on farther to our right."[40]

In his coverage of the end of the First Corps' march, academic historian Edwin B. Coddington again advanced his belief that Hood was then marching ahead of McLaws and never stopped in the rear of McLaws' division. "At Pitzer's Schoolhouse it [McLaws' division] turned to the left on the crossroad to the Peach Orchard, while Hood's division up ahead continued south toward the Emmitsburg Road," Coddington concluded. Virginia-born historian Clifford Dowdey made a similar claim in his *Lee & His Men at Gettysburg* (1958): "While McLaws was making his personal reconnaissance and trying to hurry his troops forward, Hood's men passed southward beyond his division, going into position to open the assault on his right." Dowdey's book contains no footnotes or endnotes, but it is clear Coddington drew on a portion of Lafayette McLaws' July 7, 1863, letter to his wife, in which the division commander described how he "was directed not to assault until General Hood was in position. Gen H [Hood] had gone around above me to the right." In using this source to allege that once the Confederates reached Pitzer's Schoolhouse, Hood's division was marching ahead of McLaws and immediately advanced toward the extreme right, Coddington was undoubtedly depending on McLaws' tangled verbiage that Hood "had gone around above me to the right." Like the positional phrase "to the front of," we now see the use of "around above," both of which actually refer to the real keyword, "right." McLaws was not saying Hood was leading the column at the end of the march, as in farther east of him; rather, he was pointing out that Hood had been directed farther to the right or south of him. In moving to the extreme right of the Confederate battle line, Hood would then, as McLaws described, be positioned "above me to the right." Furthermore, and perhaps even more importantly, the cited content in McLaws' letter is not a relevant source to use when discussing McLaws' and Hood's actions once the former was "at Pitzer's Schoolhouse." The passage in McLaws' letter describes events that occurred not at the end of the march, but actually well after he reached Pitzer's Schoolhouse. In fact, McLaws was not told to delay his attack and wait for Hood to get into position until *after* he passed Pitzer's Schoolhouse, *after* he formed his brigades in Pitzer's and Biesecker's Woods, and *after* he was directed multiple times to attack—all while Hood was either located in McLaws' rear or still in the process of moving and forming to the extreme right. In short, we cannot use evidence describing an advanced point in First Corps attack preparations to attempt to prove a misleading narrative about an earlier point at the end of the First Corps march.[41]

Hood's initial post-march position behind McLaws' division and his subsequent move to McLaws' right almost brings us back full circle to Longstreet's curious statements about ordering "the rear division to double on the front" to "save time." The multiple recollections recounted above confirm Hood's division initially formed in the rear of McLaws' division ("double on the front") upon finishing the march. These recollections, coupled with the fact Lee and Longstreet almost immediately ordered McLaws' division to initiate the attack, verifies that the First Corps commander made the rather remarkable real-time decision toward the end of the march to modify the divisions' deployment to an attacking column in depth with McLaws in front and Hood in support, as opposed to an adjacent deployment with McLaws on the left and Hood to the right.[42] Indeed, Longstreet's actions and dialogue with McLaws in the lead-up to those near-immediate attack orders show a commander not looking for opportunities to further delay the assault with an extended deployment, but one who was keen on getting it started. Even before the march ended, Longstreet was already asking McLaws how he intended to attack. When McLaws expressed some hesitancy and signaled he would make that determination upon seeing what was in his front, Longstreet dismissed his caution and stressed the need for rapid action: "There is nothing in your front; you will be entirely on the flank of the enemy." It is clear McLaws then recognized Longstreet was looking for prompt action, informing his chief that he would "then … continue my march in columns of companies, and after arriving on the flank as far as is necessary will face to the left and march on the enemy." In replying to McLaws' proposed plan with a curt "that suits me," it appears Longstreet was convinced he had made his intentions for swift movement sufficiently clear. For skeptics of postwar accounts, McLaws confirmed the spirit of these details in his post-battle letter to his wife, written less than a week after the battle: "General Longstreet sent word that he was satisfied there was but a small force of the enemy in front and that I must proceed at once to the assault. On examination it was discovered that the enemy were in much greater force than was expected, and the assault was delayed.... I was directed not to assault until General Hood was in position." Furthermore, in his after-battle report written in October 1863, Joseph Kershaw—at the head of McLaws' division throughout the march—recounted having a similar conversation with Longstreet about attack instructions as early as when the column reached Pitzer's Schoolhouse.[43]

In sum, it appears Longstreet's *initial,* modified strategy—formulated toward the end of the march and before he and Lee recognized the Federals were not where they expected them to be, forcing them to push Hood farther to the right—was to limit deployment time ("save time"), get the attack going as soon as possible, and resultantly, gain and attack up the Emmitsburg Road toward the presumed location of the Federal left with two-division depth, not a two-division-wide front. Most telling was that Lee and Longstreet ordered McLaws to attack while Hood was still in his rear. It was only after the Confederate High Command fully caught onto the unforeseen situation in its front along the Emmitsburg Road, and beyond, that it pushed Hood to the extreme right, or as McLaws recollected, "The firing on my command showed to Hood in my rear that the enemy was in force in my front and right, and the head of his column was turned by General Longstreet's order to go on my right." Likewise, William Pendleton wrote in his official report of this moment, "Colonel [E.P.] Alexander, by General Longstreet's direction, proceeded to explore the ground still farther to the right, and Henry's battalion, accompanying Hood's division, was thrown in that direction. Upon these, as soon as observed, the enemy opened a furious cannonade." In fact, we know that after balking at several of Lee and Longstreet's repeated orders to commence the attack, McLaws finally relented and signaled he would advance (within "five minutes" time) before receiving a last-minute communication to pause and wait until Hood fully got into position on his right. "But while collecting my staff to send the orders for a simultaneous move of the whole line, a courier dashed up with orders for me to wait until Hood got into position," McLaws recollected. The attack plan had again been altered, this time to an adjacent two-division-wide deployment with Hood on the extreme right (who would now open the assault) and McLaws on the left connecting with Richard Anderson's Third Corps division still farther to the left and near the Confederate center.[44]

So, what has this in-depth analysis of Longstreet's countermarch on the afternoon of July 2 yielded? Perhaps, first and foremost, it has again exposed the overarching narrative that has pervaded nearly all coverage of Longstreet's Gettysburg performance since the postwar years: a slow, sulking Longstreet, needlessly delaying operations.

The reality of what happened in the lead up to, during, and just after Longstreet's march and countermarch was a little more nuanced and a lot less dramatic, less full of stories about personal vendettas and sabotage and more on how events and circumstances clearly affected Confederate decisions and movements during these hours.

First of all, any discussion and understanding of Longstreet's countermarch must start with a concentrated emphasis on Lee's concealed march order. Many analyses of Longstreet's actions on July 2, particularly when questioning what inhibited Longstreet from beginning his march earlier, end with the arrival of Law's brigade around noon; however, Law's arrival was not the only thing Longstreet (and Lee) were awaiting. Additional reconnaissance activities were ongoing around that time to locate a concealed route for Longstreet's divisions to the extreme Confederate right. These reconnaissance, as we have seen from the accounts of McLaws and Kershaw, were not completed until as late as 1:00 p.m. Therefore, with this in mind, we see how Lee's concealed march order actually proved instrumental in further delaying the start of Longstreet's march into the early afternoon hours of July 2. Additionally, the implications of the concealed march order reared their head once again when Longstreet's column reached the elevated point of contention near Black Horse Tavern. Indeed, it is not an exaggeration to say Lee's concealment order essentially forced the countermarch. In sum, Hood's and McLaws' protracted, relative idleness into the early afternoon hours because of ongoing reconnaissance activities to identify a concealed route, coupled with Longstreet's decision to countermarch near Black Horse Tavern, fully exemplified that concealment, not speed, was the Confederates' primary mode of the day.

What actually happened near Black Horse Tavern, particularly as it relates to Longstreet's actions and decisions there, is another topic that has been muddled over the decades. First, as seen principally through McLaws' recollections of his dialogue with Longstreet near the elevated point, along with Joseph Kershaw's postwar testimony, we see that Longstreet made the decision to countermarch rather rapidly, perhaps within five minutes' time, as Kershaw suggested. There is no evidence Longstreet vacillated at Black Horse Tavern or fulfilled the dominant historiographic caricature that he was looking for any and every opportunity to delay the attack. Furthermore, there is also no reliable evidence that Longstreet carelessly allowed his marching column to pass over the elevated point, exposing his men to signalmen on Little Round Top. The primary source record, particularly when it comes to what Federal signalmen actually reported, does not lend credence to this pervasive assertion. To the contrary, Longstreet's column went unseen by the Federals until sometime during the countermarch. With the signalmen on Little Round Top reporting a heavy column of infantry proceeding toward the Federal right, the countermarch actually served to unknowingly and unintentionally throw the Federals off as to the ultimate destination of the Confederate column.

Along with mistaken assertions, a severe case of armchair generalship has often plagued the portrayal of Longstreet's countermarch. A number of Gettysburg historians and pundits have sometimes descended into making suggestions about what Longstreet should have or could have done when executing the countermarch, insinuating that if only their advice had been heeded, the countermarch would have been easier, less confusing, and quicker. Of course, I am referring to the regularly made assertion that Longstreet should have about-faced his column and let Hood lead the countermarch and initiate the attack. This argument ignores several things. The first is that officers like Longstreet and McLaws would have been aware of and trained in a specific way to conduct countermarches as defined by the tactical training manuals of the time, like *Hardee's Tactics*. Furthermore, the column would be countermarching along McLaws' *personal* route, while the intention, at least since the mid-morning hours, had been for McLaws to lead the assault. Additionally, Longstreet had mere minutes to make a decision and then begin executing the countermarch. This was no time to improvise. McLaws' execution of the countermarch, with the heads of the column peeling back to the right and left, was the defined, by-the-book way of conducting that maneuver. That said, those who have alleged Longstreet should have about-faced the column need not be completely discouraged; for once McLaws began executing the countermarch and Longstreet noticed some overlapping and confusion occurring, he made that very suggestion to McLaws, who insisted he retain the lead of the column and lead the attack. Longstreet ultimately acquiesced to McLaws' request; however, the important point to stress here is that Longstreet did in fact make the recommendation, signifying he was not oblivious to or satisfied with the countermarch's knotty progress and actually sought potential ways to remediate the situation.

Furthermore, analysis of the countermarch reveals that a number of historians have been led astray by some misleading postwar accounts from John Bell Hood and James Longstreet himself. Hood's June 1875 letter to Longstreet and the former First Corps commander's first major article on the battle in 1877 suggest Longstreet gave up on concealment sometime during the resumed march along the banks of Willoughby Run and pushed Hood forward by a more direct, overt route to the front of McLaws. Piecing together the post-battle and postwar testimony of several other officers who were present during the march and countermarch suggests Hood's and Longstreet's postwar recollections, in those specific cases, were either disingenuous or misremembered. There is no reliable evidence to suggest Hood had advanced unconcealed or pushed in front of McLaws' division during the latter stages of the march; rather, in accounts ranging from Evander Law, William Oates, Joseph Kershaw, Lafayette McLaws, to others, it is apparent that the First Corps retained its order of march throughout, with McLaws in the lead and Hood trailing.

Finally, a close analysis of Longstreet's countermarch and resumed march (along Willoughby Run to Black Horse Tavern Road to Millerstown Road) also reveals some potential clarifying details about what Longstreet appears to have had in mind for an initial, modified attack plan as the First Corps column passed Pitzer's Schoolhouse and approached Warfield Ridge. The multiple accounts of Kershaw, Longstreet, and McLaws especially afford details suggesting that during the final approach Longstreet considered severely limiting deployment time and sought to attack as soon as possible upon reaching Warfield Ridge through an assault in depth up the Emmitsburg Road—McLaws in front, with Hood in some sort of supporting role from behind. Indeed, it is clear the decision to move Hood to the right alongside McLaws was not made until Lee and Longstreet fully recognized the Federals were out in force along the Emmitsburg Road, with their line extending farther to the Confederate right than had been anticipated. In the meantime, and before Hood was moved to the right, Lee and Longstreet had revealingly and forcefully issued repeated orders to McLaws to commence the assault. It is clear that when Lee and Longstreet repeatedly issued these attack orders, Hood was not then positioned on McLaws' right, and obviously—considering Lee and Longstreet were at that very moment ordering McLaws to attack—had not yet been informed that his division would now open the assault.

Essay 5

Under Hill or Longstreet?

Anderson's Division on July 2

General Hill was ordered to threaten the enemy's center, to prevent re-enforcements being drawn to either wing, and co-operate with his right division in Longstreet's attack.—Robert E. Lee

One of the more persistent myths about Longstreet's Gettysburg performance that has increasingly taken root in recent years is the argument that Major General Richard H. Anderson's Third Corps division was put under Longstreet's command during the July 2 attack. Some seasoned historians of the battle may be rolling their eyes right now, perhaps thinking there is absolutely no way this argument is making the rounds, but alas it is. Indeed, on multiple occasions at different speaking events I have been asked, "Wasn't Anderson under Longstreet on July 2?" or the similar, but more forcefully leading, "Wasn't Anderson Longstreet's responsibility on July 2?" The reason I say the latter question is leading is because it is obviously couched in the belief that since Anderson was under Longstreet on July 2, it was ultimately Longstreet's fault—not Anderson's, Third Corps Commander Ambrose Powell (A.P.) Hill's, or Lee's—that only three of Anderson's five brigades fully engaged and continued the attack north of John Bell Hood's and Lafayette McLaws' divisions on July 2.

Due to the frequency with which I have run into these questions about Anderson's division on July 2 and whose command he was under, A.P. Hill's or Longstreet's, I think it is important this topic be fully explored, analyzed, and addressed. Put simply, students of the battle must be getting this argument from somewhere—a book, a battlefield tour, a message board, a roundtable speech, or a social media discussion group. While I may not be able to pinpoint where exactly this assertion has been made, I can mine the primary and secondary source record to ascertain where this argument likely originated, how it has been perpetuated, and weigh its overall merits.

What may surprise some historians is that students of the battle are actually justified in having questions about who commanded Anderson's division during the Confederates' main July 2 attack. Indeed, as we will see, some select, popular, and at times surprising secondary sources from the postwar years to modern times have likely sown palpable confusion about the identity of Anderson's direct superior on July 2.

Before we get into exploring who originated and perpetuated the myth of Anderson under Longstreet on July 2 and ascertaining the truth using primary source evidence, it is necessary we establish a baseline of who Major General Richard H. Anderson was and his record leading up the Battle of Gettysburg. This baseline is especially important when it comes to Anderson and Gettysburg since it is that pre-Gettysburg record itself that has so often led to and ultimately justified much of the confusion surrounding his command on July 2.

One need not delve too deeply into research to find that "Fightin' Dick" Anderson actually had quite a lot in common with Longstreet. They were both born in South Carolina; Anderson in central Sumter County and Longstreet in western Edgefield County. They were both born in 1821, Anderson on October 7 and Longstreet on January 8. With their birthdays in such close proximity, then it was not at all surprising they both attended the United States Military Academy at West Point from 1838 to 1842. Perhaps a little more unexpected was that both men were academically average to poor students at West Point; Anderson graduating 40th in a class of 56 cadets and Longstreet 2nd from the bottom at 54th. During the Mexican War (1846-1848), both Anderson and Longstreet fought in many of the major battles, like Contreras (August 19, 1847), Molino del Rey (September 8, 1847), and the fight for and capture of Mexico City (September 12-14, 1847).

During the Civil War, a near-foolproof rule emerged when it came to Longstreet and Anderson, namely, wherever Longstreet was located, Anderson was undoubtedly nearby. Longstreet first saw action during the Civil War as a brigadier general of three Virginia infantry regiments at the Battle of Blackburn's Ford (July 18, 1861), a precursor to the Battle of First Manassas/Bull Run (July 21). Anderson did not participate in either of those battles and would not join what was then the Confederate army of the Potomac until February 1862. Commissioned a brigadier general, Anderson would serve under Longstreet, who had been promoted to major general in October 1861. Praising Anderson's actions at the Battle of Williamsburg on May 5, 1862, Longstreet wrote that the "disposition of his forces and manner of leading them into action displayed great ability and signal gallantry and coolness." Both men were at the Battle of Fair Oaks/Seven

Maj. Gen. Richard H. Anderson, CSA (Wikimedia Commons).

Pines (May 31–June 1); Anderson temporarily assuming command of a division and earning his aforementioned nickname, "Fightin' Dick," while Longstreet essentially served as a wing commander and got his first taste of what verbally issued orders can do to the execution of a planned attack, ultimately delivering a rather underwhelming performance.

Following Joseph Johnston's wounding at Seven Pines, Robert E. Lee's ascent to the command of what was renamed the Army of Northern Virginia, and the conclusion of Lee's opening salvo as commander during the Seven Days Battles (June 25–July 1, 1862), Anderson was promoted to major general on July 14 and assumed command of what had been Benjamin Huger's division. After the Seven Days Battles, Lee reorganized the army into two wings, one under Longstreet and another under Thomas "Stonewall" Jackson, with Anderson falling under the former's wing. Therefore, Anderson served in Longstreet's command: at the Battle of Second Manassas in late August; at the September 17 Battle of Antietam/Sharpsburg near the Henry Piper Farm-Sunken Road (or "Bloody Lane") sector of the field, where he was wounded in the thigh; and in a rather limited role at the Battle of Fredericksburg in December.

During the spring 1863 campaign, Anderson would continue to fight under Longstreet's wing of the army, but the two generals would fight in separate theaters as Longstreet besieged Suffolk, Virginia, and gathered vital foodstuffs for the army in April–May 1863. Anderson's and McLaws' divisions of Longstreet's wing stayed behind and fought at the Battle of Chancellorsville (April 30–May 6), with Anderson attacking the Federal left on May 2 (while Jackson attacked the right) and both divisions siphoned off on May 3 to defend the army's rear against John Sedgwick's Federal Sixth Corps. In the meantime, Longstreet was in far southeastern Virginia with John Bell Hood's and George Pickett's divisions of 15,000 men. Anderson's solid performance in the battles leading up to the Gettysburg Campaign resulted in Lee seriously considering the South Carolinian for corps command when the army was reorganized into three corps post–Chancellorsville and upon Jackson's untimely death on May 10; however, Lee ultimately chose the Virginians Richard S. Ewell and A.P. Hill for command of the Second and Third Corps, respectively. Even so, Lee then deemed Anderson, along with John Bell Hood, "capital officers," with both men "improving ... and will make good corps commanders, if necessary."

This short summary of Anderson's military career up to the Battle of Gettysburg serves to highlight the great extent to which the division commander fought under Longstreet from 1862 to mid–1863. This stable trend would change during the Gettysburg Campaign. Once Hill was given command of the Third Corps, Lee was forced to pull units from both Jackson's (now Ewell's Second Corps) and Longstreet's command to fill out that newly formed fighting force; Anderson's division was one of them. As we will see, a number of historians have used this close association between Anderson and Longstreet in the leadup to Gettysburg to argue that Anderson was only comfortable fighting under Longstreet and his placement under Hill led to much of the confusion and misunderstanding on July 2.[1]

So, what happened on July 2 with Anderson's division? We will not go into great detail on this topic, since (1) this essay is only meant to establish who Anderson's

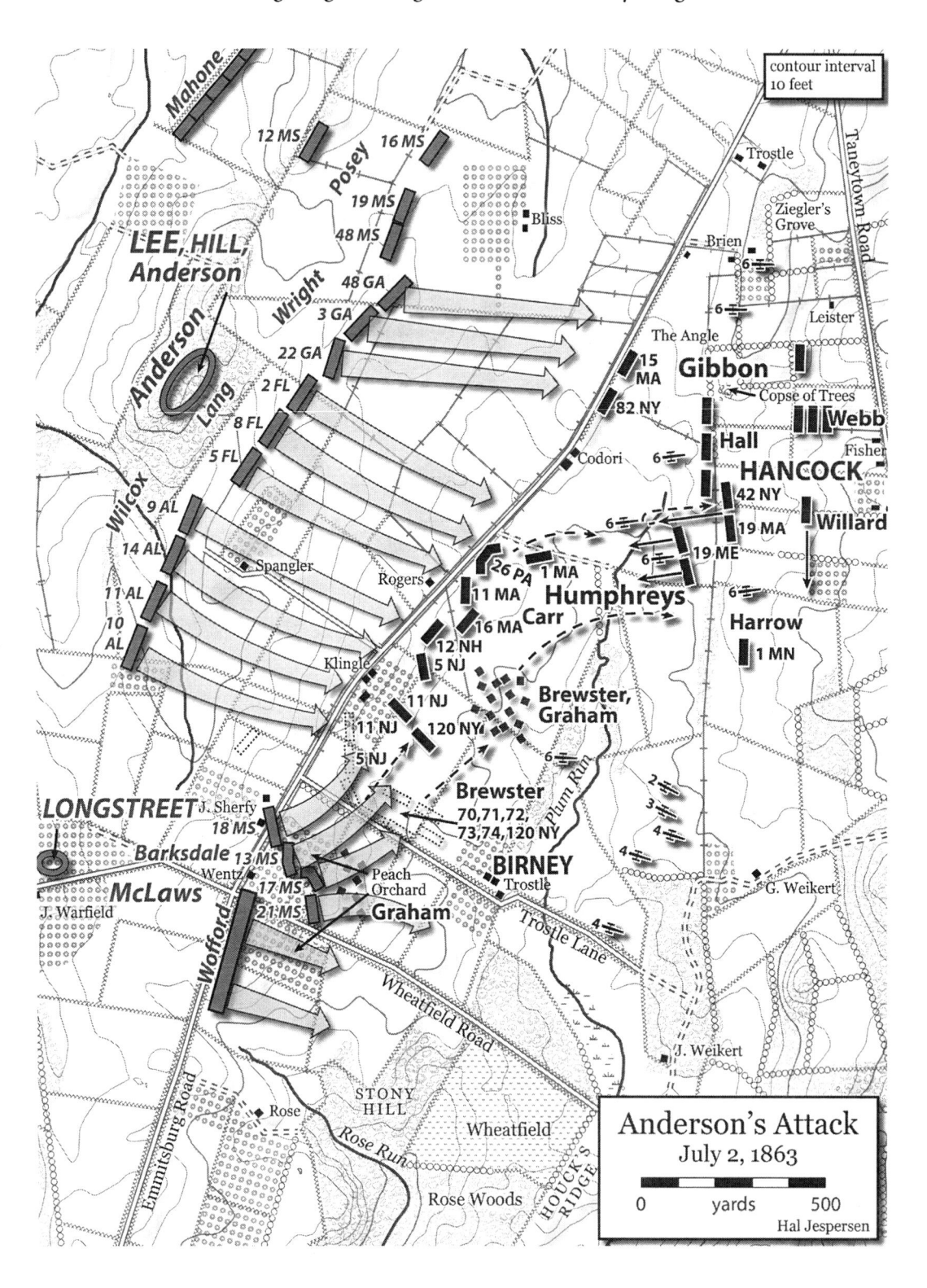

Anderson's Attack, July 2, 1863.

direct superior was on July 2, Hill or Longstreet, and (2) I, and many others, have already fully covered what happened on Anderson's front during Longstreet's July 2 attack in other published articles and books.[2] That said, a brief summary is in order.

The Confederate High Command's intention to include Anderson's division as part of the army's attack plan developed quite early on July 2. Anderson's five brigades of Cadmus Wilcox, Edward Perry (under David Lang),[3] Ambrose Ransom "Rans" Wright, Carnot Posey, and William Mahone collectively made up A.P. Hill's only fresh division following the heavy fighting on July 1, where Harry Heth's and William Dorsey Pender's divisions took leading roles in pushing the Federal First Corps off the ridges west of town. Therefore, during the morning hours of July 2, when Lee was mulling over initiating an attack on his extreme right with Longstreet's corps, Lee's "Old Warhorse" expressed concern he did not have Pickett's division on hand, which had hitherto been guarding the army's wagon trains in Chambersburg. Responding to this concern, Lee assured Longstreet that Anderson's division would make up the difference, supporting Longstreet's two available divisions of Hood and McLaws and continuing any attack made against the Federal left just to the north of them and on their left.[4]

Once Lee settled on making his main attack with Longstreet's corps around the 10 a.m. hour, Anderson's division was soon set in motion to take position to the right of Pender's division, extending the Confederate battle line along Seminary Ridge from near the David McMillan house as far south as the northern edge of Pitzer's Woods. Anderson completed his move to Pender's right and began situating his brigades on what was then the army's extreme right flank around noon, expecting to see Longstreet's men take position on his right momentarily.[5]

For reasons discussed in depth elsewhere, Longstreet's two divisions did not arrive at their attack jump-off points just east of Pitzer's Schoolhouse until the 3 p.m. hour, and after being forced to make further adjustments to their attack plan because of events and circumstances, did not launch their assault until around 4:30 p.m.[6] In any case, once Longstreet's attack got online and the eight brigades of Hood's and McLaws' division were all sent in and engaged, it was Anderson's turn to support Longstreet's left and continue the attack farther north against Cemetery Ridge. As planned, Wilcox's Alabama brigade and Lang's Florida brigade continued the attack to the left of William Barksdale's brigade against Andrew Humphrey's Federal Third Corps division along the Emmitsburg Road. Pushing this Federal division back toward Cemetery Ridge, Wilcox and Lang were soon joined, as intended, by Ambrose Wright's Georgia brigade on Lang's left. Between approximately 6:45 and 7:30 p.m., Wright's three regiments of the 48th, 3rd, and 22nd Georgia—deployed left to right respectively, with support from the 2nd Georgia Battalion—attacked just to the left of the Codori Farm, pushing two regiments of Federal infantry and a battery of artillery rearward from the Emmitsburg Road to Cemetery Ridge. Proceeding farther east toward the Federals' main line, Wright's 22nd Georgia and a portion of the 3rd Georgia secured a brief foothold on the ridge just to the south of the Copse of Trees, before being overpowered by Norman J. Hall's and Alexander Webb's Federal Second Corps brigades (John Gibbon's division), five companies of the 13th Vermont (George Stannard's brigade,

A portion of Brig. Gen. Ambrose Wright's brigade achieved a brief foothold on Cemetery Ridge near this location on July 2. The view here is looking northward up Cemetery Ridge toward the famous Angle and Copse of Trees (Author's Collection).

Abner Doubleday's First Corps division), and stout fire from multiple artillery batteries.

Another key reason Wright's stay on Cemetery Ridge proved so brief was because the supporting brigade to his left, commanded by Carnot Posey, advanced about 100 to 150 yards to the east of the Bliss Farm with only two of his regiments, the 48th and 19th Mississippi. The 16th Mississippi remained near the Bliss Farm and Posey's fourth regiment, the 12th Mississippi, never even made it that far east. Even more puzzling were the actions, or rather the inaction, of the Virginia infantry brigade to Posey's left under William Mahone, which failed to budge at all from its original position on Seminary Ridge throughout the course of the attack.[7] In the end, only three of Anderson's five total brigades managed to participate in any meaningful way during the Confederates' main July 2 attack.[8] Across Hill's entire corps of three divisions—Anderson, Heth, and Pender—13 brigades in total, only 3 attacked on July 2. Also noteworthy is the fact that Ambrose Wright stressed just days after the battle how the plan for Hill's corps on July 2 not only included Anderson's division, but Pender's and Heth's as well. "Anderson's division, being next to Longstreet's left, was to commence the pursuit, which was to be followed up immediately by Pender's and Heth's divisions," Wright claimed.[9]

What happened? Did some sort of confusion on Anderson's part about whether he was under Hill or Longstreet lead to the mismanagement of his division's assault on July 2? Was Longstreet really supposed to be overseeing Anderson's attack, as well? Before we move into this analysis in earnest, it is worth mentioning two additional, key anecdotes from Anderson's front to keep in mind as serious food for thought. First, British observer and army officer Arthur J. L. Fremantle's recollections of the second day confirm Lee was physically located with A.P. Hill throughout the July 2 attack, which would have placed both the commanding general and the

Essay 5. Under Hill or Longstreet?

Third Corps commander on Anderson's front during that division's attack, and secondly, Fremantle emphasized that Lee "only sent one message, and only received one report" during the attack, with that one report likely being a note from Longstreet "soon after 7 [p.m.]" (and just when Wright was making his promising attack), when the First Corps commander reported that "we are doing well." So, in sum, here we have Anderson, Hill, and Lee (division, corps, and army commands) all physically located on Anderson's front during his attack; Lee receiving an encouraging note from Longstreet around the time Wright attacked; and yet, instead of Anderson's entire division being sent forward, we have the two brigades of Posey and Mahone, over 2,800 men, not advancing to support the attack, as intended.[10]

For those who still doubt historians and students of the war could ever seriously come to believe Anderson was actually temporarily placed under Longstreet's command during his July 2 assault, this section of the essay should prove interesting. Indeed, it is actually not an exaggeration at all to say that four published works likely sitting on most Gettysburg scholars' and enthusiasts' bookshelves right now have, to lesser and greater degrees, advanced and perpetuated the Anderson under Longstreet assertion.

The first culprit, and perhaps the original source, that made this contention is rather surprising. None other than James Longstreet himself advanced this claim in his widely read memoirs, *From Manassas to Appomattox*. As I established in *Longstreet at Gettysburg* and in other essays in this collection, Longstreet's Gettysburg writings were mostly accurate and consistent, however, as was the case with all postwar writings on the Civil War, not without error. Like some discrepancies in Longstreet's writings about the First Corps march, countermarch, and resumed march on July 2, there are similar variations across the general's postwar accounts regarding the role and status of Anderson's division on the second day. In his memoirs, the first detail Longstreet appears to go back and forth on is how many brigades in

Brig. Gen. Ambrose R. Wright, CSA (Library of Congress).

Anderson's division were ordered to support his attack. Longstreet first emphasizes, "The battle was to be opened on the right by two divisions of the First Corps, supported on their left by four brigades of Anderson's division." Four pages later, Longstreet likewise notes, "Four brigades of Anderson's division were ordered to advance in echelon [sic] in support of my left." So, between these two sentences, we see Longstreet maintaining that four brigades of Anderson's division were ordered to support his attack. Of course, Anderson's division, as already established, consisted of five brigades. Did Longstreet momentarily forget this detail? The evidence does not suggest that was the case, considering that between those two sentences Longstreet spelled out that "Anderson's division deployed—Wilcox's, Perry's, Wright's, Posey's, and Mahone's brigades from right to left." Longstreet was clearly aware Anderson had five brigades in his command. Yet, we now turn to the smoking gun of sorts, where not only did Longstreet again set the number of supporting brigades from Anderson's division at four, not five, but proceeded to contend that those "four brigades of the right of the Third Corps *were assigned as part of my command* [emphasis added]."[11]

What are we to make of this statement from Longstreet in 1896 that suggests four brigades from Anderson's division "were assigned as part of my command"? Is this statement corroborated by any of Longstreet's other postwar accounts or his official report? It would not appear so. Some of the confusion over how many brigades were to support his two divisions persisted; however, Longstreet never made any similar statement to the one in his memoirs about Anderson's division being "assigned as part of my command." In his earliest postwar recounting of his actions at Gettysburg in November 1877, Longstreet maintained: "I realized that the fight was to be a fearful one; but being assured that my flank would be protected by the brigades of Wilcox, Perry, Wright, Posey, and Mahone, moving en echelon." Note Longstreet's listing of all five of Anderson's brigades. Lee's "Old Warhorse" also noted: "Touching [on] the failure of the supporting brigades of Anderson's division to cover McLaws' flank by echelon movements, as directed, there is little to be said. Those brigades acted gallantly, but went astray early in the fight." It is unknown what Longstreet meant by Anderson's brigades going "astray early in the fight," considering they were some of the last units to attack on that front on July 2, but of greater significance here is the fact Longstreet took no ownership whatsoever of any of Anderson's brigades and certainly made no allusion to their being part of his command. Similarly, in Longstreet's *Battles and Leaders* account of the late 1880s, he returned to the fickle contention that Hood's and McLaws' divisions would attempt to attack up the Emmitsburg Road, "with *a part* [emphasis added] of R.H. Anderson's division following the movements of McLaws to guard his left flank." Like his earlier account from 1877, Longstreet also made no mention of having any control over Anderson's division and instead clearly linked that command with the Third Corps commander: "Hill made no move whatever, save of the brigades of his right division that were covering our left."[12]

What of Longstreet's official report, written just a few weeks after the battle? Was the general's statement in his memoirs reflected anywhere in that primary source account? No. Longstreet merely explained how on July 2 the Federals were "driven from point to point, however, until nearly night, when a strong force met the brigades of Major-General [R.H.] Anderson's division, which were co-operating upon my left, drove one of them back, and, checking the support of the other, caused my left to be somewhat exposed and outflanked." Here in 1863, we see Longstreet rather loosely describing how Anderson was "co-operating" on the left of McLaws, with the intention of assisting in the protection of his attack's left flank. Longstreet did not explicitly mention anything about Anderson being placed under his command. The absence from Longstreet's report of so much as an acknowledgment of something so significant as being handed temporary command of one of Hill's divisions is telling in and of itself and by default would suggest Anderson remained under his corps commander, Hill, though, to fully confirm Anderson's command placement on July 2, other primary sources must also be consulted.[13]

What widely read secondary sources have alleged Anderson was under Longstreet's command during the Confederates' main July 2 attack? Also, upon what primary source material do these accounts base their claim? Mid-twentieth-century popular historian Clifford Dowdey, who was born, spent most of his life, and died in Richmond, Virginia, was the first to advance the Anderson under Longstreet on July 2 assertion in his widely read 1958 book, *Lee & His Men at Gettysburg: Death of a Nation*. Dowdey, a passionate admirer of Robert E. Lee and uncompromising critic of James Longstreet, nevertheless seemed to indict Lee in causing much of the confusion over Anderson's role on July 2:

> As for Anderson, recently transferred out of Longstreet's corps, Lee seemed uncertain as to his proper placement in the command situation. As if to avoid offending sensitive Hill by removing a division that had not yet fought with his corps, and yet to allow Longstreet to call on Anderson without going through Hill, Lee instructed Anderson to 'cooperate … in Longstreet's attack.' This order was the vaguest he ever gave. He did not specify whether Anderson was to act under the orders of Longstreet, commanding the attack, or of Hill, his new corps commander, or Lee's own.

Undoubtedly, Dowdey crafted an intricate and enticingly persuasive web of assertions throughout the course of these four sentences. He began by falling back on the timeless allegation that since Anderson served under Longstreet up until the Gettysburg Campaign, palpable uncertainty was produced over where his division now fit in the army. This argument is tenuous, upon considering Lee had just reorganized the army into three corps and would certainly have had the wherewithal to recall he placed Anderson under Hill's command, not Longstreet's. Citing Lee's January 1864 official report, Dowdey claimed, "Lee seemed uncertain" about where Anderson fit in the army's command structure, quoting a small portion of a sentence in Lee's report to advance a misleading narrative. The full quote from Lee's report is: "*General Hill* [emphasis added] was ordered to threaten the enemy's center, to prevent re-enforcements being drawn to either wing, and co-operate with *his* [emphasis added] right division in Longstreet's attack." Nowhere in Lee's account does the commanding general mention temporarily reneging on his reorganization decision and giving Longstreet command of Anderson's division; in fact, he explicitly delineates "General Hill was ordered to threaten" and "General Hill was ordered to … co-operate," not General Longstreet. Lee used the possessive "his right division," clearly referring to Hill. What part of

Lee's full sentence would indicate "Lee seemed uncertain" about Anderson's "proper placement in the command situation"? Nevertheless, Dowdey proceeded to advance the unfair conclusion that Lee's orders regarding the use of Anderson were the "vaguest he ever gave" and produced unmistakable confusion as to who his direct superior was on July 2—Longstreet, Hill, or Lee himself.

Furthermore, in Dowdey's second sentence, the Virginian author crafted an exceedingly drama-filled situation, advancing blatant conjecture about the supposed thoughts and feelings of Lee, Hill, and Longstreet. To Dowdey, when it came to Anderson, Lee was most worried about walking the tightrope of placating his two subordinates—not "offending sensitive Hill" and mollifying Longstreet through making some kind of pseudo-arrangement, whereby his "Old Warhorse" was "allow[ed] ... to call on Anderson without going through Hill." How do we know Lee was worried about offending Hill? Likewise, upon what evidence was the assertion based that Lee constructed a situation whereby Longstreet could bypass Hill and unilaterally direct Anderson during the attack? Dowdey's book contains no footnotes or endnotes, so other than the abbreviated sentence from Lee's report in the narrative, he gave no hint as to what sources supported these conclusions. I was personally unable to find anything in the primary source record that would lend credence to Dowdey's psychologically based scenario.[14]

Just five years after Dowdey's *Lee & His Men at Gettysburg* emerged, Mississippi-born historian and novelist Shelby Foote's *Fredericksburg to Meridian*, the second volume of his epic *The Civil War: A Narrative*, was published. Some historians and students of the war dismiss Foote's work because of its narrative, historical fiction-like style and lack of footnotes or endnotes; however, especially following his appearance on documentary filmmaker Ken Burns's popular 1990 TV series on the Civil War, Foote's works have become increasingly popular and influential in the Civil War community. Therefore, irrespective of any formal concerns some may have with Foote's *Narrative*, his works' popularity cannot be disputed; so, love them or hate them, since

Lt. Gen. A.P. Hill, CSA (National Archives).

they are widely read, we cannot ignore the effect of Foote's conclusions on generations of Civil War readers.

Foote's commentary on the topic of Anderson on July 2 was similar to Dowdey's, with slight variation. Foote held that "the fault was primarily Anderson's," with typical justification: "Missing the firm if sometimes heavy hand of Longstreet, under whom he had always fought before—except of course at Chancellorsville, where Lee himself had taken him in charge—he was unaccustomed to Hill's comparatively light touch, which allowed him to be less attentive to preparatory details." Here, Foote presented the familiar argument that Anderson had been under Longstreet since the very beginning of his time in the army and was not used to any other direct superior. Curiously, he also seemed to imply Anderson was incapable of independent thought or commanding on his own, always needing someone senior there to direct his actions and decisions during an attack. Foote's assertion was almost certainly influenced by Longstreet staffer Gilbert Moxley Sorrel's comment about Anderson's temperament: "Major General Richard H. Anderson … was rather an interesting character. His courage was of the highest order, but he was indolent. His capacity and intelligence excellent, but it was hard to get him to use them…. He had served well as a brigadier general, and now with Longstreet, commanding a division, had more to do. Longstreet knew him well and could get a good deal out of him, more than any one else."[15]

For the purposes of this essay, Foote's next assertion was even more consequential. "Furthermore, Hill had understood that his right division was more or less detached to Longstreet, whereas Longstreet had interpreted Lee's instructions merely to mean that Hill would be in support and therefore still in command of his own troops," Foote argued, before concluding, "Consequently, neither [Hill nor Longstreet] exercised any control over Anderson, who followed suit by leaving the conduct of the attack to his subordinates, with the result that it broke down in midcareer."

It is unknown what source Foote was relying on to make these claims, since, as already stated, his books did not contain footnotes or endnotes. That said, what is clear was Foote could not have been consulting A.P. Hill's or Richard Anderson's official reports, since those primary source documents controvert his claims entirely. Like Dowdey, who in relation to this topic only provided a misleading abridged quote from a sentence of Lee's report and never quoted anything from Hill's or Anderson's report, or Longstreet's for that matter, Foote appears to have ignored some or all of these reports. For one, Hill's report intimated nothing about an understanding Anderson's division was under Longstreet, or as Foote put it "more or less detached to Longstreet," during the July 2 attack. In fact, Hill's report, like Lee's—when the commanding general's commentary on this topic is presented in its entirety—clearly shows the Third Corps commander understood he retained responsibility for Anderson and any support that division afforded Longstreet's men. Hill wrote:

> The corps of General Longstreet (McLaws' and Hood's divisions) was on my right, and in a line very nearly at right angles to mine. General Longstreet was to attack the left flank of the enemy, and sweep down his line, and *I was ordered to co-operate* [emphasis added] with him with such of my brigades from the right as could join in with his troops in the attack.

Matching the verbiage in Lee's report, "General Hill was ordered to ... co-operate," Hill noted, and "I was ordered to co-operate." Neither Lee nor Hill, nor Longstreet for that matter, ever mentioned anything in their reports about Anderson reporting to Longstreet or the First Corps commander directing Anderson's movements. If that had been the case, it is more than likely Hill, Lee, or Longstreet would have included that critical piece of information in at least one of their reports. We can make this assumption because Hill included that exact piece of information when it came to his report's July 3 section. On July 3, Hill penned:

> I was directed to hold my line with Anderson's division and the half of Pender's (now commanded by General Lane), and to order Heth's division (commanded by Pettigrew), and Lane's and Scales' brigades, of Pender's division, *to report to Lieutenant General Longstreet as a support to his corps in the assault* [emphasis added] on the enemy's lines.

It now being established that Anderson was Hill's responsibility, what of Foote's comment about negligence in exercising control over Anderson during the July 2 attack? With the understanding that Anderson remained under Hill's purview, it was none other than the latter's responsibility to exercise "control over Anderson," either from the onset (if Hill desired) or if execution happened to go sideways. In his report, Hill acknowledged his awareness that the execution of Anderson's attack, particularly the lack of support afforded the three attacking brigades, did indeed go sideways, but then seemed to dodge overall responsibility. "Soon after McLaws moved forward," he wrote, "General Anderson moved forward the brigades of Wilcox, Posey, and Wright, en echelon.... The enemy threw forward heavy re-enforcements [sic], and no supports coming to these brigades, the ground so hardly won had to be given up." Here, Hill clearly divulged that in directing the attack, he more or less gave Anderson an entirely free hand, to the point that even when Hill noticed "no supports coming to these brigades," the Third Corps commander apparently did little but acknowledge that all the progress made by Wilcox, Lang, and Wright "had to be given up." With Hill having Posey's and Mahone's brigades available, along with Pender's and Heth's divisions to the left and rear of Anderson, respectively, and now acting in his newly minted capacity as corps commander working across divisional lines, whose responsibility other than Hill's was it to ensure support to his attacking brigades? Certainly, Anderson shares some responsibility too, particularly for Posey's and Mahone's inaction, and perhaps to a certain degree Lee, who was with Hill at the time; however, in the end, it was A.P. Hill's corps.[16]

Both Anderson's official report and several of his brigade commander's reports confirm the claim that Anderson was the primary officer charged with responsibility to initiate and manage his division's attack. That said, what these reports make equally clear—and what Foote got right—was that once Anderson issued orders for some of his brigades to advance, for the most part he proceeded to take his own Hill-at-Gettysburg-like, hands-off approach. A.P. Hill was practically a nonentity in all these reports and Longstreet was referred to only so far as McLaws' division served as a timer of sorts for when Anderson's rightmost brigades were to proceed to the attack. Furthermore, Longstreet was neither described in these reports as some sort of temporary corps commander for Anderson's men, nor as someone who was serving in some kind of attack oversight capacity north of McLaws.

Characteristic of these conclusions was the content of Anderson's report, where the division commander established his central role in ensuring his right brigade's (Wilcox's) initial timing was in sync with the progress of Longstreet's left. "I was ... ordered to put the troops of my division into action by brigades as soon as those of General Longstreet's corps had progressed so far in their assault as to be connected with my right flank," Anderson noted, while adding that around 5:30 p.m. McLaws' division "advanced so far as to call for the movement of my troops" with "the advance of Mc-Laws' [sic] division ... immediately followed by the brigades of mine, in the manner directed." The contents of Cadmus Wilcox's report verified Anderson's commentary, when the brigade commander recollected that "my instructions were to advance when the troops on my right should advance, and to report this to the division commander, in order that the other brigades should advance in proper time." Likewise, Ambrose Wright, commanding the middle brigade in Anderson's battle line, contended: "About noon, I was informed by Major-General Anderson that an attack upon the enemy's lines would soon be made by the whole division.... I was instructed to move simultaneously with Perry's [Lang's] brigade, which was on my right, and informed that Posey's brigade on my left, would move forward upon my advance." And finally, David Lang recalled how "about 5 p.m. I received an order from General Anderson to the effect that General Longstreet was driving back the enemy's left, and that Wilcox would advance whenever General Longstreet's left advanced beyond him. I was ordered to ... advance with General Wilcox.... At 6 p.m., General Wilcox having begun to advance, I moved forward." What do all these accounts have in common? For one, no mention was ever made of Longstreet having any sort of direct role in managing Anderson's brigades or Anderson himself.[17] Additionally, they highlight Anderson's rather proactive approach in the lead-up to the attack to ensure that at least his initial brigades advanced at the proper and intended moment to support Longstreet's left flank.

Follow-on content from these and other reports, like Carnot

Brig. Gen. Cadmus Wilcox, CSA (Library of Congress).

Posey's and William Mahone's, further amplify the degree to which many of Anderson's brigadiers naturally continued to view him as the primary officer directing the attack, while concurrently shedding light on how and when the Third Corps division's attack began to be mismanaged and resultantly break down. As you will recall, upon advancing, Ambrose Wright was under the impression Posey's brigade would near simultaneously advance on his left in line with the intended en echelon attack plan for Anderson's division. However, according to Wright's report, once he neared the Emmitsburg Road, Posey was nowhere to be found, thus exposing his left flank. Wright then described how he attempted to notify Anderson, hoping the division commander might take steps to remediate the unforeseen situation: "I dispatched my aide-de-camp, Capt. R.H. Bell, with a message to Major-General Richard Anderson, informing him of my own advance and its extent, and that General Posey had not advanced with his brigade on my left." In response to this dispatch, Wright described how Anderson instructed the brigadier "to press on; that Posey had been ordered in on my left, and that he (General Anderson) would reiterate the order." In another post-battle account, Wright represented Anderson as providing assurances "that both Posey and Mahone had been ordered in," while in the meantime urging the Georgian brigade to "go on." Ultimately, Wright was afforded no support from Posey or Mahone on his left, and Lang's and Wilcox's brigades on his right were soon compelled to withdraw, leaving both his flanks exposed and forcing his own retreat.

Carnot Posey's rather peculiar official report provides little insight as to his general orders on July 2 or what happened with his brigade that day. That said, Posey did reference "the major-general" several times in his report, while never mentioning anything about Longstreet. William Mahone's report, consisting of "a few brief remarks," is even less informative, though its concise acknowledgment that "the brigade took no special or active part in the actions of that battle beyond that which fell to the lot of its line of skirmishers," is probably evidence enough to further verify that something went seriously awry on Anderson's front on July 2. Further confirming this conclusion was that Posey, Wright, and Wilcox each asked Anderson for support during the attack; Wilcox a total of three times.[18] Wilcox later reported that on one of those occasions, he had sent his adjutant rearward to Anderson's headquarters, which was located "back in the woods." Upon arriving there, the adjutant apparently found Anderson's horse tied to a tree "and all his staff lying on the ground (indifferent) as tho' nothing was going on." Still smarting years later, Wilcox alleged: "I am quite certain that Gen'l A. never saw a foot of the ground on which his three brigades fought on the 2nd July." The account of what happened with Mahone's brigade during the attack is perhaps even more surprising. Allegedly, during the attack, Anderson sent Mahone orders to advance, whereby the brigadier responded that he already had orders from Anderson to stay put where he was on Seminary Ridge. The staff officer, Lieutenant S.D. Shannon, then proceeded to reiterate that the new order originated with Anderson. No matter, Mahone replied; he already had his orders from Anderson and proceeded to maintain his brigade's idle state throughout the remaining minutes of the division's attack.[19]

Reflecting, in a general sense, on Anderson's July 2 attack, it is quite clear the division had extraordinarily little chance to achieve any lasting or significant Confederate success that day, particularly without support from another Third Corps division. Three main difficulties were working against Anderson's division on July 2. The first issue was Anderson's brigades were in no way, shape, or form attacking in depth. Unlike Longstreet's two divisions, which were initially positioned with two brigades in front and two behind, Anderson's attack was executed with a mere single brigade depth. This arrangement was likely instituted because of the second issue: the fact that Anderson was forced to attack over a front nearly as broad as Longstreet's (1,750 versus 2,500 yards, respectively[20]), and apparently with only his own division at his disposal. As a result, Anderson's brigades were stretched out side-by-side to cover the distance, effectively diluting their overall force of attack. The last issue gets us back to the command issues that plagued Anderson's attack on July 2. As noted in Wilcox's recollections of that day, Anderson was said to be located well back from the front—perhaps several hundred yards behind it—and resultantly, would have been unable to exercise close supervision over the attack. Furthermore, even when the evidence indicates Anderson did indeed attempt to push Posey and Mahone forward to support his other three brigades, there is no suggestion he attempted to follow up with the two brigadiers to ensure those orders were carried out. Likewise, where was Hill? And what about the commanding general, who was co-located with Hill? Instead of focusing on Anderson, Hill, or Lee with respect to the obtuse handling of Anderson's division on July 2, a number of historians have seemingly attempted to return the focus to Longstreet—an observation that leads us into the last, widely read, secondary source we will explore in this essay that has alleged Anderson was under Longstreet's temporary command during the July 2 attack.

Academic historian Allen Guelzo's popular, one-volume history of the Battle of Gettysburg, recently published in 2013, is one of the better battle narratives with respect to its more reasonable coverage of Longstreet's performance. That said, when it comes to covering Anderson's division on July 2, Guelzo joins some past authors in clearly and misleadingly suggesting Anderson was placed under Longstreet's command. Picking up on the morning of July 2 when Longstreet expressed his concern to Lee over not having Pickett's division available to participate in a First Corps–led attack, Guelzo writes, "Lee assured Longstreet that he could make up the deficit in numbers by borrowing Richard Heron Anderson's division from Powell Hill." The use of those two words, "borrow" and "from," suggest Hill was forced to temporarily relinquish command of Anderson's division and essentially had it taken away from him for the duration of the attack. Further clarifying his position, Guelzo later maintains, "[Anderson] was assigned to division command in Powell Hill's corps, where he did not hesitate to make his displeasure with Hill known to a sympathetic Longstreet…. When Lee authorized Longstreet to substitute Anderson for George Pickett's division, he could not have made Longstreet or Anderson a more mutually agreeable gift." Guelzo, like Dowdey and Foote before him, draws attention here to the lengthy history of association in the army between Anderson and Longstreet and the extent to which Anderson preferred the command style of Lee's "Old Warhorse" over A.P. Hill, strongly hinting it was almost inevitable Anderson be handed over to Longstreet on July 2. The academic historian also adds "substitute" to the previously mentioned "borrow" in describing what he believed happened with Anderson's division on July 2. Guelzo essentially claims Anderson was substituted for Pickett, which is essentially true; however, he then adds a qualifier about how this substitution presented Anderson and Longstreet with a "mutually agreeable gift"—suggesting Longstreet was happy he again had command of Anderson, and likewise, Anderson was pleased he again found himself under Longstreet.

Leaving no room for uncertainty as to what Guelzo is implying, he also advances the claim that at one point during the morning of July 2, "Hill and Longstreet peeled away and sat down to discuss the intricacies of temporarily transferring command of Anderson's division." In examining the endnote associated with Guelzo's claim, a secondary source, James L. Robertson, Jr.'s, *General A.P. Hill: The Story of a Confederate Warrior*, is listed. Analyzing the pages of Robertson, Jr.'s, book listed in the endnote, 216 and 221–222, the first page merely describes how in the early morning hours of July 2, Hill and Longstreet met with Lee, where the generals briefly talked and examined a map. The only other detail on page 216, somewhat related to the topic at hand, was when Robertson, Jr., indicated once Lee decided on a battle plan for the day, "Hill's corps was to 'cooperate' in the assault." In other words, there is nothing on this page about a Hill-Longstreet meeting discussing the transfer of Anderson's division from the former to the latter. Moving forward to pages 221–222, we find that Robertson, Jr., has already moved on from July 2 to "Friday, *July 3* [emphasis added]." Near the bottom of the page, Robertson turns to describing how on the morning of July 3, Hill and Longstreet "strolled away a short distance and sat down on a fallen log," where they "reached agreement on the disposition of troops." What this examination indicates is that the pages cited from Robertson, Jr.'s, book collectively have nothing to do with a discussion about "intricacies of temporarily transferring command of Anderson's division" on July 2, and in the case of pages 221–222, have nothing whatsoever to do with July 2, and actually describe events on July 3.[21]

As one might expect, the relationship between Ambrose Wright and Richard Anderson went south rather quickly after the Battle of Gettysburg. Wright, who was well known for his combativeness and candid nature, believed Anderson, along with Lang, Posey, and Mahone, had left his Georgia brigade out to dry at the center of the battle, squandering what he (and others since) has characterized as one of the Confederate army's best opportunities to break through the Federal line on Cemetery Ridge. Just five days after the battle, Wright penned a revealing and scathing letter to his wife, not only describing his brigade's actions on each day of the battle, but also pointing out which of his superior officers and fellow brigadiers he believed dropped the ball on July 2. The private letter would have been harmless enough, if it had not somehow found its way into the July 27, 1863, edition of the Georgia *Daily Constitutionalist*. Besides some details Wright included in the letter about asking Anderson for support from Posey (and never getting it) and claiming that Lang's brigade "gave way, and shamefully ran to the rear," the sentence that undoubtedly got his superior officer Anderson's attention was when Wright declared: "Thus we were perfectly isolated from any portion of our army, a mile in its advance, and although we had gained the enemy's works and captured his guns, we were about to be sacrificed to the bad management and cowardly conduct of others." Soon after seeing the article,

Anderson had Wright arrested and attempted to have his brigadier court-martialed for "disobedience towards superior officers and for matters connected with publications which appeared in the Augusta constitutionalist." The drama did not last for too long; with Wright acquitted of charges in August 1863. Ultimately, Anderson also made it clear he did not want any of his subordinate brigadiers blamed for what happened on July 2 and that if anyone should be held responsible, as their direct superior, he should.[22]

As for Anderson's and Longstreet's hitherto close association leading up to the Battle of Gettysburg, that would more or less continue until the army's surrender at Appomattox. After Longstreet's severe wounding during the May 1864 Battle of the Wilderness, it was none other than Anderson who took command of the First Corps until Longstreet's return in October. On May 31, Anderson was even temporarily promoted to the rank of lieutenant general, and once Longstreet returned, Anderson would not be relegated to divisional command. In a sign of how well Lee thought he performed at the corps level, Anderson was given command of the new Fourth Corps, which survived until its near-total dissolution at the Battle of Sailor's Creek on April 6, 1865, and subsequent merger with the Second Corps on April 8—just one day before the army surrendered at Appomattox Courthouse.[23]

It is largely because of this close association between Longstreet and Anderson in the Army of Northern Virginia prior to (and to a certain extent after) Gettysburg that historians have sometimes been misled into embroiling Longstreet in Anderson's and Hill's (and Lee's?) "bad mismanagement," as Ambrose Wright characterized it, at the center of the Confederate line on July 2. Indeed, over the decades and up to the present day, some well-known historians have seen fit to advance conjecture based on no, twisted, partial, or faulty evidence that Anderson was in some way placed under Longstreet's command upon George Pickett's absence on the second day of the Battle of Gettysburg. Granted, and unfortunately for Longstreet's sake, Lee's "Old Warhorse" perhaps started this whole misconception when he wrote in his 1896 memoirs (and in none of his other post-battle or postwar accounts) that four of Anderson's brigades "were assigned as part of my command" during the Confederates' July 2 attack on the Federal left and center. Nevertheless, a careful reading of, most significantly, the official reports of key players like Lee, Hill, Anderson, Longstreet, and the five brigadier generals under Anderson, collectively controverts both Longstreet's statement in his memoirs, and the cited historians' allegations. The evidence is overwhelming that Lee intended Anderson to be a substitute division, in Pickett's absence, and to cooperate with Longstreet in continuing the attack north of McLaws; however, equally overwhelming is the evidence confirming Anderson remained under A.P. Hill's command and orders, not Longstreet's.

In closing, perhaps the most important question to be asked is the simple, but often elusive: Why? Why would some historians advance the false narrative that Anderson was under Longstreet during the Confederates' July 2 attack on the Federal left and center? Based on my experience and observation, modern-day Longstreet critics have undoubtedly attempted to use this particular historical error—present in several popular and easily accessible books on the battle—to advance a misguided story line. Their narrative often goes something like this:

Anderson's division was actually Longstreet's responsibility on July 2 and that is why Hill and Lee never stepped in to remediate any issues on Anderson's front, or Anderson's division wound up not fully attacking on July 2 because Longstreet exercised no management or oversight of it, as Lee had expected.

I have heard variations of this storyline over the course of the last fifteen years researching and studying the topic of Longstreet's Gettysburg performance and, most recently, at some book events since the publication of *Longstreet at Gettysburg*. I have also regularly seen it rehashed on popular Civil War message boards and Gettysburg discussion groups on social media. It is hard to shake the sense that this concocted narrative based on secondary source historiographical error is yet another offshoot of the anyone-but-Lee-is-to-blame vestige that emerged in the years after Lee's death. In essence, to those who subscribe to this myth, there must be some kind of justification to explain away why Lee, co-located with Hill, neglected to apply pressure to Anderson's attack unfolding right in front of him. In attempting to shift blame, attention is unsurprisingly diverted to the usual culprit. Longstreet—still smarting from having his tactical suggestions rejected by Lee in the early morning hours—must have been involved with the debacle, neglecting his duty to oversee Anderson.

For historians and students of the Battle of Gettysburg it is well beyond time to point out and reject such false narratives, which unfortunately have been passed down in popular secondary sources from generation to generation. For all intents and purposes, one need only consult the primary source record to verify Anderson's division remained under A.P. Hill's command and orders on July 2, and no amount of twisting the evidence otherwise can change that well-documented fact.

Essay 6

Suppressed No More

Helen Longstreet's Lee and Longstreet at High Tide

It is the carefully sifted story of the records and contemporaneous witnesses.... The reader will perceive that at last it is the story of the records.
—Helen Longstreet

She was not called the "Fighting Lady" or the "Fighting Widow" in vain. In every facet of her 99-year-long life, Helen Dortch Longstreet, the second wife of former Confederate Lieutenant General James Longstreet, cultivated a fervent spirit of determination, resiliency, and vigor. How appropriate, then, it was for Thomas J. Herbert, the Governor of Ohio in 1947, to write Helen upon the presentation of her portrait to the Georgia State Law Library by "Americans North and South" and soon displayed in the Georgia State Capitol Building: "To a gallant lady who not only has the courage of her convictions, but the energy and unselfishness to pursue them."[1]

Indeed, nearly three-quarters of a century earlier, in 1878, a 15-year-old Helen undertook newspaper editor duties for her father James Speed Dortch's *The Weekly Tribune*, in Carnesville, Georgia, only to take on full ownership of the paper by 1888. Helen also found time to pursue higher education twice in the 1880s, both at the Georgia Baptist Female Seminary (now Brenau University) in Gainesville, Georgia, and the Collegiate Institute of Notre Dame in Baltimore, Maryland. While studying history, geography, math, French, German, and Latin, among other subjects at Notre Dame from 1887 to 1889, Helen was alone presented with an award for "Successful Application to Study" in her first year at the institute. She returned to Georgia in the 1890s and by 1894, was editor and publisher for the Milledgeville, Georgia, *Daily Chronicle*; served as private secretary for Georgia governor William Yates Atkinson; and worked as assistant state librarian—the first woman to hold that position.[2]

In the years after her seven-year marriage to James Longstreet (1897–1904), Helen never remained idle and there was rarely a dull moment. One of the most acute examples of Helen displaying her incomparable dynamism was when serving as postmistress of Gainesville, Georgia, in the immediate years after General Longstreet's death. Now in her 40s and living alone, the widow Longstreet once awoke late in the night—around 2 a.m. in the morning—to the sound of rustling in her house. Helen's first instinct was to grab her pistol and investigate the noise. Soon enough, she noticed a burglar in the dining room rummaging through her table silver. When she made her presence known, the man attempted to escape through a nearby window, whereby Helen opened fire. The surprised robber turned and shot at Helen once with his own pistol, missing her; however, this effrontery only served to cause the postmistress to empty her entire barrel of bullets at the man, apparently hitting him at least once during his escape. The next day, the local newspaper naturally reported that "the firing alarmed the quarter of the city in which Mrs. Longstreet resides and caused a crowd to gather." Such was how Helen Dortch Longstreet dealt with robbers.[3]

When her environmental and political foes cropped up in the years after her husband's death, Helen of course would not wield a fully loaded pistol, but instead a biting pen and an unwavering voice. From 1911 to 1913, Helen led the fight against the Georgia Power and Railroad Company, which planned to build a dam at Tallulah Falls, known as the "Niagara Falls" of the South. The project would create a significant hydroelectric power source but would concurrently divert the water flow of the Tallulah River away from the falls to the detriment of the area's booming environmental and economic assets. Helen would derisively and unsurprisingly refer to her opponents in the railroad company as nothing but "commercial pirates and buccaneers." Helen was also regularly drawn to politics, fervently supporting former President Theodore Roosevelt's Progressive Party (more popularly known as the "Bull Moose Party") in 1912, even to the point of serving as a delegate to the party's convention. For a time in the 1930s, Helen moved to the U.S. Virgin Islands and sought to draw attention to poor living conditions and the predominance of political corruption on the islands. Just 12 years before her death and well into her 80s, the "Fighting Lady" embarked on the last significant political battle of her life when she ran an unsuccessful write-in campaign against the staunch segregationist, Democrat governor of Georgia, Herman Talmadge. Though it proved a fruitless attempt in the end, highlights of the widow Longstreet's bold campaign platform called for upholding civil rights, supporting state welfare institutions, unmasking the Ku Klux Klan, and severely opposing Communism, which she believed sought to "destroy the Christian Church and to enslave mankind."[4]

Helen again displayed her fortitude and pluck during World War II, when she worked as a riveter at the Bell Aircraft Plant in Marietta, Georgia. The "Fighting Lady," then in her early 80s, helped build B-29 bombers, enthusiastically proclaiming, "I am going to assist in building a plane to bomb Hitler and the Son of Heaven to the Judgement Seat of God," while explaining, "I was the head of my class in riveting school. In fact, I was the only one in it." Tellingly of Helen's continued liveliness and sharpness, her foreman, R.E. Harben, stated of her, "She has never been absent a single day, not tardy a single minute, during her nearly two years of service. Her work, in quantity and quality, ranks with the best that has been done in this great plant. She has richly earned the highest merit rating."[5]

Growing up in the newspaper world and working as a librarian in Georgia, Helen was no stranger to journalism, editing, researching, and writing. Indeed, it was when she worked as assistant state librarian in Atlanta, Georgia, in the mid–1890s that her relationship with James Longstreet blossomed. At the time, the general was writing his memoirs, *From Manassas to Appomattox*, and apparently made frequent visits to the State Library to conduct research, and likely to see the assistant state librarian. Helen later maintained that Longstreet "often pressed me into service in the preparation of speeches which he was called upon to deliver throughout the country, one of the most notable being made at a banquet on General Grant's birthday in New York City." A few years later, and shortly after their marriage in 1897, Helen also edited and revised the second edition of the general's memoirs and apparently joyfully served as Longstreet's secretary of sorts, keeping track of his "voluminous correspondence to make sure that the letter of no loyal soldier ever went unanswered." After her husband's passing in 1904 until her death in 1962, Helen continued to pursue her passion for writing. She penned numerous books and essay collections, with some of the more significant ones being *Woodrow and the Granddaughters of a President: A Political Criticism* (1916); *In the Path of Lee's "Old Warhorse"* (1917); *Travail of the New Slavery: A Novelette* (1917); *Trail of the Spoilsmen in the Gainesville, GA., Post Office: Essays* (1922); and *Sure Road to World Peace: A Call for Peace* (1946).[6]

Astute students of the Civil War will note that in this list of notable works by Helen Longstreet, I have left out the most significant, *Lee and Longstreet at High Tide: Gettysburg in the Light of the Official Records*, published in the months after James Longstreet's death. With this short introduction to Helen's rather extraordinary life, we can now turn to the main focus of this essay: an analysis of Helen's 1904 book, which the widow Longstreet intended to be a bulletproof defense of her deceased husband's military career, and especially his performance at the July 1863 Battle of Gettysburg. In all actuality though, the succinct overview of Helen's passionate life in the preceding pages can be used as a prism through which we can better understand how she approached and dealt with anyone who saw fit to disparage her late husband's military record, and above all his actions at Gettysburg.

Understandably, whenever someone hears the word "defense" associated with a historical work, they immediately assume the author has an agenda. This is certainly a reasonable assumption. The issue with equating "defense" and "agenda," in this case as a means to immediately dismiss a work such as Helen Longstreet's *Lee and Longstreet at High Tide*, is that it ignores the fact that while most historians writing on the Longstreet-Gettysburg topic over the last century-plus may have been careful about embracing defenses of Longstreet over fear of agenda, bias, and reliability, they have seldom chosen to exercise that same caution when assessing attacks against Longstreet and any resulting agenda, bias, and reliability issues inherent in those attacks. In a number of instances, these historians actually appear to have cast agenda, bias, and reliability to the wind, perhaps so as to satisfy their own agendas, leave unchallenged the long-congealed status quo conclusions on the Longstreet-Gettysburg topic, or out of some sort of fear of making waves in the Civil War author community. Indeed, for decades, historians have thought it acceptable to widely use and trust much of the biased and agenda-driven documentation originating in the postwar years—documentation often jam-packed with Lost Cause-influenced narratives on the Gettysburg battle from the likes of Jubal Early, William Pendleton, and other former Confederate officers. These narratives often held that Robert E. Lee was the perfect general in every respect and James Longstreet was altogether flawed in many respects. Regarding Gettysburg specifically, this cabal of postwar writers was adamant Lee devised reasonable strategic and tactical plans both for the campaign and at the three-day battle, respectively, and it was especially because of Longstreet's alleged shortcomings that he failed at the Confederate "High Tide."[7] Describing this tenacious trend, Helen wrote, "Short-sighted partisans seemingly argued that the disparagement of Longstreet was necessary to save the military reputation of Lee. But Lee's great fame needed no such sacrifice." Perhaps most unfortunate in this cycle of trusting tainted and agenda-driven postwar narratives has not been its effect on other historians, but actually its effect on students of the war. Historians' audience—readers—has been digesting secondary sources with these hardened interpretations on the Longstreet-Gettysburg Controversy for well over a century now and it is a monumental challenge in many cases to get people to change their minds from long-standing narratives, however well-argued to the contrary.[8]

In the case of Helen Longstreet's 1904 book, it is often said by Longstreet critics, or even by reasonable skeptics of "defenses," that the work is biased and unreliable. Perhaps it is not a coincidence that similar charges have been leveled over the years against all of James Longstreet's postwar writings, and most commonly his 1896 memoirs, *From Manassas to Appomattox*.[9] In dismissing Helen's book, they claim she was only two months old when the Battle of Gettysburg was fought and therefore was not a firsthand observer or participant in the battle. Further, they contend she clearly wrote her book out of resolute defense of her husband, to try to dispel all criticism of Longstreet's Gettysburg performance. Lastly, they will also draw attention to when the book was published—1904—41 years after the battle was fought and therefore, they allege, any conclusions she drew were purely speculative and muddled by the simple passage of time.

Before getting into an in-depth analysis of Helen's interpretation of Longstreet's actions at Gettysburg as presented in her book, it would only be appropriate to briefly address these arguments. As to the first charge that Helen was but a baby when Longstreet fought at Gettysburg and therefore anything she wrote was blind speculation is like arguing that any historians not physically present at the historical event they are covering should never write about that event. In composing *Lee and Longstreet at High Tide*, Helen was participating in the historical trade and employing methods of historical research and writing. She indicated as much in the preface to her book, describing her work as "the *carefully sifted story of the records and contemporaneous witnesses*, [emphasis added] and for clearness I have here and there introduced General Longstreet's personal version of some of the disputed points. But the reader will perceive that at last it is the story of the records." In contending that her book is the "story of the records," naturally one would then ask the logical follow-on question: What records? Helen answered that question too—maintaining that not only did she draw upon Longstreet's *From Manassas to Appomattox*, the general's "stores of knowledge" and a "treasure-house of memories" (Helen began writing her book before Longstreet's death), but also, most importantly, she relied on Captain Leslie J. Perry, who had been employed in the War Records Office, and from 1889 to 1899, worked intimately on the compilation of the *Official Records*, more formally known as the *War of the Rebellion: A Compilation of the Official Records of the Union and Confederate Armies*. Every seasoned historian who has written about a Civil War–related topic will be amply aware of the significance of these records, which summarily contain Union and Confederate after battle reports and correspondence, for compiling a historical work. Helen's use of the *Official Records* is confirmed when she quoted from and analyzed several key official reports over the course of her narrative.[10]

Further on this argument, in maintaining that Helen was too far removed in time from the Battle of Gettysburg to offer anything beyond speculation, critics and skeptics are implicitly suggesting that those who were physically present at the battle, no matter where they were located on the battlefield, automatically produced more reliable accounts. But, objective historians and students of the war must equally consider the suspect reliability of Longstreet's postwar critics, nearly all of whom were participants in the battle. What firsthand knowledge did Jubal Early, a division commander in Richard Ewell's Second Corps located on the Confederate left at Gettysburg, have of Confederate First Corps events on the right flank? What of John B. Gordon, a brigadier general also in the Second Corps, who matter-of-factly wrote of his brigade's role on the second and third days of the battle, "The movements during the succeeding days of the battle, July 2 and 3, I do not consider of sufficient importance to mention"? What of Fitzhugh Lee, a brigadier general in James Ewell Brown (J.E.B.) Stuart's cavalry division who saw no action at Gettysburg until the third day at East Cavalry Field? The list goes on and on. Longstreet critics and Helen skeptics might well then ask, what of William Pendleton, Lee's chief of artillery? Surely, he had a broader view of Confederate tactical operations at Gettysburg. One of the many problems with relying on Pendleton, as we will see later in this essay, is that he had serious credibility issues. Not only was Pendleton the principal postwar originator of the completely fictitious "Sunrise Attack" theory, but even more suspicious was that his official after-battle report is at complete variance with most everything he wrote in the postwar years.[11]

To the offshoot charge that Helen's book is speculative and unreliable simply because it was published in 1904, not only can we again return to the fact that the widow Longstreet was then taking on the role of the historian in crafting her interpretation, but it also begs the question: How many other books and source documents written in the early 20th century have historians put their trust in and regularly employed to compose their own histories? The answer is many. A few key ones come to mind immediately, namely, John B. Gordon's *Reminiscences of the Civil War* (1903), James Power Smith's "General Lee at Gettysburg" (1905), Walter Taylor's *General Lee: His Campaigns in Virginia 1861–1865 with Personal Reminiscences* (1906), and E.P. Alexander's *Military Memoirs of a Confederate* (1907). When subjected to close scrutiny and cross-referenced with additional source documentation—even documentation written by the same author—these works and many others of the postwar period are found to be chock-full of fallacies, inconsistencies, and conjecture, of course, some more than others. No more should we write off Helen's book simply because it was written so many years after the battle than we should engage in a complacent examination of Gordon's, Smith's, Taylor's, and Alexander's writings of the same time period.

As to the critics' and skeptics' charge that Helen wrote her book with the primary goal of defending her husband and therefore entered the controversy with an agenda, that point is conceded; however, no less conceded is the fact that the chief agenda of the postwar anti–Longstreet group was to defend Robert E. Lee's every action and decision at whatever expense to Longstreet. Just a few years before his death, Longstreet himself shrewdly articulated this reality when asserting that "no Southern writer dares to admit that General Lee ever made a military mistake." Students of the war must be cognizant of the extreme extent to which many postwar Longstreet critics played fast and loose with the "facts" and advanced fictional or misremembered reminiscences to fulfill that agenda. Despite this reality, many historians have chosen to rely heavily on several of these tainted accounts when composing their own battle narratives and have not shown a comparable level of the suspicion of bias and reliability regularly applied to Helen Longstreet's, or James Longstreet's, writings for that matter. Perhaps the most egregious example of this occurrence can be found in Virginian Douglas Southall Freeman's four-volume, *R.E. Lee: A Biography*, where in 1934—60 years after the "Sunrise Attack" theory was fully debunked—the historian was still claiming that in the early morning hours of July 2, Lee had expected to see Longstreet's divisions in battle formation, ready to attack the Federal left.[12]

All these anti–Longstreet charges and pro–Longstreet responses ultimately beg the question: Who are we to believe? The trouble-free and easy response would be for us to just throw up our hands and declare we will never know; the primary and postwar record is just too convoluted, while the mountain of Gettysburg-related secondary source historiography further obscures the quest for truth. This ever-present mindset would ultimately preserve much of the status quo when it comes to this topic, since unsurprisingly, readers typically come to believe whatever point of view is published the most (not often having the time to wade through the tangled webs of primary source and postwar documentation themselves), and in this case, the sheer number of anti–Longstreet or anti–Longstreet-leaning books and articles have far outweighed the contrary point of view over the last century. This quantitative disparity alone demonstrates how effectively the postwar anti–Longstreet group of writers carried out their agenda against Longstreet.

A quick dismissal of Helen's book simply because the author was General Longstreet's wife, or even more simply because the author's last name was "Longstreet," would cause one to miss the fact that Helen clearly understood and articulated the historian's craft. Explaining her motive for writing the book, she sagaciously maintained, "But for the benefit of the present—of the young, the busy, who have neither time nor inclination to study the records, and for that sentiment that is increasingly shaped by the public press,—for these and other reasons it appears fitting that in this hour historical truth should have a spokesman on the Gettysburg contentions. In the absence of one more able to speak, this little story of the truth is written." The "Fighting Lady" emphasized, perhaps too optimistically, that she was part of a generation moving on from the "drama of the great 'Lost Cause' … a generation that seeks the truth, unwarped and undistorted by passion, and can face the truth." Helen equally recognized the long-term repercussions for historical truth if she failed to plainly convey her thoughts on the Longstreet-Gettysburg controversy, writing, "This hour does not clamor for the charity of silence, but for the white light of truth which I reverently undertake to throw upon the deeds of [General Longstreet]." Most importantly, Helen spoke directly to that omnipresent question about who we should and should not believe and how we are to induce and discern truth, all of which is worth quoting in full:

> The cold historian of our Civil War of a hundred years hence will not go for truth to the picturesque reminiscences of General John B. Gordon, nor to the pyrotechnics of General Fitzhugh Lee, nor yet to the somewhat hysterical ravings of Rev. Mr. [William] Pendleton and scores of other modern essayists who have sought to fix the failure of Gettysburg upon General Longstreet. The coming chronicler will cast aside the rubbish of passion and hate that followed the war, and have recourse to the nation's *official war records*, and in the cool, calm lights of the *letters and reports of the participants, written at the time* [emphasis added], will place the blunder of Gettysburg where it belongs. Longstreet's fame has nothing to fear in that hour.[13]

Despite how alluring and seductive the postwar, Lost Cause, anti–Longstreet group's writings have been to many legitimate historians over the decades, Helen's characterization of them as "picturesque," "pyrotechnics," "hysterical ravings," and "rubbish of passion and hate" was not only ahead of her time, but even more importantly, a completely fair and reasonable assessment of their worth to objective Civil War history. It must be remembered that the primary means through which the anti–Longstreet group perpetuated its distorted views on Longstreet's performance at Gettysburg was through the Southern Historical Society (SHS), founded in 1869, with its publication vehicle, the *Southern Historical Society Papers (SHSP)*, printed in some form between 1876 and 1959. Echoing Helen Longstreet's observations, perhaps just in a more academic fashion, is historian Richard D. Starnes' commentary on the SHS: "The Society was *uninterested in academic history, with its emphasis on objective evaluation of facts, sources, and interpretations* [emphasis added]. Rather, the organization dedicated itself to the creation of a Confederate historical memory." Starnes further sharpened this monumental point by emphasizing that "historical memory is an individual's or a group's recollection of past events. Historical memories do not represent the past as it occurred, but rather the past as it is perceived." It is tempting to italicize Starnes' entire quotation here because of its supreme importance to a foundational understanding of what undergirded the postwar anti–Longstreet group's writings, and resultantly, many Gettysburg battle narratives and interpretations that have followed over the years. At its core, the SHS sought to perpetuate the very definition of a historical agenda, not objective history firmly based in examining and comparing sources and weighing a body of evidence. Perhaps most significantly, a solid understanding of the SHS's original aims, as recounted above, serves to highlight how important it is for students of the war today to tread very carefully and cautiously when reading (and internalizing) many studies on the Battle of Gettysburg (and even on the Civil War more generally).[14]

Contrary to the SHS's goals and priorities of creating and advancing historical memory, Helen's "cold historian" statement demonstrates a clear awareness of how to properly conduct historical research and use the official record to inform and make educated conclusions, which should, at the very least, instill some preliminary confidence in skeptics that she was not simply relying on her last name, General Longstreet's writings, or pure emotion to write *Lee and Longstreet at High Tide*. And as one begins to carefully read and examine Helen's take on the Longstreet-Gettysburg controversy, one cannot help but come away with the overwhelming impression she not only had a proven awareness of the historical trade (likely through her background as a journalist), but further, was more than capable of employing that awareness to write the earliest, and still one of the finest, published accounts addressing Longstreet's actions at the Battle of Gettysburg.

Indeed, Helen's analysis in her 1904 book has not only stood the test of time and remained largely accurate to this day, but many of her assertions, as we will see, were ahead of her time. Just one remarkable example was her clear contention that the Confederate High Command never designated Little Round Top as an attack objective on July 2; rather, Lee's sights were on gaining and attacking up the Emmitsburg Road, with seizure of the Joseph Sherfy Peach Orchard as the first step in that process. This argument was not fully explored or given the attention it deserved until some recent publications, but here was Helen over 100 years ago making that very same case.[15]

In crafting and documenting my analysis for this essay, I thought it not only appropriate, but instructive to compare many of Helen's conclusions with John B. Gordon's anti–Longstreet writings in his *Reminiscences of the Civil War*—not merely because they were published at almost the exact same time or because they offer clear contrasting points of view, but because in all actuality Gordon's book proved *the* impetus for Helen's decision to write *Lee and Longstreet at High Tide*. In fact, although Helen spent some time addressing William Pendleton's postwar allegations and writings, her book can most accurately be considered a direct response to *Reminiscences of the Civil War*. The Widow Longstreet confirmed this assertion in her poignant story about the impetus for her book project and her husband's suppressed reaction to Gordon's charges in the last months of his life:

> General John B. Gordon, during recent years, did General Longstreet injustice. I know he caused him much pain. At a time when General Longstreet was suffering horribly,—one eye had already been destroyed by the dreadful disease; he had long been deaf and paralyzed from war service; the wound in his throat was giving him severest pain,—at this sad time General Gordon revived the old, threadbare story that he had disobeyed orders at Gettysburg. But when a reporter from one of the New York dailies called to interview him about General Gordon and his charges, he refused to say one word. It was then that I said, "If you will not reply to General Gordon, I will. And in the future, so long as I shall live, whenever your war record is attacked, I will make answer." And so it happened that the little story of Gettysburg was written while General Longstreet was nearing the grave. During these last, sorrowful days he had heard that General Gordon was not in good health, and he asked me, with touching concern, about his condition. I expected to tell General Gordon of these occurrences, but I never saw him again. The Reaper gathered him in, ten days after General Longstreet answered the call.[16]

It is curious, but increasingly unsurprising, that of the six major, one-volume studies of the Battle of Gettysburg published since the mid-twentieth century—Glenn Tucker's *High Tide at Gettysburg* (1958), Clifford Dowdey's *Lee and His Men* at Gettysburg: The Death of a Nation (1958), Edwin B. Coddington's The Gettysburg Campaign: A Study in Command (1968), Stephen B. Sears' Gettysburg (2003), Noah A. Trudeau's Gettysburg: A Testing of Courage (2003), and Allen C. Guelzo's Gettysburg: The Last Invasion (2013)—only Tucker's book sourced Helen's work in the bibliography section. Conversely, every volume except for Guelzo's, which contains notes but no bibliography, lists Gordon's book as a source. However poor a source it is in many respects, I do not question other historians' judgment for including *Reminiscences of the Civil War*; after all, Gordon was certainly a participant in the battle. What I do find perplexing and troubling is the exclusion of Helen Longstreet's book, especially since large portions of these books attempt to address the Longstreet-Gettysburg controversy. How could historians exclude a book that provides copious insights into Longstreet and his actions at the Battle of Gettysburg and whose author clearly delved into the *Official Records* (likely with the help of Captain Leslie J. Perry), while including Gordon's book, which actually contains very little commentary on Gettysburg and is entirely based on dated, personal reminiscences and recollections of what others wrote in the postwar years?[17]

In her book, Helen cut right to the core problem with Gordon's *Reminiscences of the Civil War*. "He simply reiterates the old charges in full, produces no evidence in their support, and gratuitously endorses a false and cruel verdict," Helen contended, before deeming "his contribution ... of no historical value. It carries inherent evidence that General Gordon made no critical examination of the documentary history of Gettysburg." Closing that thought with the cutting statement—"He assumes to render a verdict on the say-so of others"—she then proceeded to pick up on the following page with the equally penetrating observation that "his [Gordon's] testimony is obviously of the hearsay kind. In fact, as will be observed from his own admission, it is no more than his own personal conclusions, wholly deduced from the assertions of others, based on an assumed state of facts which did not exist." Just as she dealt with the robber trying to steal her table silver, Helen unloaded the entire barrel on the

John B. Gordon in the postwar years (Library of Congress).

integrity of Gordon's book, yet historians have overwhelmingly ignored Helen's work and consulted the former Georgia officer's. Throughout the remainder of this essay, we will examine the merits and shortcomings of Helen's pro–Longstreet and Gordon's anti–Longstreet arguments, using their books as a lens to discern which side had the more truthful and better supported argument when held up against the primary and cross-referenced postwar record. In engaging in this analysis, it is hoped that we can provide some answers to that ubiquitous question about whom we should believe.[18]

Realistically, John B. Gordon's criticism of James Longstreet's actions at Gettysburg only spanned a few pages in his *Reminiscences of the Civil War*.[19] That said, the widely circulated *Scribner's Monthly* magazine went on to print Gordon's entire Gettysburg chapter in its July 1903 issue. Additionally, no matter how briefly and slapdash Gordon outlined his criticisms against Longstreet, his commentary covered nearly all of the core anti–Longstreet group beliefs as they pertained to Gettysburg in the postwar years and beyond. First, the former Confederate major general claimed Lee ordered Longstreet to attack early on the morning of July 2, but Longstreet single-handedly delayed the attack until the late-afternoon hours. In doing this, Gordon alleged Longstreet cost the Confederates the opportunity of seizing Little Round Top, which he characterized as "the key to the position" that could have been occupied "in the morning without firing a shot or losing a man." Second, Gordon held that Lee ordered Longstreet to attack at "daybreak" on July 3, but Longstreet again single-handedly delayed that attack until the afternoon hours. Born out of this second criticism was Gordon's assertion that Lee had actually ordered Longstreet to use "three divisions of his corps, and two divisions of A. P. Hill's corps" during the July 3 attack. In making this statement, Gordon alleged Lee had intended for Longstreet to use his other two, First Corps divisions of Lafayette McLaws and John Bell Hood, along with George Pickett's (First Corps), Harry Heth's (Third Corps), and part of William Dorsey Pender's (Third Corps) division, in the attack. As an overarching charge tacked onto these claims, Gordon contended that Longstreet neither "cheerfully," "promptly," "cordially," "intelligently," nor "vigorously" executed his orders on the second and third days; engaged in intentional delay tactics; and demonstrated a general lack of cooperation. In a last twist of the knife, Gordon included his belief that Lee died "believing that he lost Gettysburg at last by Longstreet's disobedience of orders," and that "the testimony on this point is overwhelming."[20]

In making these charges, Gordon was confident all "impartial military critics, after thorough investigation, will consider the following as established." In Gordon's mind, the case was closed; that upon careful examination of the primary source record, all current and future objective history would confirm his claims. Unfortunately for the former Confederate brigadier at Gettysburg, the unsubstantiated nature of his allegations and the slapdash way in which he articulated them exposed Gordon's own partiality, lack of "thorough investigation," reliance on faulty memory, and trust in his and others' dubious postwar conclusions. Published just a few months later, Helen Longstreet's thorough and better-documented response fully unmasked Gordon's bias and the many shortcomings of his charges against General Longstreet's Gettysburg performance, bluntly describing his "assumption" in one instance as "based upon other assumptions founded upon an erroneous presumption."[21]

Gordon's initial allegation that Lee ordered Longstreet to attack early in the morning on July 2 was merely a less precise, watered-down version of what was first asserted by the Army of Northern Virginia's Chief of Artillery, William Pendleton, in January 1873. Pendleton stated at that time, thirty years before Gordon's book, "The ground southwest of the town [Gettysburg] was carefully examined by me after the engagement of July 1.... Its practicable character was reported to our commanding general. He informed me that he had *ordered Longstreet to attack on that front at sunrise next morning.*" Jubal Early, a Confederate Second Corps division commander at Gettysburg, and the Reverend John William Jones, a Confederate chaplain during the war and Secretary of the Southern Historical Society for 14 years after the war, quickly came to the support of Pendleton in the mid–1870s to perpetuate this allegation. Early's support was no surprise either; in a January 1872 address, "The Campaigns of Robert E. Lee," he actually became the first former Confederate to adamantly allege Lee would have certainly won the Battle of Gettysburg had it not been for Longstreet's defiance and slowness. Gordon employed the word "daybreak" when alleging Lee ordered Longstreet to attack early on July 3; however, he avoided the use of "sunrise" or "daybreak" in describing the time when Lee apparently ordered Longstreet to attack on July 2. Rather, he claimed Lee intended Longstreet to make his assault "early the morning of the second day"—a more imperceptible allegation and a clear step back from Early and Pendleton's earlier "sunrise" claims.[22]

Perhaps by 1903, Gordon had realized Pendleton's "Sunrise Attack" theory had completely run its course of believability. Indeed, in her book, Helen spent nearly ten pages addressing the "Sunrise Attack" allegation, ensuring her readers understood Pendleton's claim was a total fabrication based on no evidence whatsoever. Most of those pages were used to re-display correspondence sent to James Longstreet in the mid–1870s from other former Confederate officers and later published in his memoirs. All the authors of these letters to Longstreet—Lee's adjutant general, Colonel Walter H. Taylor; two of Lee's aides, colonels Charles Marshall and Charles S. Venable; Lee's military secretary Armistead Lindsay (A.L.) Long; and one of Longstreet's staff members, Colonel John W. Fairfax—claimed no knowledge of any order that he was to attack at sunrise on July 2. As if that was not enough, Helen also included an excerpt from a published article written by Lafayette McLaws in the 1870s, along with a letter from John Bell Hood to Longstreet, which she pulled from Hood's memoirs, *Advance and Retreat*. Both additional sources either explicitly or implicitly through supplementary detail discounted Pendleton's "Sunrise Attack" allegation.[23]

Just when the reader may have thought Helen was done with Pendleton and had beyond sufficiently proven her case, she returned to the former artillery chief a few pages letter to use his official battle report—dated September 12, 1863—to demonstrate he was "an oral falsifier of history ... established by his own hand." Helen explained that in 1895—when, as assistant state librarian, she was helping General Longstreet with research for his memoirs—Captain Leslie J. Perry, then working on the compilation and publication of the *Official Records*, located Pendleton's official Gettysburg report and informed them of the stark differences between its contents and what the former chief of artillery had said in 1873. In short, Pendleton's report—a large portion of which Helen included in her book—described a frenzy of Confederate reconnaissance activity around midday on July 2. The report showed there was absolutely no dearth of activity on the Confederate side throughout the morning hours as the Confederate High Command, engineers, and other officers continued to attempt to gain a better understanding of the contours of the Federal left. Pendleton even admitted in his report that he first examined the Federal position "soon after sunrise." With initial surveys after sunrise and continued reconnaissance activity throughout the morning, you simply cannot have a Confederate assault on the Federal left at sunrise. Beyond logically making her point, Helen also included a footnote to Pendleton's report, indicating its location in the *Official Records*: "For General Pendleton's official report, see Part II., Vol. XXVII., War Records, pp. 346–354. That is the volume in which will be found all the other Confederate reports referred to in the text." Whether Helen had subsequently accessed Pendleton's report and noted its location in the *Official Records* herself, or whether Perry had passed along its location is not a question of great significance; rather, the mere inclusion of the footnote is most significant in that it is an outward, visible expression of the seriousness in which Helen took her role as historian in composing her book. It certainly was not required that she include such detailed footnotes; in contrast, Gordon's book contains not even one.[24]

Though Longstreet critics have been even more reluctant to give it up over the years, Gordon's early morning attack assertion was equally as fanciful as Pendleton's "Sunrise Attack" theory. In dismantling Gordon's claim, Helen outlined a solid case of well-supported points that realistically should have settled the Longstreet-Gettysburg controversy over a century ago as it pertains to the second day. Whereas Gordon simply threw out an unsupported platitude about Lee's supposed intent to attack early on July 2—a typical mode of argument still employed by Longstreet critics to this day—Helen actually presented substantial evidence that showed Lee was unable to issue Longstreet's attack orders until the late morning hours and the First Corps commander was unable to attack the Federal left until he ultimately did around 4:30 p.m. Helen focused on the often-ignored or overlooked fact that Lee demonstrated considerable uncertainty on the morning of July 2 as to where he wanted to initiate his main point of attack. "As late certainly as eleven o'clock, if not noon," Helen wrote, "General Lee and his staff-officers were still rambling all over a front six miles long, yet undetermined either as to the point or proper route of attack." This is really the core point to be made against claims the First Corps commander single-handedly delayed a Confederate attack from happening on the morning of July 2. An essential extension of that point, which Helen also documented, was Lee's indecision as to what to do with Richard Ewell's Second Corps on July 2, which resulted in multiple staff officers and personal trips to the Confederate left to ascertain if there was a better opportunity to initiate an assault from that front. The widow Longstreet observed, "At sunrise of the 2d, General Lee himself did not know where to attack. He did not know as late as ten or eleven o'clock. His mind was not fully made up until after he came back from Ewell's front ... and had made the final examination on the right." On top of consulting General Longstreet's writings, it appears Helen drew on two primary sources to come to these conclusions: a May 11, 1875, letter from Charles Venable to General Longstreet, and Pendleton's official report. In the Venable-to-Longstreet letter, the former aide to Lee described his assignment and Lee's uncertain state of mind on the morning of July 2:

> About sunrise on the 2d of July I was sent by General Lee to General Ewell to *ask him what he thought of the advantages of an attack on the enemy from his position* [emphasis added]. (Colonel Marshall had been sent with a similar order on the night of the 1st.) General Ewell made me ride with him from point to point of his lines, so as to see with him the exact position of things. Before he got through the examination of the enemy's position, *General Lee came himself to General Ewell's lines* [emphasis added]. In sending the message to General Ewell, General Lee was explicit in saying that the question was whether he should move all the troops around on the right and attack on that side.[25]

It is equally clear that Helen drew much information about Confederate reconnaissance activity on the morning of July 2 from Pendleton's report. Helen's description of that activity, noting how "his [Lee's] staff-officers, Pendleton, Long, Colonel Walker, and Captain Johnston, by Lee's orders, had been examining the ground to the right. Upon Lee's return from the left he rode far to the right and joined Pendleton," coincides with details Pendleton afforded in his report. Helen reasonably concluded from these particulars that "not until then was the attack on the enemy's left by Longstreet finally decided upon. Longstreet said it was not earlier than eleven o'clock when he received his orders to move; from the time consumed by Lee and his staff it was probably later."

The "Fighting Lady's" contention that Lee issued Longstreet's orders around 11 a.m. or later—perhaps as late as noon—is an even more sensible assertion when coupled with additional events and circumstances that served to delay a Confederate attack on July 2. Helen identified and covered a number of these as well, starting with Lee's concealed marching order, which called for Longstreet's two divisions to march along a hidden route to the extreme Confederate right. Of course, before being able to execute a concealed march, first a concealed route had to be found. Though Helen never explicitly maintained Lee ordered his engineer, Captain Samuel Johnston, to locate a concealed route in the late morning hours, she did demonstrate an awareness that Johnston was involved "by Lee's orders" with "examining the ground to the right." Though Helen did not mention them in her book, additional postwar testimonies from Captain Johnston himself and Lafayette McLaws further lent credence to the claim the engineer was involved with reconnaissance duties to locate a concealed route to the right. Along with these scouting activities in preparation for the hidden march, its execution would consume yet more time, especially once it was found that the supposedly concealed route was not so concealed after all. Once the Confederates reached Black Horse Tavern it was discovered that if the march proceeded, Federal signalmen on Little Round Top would observe the column. Therefore, in continued accordance with Lee's concealed marching order,

Longstreet's men were forced to countermarch and pursue another route. Helen noted the consequences of this unforeseen delay ultimately triggered by Lee's directive: "By order of Lee, Longstreet was compelled to move by back roads and lanes, out of sight of the enemy's signal officers on [Little] Round Top. His troops actually marched six or seven miles to reach the point of deployment." Helen also drew attention to the delay caused by the column being led to what would have been an exposed point, asserting, "To avoid the observation of the enemy, [the march] was necessarily slow at best, and made doubly so by the mistakes of Pendleton's guides, who put the troops upon the wrong routes."[26]

Along with Lee's indecision over the point of attack and what to do with Ewell's corps, ongoing reconnaissance activities throughout the morning hours, and the repercussions of the commanding general's concealed marching order, Helen also hit on another major justification for delay on the morning of July 2: the absence of Evander Law's brigade of Hood's division until around noon. With the absence of Pickett's division, Law's brigade made up one-eighth of the First Corps attack force on July 2 and therefore would have very likely proven a critical deficiency for Longstreet. Helen touched on Law's brigade twice, each time only briefly in her narrative, underscoring the great distance ("not less than twenty miles away") the unit had to march to reach Gettysburg despite leaving very early in the morning on July 2, and the time of day it reached the battlefield ("about noon"). In not directly spending much time addressing this particular point, perhaps the widow Longstreet figured that Daniel Sickles, former Federal Third Corps commander at Gettysburg, had provided ample coverage in his introduction to her book. The former Federal corps commander accurately analyzed this topic: "Moreover, if the assault had been made in the morning, Law's strong brigade of Alabamians could not have assisted in the attack, as they did not arrive on the field until noon." Additionally, in her chapter, "Longstreet's Version of the Operations of July 2," Helen included a long excerpt from an article General Longstreet wrote in 1877, titled, "Lee in Pennsylvania," which not only underscored Law's absence until noon, but also touched on the key fact that upon receiving orders to move for the first time around 11 a.m., Longstreet asked Lee's permission to await Law's arrival and the commanding general consented to that request.[27]

Undoubtedly one of the most impressive arguments Helen Longstreet made in her 1904 book was pointing out the fact that Lee's orders for Longstreet on July 2 were to gain and attack up the Emmitsburg Road, and that the Confederate High Command never designated Little Round Top as an attack objective for the assault. In making this argument, Helen addressed another of Gordon's unsupported platitudes, in which he claimed Little Round Top was the key position and by attacking in the late-afternoon hours Longstreet missed the opportunity to seize it easily in the morning. To dismantle Gordon's heedless claim, Helen collectively employed three primary source documents: the official reports of Lee, Longstreet, and Richard Anderson, a Third Corps division commander at Gettysburg whose command was positioned on Longstreet's immediate left on July 2. In a paragraph so remarkable for its time as to warrant quoting in full, Helen established that Longstreet had been directed to attack up the Emmitsburg Road, first to seize the elevated ground at and around the Joseph Sherfy Peach Orchard, and then to press on toward Cemetery

Ridge and Cemetery Hill, both being terrain features located north of Little Round Top:

> It is competent to point out that Longstreet's orders from General Lee were "to move around to gain the Emmitsburg road, on the enemy's left." In short, he was "to attack up the Emmitsburg road," as all the authorities agree. He therefore could not well "occupy" Little Round Top up the Emmitsburg road, because it was but a fraction less than a mile to the east of that road. It is as clear as noonday that Lee had no thought at first, if ever, that Little Round Top was the "key to the position." Lee merely contemplated driving the enemy from some high ground on the Emmitsburg road from which the "more elevated ground" of Cemetery Hill in its rear, more than a mile to the northward of Little Round Top, could be subsequently assailed.

To support this notable assertion, Helen cited one of Lee's official reports, written July 31, 1863, in which the commanding general discussed how Longstreet had been directed to seize and hold some "desired ground" that could be used by "our artillery ... in assailing the more elevated ground beyond, and thus enable us to reach the crest of the ridge." As Helen pointed out, Lee's "desired ground" was the Peach Orchard and the adjacent high ground along the Emmitsburg Road, and "the crest of the ridge"—the primary objective—referred, of course, to Cemetery Hill, or as Helen put it, "It was the 'crest of the ridge,' not the [Little] Round Top, that Lee wished to assail. His eye, from the first, appears to have been steadily fixed upon the Federal centre. That is why he ordered the 'attack up the Emmitsburg road.'" Helen also proceeded to use Longstreet's and Anderson's official reports as compounding evidence to support her argument that "Lee's orders were imperative" and that "Longstreet was ordered to attack a specific position 'up the Emmitsburg road,' which was *not* Little Round Top, as assumed by Gordon." Hammering this point home again, Helen effectively summarized:

> After the war it was discovered that a very early attack on Little Round Top would perhaps have found it undefended, hence the afterthought that General Longstreet was ordered to attack at sunrise. But whatever the hour Longstreet was ordered to attack, it was most certainly not Little Round Top that was made his objective.

Before moving on, it is also well worth mentioning that like she did in the section of her book on Pendleton's "Sunrise Attack" theory, Helen again provided the reader the precise origin of her primary source information: writing in reference to Lee's report, "It is found at page 305 *et seq.*, of Part II., Vol. XXVII., of the printed War Records, easily accessible to everybody"; and on Longstreet's report, "It was written July 27, 1863. On page 358 of the same book he says."[28]

Once the "Sunrise Attack" theory began rapidly losing credibility (though it still persists in some Civil War circles even to this day), the postwar anti–Longstreet persons made some strategic changes to their agenda in the last two decades of the nineteenth century. Along with broadening their critique of Longstreet's alleged actions in the lead-up to his late afternoon attack on July 2—seamlessly shifting their claim from Lee ordered Longstreet to attack at sunrise to Lee intended for Longstreet to attack in the early morning, or even less precisely, in the morning—they also began pushing the contention that Lee expected his "Old Warhorse" to, as Gordon claimed, attack at "daybreak" on July 3.[29]

It would appear a number of historians have seriously and regularly entertained this argument. Fully indulging in this allegation, they have immediately pivoted to analyzing the merits of another follow-on charge that has metastasized over the years, namely that Longstreet neglected to have Pickett's division ready to resume *some kind* of attack on the Federal left or left center, *sometime* early in the morning on July 3. None of the details have ever really been fleshed out, but apparently that is of little importance; rather most historians who have chosen to go down this path seem to settle on the belief that Lee expected Longstreet and Ewell to attack simultaneously in the early morning hours of July 3. In their view, Longstreet really lost touch with reality by the overnight hours of July 2–3 and apparently decided to take matters into his own hands and altogether ignore Lee's attack orders. To them, not having Pickett fully up until the mid-morning hours was unconscionable and clearly demonstrated Longstreet's neglect or unruliness at best, and insubordination at worst.[30]

If these historians had consulted *Lee and Longstreet at High Tide* and examined how Helen Longstreet cogently responded to Gordon's claim in 1904, much time, energy, and ink would have been spared in the last century. Helen cut right to the heart of the matter in just six words: "Lee himself mentions no such order." Indeed, there is no evidence for Gordon's "daybreak" order. Not one officer ever came forward after the battle, just after the war, or in the postwar years with convincing testimony or documentation that afforded specifics on this supposed order. The limited information we do possess concerning Lee's overnight plan for July 3 was also accurately summarized by Helen: "In his [Lee's] final report, penned six months afterwards, he merely mentions that the 'general plan was unchanged,' and Longstreet, reinforced, ordered to attack 'next morning,' no definite hour being fixed." Indeed, if Lee had ordered Longstreet to attack at daylight some time during the overnight hours, what units was Longstreet directed to use in this assault? Where was he ordered to attack? What specific time was he to attack? Helen leveraged Longstreet's official report, which she effectively emphasized would have "passed through Lee's hands…[and been] returned … to the subordinate for correction if there were errors in it," to show Longstreet was unaware of any order or specific plan of attack until he met with Lee in the early morning hours of July 3. It was only then that Lee divulged some specifics on his "unchanged" tactical plan, or as Longstreet wrote in his official report, "the commanding general joined me, and ordered a column of attack to be formed of Pickett's, Heth's, and part of Pender's divisions, the assault to be made directly at the enemy's main position, the Cemetery Hill."[31]

In all actuality, both Longstreet's report and Helen's commentary did not tell the full story, neglecting to mention that Lee did initially come to Longstreet with a near—"unchanged" tactical plan. During their early morning meeting, Lee first called for Longstreet to renew the attack with Hood's and McLaws' divisions against the Federal left center (over much of the same ground they had fought on July 2), supported by Pickett's fresh division. It was only after Longstreet pushed back on this initial proposal by indicating Hood and McLaws represented the army's right flank that Lee agreed to change the principal assault units from McLaws, Hood, and Pickett to Pickett, Heth, and two brigades from Pender's division. Elsewhere in her book, Helen included an excerpt from Lee's report that plainly called attention to these two distinct plans, Lee's initial and the modified:

General Longstreet was delayed by a force occupying the high rocky hills on the enemy's extreme left, from which *his troops could be attacked in reverse as they advanced*. His operations had been embarrassed the day previous by the same cause, and *he now deemed it necessary to defend his flank and rear with the divisions of Hood and McLaws* [emphasis added]. He was therefore reinforced by Heth's division and two brigades of Pender's.

Though this information is necessary for a more comprehensive understanding of how Confederate planning developed in the lead-up to the Pickett-Pettigrew-Trimble Charge, we need not become buried in detail. Helen easily addressed Gordon's base claim of a planned daybreak attack on the First Corps' front by stressing that no evidence has ever been produced showing Lee issued Longstreet any specific attack order during the overnight hours of July 2–3. To the contrary, Longstreet's official report, which would have landed squarely on Lee's desk, claimed he was first issued specific orders when the commanding general joined him in the early morning hours of July 3.[32]

As a separate, but related, part of Gordon's daybreak claim, Longstreet was also criticized for not attacking until the afternoon hours on July 3. Helen easily tossed aside this criticism, as well, in underscoring the significant effect Lee's decision to use units from multiple corps had on the timing of Longstreet's July 3 assault. "No early attack was possible under the conditions imposed by Lee to use Pickett's, Pettigrew's, and Pender's troops, widely separated," Helen maintained, while also drawing attention to Lee's statement from one of his official reports: "The morning was occupied in necessary preparations." In short, Helen rationally deduced that Lee's decision to combine troops from two different corps—the First and Third Corps—to make the attack would inevitably require more coordination, planning, and time, than an assaulting column made up of men from the same corps.[33]

To round out Gordon's accusations against Longstreet's actions on the third day, we must turn to Helen's rebuttal of another one of his "facts established": that Lee intended his "Old Warhorse" to send Hood's (Law) and McLaws' divisions forward with the initial attack. Gordon's contention that Longstreet was to use all three of his First Corps divisions, plus Heth's (Pettigrew) and half of Pender's (Trimble) division, has precipitated many speculative beliefs over the decades that Lee intended for more infantry support to be afforded to Pickett, Pettigrew, and Trimble, both from the beginning and throughout the attack. Resultantly, all kinds of theories have surfaced, ranging from the use of Hood's and McLaws' divisions; Cadmus Wilcox and Edward Perry's (David Lang) Third Corps brigades; additional Third Corps brigades located in Long Lane; to, in the utmost extreme, an entire "second wave" of infantry.

Helen's astute and informed response to Gordon's baseless assertion about the intended use of Hood and McLaws is instructive and once again shows the wide disparity of reliability between the former Confederate brigadier's and the "Fighting Lady's" contentions. In debunking Gordon, Helen did not rely on hearsay or perhaps something General Longstreet had told her before his death; rather, she demonstrated her professionalism, returning to the primary source record and emphasizing what Lee wrote in one of his official reports. Already quoted above, but worth revisiting is Lee's statement: "He [Longstreet] now deemed it necessary to defend his flank and rear with the divisions of Hood and McLaws. He was therefore reinforced by Heth's division and two brigades of Pender's." Characterizing Gordon's charge that "Longstreet was culpable in not sending McLaws and Hood to the attack with Pickett" as yet another "old story," Helen went on to provide some amplifying and cutting commentary as only she could:

> Lee's own utterances show that McLaws and Hood were not to join in the Pickett attack, but, on the contrary, were excluded for other vital service by Lee's specific directions. It is true this was done upon Longstreet's strenuous representations that twenty thousand Federals were massed behind the Round Top to swoop down on the Confederate flank if Hood and McLaws were withdrawn. After viewing the ground himself Lee acquiesced.... Lee was made aware by his own personal observations and by Longstreet's explanations that it was impossible to withdraw Hood and McLaws.

A few paragraphs later, Helen concluded her rebuttal, once again reiterating her main point, that on the morning of July 3, Longstreet expressed a valid argument that Hood's and McLaws' divisions represented the army's right flank and that Lee had given Longstreet his express permission to hold the two divisions in place for that very reason, while also stressing that Hood's and McLaws' men were in no condition to do much of anything after their blistering fight on July 2.

> The troops of Hood and McLaws, in view of their enormous losses [on July 2], were in no condition to support Pickett effectively, even had they been free for that purpose. But it has been shown above by the testimony of both Lee and Longstreet that they were required to maintain the position they had won in the desperate struggle of the evening previous to prevent the twenty-two thousand men of the Union Fifth and Sixth Corps from falling en masse upon Pickett's right flank, or their own flank and rear had they moved in unison with Pickett.[34]

One of Gordon's more all-encompassing accusations against Longstreet's Gettysburg performance may get the postwar prize for number of adjectives used to negatively describe the First Corps commander's alleged actions on July 2–3. In Gordon's view, Longstreet did not "cheerfully," "promptly," "cordially," "intelligently," nor "vigorously" execute his orders on the last two days of the battle. Attempting to definitively prove or disprove whether Longstreet was cheerful or cordial on July 2 and 3 wades quite deeply into the murky waters of speculation. In all actuality, Gordon never really attempted to prove anything; indeed, as with the rest of his claims, he just made an unsupported blanket statement—often an effective mode of argument that easily persuades those who are presupposed to believe it, as many in the South were during the postwar years. Furthermore, this particular allegation about Longstreet's mood was particularly suspect coming from Gordon given there is no evidence suggesting the Second Corps brigadier at Gettysburg even saw Longstreet during the battle. Helen effectively drew attention to this fact in her own narrative: "Both South and North there is a widespread impression that Gordon was a conspicuous figure at Gettysburg. This is erroneous. He was merely a brigade commander there, stationed five miles from Longstreet. It is not certain that he personally saw either Lee or Longstreet while the army was in Pennsylvania." Depending what point on Warfield Ridge you use as a starting point for Longstreet's July 2 position, Gordon's location was more accurately between two and three miles northeast of Longstreet. That detail aside, this realization more importantly leads to the next logical question—what source was Gordon relying on to claim Longstreet was not cheerful or cordial in executing his orders on July 2 and 3? Gordon provided no hint as to his source of information and so we can safely assume this was yet another claim based on hearsay from something another writer alleged in the postwar years.[35]

Alleged lack of cheerfulness and cordiality thus addressed, we now can move on to Gordon's allegation that Longstreet executed his orders slowly, without vigor, and unintelligently at Gettysburg, which Helen addressed directly with several pieces of evidence. First, Helen identified and understood that embedded in Gordon's contention as it related to the second day was, once again, his false belief Lee intended Longstreet to seize Little Round Top. This postwar anti–Longstreet group belief has already been amply covered in this essay, but it is worth reiterating here that almost always when anyone criticized Longstreet in the postwar years (and beyond) for not attacking early or quickly enough on July 2, they did so with the previous false assertions that Lee realized early on July 2 that Little Round Top was the key terrain feature on the southern end of the battlefield and had ordered Longstreet to seize it. Both presuppositions are false. Lee neither designated Little Round Top as key terrain in the lead-up to Longstreet's attack nor did he ever order Longstreet to take it on July 2. Helen not only accurately framed Gordon's contention about Longstreet's alleged slowness around Little Round Top, but she rightly characterized the claim as "'the milk in the cocoanut [sic]' of the charges against Longstreet," while shrewdly discerning that "without consulting the records Gordon has merely followed the lead of some of General Lee's biographers, notably Fitzhugh Lee, who asserts his illustrious uncle [Robert E. Lee] 'expected Longstreet to seize Little Round Top on the 2d of July.' The records clearly show that nothing was farther from General Lee's thoughts."[36]

Regarding alleged slowness, we have already established Longstreet could only execute his orders as quickly as he received them. Many authors over the years have become wrapped up in declaring, "It was Longstreet's responsibility to…." When it comes to taking major actions like moving two divisions to their attack positions along a concealed route, it was not Longstreet's responsibility to do so until he was ordered by his superior. In summary, Helen drew much attention in her book to Lee's indecision throughout the morning hours on July 2, Longstreet's lack of orders until 11 a.m., the consent to wait for Law's brigade, and the many ongoing reconnaissance activities until the late morning hours. Further, Helen employed an 1877 letter to Longstreet from former Longstreet aide John W. Fairfax that slices like a hot knife through butter all three of Gordon's "promptly," "intelligently," and "vigorously" adjectives. Fairfax's letter was an especially valuable source given the former aide was not only a Virginian, but also someone who deeply admired and loved Robert E. Lee (though not to the point of worshipping him as a saint). Concerning Gordon's "promptly" claim, Helen recounted Fairfax's recollection that "you [Longstreet] and General Lee were together the greater part of the day up to about three o'clock or later." This reminiscence, corroborated in other postwar accounts, would naturally precipitate the question: How would Longstreet have gotten away with being intentionally and obviously slow if Lee was physically located with or near him for most of the day up until the 3 p.m. hour or later? Fairfax covered Gordon's "intelligently" claim too when recollecting how John Bell Hood repeatedly petitioned

Longstreet—both through aides and personally—to take his division around Big Round Top in an attempt to flank the Federal left, with the First Corps commander stating, "It is General Lee's order; the time is up,—attack at once." Of course, as has already been established, General Lee's orders were to attack up the Emmitsburg Road. With Fairfax's recollection and this key fact in mind, logically speaking, if Longstreet attacked unintelligently on July 2—perhaps in not fully directing his divisions' might entirely against the postwar anti–Longstreet Holy Grail, Little Round Top—it was actually because he was acting on and carrying out the unintelligent orders that originated not with himself, but with his chief. Lastly, regarding Longstreet's alleged lack of vigor, Helen's use of Fairfax's letter afforded her the opportunity to highlight his last sentence: "General Hood charged, and I spurred to report to you [Longstreet]; found you with hat in hand, cheering on General McLaws' division." Would a sulky and moping Longstreet be found enthusiastically "cheering on" and personally leading his troops into battle? In this case, Fairfax was undoubtedly referring to Joseph Kershaw's brigade of McLaws' division; however, Longstreet also took charge of when to send William Barksdale's brigade forward and personally led William Wofford's brigade into battle.[37]

Speaking of vigor, Helen also included a lengthy excerpt from Longstreet's first postwar article on the battle, published in the *Philadelphia Weekly Times* in 1877, which drew attention to the lack of gusto exhibited on A.P. Hill's and Richard Ewell's front during Longstreet's attack on July 2. In her book's fifth chapter, titled "Longstreet's Version of the Operations of July 2," Helen integrated Longstreet's well-supported claim that he had been "assured ... my flank would be protected by the brigades of Wilcox, Perry, Wright, Posey, and Mahone, moving en echelon, ... that Ewell was to co-operate by a direct attack on the enemy's right, and Hill to threaten his centre ... attack if opportunity offered, and thus prevent reinforcements from being launched either against myself or Ewell." The former First Corps commander's account, as presented, was mostly accurate with the minor exception that, according to Lee's January 1864 battle report, Ewell had more precisely been ordered to make a demonstration against the Federal right simultaneous with Longstreet's attack, to be converted into a real attack if the opportunity arose. Nevertheless, whether a demonstration or an attack, Ewell failed to apply the necessary pressure to the Federal right flank during Longstreet's attack to ensure Union reinforcements could not be shifted against the Confederate divisions of Hood, McLaws, and Richard Anderson, who were besieging the Federal left and center. Likewise, A.P. Hill (and Lee, who was located on Hill's front once Longstreet's attack began on July 2) neglected to ensure, at the very least, all five brigades of Anderson's division engaged. Resultantly, only Wilcox, Perry (under Lang), and Wright attacked; Posey saw limited action; and Mahone never advanced at all.[38] Of course, unlike Helen's inclusion of Longstreet's substantiated recounting of these failings, Gordon's Lost Cause–inspired focus on pushing an agenda of historical memory over producing objective history led him to completely omit the shortcomings of the Virginian generals, Ewell[39] and Hill, in his coverage of the July 2 battle.

Lastly, with respect to Gordon's claim that Longstreet did not promptly, intelligently, or vigorously handle the Pickett-Pettigrew-Trimble attack on July 3, Helen once against returned to the *Official Records* and Lee's official report—specifically the commanding general's assertion that "the morning was occupied in necessary preparations, and the battle recommenced in the afternoon of the 3d." Helen tacked on an additional, astute observation that "time was not an essential element in the problem of the 3d. The Federal army was then all up," before establishing later in her narrative that Lee was an active participant in the planning and preparation for the July 3 attack: "General Lee was for a time personally present while this work was going on, conversing with Pickett concerning the proper dispositions and making various suggestions. He therefore knew by personal observation, before the charge was made, exactly what troops were included and what were not."[40] Indeed, there are many accounts that describe Lee and Longstreet working collaboratively on the morning of July 3 to prepare for the attack and to ensure all the principal officers understood their roles and responsibilities.[41] Of course, Longstreet was the attack commander and had the principal responsibility of planning and executing the assault, but that does not detract from the fact that Lee was with or near Longstreet throughout the morning hours and most certainly would have pointed out any major errors or oversights in preparation.[42] Helen went into little additional detail on the intricacies of Longstreet's July 3 attack, probably since most of Gordon's accusations were July 2-focused and maybe even more likely because she clearly believed July 3 was a tragic event, but ultimately a moot historical topic. "It is admitted by almost if not quite all authority on the subject that Pickett's charge was hopeless," she pronounced, before further maintaining that the assault "proved the most disastrous and destructive in Confederate annals" and "was, in fact, the death-knell of the Southern republic."[43]

Not only did Helen address specific points of contention related to Longstreet's tactical performance at Gettysburg, but she also spoke to the Longstreet-Gettysburg controversy more broadly by emphasizing what has probably always been the most effective argument against detractors' allegations: the continuation of Robert E. Lee and James Longstreet's close personal and professional relationship well after the Battle of Gettysburg. How could Lee stand to have a direct subordinate around him who had sulked, dragged his feet, and sabotaged attack plans when he did not get his way, as critics have claimed? Why would Lee want to continue to work with someone who, as critics have also alleged, deliberately defied or ignored his orders? Further, why would Lee continue to have a personal relationship, even after the war, with a former subordinate whose insubordination caused the Confederate loss at the most important battle of the war, as Gordon alleged? Throughout his time as commander of the Army of Northern Virginia, Lee consistently had subordinates he considered incompetent, ineffectual, or irascible transferred out of the army to another theater of action,[44] but here was Longstreet who, according to many of his critics over the decades, demonstrated all of those negative qualities at Gettysburg, but somehow managed to remain in Lee's good graces as his senior and principal subordinate right down to the surrender at Appomattox. Framing the entire controversy in this way, as Helen does in *Lee and Longstreet at High Tide*, truly exposes the absurdity of the overwhelming majority of allegations made against Longstreet's Gettysburg performance since the 1870s.

Gordon's claim of "overwhelming" testimony showing Lee died "believing that he lost Gettysburg at last by Longstreet's disobedience of orders" fits nicely into that category of absurd allegations that has nevertheless tacitly seeped into many Gettysburg battle narratives over the last century.[45] Broad and sensational statements like these are more easily believed and perpetuated than well-documented, lengthy, and sometimes necessarily complex explanations to the contrary. Further, even when these broad statements are not believed exactly as they are presented when taken in full, the damage is typically already done and leads to misguided belief in other less salacious accusations against Longstreet's Gettysburg performance.

To Helen, Gordon's allegation possessed a "gauzy character," suggesting her belief it was an elusive or vague story designed to thinly veil whatever was underneath—in this case, the truth. As Helen pointed out, nothing has ever been found in Lee's public or private correspondence during or after the war indicating he always or even increasingly thought he lost at Gettysburg because of "Longstreet's disobedience of orders." As Helen emphasized, the contrary was true—Lee and Longstreet continued to maintain a very close personal and professional relationship after Gettysburg. Helen quoted extensively from several letters between Lee and Longstreet in the months and years after the July 1863 battle. Less than 90 days after Longstreet was allegedly ignoring Lee's orders and despising him for his tactical approach on the second and third days at Gettysburg (as Gordon and others alleged), Longstreet wrote to Lee while in Richmond preparing two of his divisions to join Braxton Bragg's Army of the Tennessee in Georgia: "If I did not think our move a necessary one, my regrets at leaving you would be distressing to me…. Our affections for you are stronger, if it is possible for them to be stronger, than our admiration for you." Lee soon wrote back after Longstreet's actions largely facilitated the Confederate victory at the Battle of Chickamauga: "My whole heart and soul have been with you and your brave corps in your late battle…. Finish the work before you, my dear General, and return to me. I want you badly, and you cannot get back too soon." In yet another letter to Longstreet in October 1863, Lee reiterated his ceaseless affection and dependence on Longstreet: "But I missed you dreadfully, and your brave corps. Your cheerful face and strong arms would have been invaluable. I hope you will soon return to me. I trust we may soon be together again. May God preserve you and all with you." Just six days before Lee sent this letter to Longstreet, his "Old Warhorse's" first wife, Maria, gave birth to a son in Petersburg, Virginia, on October 20—Longstreet's first child following the January–February 1862 deaths of three of his children, who tragically died during a scarlet fever epidemic in Richmond. Tellingly of his affection for his commanding general, Longstreet named his new son Robert Lee Longstreet—after General Lee—who even agreed to be his namesake's godfather. The significance of this fact cannot be overstated. Here, a few months after the Battle of Gettysburg, was James Longstreet naming his newborn son after the man he supposedly could no longer tolerate and wanted to get away from because of tactical differences at Gettysburg. Likewise, here was Robert E. Lee agreeing to be godfather to the son of a subordinate whose derelict and insubordinate actions, according to Gordon and others, cost him the victory at Gettysburg.

A few months after the Army of Northern Virginia's surrender at Appomattox

Courthouse, as Lee and Longstreet returned to civilian life, the former commanding general wrote a letter to his senior subordinate that not only fully demonstrated the depth of his love for Longstreet, but also where he ranked Longstreet in military ability:

> I am delighted to hear that your arm is still improving & hope it will soon be restored. You are however becoming so accomplished with your left hand, as not to need it. You must remember me very kindly to Mrs. Longstreet & all your children. I have not had an opportunity yet to return the compliment she paid me. I had while in Richmond a great many inquiries after you, & learned that you intended commencing business in New Orleans. *If you become as good a merchant as you were a soldier I shall be content. No one will then excel you, & no one can wish you more success & more happiness than I. My interest & affection for you will never cease, & my prayers are always offered for your prosperit* [emphasis added]—I am most truly yours R E Lee

"No one will then excel you." These are Lee's words that bear repeating over and over. No one means no one. Not Jackson, Stuart, Ambrose Powell (A.P.) Hill, and certainly not the postwar Lee worshippers, Jubal Early and John B. Gordon, among others. Does the content and tone of Lee's letter sound like a general still stewing over a subordinate's alleged disobedience of orders at the battle many believed determined the Confederacy's fate? As if these examples were not enough to convince those who persist in alleging Lee and Longstreet's relationship was strained after Gettysburg or that, as Gordon claimed, Lee believed Longstreet's actions there cost him the victory, Lee wrote one of Longstreet's business partners in New Orleans just a week after he sent the correspondence quoted above: "I do not consider my partnership with him [Longstreet] yet dissolved, and *shall not let him go during life*" [emphasis added]. Collectively, all these examples beg the questions: Was this correspondence demonstrative of a relationship embittered over the Southern loss at Gettysburg? Further, does it show any sign that Lee felt betrayed by anything Longstreet allegedly did at Gettysburg? Had affection and trust been lost? Based on the primary source evidence, as presented above and in Helen's book, the answer must be a resounding no, or as the "Fighting Lady" appropriately summarized, "Their [Lee and Longstreet] personal friendship continued after Gettysburg as it was before. It was of the closest and most cordial description. General Lee always manifested the highest regard for General Longstreet, and continued to manifest undiminished confidence in his military capacity, fighting qualities, and subordination. There is no manifestation of a withdrawal of that confidence after Gettysburg."[46]

Another effective mode of argument Helen deployed against Gordon's claim was that Longstreet's detractors did not begin attacking his Gettysburg performance until after Lee's death. Indeed, Longstreet had publicly voiced his support for reconciliation between North and South as early as 1867, became a Southern Republican and Catholic, and questioned Lee's judgment at Gettysburg in a series of interviews in which he participated for William Swinton's 1866 book, *Campaigns of the Army of the Potomac*, all well before Lee's passing in October 1870. However, Pendleton, Early, and Jones, the three initial critics, did not begin their campaign against Longstreet until January 1872.[47] If Longstreet committed all these unforgivable sins before Lee's death and these critics were most peeved about Longstreet's commentary on Lee's judgment at Gettysburg, why would they wait until after their protagonist passed to attack Longstreet? If their contentions regarding Longstreet's Gettysburg performance were so foolproof and Lee had apparently increasingly come to believe he lost the battle because of something Longstreet did or did not do, why not roll out those charges before Lee died?

Helen convincingly argued that Lee would not have approved of the anti–Longstreet group's coordinated assertions against his "Old Warhorse" and would have clearly expressed that disapproval. As General Longstreet wrote in several of his postwar writings, Helen reiterated, "He [Longstreet] has always regretted deeply that this discussion was not opened before the death of General Lee. If the charges so vehemently urged had been preferred or even suggested in Lee's lifetime, Longstreet does not believe they would have needed any reply from him. General Lee would have answered them himself and set history right." Helen further observed, "Not one word appears to have been published openly accusing him [Longstreet] of disobedience at Gettysburg until the man [Lee] who could forever have silenced all criticism was in his grave," while stressing with some degree of sarcasm that "the cruel slander" claiming Longstreet "had disobeyed Lee's most vital orders, causing the loss of the Gettysburg battle and the ultimate fall of the Confederate cause" was a "strange discovery ... not made until some years after the battle and General Lee's death. Thereafter for two decades the South was sedulously taught to believe that the Federal victory was wholly the fortuitous outcome of the culpable disobedience of General Longstreet."[48]

Helen employed another effective mode of argument when addressing Gordon's last contention, which has often been overlooked by those seeking to refute similar claims over the decades. In their attempt to defend Lee's every wartime action and decision, especially every one he made at Gettysburg, the postwar anti–Longstreet group actually wound up hurting him. Indeed, a large consequence of the focus on and longevity of the Longstreet-Gettysburg controversy—soon smoldering on into its 15th decade of debate—has been that many of Lee's mistakes and shortcomings at the battle have been increasingly and more sharply exposed. Additionally, in twisting the record and pushing an agenda in the way they did to libel Longstreet—putting words in Lee's mouth and thoughts in his head by way of fabrication and speculation—the postwar anti–Longstreet group actually created little more than a distorted postwar construction of their former chief, who could unfortunately no longer think and speak for himself. Helen pointed out that the creation of this artificial Lee was ultimately unnecessary: "Short-sighted partisans seemingly argued that the disparagement of Longstreet was necessary to save the military reputation of Lee. But Lee's great fame needed no such sacrifice." Former Confederate president Jefferson Davis, while certainly no close friend to Longstreet, nevertheless grew to understand the clear, negative effect Lee's postwar "eulogists" had on the Virginia general in their attempt to defend him at all costs to the detriment of others. Like Helen, Davis noted how Lee's reputation "needs no ornamentation," while he denounced postwar efforts to fashion a "foundation of fiction in disparagement of others" and, likewise, a "fictitious elevation at the expense of others." In highlighting the boomerang effect of how the anti–Longstreet group's attempt to defend Lee wound up backfiring on itself and its protagonist, Helen shared a pertinent quote from Captain Leslie J. Perry of the War Records Department: "Many illusions of Lee's misguided friends ... are unwittingly doing deadly injury to his military fame by magnifying the mistakes of Gettysburg and ascribing them to another." Asserting similarly on the consequences of this boomerang effect, Helen claimed that even as early as her time of writing in 1904, "most" students and historians of military history "severely criticize Lee's operations from start to finish, particularly the hopeless assaults he persisted in making, and for the lack of concert. It is held generally now that the dreadful result fully justified Longstreet's protests against attacking the Federals in that position."[49]

Like any book covering some aspect of the Battle of Gettysburg, Helen's was not perfect. One minor and two larger deficiencies should be pointed out and addressed. As to the smaller error, Helen contends in the fourth chapter of her book, titled "Gordon's 'Established Facts' and Pendleton's Fulminations," that William Pendleton was the first ex-Confederate officer in the postwar years to attempt to hoist the blame for the South's loss at Gettysburg on Longstreet. Of course, Helen was referring to Pendleton's infamous "Sunrise Attack" speech he gave in Lexington, Virginia, on January 17, 1873. "The first positive utterance holding General Longstreet responsible for the defeat at Gettysburg, through failure to obey Lee's orders, came from Rev. Dr. William N. Pendleton," Helen charged. Pendleton was actually not the first, though; that honor, and he most certainly would have considered it one, belongs to Jubal Early, who alleged a year earlier on January 19, 1872, "He [Lee] then determined to make the attack from our right on the enemy's left, and left us for the purpose of ordering up Longstreet's corps in time to begin the attack at dawn next morning. That corps was not in readiness to make the attack until four o'clock in the afternoon of the next day."[50]

Helen's first sizable mistake was advancing speculation on the issue of Longstreet's two alternate tactical proposals at Gettysburg. On the evening of July 1 and again on the morning of July 2, Longstreet proposed to Lee that the army execute a turning movement off the Federals' left flank; locate and occupy a good defensive position between the Federal army and the strategically important Northern cities of Baltimore and Washington, D.C.; and invite the Federals to attack them in position. In this first instance, Longstreet advocated for a redeployment of the army, followed by the use of the tactical defensive. The second of Longstreet's proposals germinated during the overnight hours of July 2 and into the early morning of the third day. Very likely resulting from Longstreet's recognition that Lee was fixed upon continuing the tactical offensive on July 3 (and probably inspired by Hood's findings just before his division's July 2 attack), he explored and apparently was prepared to set in motion a plan to move some or all his corps—exactly how much is unclear— around the Round Tops to attack the Federals in the flank and rear. Note that in this second instance, Longstreet demonstrated he was resolved to the fact that the army would remain at Gettysburg, and in attacking around the Round Tops in that fashion, would obviously have employed the tactical offensive. On Longstreet's first proposal, the turning movement, Helen alleged it "was far more promising of success" in comparison with "attacking the Federals in that position" at Gettysburg. On the second proposal, the flank attack on July 3, Helen believed it "was the only daylight attack possible from Longstreet's front on the morning of the 3rd" and characterized it as "the feasible early attack." The issue here is not whether Helen was reasonable or unreasonable in her assessment of the feasibility of Longstreet's proposals, rather, the issue is that she entertained speculation and advanced any opinion at all on their feasibility. In doing so, she strayed from her disciplined adherence to the otherwise rather academic approach she took in analyzing and prosecuting her case. Advancing hypothetical speculation, and even worse, trying to prove supposition one way or the other, is simply not the territory of a historian or a writer engaging in the historical trade.[51]

The final mistake is more of a tongue-in-cheek observation than an earnest criticism. On multiple occasions in her book, Helen advanced what turned out to be her mistaken prediction that Longstreet's war record, and specifically his actions at Gettysburg, would need no future defense. Naïve to the weighty influence the postwar Lost Cause, anti–Longstreet narrative would have on many future historians after 1904, Helen declared that Longstreet's "war record … stands unassailable—needing no defenders," while revealing that in the general's last years he even "deemed it unnecessary to make defence of his military integrity, save such as may be found in his memoirs, 'Manassas to Appomattox,' [sic] published nearly ten years since. He has held that his deeds stand on the impartial pages of the nation's records—their own defender."[52] Helen was on to something in that last sentence, at least when it comes to Longstreet's "deeds" at Gettysburg. The primary source record does indeed serve as Longstreet's "own defender"—that is, when it is used fairly, examined objectively, and without strings attached to any personal agenda or bias. Indeed, as events turned out, Helen and her aging husband were not much for reading the tea leaves at the turn of the twentieth century. Because of how effectively the postwar anti–Longstreet cabal carried out its work, Longstreet's record, especially as it pertained to Gettysburg, would certainly require help from others in the decades to follow.

If there is one incontrovertible thing to be said about Helen Longstreet, it is that she was a fighter. Whatever she did, she gave it her all. Whatever her passion—and she had many throughout her near-century-long life—she attacked it head-on. Despite her enduring zeal for political, environmental, and conservational issues, her greatest passion was always her late husband, General Longstreet. And even though she was undoubtedly a fighter, she had a vast capacity to love and her passion for defending General Longstreet's military record was almost certainly never born out of hate for his detractors, but instead from an undying love and admiration for Lee's "Old Warhorse."

Indeed, Helen and General Longstreet's relationship, briefly initiated in the mid–1880s and then quickly blossoming a decade later, was nothing if not a testimonial of each one's capacity to love deeply. Helen first met General Longstreet at the young age of 21 when she was attending Georgia Baptist Female Seminary in 1884. Longstreet's only daughter, Louise "Lulu" Longstreet (later Whelchel), then only 12 years old, was also a student at the seminary and Helen later described how Lulu regularly invited her and some other girls to Longstreet's home, where they "viewed with much awe the swords, pistols, and other war relics." Longstreet was then serving as a U.S. marshal for northern Georgia[53] and spent the weekdays in Atlanta before returning to Gainesville each weekend. On one afternoon in November 1884, while Lulu, Helen, and a few other girls were at Longstreet's house, perhaps admiring his war memorabilia as was their custom, the general himself rode up "from the [Gainesville] station on a big mule." A brief, but memorable conversation, at least for Helen, was struck up between the then-21-year-old and Longstreet, whereby the general asked her name. Upon learning her last name was "Dortch," Longstreet expressed some elusive familiarity and Helen quickly proceeded to inform him her uncle was Lewis Dortch, who had served in Longstreet's First Corps and died at the May 1864 Battle of the Wilderness on the same day the general received his near-fatal wound. In the ensuing moments, Longstreet proceeded to kiss Helen on both cheeks out of respect and compassion for her uncle's memory, while expressing fondness for her "gold" braids of hair. "They are like the sunshine on the leaves out there!" Longstreet exclaimed, pointing to the colorful blanket of autumn leaves strewn about his property. Helen later admitted of this moment: "Looking back across the years I know that life has given me few moments of ecstasy to equal that one."[54]

As has already been recounted, Helen and General Longstreet did not meet for a second time until ten years later, when Helen was the assistant state librarian in Atlanta and Longstreet was busy conducting research for and writing his memoirs. On one of those visits from Gainesville to the State Library in Atlanta, Longstreet informed Helen that his train would arrive late after the library closed and so he would call on her at her house. To fully do justice to the rest of this tender story, Helen's own narrative is worth quoting in full:

> He was waiting in the reception hall by the stairway as I came down to meet him. My foot caught in the tangle of my train as I descended and near the foot of the stair I literally fell headlong into his arms, which were outstretched to catch me. Before I could regain my breath or feet, he was kissing me on one cheek and then on the other. "Oh!" I stammered finally, "will you never let me go?" "Not while life lasts," he answered.[55]

Outdoing even this hallmark moment was a letter General Longstreet penned Helen in the summer of 1897, shortly before their wedding at the Governor's Mansion in Atlanta on September 8. Helen was then in Lithia Springs, Georgia, and apparently Longstreet would travel the 70 miles from Gainesville every weekend to see her. In the interim, he would send her a letter every day. Looking back years later in 1917, Helen described this collection of letters' physical state as "yellow with the weight of twenty years," while characterizing their sentimental value as nothing but "sacred." In this one particular letter, the 76-year-old, soon-to-be groom revealed to his 34-year-old, soon-to-be bride a reflective prayer he had beseeched to God the evening before: "Last night I found myself praying for the love that might move my God to take me closer to His love; then it came to me that the love of my Helen in all her preciousness and sweetness was God's answer." Though Longstreet divulged he was occasionally plagued by moments of doubt with respect to their 42-year age gap— "It sometimes comes to me that your youth should not be linked with my old age, and our ways might be separate"—those fleeting moments were always surmounted by his overwhelming "thought that God could not find those ways and it would be folly for us to try to find them." "We will make the journey together and let us hope to make it joyful and acceptable before Him.... God bless you and keep you ever fair and more and more lovely," Longstreet affectionately concluded.[56]

In the summer of 1898, the newlyweds departed for the Republic of Mexico for their honeymoon, where they visited several Mexican-American War battlefields on which General Longstreet had seen combat over a half century before in 1846–1847. Helen later declared that "the battle-fields ... were of supreme interest," while unsurprisingly contending they were that much more comprehensible and enjoyable with General Longstreet by her side: "It was my great privilege—to-day a cherished memory—to go over the fields that stretch away from Chapultepec with a war-worn soldier who fifty years earlier had there learned his first lessons in real warfare."[57] As their seven-year marriage undoubtedly slipped by too quickly before Longstreet's death in January 1904, the couple split enjoying time in their small home in Gainesville with traveling the country together for the general's duties as U.S. Commissioner of Railroads,[58] and to attend numerous battle anniversaries, veterans events, and monument unveilings.

On top of her *Lee and Longstreet at High Tide* publication just after the general's passing, Helen continued to write articles on Longstreet, which were either printed as stand-alone essays in newspapers or included in some of her other books. In addition to writing, Helen also made many speeches on Longstreet in the first half of the twentieth century, continuing to tout and defend his military record. Following Helen's time of political activism in the Virgin Islands throughout the early-to-mid–1930s, where she even applied to be lieutenant governor of St. Croix in 1933, her passion to truly memorialize General Longstreet for future generations reached its zenith in the late 1930s. She helped to inaugurate the Longstreet Memorial Association on the 75th anniversary of the Battle of Gettysburg in 1938 to "meet the revived slander [against Longstreet] and to correct a long neglect"; commissioned a painting of General Longstreet by artist Howard Chandler Christy that was unveiled at the September 1939 New York World's Fair[59]; and in the years leading up to World War II, pushed to have an equestrian statue of Longstreet erected on the Gettysburg Battlefield. Though Helen mused in March 1940 that "General Longstreet ... will soon stand among statues of the great commanders that have long adorned Pennsylvania's great field.... The 'Old Warhorse' mounted again on Hero, will call from the shadows of the Round Tops and the scarred passes of Devil's Den, until marble and bronze crumble," the statue was not to be and the idea was disrupted and ultimately scrapped due to the onset of America's involvement in World War II.[60]

Helen Longstreet made sure her love and respect for General Longstreet extended beyond the grave and was made apparent. Just after Helen's death in 1962, the widow Longstreet's niece, Mrs. R.H. Rumph, revealed Helen "left explicit, written instructions ... she not be buried in Gainesville" at the Longstreet family plot in Alta Vista Cemetery. Rumph affirmed she was "complying with her aunt's request" and never disclosed any details as to the underlying reasoning behind Helen's crypt internment in a rather random, lower-level alcove of Westview Cemetery Abbey in Atlanta. Direct descendants of General Longstreet have since provided the explanation, noting how Helen did not think it appropriate or respectful to be buried with Longstreet's first wife of over 40 years (1848–1889) and so the loyal "Fighting Lady" chose to be interred 60 miles southwest of the man she spent so many of her waking years honoring and defending.[61]

Besides her enduring love and respect for him, what was so remarkable about General Longstreet that he remained Helen's deepest passion for the last 58 years of her life? Perhaps it was the fact that she saw so much of herself in Longstreet—that same fighting spirit and indomitable energy, that same reverence for authenticity and candidness despite the cost. Indeed, Helen once described how Longstreet had "always been a figure of more sublime courage in the gathering storms of '67 and the years that followed than on any of the brilliant fields of the Civil War," while admitting that she "love[d] best to think of him, not as the warrior leading his legions to victory, but as the grand citizen after the war ... ended, nobly dedicating himself to the rehabilitation of his broken people, offering a brave man's homage to the flag of the established government, and standing steadfast in all the passions, prejudices, and persecutions of that unhappy period." At long last, Helen concluded that her passion and admiration for Longstreet ultimately stemmed from his "love ... honor and soul [which] crystallized into a being of wonderful majesty, immovable as Gibraltar." To Helen, even the infirmities of Longstreet's last years, "Blindness, deafness, paralysis, the decay of physical faculties, failed to move his dauntless courage or quell his splendid determination."[62]

James Longstreet with his second wife, Helen Dortch Longstreet, in 1901 (The Longstreet Society).

Instances of Helen Longstreet's demonstration of love for and loyalty to Longstreet for five decades after his death were manifold: the continued articles and speeches, the Longstreet Memorial Association, the commissioning of the massive painting of the general, and the push to erect an equestrian statue of Lee's "Old Warhorse" on the Gettysburg Battlefield. However, none of these weighty tributes would ever top the combination of ferocity and precision she brought to bear in the

Exterior, Westview Cemetery Abbey, Atlanta, Georgia. When Helen Longstreet died in May 1962, she was laid to rest just inside the bottom left alcove's glass doors (Author's Collection).

composition of her 1904 book, *Lee and Longstreet at High Tide*. Despite her adherence to tried-and-true methods of historical scholarship while showing a dedicated dependence on the use of the *Official Records* and other primary source documentation to support her arguments and counter-arguments, most historians over the years have chosen to pan Helen's work for insufficient and misguided reasons. Falsely maligning her writing as biased and speculative, these same historians have apparently deemed it prudent to trust many of the postwar anti–Longstreet group's writings in fashioning their own battle interpretations and narratives, despite that group's proven track record to regularly advance dubious hearsay accusations (such as all of Gordon's allegations in his *Reminiscences*, for example) and sometimes devise completely fabricated stories (such as Pendleton's "Sunrise Attack" theory). Many postwar anti–Longstreet group writings have been given a pass over the years and remain mainstay sources—at least enough to be considered, if not consulted—while Helen Longstreet's work has rarely even been given a fighting chance. Such has been the unfortunate way of things undergirding most treatments of the Longstreet-Gettysburg Controversy since the early 1900s.

Perhaps this persistent trend in historical methodology should not altogether come as a big surprise today upon considering the typical treatment of and reaction to James Longstreet's postwar writings. Indeed, one of the major overlooked legacies of the postwar anti–Longstreet group's concerted agenda against Lee's "Old Warhorse" was the continued denigration of his writings; labeling anything written by an author with last name "Longstreet" a fabrication and untruth.[63] The residue of this legacy blatantly manifested itself as recently as 1993, with the publication of Robert K. Krick's essay, titled, "If Longstreet Says So.... It is Most Likely Not True." Limiting oneself only to the very first page of the essay, Krick characterizes Longstreet's postwar writings as "late-life posturing" and "poisonous ventures"

Essay 6. Suppressed No More 169

that "reveal[ed] glimpses of his [Longstreet's] soul that left observers repulsed," while concurrently making his Lost-Cause–inspired stance clear in stating Longstreet "stray[ed] from the demonstrable truth and regularly contradict[ed] his own accounts from one [postwar] article to the next." Krick even quotes from a postwar Petersburg, Virginia, newspaper that described Longstreet's writings as "vaporings of senility and pique," leading the historian to claim this characterization "echoed the views of millions of Southerners."[64]

Top: Interior, Westview Cemetery Abbey, Atlanta, Georgia. Site of Helen Longstreet's crypt internment. The author has marked her final resting placing with an arrow. *Bottom:* Close-up of Helen Longstreet's grave marker. "Widow of Gen. Jas. Longstreet"—a fitting memorial for a woman whose greatest passion was defending her late husband's memory (Author's Collection).

The reader will have to go elsewhere for a fuller analysis of James Longstreet's postwar writings,[65] but suffice it to remind readers here that a quotation from a postwar Virginia-based newspaper should not necessarily be considered a bellwether source of non-partiality when it comes to judging the actual merit of the non–Virginian James Longstreet's postwar writings.[66] Neither should the integrity of Longstreet's writings be determined based on their numerical unpopularity in a postwar South that largely despised his political decisions and his questioning of Virginia general (and postwar marble man) Robert E. Lee's tactical judgment at the "High Tide of the Confederacy." Additionally, all the ways in which Krick labels Longstreet's postwar writings could in fact just as easily be turned around and applied to the postwar anti–Longstreet group of writers. Did they posture? Did they inject poison into the Gettysburg source record? Did they reveal glimpses of their souls? Did they often stray from the demonstrable truth? Any reasonable historian and student of the war would have to admit that the answer to all these questions is "yes."

Yet, what in fact matters most to our understanding of the Gettysburg battle and Longstreet's actions is not the fulfillment of some partisan historical agenda, one way or the other, but actually getting to the truth of the matter, or at least closer to the truth by way of a detailed examination of the primary source record, coupled with careful cross-referencing of postwar documentation. Touching on what she believed to be the value of Longstreet's writings specifically, Helen Longstreet observed, "How closely he is confirmed in all essential particulars by the records is marvellous [sic]. In this regard it is to be noted that in all these controversies his statements have always stood analysis in the light of all the evidence far better than those of his reckless critics," while also contending "Nobody familiar with his [Longstreet's] open character and candid manner of discussing its [Gettysburg's] various phases can doubt for one instant that he tells the details of Gettysburg exactly as they occurred, in so far as his personal part was concerned." Undoubtedly, not everything Longstreet wrote in the postwar years about Gettysburg was accurate; perfection eluded every postwar writer who participated in the battle to lesser and greater degrees. In many of Longstreet's earlier writings in the 1870s and 1880s, he was largely constrained to personal recollection, dependence on the limited sources he possessed, and correspondence with other surviving officers. The compilation of the *Official Records* associated with the Battle of Gettysburg (Volume 27 in three parts) did not commence until the late 1880s, with publication in 1889. Longstreet did have some access to those records via Helen and Captain Leslie J. Perry when researching and writing *From Manassas to Appomattox* in the 1890s. Like his other writings, when weighed upon the whole, Longstreet's memoirs were consistent and reliable; albeit marred with a noticeable (and understandable, by that point) bitterness toward his detractors and resentment toward the glowing postwar treatment of other officers (like "Stonewall" Jackson, for example), which led him to stray at points into making unnecessary and misleading accusations of his own. Overall, as I have written and stated elsewhere, I agree with academic historian William Garrett Piston's evenhanded characterization of Longstreet's postwar writings on Gettysburg: "While his account of the battle was not without errors, it was essentially accurate. Indeed, his writings may have won considerable approval had he taken into account, when composing them, that Lee had become a saint."[67]

The perpetuation of the often-stated, "You cannot trust any of Longstreet's writings" (just like the ever-prevalent, "Lee intended for Longstreet at Gettysburg to") needs to be accurately and properly framed for what it is—another vestige of the postwar Lost Cause, anti–Longstreet group's agenda that has managed to survive into the present day. As a natural extension of that commonplace statement, Helen Longstreet's *Lee and Longstreet at High Tide* has just as regularly been summarily dismissed over the decades as biased and speculative. To the contrary, when it comes to analysis and coverage of the Longstreet-Gettysburg Controversy, it is well beyond time for the dependence on long-standing historical methodologies and dated mindsets, along with their resulting tainted interpretations, to cease and reform. As part of that reform, before writing a new work that attempts to touch on this long-standing controversy, perhaps it is high time for Gettysburg historians to crack open a copy of Helen Longstreet's *High Tide* and carefully consider her amply researched (for the time) arguments and counter-arguments, which are frequently articulated in an even more cogent and disarming way than her late husband was ever able to muster against his critics. In closing her book, Helen summary outlined the vital source of evidence on her side and the truth revealed therein, which is only fitting and appropriate to end with here:

> The personal letters and official reports of Robert E. Lee, reproduced in this work, clearly established that from Gettysburg to Appomattox Longstreet continued to be Lee's most trusted Lieutenant; their mutual affection and admiration had no diminution. The official reports of Lee and Pendleton herein given make it clear as noonday that Longstreet disobeyed no orders of his chief at Gettysburg, and was at no time "slow" or "obstructive" on that great field. The man who, under the weight of official evidence massed in this little story, can still raise his voice to assert that "Longstreet was slow and balky" at Gettysburg, takes direct issue with the official reports of Robert E. Lee and the Rev. Mr. Pendleton, and his becomes a quarrel with the war records.... This is the story, short enough for the busy; clear and straight enough for the young. It is the story of sentiment as well as reverence and admiration, growing up from childhood, of him who led the forlorn hope at Gettysburg. But behind the sentiment is the unassailable truth. It is undeniably the story of the records, of the events exactly as they occurred. It is fully corroborated by all the probabilities; in no part disputed by one.[68]

Chapter Notes

Essay 1

1. J. William Jones, D.D., "The Longstreet-Gettysburg Controversy: Who Commenced It," *Southern Historical Society Papers*, 23: 348. Hereafter cited as *SHSP*; John Wesley Brinsfield, *The Spirit Divided: Memoirs of Civil War Chaplains: The Confederacy*, 192–194; *A Guide to the J. William Jones Papers, 1861–1892*. Accession 21294. Personal papers collection, The Library of Virginia, Richmond, Virginia, https://ead.lib.virginia.edu/vivaxtf/view?docId=lva/vi01129.xml; David S. Williams, "J. William Jones (1836–1909)," *New Georgia Encyclopedia*, https://www.georgiaencyclopedia.org/articles/history-archaeology/j-william-jones-1836-1909.

2. *SHSP* 4: 49–87; *SHSP* 5: 52–87, 162–194, 257–287; Thomas L. Connelly and Barbara L. Bellows, *God and General Longstreet: The Lost Cause and the Southern Mind*, 34; Cory M. Pfarr, *Longstreet at Gettysburg: A Critical Reassessment*, 11.

3. Jones, "The Longstreet-Gettysburg Controversy," *SHSP* 23: 342–343; James Longstreet, "Lee in Pennsylvania," *Annals of the War*, 434.

4. Jones, "The Longstreet-Gettysburg Controversy," *SHSP* 23: 343–344; *A Guide to the J. William Jones Papers*, https://ead.lib.virginia.edu/vivaxtf/view?docId=lva/vi01129.xml.

5. William Swinton, *Campaigns of the Army of the Potomac: A Critical History of Operations in Virginia, Maryland and Pennsylvania, from the Commencement to the Close of the War, 1861–1865*, 340–341; Jones, "The Longstreet-Gettysburg Controversy," *SHSP* 23: 343.

6. Swinton, *Campaigns of the Army of the Potomac*, 340; *The War of the Rebellion: A Compilation of the Official Records of the Union and Confederate Armies*, 128 vols. (Washington D.C., 1880–1901), Series 1, Vol. 27, Pt. 2, 318, Hereafter cited as *OR*. All references are to Series 1 unless otherwise noted.; Walter Taylor, "The Campaign in Pennsylvania," *Annals of the War*, 305–307; Pfarr, *Longstreet at Gettysburg*, 24–27; Jones, "The Longstreet-Gettysburg Controversy," *SHSP* 23: 344; James Longstreet, *From Manassas to Appomattox*, 384.

7. Pfarr, *Longstreet at Gettysburg*, 170–171; Gilbert Moxley Sorrel, *At the Right Hand of Longstreet: Recollections of a Confederate Staff Officer*, 80; James Longstreet, "Lee in Pennsylvania," *Annals of the War*, 432.

8. Swinton, *Campaigns of the Army of the Potomac*, 340–341; Jones, "The Longstreet-Gettysburg Controversy," *SHSP* 23: 343–344.

9. James D. McCabe Jr., *Life and Campaigns of General Robert E. Lee*, 393–395.

10. Jones, "The Longstreet-Gettysburg Controversy," *SHSP* 23: 343–345; William Garrett Piston, *Lee's Tarnished Lieutenant: James Longstreet and His Place in Southern History*, 125; James Longstreet, "Lee in Pennsylvania," *Annals of the War*, 414–415.

11. Jones, "The Longstreet-Gettysburg Controversy," *SHSP* 23: 344; Jubal Early, *The Campaigns of Robert E. Lee, An Address Before Washington and Lee University, January 19, 1872*, http://leefamilyarchive.org/reference/addresses/early/index.html.

12. James Longstreet, "Lee's Right Wing at Gettysburg," *Battles and Leaders*, 3: 351; Pfarr, *Longstreet at Gettysburg*, 10–11, 53, 90, 114.

13. James Longstreet, "Lee in Pennsylvania," *Annals of the War*, 437–438; Jefferson Davis, *The Rise and Fall of the Confederate Government, Volume II*, 440–441; "Letter from General C.M. Wilcox, March 26, 1877," *SHSP* 4: 114; James Longstreet, "Lee's Right Wing at Gettysburg," *Battles and Leaders*, 3: 351.

14. "Letter from General J.A. Early, March 12, 1877," *SHSP* 4: 64; "Supplement to General Early's Review.—Reply to General Longstreet," *SHSP* 4: 286–287.

15. Fitzhugh Lee, "A Review of the First Two Days' Operations at Gettysburg and a Reply to General Longstreet," *SHSP* 5: 178–180.

16. Cadmus Wilcox, "General C.M. Wilcox on the Battle of Gettysburg," *SHSP* 6: 105.

17. James Longstreet, "Lee in Pennsylvania," *Annals of the War*, 414–415; William Youngblood, "Unwritten History of the Gettysburg Campaign," *SHSP* 38: 318; James Longstreet, "The Mistakes of Gettysburg," *Annals of the War*, 632.

18. James Longstreet, "The Mistakes of Gettysburg," *Annals of the War*, 632; Jones, "The Longstreet-Gettysburg Controversy," *SHSP* 23: 347; Pfarr, *Longstreet at Gettysburg*, 121–135, 143–144.

19. Pfarr, *Longstreet at Gettysburg*, 36–37, 47, 66–67, 114; Fitzhugh Lee, "Letter from John B. Bachelder, Esq." in "A Review of the First Two Days' Operations at Gettysburg and a Reply to General Longstreet," *SHSP* 5: 174; Bachelder wrote, "The best chance for a successful attack was within the first hour, and unquestionably the great mistake of the battle was the failure to follow the Union forces through the town, and attack them before they could reform on Cemetery Hill."

20. John M. Archer, *East Cemetery Hill at Gettysburg: "The Hour Was One of Horror,"* 69, 72, 75, 77; Harry W. Pfanz, *Gettysburg: Culp's Hill & Cemetery Hill*, 213, 238. Bradley M. Gottfried, *The Maps of Gettysburg: An Atlas of the Gettysburg Campaign, June 3—July 13, 1863*, 224; Glenn Tucker, *High Tide at Gettysburg: The Campaign in Pennsylvania*, 296–299; Gordon's brigade of Early's division was not the only potential reinforcement withheld during this attack. Three brigades from Maj. Gen. Robert Rodes' division were supposed to attack Cemetery Hill simultaneously with Early's division from the northwest; however, for reasons unexplained, Rodes did not even begin moving his men into place in preparation for advancing until Early's attack was already underway. Also a mystery was Rodes' apparently turning over tactical command of the attack to one of his brigadiers, Stephen Ramseur, at the last minute. Ramseur wound up advancing the brigades halfway to their objective before determining they were too late and the Federal position was too strong. Ramseur halted the command and ordered a quiet withdrawal to Long Lane.

21. Douglas Southall Freeman, *Lee's Lieutenants: A Study in Command*, One-Volume Abridgment, ed. Stephen W. Sears, 745–749, 751, 758–761, 765, 768–769; Bryce Suderow, e-mail message to author, April 20, 2022. Author and Historian Bryce Suderow was very helpful in providing details about the last days of Jubal Early's Confederate career. He noted that when John B. Gordon returned to Petersburg, Virginia, with the Second Corps in December 1864, Early's Army of the Valley remained in the Shenandoah Valley with only one division of infantry and a cavalry division under Thomas Rosser. Commencing in 1865, Early commanded altogether about 2,000 infantry in the single division left to him. In the major defeat he suffered at Waynesboro, Virginia, on March 2, 1865, Early's army was destroyed, with the Federals capturing about 1,600 men. When Lee relieved Early of his command in late March 1865, he was replaced with Lunsford Lomax. Despite Early's series of defeats from late 1864 to early 1865, Suderow emphasized that "if you read Lee's order relieving Early of command, you will see that he did so reluctantly."; Jubal Early, *A Memoir of the Last Year of the War for Independence, in the Confederate States of America: Containing an Account of the Operations of His Commands in the Years 1864 and 1865*, 131; Thomas J. Goree, *Longstreet's Aide: The Civil War Letters of Major Thomas J. Goree*, ed. Thomas W. Cutrer, 143–149; J. Tracy Power, "Jubal A. Early (1816–1894)," *Encyclopedia Virginia*, https://www.encyclopediavirginia.org/Early_Jubal_A_1816-1894; Kathryn Shively Meier, "Jubal A. Early: Model Civil War Sufferer," *J19: The Journal of Nineteenth-Century Americanists*, Volume 4, Number 1, Spring 2016, 206–214; Pfarr, *Longstreet at Gettysburg*, 6–9.

22. Pfarr, *Longstreet at Gettysburg*, 145–147, 152–155; Pendleton's report can be found in *OR* 27/2: 346–354. Note especially this section of the report: "This front was, after some time, examined by Colonel [William P.] Smith and Captain Johnston (engineers), and about midday General Longstreet arrived and viewed the ground. He desired Colonel [E.P.] Alexander to obtain the best view he then could of the front. I therefore conducted the colonel to the advanced point of observation previously visited. Its approach was now more hazardous, from the fire of the enemy's sharpshooters, so that special caution was necessary in making the desired observation. Just then a sharp contest occurred in the woods to the right and rear of this forward point. Anderson's division, Third Corps, had moved up, and was driving the enemy from these woods....These woods having been thus cleared of the enemy, some view of the ground beyond them, and much farther to the right than had yet been examined, seemed practicable. I therefore rode in that direction, and, when about to enter the woods, met the commanding general, en route himself for a survey of the ground."

23. It is worth noting that in Pendleton's January 1873 account, he described Longstreet's reaction quite differently and alleged that "at first General Longstreet dissented, but on second thought preferred that himself should be represented with the rest." Frank P. Cauble, *The Surrender Proceedings: April 9, 1865, Appomattox Court House*, 3rd Edition, The Civil War Battles and Leaders Series (Lynchburg, VA: H.E. Howard, 1987), 9–12; Bryce Suderow and Patrick A. Schroeder (Historian, Appomattox Court House National Historical Park), e-mails to the author, April 20, 2022; Michael E. Haskew, *Appomattox: The Last Days of Robert E. Lee's Army of Northern Virginia*, 180–181; Glenn Tucker, "Longstreet: Culprit or Scapegoat?" *Civil War Times Illustrated*, Volume 1, 1962–1963, 6.

24. Thomas L. Connelly, *The Marble Man: Robert E. Lee and His Image in American Society*, 37–38; Jon L. Wakelyn, *Biographical Dictionary of the Confederacy*, 342; Susan Pendleton Lee, *Memoirs of William Nelson Pendleton, D.D.*, 39–40, 48, 58, 66, 71, 108, 172, 279–280.

25. Connelly, *The Marble Man*, 39.

26. Ibid.,, 39–42; Fitzhugh Lee, "A Review of the First Two Days' Operations at Gettysburg and a Reply to General Longstreet," *SHSP* 5: 162; Jones, "The Longstreet-Gettysburg Controversy," *SHSP* 23: 347–348.

27. Connelly, *The Marble Man*, 25, 39–40, 43–47; Catherine M. Wright, "Lee Chapel," *Encyclopedia*

Virginia, https://www.encyclopediavirginia.org/Lee_Chapel.

28. *New Orleans Times*, June 8, 1867; *Chicago Tribune*, June 10, 1867; Piston, *Lee's Tarnished Lieutenant*, 104–106; Pfarr, *Longstreet at Gettysburg*, 7–9; Jones, "The Longstreet-Gettysburg Controversy," *SHSP* 23: 348.

29. Referring to Longstreet's June 1867 article, the general's uncle, Augustus Longstreet, candidly told his nephew, "It will ruin you, son, if you publish it."

30. Jones, "The Longstreet-Gettysburg Controversy," *SHSP* 23: 348.

Essay 2

1. Helen Longstreet, *Lee and Longstreet at High Tide: Gettysburg in the Light of the Official Records*, 8.

2. Ibid., 17–21.

3. Ibid., 8, 17–18.

4. For a comprehensive analysis of the controversy surrounding Longstreet's Gettysburg performance, see Cory M. Pfarr's *Longstreet at Gettysburg: A Critical Reassessment*, William Garrett Piston's *Lee's Tarnished Lieutenant*, and Glenn Tucker's *Lee and Longstreet at Gettysburg*.

5. The Joint Congressional Committee on the Conduct of the War was established in December 1861 following the Federal defeat at the Battle of Ball's Bluff and disbanded in May 1865 at the conclusion of the war. Generally, it investigated the progress of the Federal war effort and regularly became a forum where generals accused of failure testified and responded to charges. The committee held a series of hearings in 1864 that specifically addressed the Meade-Sickles Controversy at the Battle of Gettysburg. Sixteen officers from the Army of the Potomac's high command who participated in the battle testified during these hearings. For an annotated but comprehensive account of these hearings, see Bill Hyde, *The Union Generals Speak: The Meade Hearings on the Battle of Gettysburg*. Radical Republican Senators Benjamin Wade of Ohio and Zachariah Chandler of Michigan led the committee. Wade and Chandler's hardline positions on slavery and how to deal with the South largely set the committee's tone toward being decidedly anti-Lincoln and anti–West Point. Understanding this, it was altogether unsurprising then that the committee's Gettysburg report, which came out at war's end, was generally unfavorable to Meade's performance at the battle. For additional details, see Richard A. Sauers, *Gettysburg: The Meade-Sickles Controversy*, 49–66.

6. Negative descriptions of Sickles' original position on lower Cemetery Ridge were numerous. Major Thomas Rafferty of the 71st New York and Sickles staffer Henry Tremain offered two descriptive and telling examples. Rafferty asserted that the position was "faulty," "impossible to occupy with any prospect of being able to hold it," and "quite springy and marshy, and was covered thickly with a growth of stunted bushes…and masked by the woods and the broken and rocky ground in our front, affording most excellent positions and covers for the rebels to take possession of without risk, and attack us with every advantage in their favor." Likewise, Tremain contended that the "location proved to be on low ground, easily commanded by the land in front, and running off the left." See Hessler, *Sickles at Gettysburg*, 109, and Hessler and Britt C. Isenberg, *Gettysburg's Peach Orchard*, 46.

7. It is worth mentioning that Little Round Top is yet 70 feet higher than the Peach Orchard position. See Hessler, *Sickles at Gettysburg*, 104.

8. Regarding Geary, Sickles told the Joint Congressional Committee on the Conduct of the War that when he sought to relieve the Twelfth Corps division, it "was not in position, but was merely massed in my vicinity." David Birney began posting his division on lower Cemetery Ridge at least an hour after Geary began departing the north face of Little Round Top around 5 a.m. James Hessler suggests that the discrepancy in times between Geary's departure and Birney's arrival provided "a possible explanation for the discrepancy." Hessler also cites the 141st Pennsylvania's regimental history to further support this contention. The regimental history emphasized, "Geary had moved about five o' clock in the morning, and Sickles did not receive his orders until an hour later, when being ignorant of the position Geary had held, and no officer being left to direct him, the order was imperfectly carried out." See Hessler and Isenberg, *Gettysburg's Peach Orchard*, 49. Further supporting this contention was Sickles' aide-de-camp, Henry Tremain's postwar recollection that "When your [Sickles'] troops arrived they occupied grounds at the left of the army where there were troops when there was nothing to indicate the presence of General Geary." See David L. and Audrey J. Ladd, *The Bachelder Papers*, Vol. I, January 5, 1863 to July 27, 1880, 671; It is well worth mentioning on this controversial topic that Meade wrote a private letter in March 1870 to Colonel G.G. Benedict (published in 1886), in which he directly addressed the Geary controversy, underscoring that Geary had told him that the Twelfth Corps officer had tried to "explain the position and its importance" to Sickles; however the Third Corps commander sent a reply that he "would attend to it in due time." Meade concluded from this testimony that Sickles "knew the position occupied by Geary's division, or could have known, and yet failed to occupy it." See Meade, "The Meade-Sickles Controversy," *Battles and Leaders*, 3: 414. Sickles replied to this Geary-related allegation in August 1886 and his response was rather telling in its flagrant inaccuracy—"The Twelfth Corps was never at any time until the very close of the battle on the 2nd of July, in position on the left." See Sickles, "The Meade-Sickles Controversy," *Battles and Leaders*, 416.

9. Bill Hyde, *The Union Generals Speak: The*

Meade Hearings on the Battle of Gettysburg, 44, 107; Sauers, *Gettysburg: The Meade-Sickles Controversy*, 137–140, 154; James Hessler speech, "Sickles at Gettysburg," August 13, 2013, Gettysburg Foundation; Hessler, *Sickles at Gettysburg*, 116, 266; Richard Sauers makes a persuasive argument in his *Gettysburg: The Meade Sickles Controversy* when presenting evidence that Sickles never effectively or fully deployed his corps in its original position on lower Cemetery Ridge—a shorter line than its forward position in the mid-afternoon. Sauers notes Humphrey's cramped original position north of the George Weikert Farm, near Patterson's Woods; and that by noon, Sickles had at least three brigades held in reserve: De Trobriand's of Birney's division, along with Burling and most of Brewster's brigade of Humphrey's division. Sauers also draws attention to the fact that Sickles claimed he understood the importance of Little Round Top as the key to the Federals' position; however, in his original position, he neither attempted to occupy it in force, nor even covered it with a skirmish line.

10. Sickles was worried about the army's left flank as early as 9:30 p.m. on July 1, when he informed Meade, "My impression is, if I may be allowed to make a suggestion, that our left and rear are not sufficiently guarded." Additionally, there is considerable evidence Meade either anticipated an attack against his right flank or considered launching an attack of his own from there. He undoubtedly focused most of his attention on that portion of his line well into the afternoon hours of July 2. Resultantly, when the Fifth Corps arrived on the field, Meade positioned it near his right in anticipation of using it to offensively or defensively support Henry Slocum's Twelfth Corps. Meade very well may have believed Sickles' front was least likely to see the day's main thrust of battle. See Sauers, *Gettysburg: The Meade-Sickles Controversy*, 33, 64; Hessler, *Sickles at Gettysburg*, 106, 109, 125–127; *The War of the Rebellion: A Compilation of the Official Records of the Union and Confederate Armies*, 128 vols. (Washington, D.C. 1880–1901), Series 1, vol. 27, Pt. 3, 468; Hereafter cited as *OR*. All references are to Series 1 unless otherwise noted; David L. and Audrey J. Ladd, *The Bachelder Papers*, Vol. I, January 5, 1863, to July 27, 1880, 671, 673.

11. Pfarr, *Longstreet at Gettysburg*, 73–74; Hessler speech, "Sickles at Gettysburg"; Hessler, *Sickles at Gettysburg*, 124–126, 128–129, 321; Hyde, *The Union Generals Speak*, 335–336; Sauers, *Gettysburg: The Meade-Sickles Controversy*, 146–148; Seth Williams, Meade's adjutant general, provided key testimony on the topic of Meade's alleged July 2 retreat order. Williams described the order as "a contingency which might possibly happen of the army being compelled to assume a new position." Williams recalled preparing such an order and copies were "possibly" prepared, but nothing was ever "distributed." Williams concluded, "I only know such an order was never in fact issued." Two additional convincing reasons that demonstrated Meade was not contemplating retreat on the morning and afternoon of July 2 are the non-withdrawal of the army's artillery reserve and the summoning of the Sixth Corps to Gettysburg with all possible haste.

12. One of the more candid statements about Sickles' decision comes from academic historian Allen Guelzo, who has described Sickles' move as a "chicken-brained plan." See Guelzo, *Gettysburg: The Last Invasion*, 284. Also see Edwin Coddington, *The Gettysburg Campaign: A Study in Command*, 445–447; Harry Pfanz, *Gettysburg: The Second Day*, 425, 431; Sauers, *Gettysburg: The Meade-Sickles Controversy*, 34, 153–159; Stephen W. Sears, *Gettysburg*, 269; When cast in the light of Meade's instructions to Sickles at their 11 a.m. face-to-face meeting, Sickles' disobedience of orders is rather obvious. At this meeting, Sickles asked Meade if he could post his men as his judgment saw fit, to which Meade replied, "Certainly, within the limits of the general instructions I have given to you; any grounds within those limits you choose to occupy I leave to you." Those general instructions—relayed multiple times to Sickles on the morning of July 2—were for Sickles to connect his right with Hancock's Second Corps on Cemetery Ridge and to extend his left to Little Round Top. Without getting into the murky debate over where exactly Sickles was supposed to post his troops near or on Little Round Top, it is clear that in moving his corps forward to the Emmitsburg Road position, Sickles' right was disconnected from Hancock, while his left rested not on Little Round Top, but Houck's Ridge to the west. Therefore, Sickles' move was not "within the limits of" Meade's "general instructions." It is worth mentioning that Sickles claimed on several occasions in the postwar years that he never received orders on July 2. For some examples, see Sauers, *Gettysburg: The Meade-Sickles Controversy*, 71–72. Perhaps John Gibbon, a division commander in the Federal Second Corps at Gettysburg (and temporarily in command of the corps on July 2 and early July 3, as Hancock was forced by events to take on wing command), settled the issue best when succinctly, but effectively, pointing out that "Neither did he [Sickles] receive orders to go where he did go." See Robert P. Broadwater, *Gettysburg as the Generals Remembered It: Postwar Perspectives on Ten Commanders*, 89. Equally as concise and effective was Henry Hunt's discerning statement, when he characterized the entire Meade-Sickles Controversy as "queer"—underscoring how "with Sickles' friends, it is 'which was the best line to adopt.' The real one is 'Was Sickles justified in departing from his instructions if he understood them.'" See *Blue & Gray* magazine. United States: Blue & Gray Enterprises, 1987, Vol. 5–6, 59.

13. The inherent disadvantages to a salient position are essentially that it affords an enemy the opportunity to attack the position from two sides. Sickles' salient anchored at the Peach Orchard was especially vulnerable upon recognizing both his

flanks were unprotected. A gap of about 1,100 yards separated Sickles' right flank from Hancock's left. On Sickles' left flank was the 500-yard-wide Plum Run Valley located between Houck's Ridge and the Round Tops. That said, Army of the Potomac Chief of Artillery Henry Hunt thought Sickles' advance position held some unique merit, contending, "It would, it is true, in our hands present a salient angle, which generally exposes both its sides to enfilade fires; but here the ridges were so high that each would serve as a 'traverse' for the other, and reduce that evil to a minimum." See Henry Hunt, "The Second Day at Gettysburg," *Battles and Leaders*, 3:301–302.

14. A full analysis of the "Meade-Sickles Controversy," especially as it relates to the long-standing debate over Sickles' July 2 move to the Peach Orchard, is beyond the scope of this essay. Readers are encouraged to read Hessler's *Sickles at Gettysburg*, Hessler and Isenberg's *Gettysburg's Peach Orchard*, and Sauers, *Gettysburg: The Meade-Sickles Controversy* for a comprehensive account of this topic. In his books and speeches, Hessler in particular has also persuasively drawn significant attention to Sickles' pre-Gettysburg behavior, experiences, and temperament as consequential factors that influenced Sickles' decision on July 2. For Hessler's speeches, see "Sickles at Gettysburg," August 13, 2013, Gettysburg Foundation, and "Gettysburg's Peach Orchard," August 8, 2019, U.S. Army Heritage and Education Center. Likewise, see Sauers, *Gettysburg: The Meade-Sickles Controversy*, 159–160, for a brief, but convincing commentary on Sickles' equally checkered postwar career.

15. Helen Longstreet, *Lee and Longstreet at High Tide*, 8; Pfarr, *Longstreet at Gettysburg*, 7–8, 10, 167, 172–174; Cory M. Pfarr interview, "Longstreet at Gettysburg," Pennsylvania Cable Network, PA Books, April 3, 2019.

16. Any time I have mentioned the potential merits of Sickles' July 2 move and its negative effect on Longstreet's July 2 attack at public events for my 2019 book *Longstreet at Gettysburg*, I am understandably met with skepticism and usually asked for some explanation. Two recorded examples of this occurrence are present in Cory M. Pfarr interview, "Longstreet at Gettysburg," Pennsylvania Cable Network, and Cory M. Pfarr interview, "Reassessing James Longstreet at Gettysburg with Cory Pfarr," Keith Harris, *The Rogue Historian Podcast*, November 6, 2019.

17. Hessler has frequently and critically addressed the futility of entertaining hypothetical conjecture when discussing Sickles' move to the Peach Orchard. In a general sense, he has rightly characterized "speculation" as "the bane of historians," and on this controversy in particular asserts, "The impact that Sickles' movements had on James Longstreet's attack often rests on conjecture and unsolvable what-if scenarios, rather than on analysis of what actually happened." See Hessler and Isenberg, *Gettysburg's Peach Orchard*, 121n1, 331.

Additionally, Richard Sauers in his book on the Meade-Sickles Controversy (156, 158) also issues several warnings about engaging in speculative discussions on the topic. Sauers writes, "Dan Sickles did a magnificent job of stressing this what-if scenario that many historians have fallen into the same trap and have repeated the same error of reasoning," and "any adventure into the realm of speculative history will remain just that—an adventure into the fantasy world."

18. *OR* 27/2, 358.

19. James Longstreet, "Lee in Pennsylvania," *Annals of the War*, 428.

20. *OR* 27/2, 318–319, 446; Captain Robert E. Lee, *The Recollections and Letters of General Robert E. Lee*, 102. Regarding concert of action across corps, Lee wrote in an 1868 letter, "It [the battle] was continued in the effort to overcome the difficulties by which we were surrounded, and it would have been gained could one determined and united blow have been delivered by our whole line."

21. Edward Porter Alexander, *Military Memoirs of a Confederate: A Critical Narrative*, 408.

22. Pfarr, *Longstreet at Gettysburg*, 105–117.

23. *OR* 27/1, 116, 120; Kershaw, "Kershaw's Brigade at Gettysburg," *Battles and Leaders*, 3: 338; Henry H. Lockwood's brigade was a 12th Corps unit, not 1st Corps. Meade later wrote a supplementary report to correct the mistake.

24. James Longstreet, "Lee in Pennsylvania," *Annals of the War*, 428; Hyde, *The Union Generals Speak*, 110.

25. *Ibid.*, 425; James Longstreet, *From Manassas to Appomattox*, 373; Kershaw, "Kershaw's Brigade at Gettysburg," *Battles and Leaders*, 3: 338; James Longstreet, "The Mistakes of Gettysburg," *Annals of the War*, 623.

26. Alexander, *Military Memoirs of a Confederate*, 407; James Longstreet, "Lee in Pennsylvania," *Annals of the* War, 424.

27. Ward's brigade was 2,100-strong, but his 3rd Maine and 1st U.S. Sharpshooters, 450 men combined, were detached near the Peach Orchard during the fight. That said, the 40th New York from Philippe Regis De Trobriand's brigade and the 6th New Jersey, George Burling's brigade of Andrew Humphrey's division, ultimately fought on Ward's front; Hessler, *Sickles at Gettysburg*, 164; Sears, *Gettysburg*, 275.

28. Burling's brigade of Humphrey's division had one of the more interesting experiences on July 2. The brigade was essentially distributed to different sectors of the Federal left. Initially placed in Trostle's Woods to support David Birney's Third Corps division, the 5th New Jersey remained on Andrew Humphrey's front along the Emmitsburg Road, the 2nd New Hampshire and 7th New Jersey fought at the Peach Orchard, the 6th New Jersey supported Ward's brigade in the Plum Run Valley between Devil's Den and Little Round Top, and the 8th New Jersey and 115th Pennsylvania were sent to the Stony Hill and Wheatfield sector. See "Monument to the 3rd Brigade, 2nd Division, 3rd Corps

at Gettysburg" at Gettysburg National Military Park (GNMP); Gottfried, *Brigades of Gettysburg*, 224; Hessler, *Sickles at Gettysburg*, 130, 156; Hessler and Isenberg, *Gettysburg's Peach Orchard*, 106; David Powell, "Advance to Disaster: Sickles, Longstreet, and July 2nd, 1863," *The Gettysburg Magazine*, Issue 28 (2003), 46.

29. Law was put in-charge of Longstreet's right division after Hood's wounding early in the fight.

30. James Longstreet, "Lee in Pennsylvania," *Annals of the War*, 424–425; Evander Law, "The Struggle for 'Round Top,'" *Battles and Leaders*, 3: 324.

31. Hessler, *Sickles at Gettysburg*, 329; James Hessler and Jack Drummond, "Sickles Returns," *The Gettysburg Magazine*, Issue 34 (2006), 72–73. Longstreet's statement about having "more open field in which to work" if Sickles had remained on or returned to lower Cemetery Ridge is in accordance with what James Hessler has aptly described as the "avenues of approach" factor, part of the KOCOA (Key Terrain, Observation, Cover, Obstacles, Avenues of Approach) method of evaluating "ground" on a battlefield. See Hessler's "Gettysburg's Peach Orchard" speech, August 8, 2019, U.S. Army Heritage and Education Center. Henry Hunt, Meade's Chief of Artillery, also mentioned this "avenues of approach" factor as a positive aspect of Sickles' forward position in his major postwar article on the July 2 battle, writing, "its occupation would cramp the movements of the enemy." See Hunt, "The Second Day at Gettysburg," *Battles and Leaders*, 3: 302.

32. Hessler, *Sickles at Gettysburg*, 341–342.

33. Longstreet's reference to Meade seriously considering a redeployment of his army "behind Pipe Creek" was very likely influenced by Sickles' repeated allegations to this effect over the years.

34. James Longstreet, *From Manassas to Appomattox*, 382; Helen Longstreet, *Lee and Longstreet at High Tide*, 22; Lafayette McLaws, "Gettysburg," *Southern Historical Society Papers*, 7: 77. Hereafter cited as *SHSP*.

35. Pfarr, *Longstreet at Gettysburg*, 64–65, 92–93, 95, 97, 105; *OR* 27/2: 308, 318.

36. Pfarr, *Longstreet at Gettysburg*, 69, 71–73; Law's brigade joined the rest of Longstreet's two divisions of Hood and McLaws around noon on July 2. See Law's February 1891 letter to Gettysburg historian John Bachelder in David L. and Audrey J. Ladd, *The Bachelder Papers*, Vol. III, April 12, 1886 to December 22, 1894, 1790.

37. Pfarr, *Longstreet at Gettysburg*, 49–54, 66–83.

38. For details on post-battle writers' misleading claims about the potential for the Confederates to seize Little Round Top in the morning hours of July 2, see Pfarr, *Longstreet at Gettysburg*, 92–93, 95, 105.

39. Pfarr, *Longstreet at Gettysburg*, 85; Sears, *Gettysburg*, 252.

40. *Ibid.*, 59–60, 69–71, 84–85, 88–89; *OR* 27/2: 608; McLaws, "Gettysburg," *SHSP* 7:77.

41. Daniel Sickles, "The Meade-Sickles Controversy," *Battles and Leaders*, 3: 417–418.

42. Edward Porter Alexander, *Fighting for the Confederacy: The Personal Recollections of General Edward Porter Alexander*, 238. It is important to note E.P. Alexander's opinion of Sickles' move was anything but consistent. He also wrote negatively about the 3rd Corps commander's decision, contending, "[Sickles] unwisely ordered an advance of his whole corps to hold the ground about the Peach Orchard. He probably had in mind the advantage given the Confederates at Chancellorsville in allowing them the occupation of the Hazel Grove plateau. But it was, nevertheless, bad tactics. It exchanged strong ground for weak, and gave the Confederates an opportunity not otherwise possible. They would be quite sure to crush the isolated 3rd corps. If their attack was properly organized and conducted, it might become possible to rush and carry the Federal main line in the pursuit of the fugitives." See Alexander, *Military Memoirs of a Confederate*, 392–393.

43. Mid-twentieth century journalist and historian Glenn Tucker did not believe Sickles' move aided the Federals against Longstreet on July 2. Tucker thought that absent the expected support from Ewell and Hill, "the salient he [Sickles] created gave Longstreet a good target." Tucker held that if the Federal Third Corps had stayed on or returned to lower Cemetery Ridge, the First Corps divisions would have had to perilously advance "across three quarters of a mile of open land to reach the Third Corps line." Tucker and I agree that had Ewell and Hill carried out Lee's orders as directed, simultaneous with Longstreet's attack, this entire discussion about the merits of Sickles' move would probably be moot, as the Confederates would very likely have pierced and severely threatened the integrity of the Federal position somewhere along Cemetery Ridge. The catastrophic consequences (for the Confederates) of Ewell's and Hill's limited support on July 2 aside, I would also agree with Tucker that "Longstreet would have had to change front" if Sickles' left flank was in its original location just north of Little Round Top. Undoubtedly, the Confederate High Command would have had to completely divorce itself from the guiding attack plan "up the Emmitsburg Road" and fashion an alternate strategy that very likely would have involved maneuvering a significant portion of the attack force in the vicinity of or across the Round Tops. With all this said, simply calling Sickles' Peach Orchard position "a good target" for Longstreet on July 2 is a bridge too far for me, since only the target's bulls-eye was located at the Peach Orchard. Sickles' line, particularly David Birney's division stretched down to the southern end of Devil's Den. Additionally, it is important to remember the military principle, aptly described by military historian William Glenn Robertson, that "the defense of a critical point always should begin forward of its final protective line." In this case, the critical

point was Cemetery Ridge. Coupled with the rest of the swirling circumstances and events that took place on the afternoon of July 2, Sickles' advanced position (with Federal reinforcements) turned out to be less a "good target" and more a tiger being caught by its tail. See Glenn Tucker, *Lee and Longstreet at Gettysburg*, 37–39 and Tucker, *High Tide at Gettysburg: The Campaign in Pennsylvania*, 243–244; William Glenn Robertson, "Daniel E. Sickles and the Third Corps," *The Second Day at Gettysburg: Essays on Confederate and Union Leadership*, ed. Gary W. Gallagher, 55.

44. Academic historian Kent Gramm has also weighed in on Sickles' move. In a 1997 essay, Gramm mentions the 1902 letter from Longstreet to Sickles and spends a few pages analyzing Sickles' advance position on July 2. Ultimately, he does not rule in the Federal Third Corps commander's favor. Gramm begins with the assertion that Little Round Top "was the key to the Federal position," "not the peach orchard." As previously discussed, hindsight affords us the chance to declare that Little Round Top was favorable to the Peach Orchard; however, at the time of the battle, Little Round Top did not figure into the Confederate High Command's attack objectives on July 2. Additionally, Meade demonstrated he was not overly concerned with this alleged "key" to his position in the hours leading up to the July 2, while Sickles ultimately had the same idea as the Confederates in deeming the Peach Orchard critical ground. Of course, Lee and Sickles may have been wrong in their estimation of the Peach Orchard's worth, but nevertheless, that is what they believed, and both men acted upon that belief on July 2. That said, like Tucker, Gramm accurately underscores that had Sickles not moved out to the Peach Orchard or returned to lower Cemetery Ridge, it would have required the Confederates to alter their attack plan and change front. He also correctly emphasizes that the Confederates could have used the Peach Orchard as an artillery platform, as Lee had intended, to shell Cemetery Ridge. Like William Glenn Robertson though, Gramm's best point is drawing attention to Sickles' advance position creating "a defense in depth" and the theory that if Lee "had pushed the Federals off Cemetery Ridge, there would have been no place for the Yankees to fall back to." That aside, Gramm believes that even had Sickles stayed put or returned to lower Cemetery Ridge, Meade's timely shifting of Federal reinforcements, particularly the Fifth Corps, coupled with Federal artillery fire from Little Round Top, would have proven decisive in retaining a Federal victory. "Meade would have had control over the battle, and reinforcements would not have gone in almost willy-nilly to get ground up in relative isolation. Longstreet's attack would have failed, as happened the next day.... Probably," Gramm writes. Perhaps though, I think to some degree, this prediction downplays both the potential impact of a direct Confederate attack against lower Cemetery Ridge (with no intermediary, weakening fight between the armies) and the debilitating effect Sickles' advance position ultimately had on Longstreet's July 2 attack. See Kent Gramm, "The Chances of War: Lee, Longstreet, Sickles, and the First Minnesota Volunteers," *The Gettysburg Nobody Knows*, ed. Gabor S. Boritt, 91, 95–97.

45. For additional details on communications between Lee, Longstreet, and McLaws in the minutes leading up to the Confederate High Command's recognition of this changed battlescape, see Chapter 10 of Pfarr, *Longstreet at Gettysburg*, 84–87.

46. McLaws, "Gettysburg," *SHSP* 7:70; Fitzgerald Ross, *A Visit to the Cities and Camps of the Confederate States*, 54–55; Pfanz, *Gettysburg: The Second Day*, 426.

47. Historians have largely dodged this question over the decades. Standing near the intersection of Barksdale's and Kershaw's brigades' position on July 2 (present-day location of the Longstreet Tower) and then again farther south on the Phillip Snyder Farm (near where McLaws' and Hood's divisions intersected on July 2), this author believes it would have been extremely difficult to miss the fact that the Federal line refused back from the Emmitsburg Road at the Wheatfield Road. It has been sufficiently pointed out that the Third Corps line's refusal at the intersection of the Emmitsburg and Wheatfield Roads and the extension of it all the way to Devil's Den should have squelched any attempt to attack up the Emmitsburg Road; however, that is exactly what Lee (through Longstreet) continued to order Hood to do in the lead-up to the Confederate First Corps' attack.

48. Pfanz, *Gettysburg: The Second Day*, 426; Helen Longstreet, *Lee and Longstreet at High Tide*, 24–25, 28; McLaws, "Gettysburg," *SHSP* 7:75–78; Pfarr, *Longstreet at Gettysburg*, 88–91.

49. Alexander, *Fighting for the Confederacy*, 241; Captain Justus Scheibert, *Seven Months in the Rebel States During the North American War, 1863*, ed. W. Stanley Hoole, 112–113; McLaws, "Gettysburg," *SHSP* 7:73; Pfarr, *Longstreet at Gettysburg*, 101, 105–106.

50. Despite McLaws' belief that the Federal Third Corps' move to the Emmitsburg Road clearly upset Confederate attack plans on July 2, he also criticized Sickles' decision in the postwar years. In an 1886 article, he wrote that "the word 'victory' must mean something in the more modern vernacular which is not given to it in the dictionaries" when addressing claims that Sickles' actions on July 2 constituted a Federal success. See McLaws, "The Federal Disaster on the Left," *Philadelphia Weekly Press*, August 4, 1886.

51. John B. Hood, *Advance and Retreat*, 57–58; McLaws, "Gettysburg," *SHSP* 7:71, 75; James Longstreet, "Lee in Pennsylvania," *Annals of the War*, 424; James Longstreet, *From Manassas to Appomattox*, 370; Alexander, *Fighting for the Confederacy*, 238.

52. Pfarr, *Longstreet at Gettysburg*, 130–135; *OR* 27/2: 320; McLaws, "Gettysburg," *SHSP* 7:77; Helen Longstreet, *Lee and Longstreet at High Tide*, 29.

53. For details on the unavailability of Pickett's division to support the First Corps' attack on the afternoon of July 2, see Pfarr, *Longstreet at Gettysburg*, 121–122.

54. A reasonable counterargument has been made that Meade actually stripped his right too much on the afternoon of July 2 to meet Longstreet's threat against his left. Buttressing this argument most is the fact that only one Twelfth Corps brigade under George Greene was left to defend Culp's Hill in the evening hours of July 2 against multiple attacks by the Confederate Second Corps.

55. Alexander, *Fighting for the Confederacy*, 241–242; Alexander, *Military Memoirs of a Confederate*, 393, 405; McLaws, "Gettysburg," *SHSP* 7:75.

56. When discussing direct infantry reinforcement to Hood's and McLaws' divisions on July 2 it is important to underscore the absence of Pickett's division, another result of J.E.B. Stuart's continued absence (and the Confederates' ineffective use of other available cavalry forces). Like Law's brigade of Hood's division, Pickett's division was tasked with guarding the army's trains and did not arrive in the vicinity of the battlefield until the mid- to-late-afternoon hours on July 2. Pickett started from Chambersburg to Gettysburg around 2 a.m. and marched 27 miles. Along with Pickett, recall that Lee considered moving Ewell's corps around to the Confederate right to support Longstreet's attack during the overnight hours of July 1 and early morning hours of July 2. See Pfarr, *Longstreet at Gettysburg*, 58–59, 66–67, 121–122.

57. The Gettysburg-based newspaper *Star and Sentinel* concisely and astutely summarized this argument in an article written for a Memorial Day event at Gettysburg in 1899. Reasonably docking Sickles for leaving Little Round Top "unoccupied," the newspaper just as reasonably asserted "that the exhaustion of the Confederates in driving back Sickles from the position that he had assumed had much to do with rendering [the Confederates] unable to drive the Union from its final [Cemetery Ridge] position." See Hessler, *Sickles at Gettysburg*, 357.

58. Pfarr, *Longstreet at Gettysburg*, 102–107; Tucker, *High Tide at Gettysburg*, 280; Pfanz, *Gettysburg: The Second Day*, 404; Alexander, *Fighting for the Confederacy*, 240; E.P. Alexander, "The Great Charge and Artillery Fighting at Gettysburg," *Battles and Leaders*, 3:360.

59. Brigadier General Jerome Robertson commanded the other brigade in Hood's division that attacked concurrently with Law's brigade. Robertson's official report clearly shows that, despite orders to place his left on the Emmitsburg Road and keep his right in contact with Law's left flank, Law's extreme eastward drift away from the Emmitsburg Road served to break Robertson's brigade into two pieces. Resultantly, Robertson's 3rd Arkansas and 1st Texas advanced toward Houck's Ridge (and nearer the Emmitsburg Road), while his 4th and 5th Texas followed Law's 4th, 47th, and 15th Alabama regiments toward the Round Tops. Robertson described this separation in his report, written July 17, 1863: "I was ordered to keep my right well closed on Brigadier-General Law's left, and to let my left rest on the Emmettsburg [sic] pike. I had advanced but a short distance when I discovered that my brigade would not fill the space between General Law's left and the pike named, and that I must leave the pike or disconnect myself from General Law on my right. Understanding before the action commenced that the attack on our part was to be general, and that the force of General McLaws was to advance simultaneously with us on my immediate left, and seeing at once that a mountain held by the enemy in heavy force with artillery, to the right of General Law's centre, was the key to the enemy's left, I abandoned the pike and closed on General Law's left. This caused some separation of my regiments.... As we approached the base of the mountain, General Law moved to the right, and I was moving obliquely to the right to close on him." See *OR* 27/2, 404, and Pfarr, *Longstreet at Gettysburg*, 101; Robertson more succinctly clarified his orders in a May 1882 letter to John Bachelder, stating, "My orders from Gen. Hood was [sic] to keep my left on the Emmitsburg road and in no event to leave it unless the exigency of the battle made it necessary or proper, in which case I was to use my judgement. My right joined Law....The Emmitsburg road from where we started, bears sharply to the left. While Law on my right bore to the right, which separated my brigade." See David L. and Audrey J. Ladd, *The Bachelder Papers*, Vol. II, September 6, 1880, to April 12, 1886, 860–861; Lieutenant Colonel James D. Waddell, who took over command of the 20th Georgia regiment, Benning's brigade, following the death of Colonel John A. Jones, described how, when his regiment advanced, he immediately noticed a sizable gap between Law's and Robertson's brigade, writing, "We had not advanced far before it was ascertained that there was a considerable space intervening between Law's and Robertson's brigades." See *OR* 27/2: 426.

60. Pfanz, *Gettysburg: The Second Day*, 499n68; Daniel M. Laney, "Wasted Gallantry: Hood's Texas Brigade at Gettysburg," *The Gettysburg Magazine*, Issue 16 (1997), 36; On the vulnerability of Sickles' line to flank attack via the Plum Run Valley, see K. Paul Raver, "Deception and the Citizen-General: The Sickles Faction at Gettysburg," *The Gettysburg Magazine*, Issue 31 (2004), 70, 72.

61. Hood, *Advance and Retreat*, 59; Coddington, *The Gettysburg Campaign*, 402; See Sears, *Gettysburg*, 265 for an example of this prevalent, misleading assertion, with the author claiming, "On this 2nd of July Hood's mission was essentially what Lee originally intended for McLaws....Hood determined to strike the newly found Federal left with Robertson's brigade directly, while Law on the right swung across Round Top and Little Round Top to turn the Federals' flank." Likewise, see James M. McPherson, *Battle Cry of Freedom*,

659, "Rising above the surrounding countryside, the two Round Tops dominated the south end of Cemetery Ridge. If the rebels had gotten artillery up there, they could have enfiladed the Union left. Sickles' advance had uncovered these hills. A brigade of Alabamians advanced to seize Little Round Top." Douglas Southall Freeman, in his *Lee* (p. 332), a biography of the commander of the Army of Northern Virginia, suggested that Hood's division, specifically Law's brigade, was "forced to fight their way directly toward the ridge and, where they could mount it, to turn to the left." In his later work, *Lee's Lieutenants: A Study in Command* (p. 580), Freeman again matter-of-factly stated, as if it was in accordance with his orders, "Evander Law, ... pushed his own brigade over Round Top and grappled with the enemy on Little Round Top." Longstreet biographer, Jeffry Wert, in his *General James Longstreet: The Confederacy's Most Controversial Soldier*, 273–274, acknowledges that Hood was made amply aware of his orders to "assault up the Emmitsburg Road"; however, the author then describes the progress of the attack matter-of-factly and without further explanation, contending, "They [the Confederates] found themselves on the lower slope of Big Round Top... and up the side of Little Round Top." Carol Reardon, in her U.S. Army staff ride book for Gettysburg, stresses on multiple occasions that it was always understood Law would proceed toward the Round Tops, writing: "Hood's attack plan for his four brigades seemed straightforward enough. Brig Gen. Evander M. Law's Alabamians would step off first, seize the crest of Round Top and move on Little Round Top, bypassing the III Corps' left flank at Devil's Den entirely"; "Brig. Gen. Henry L. Benning's Georgians would follow the Alabama flags, presumably to the Round Tops"; "Law's brigade split in two, with three regiments heading toward the Round Tops as planned"; and "Under Hood's original plan, Benning's Georgians should have followed the Alabamians toward the Round Tops." See Carol Reardon, *The Gettysburg Campaign: June-July 1863*, "The U.S. Army Campaigns of the Civil War," Center of Military History (U.S. Army, Washington, D.C., 2013), 36, 38.

62. Tucker, *High Tide at Gettysburg*, 252–255, 265–267; William C. Oates, *The War Between the Union and the Confederacy and Its Lost Opportunities with a History of the 15th Alabama Regiment and the Forty-Eight Battles in Which It Was Engaged*, 210. Evander Law never wrote an official report in the days and weeks following the Gettysburg battle; however, he did write a fairly lengthy postwar article. It is worth noting that in this postwar account, Law made no mention of ordering the extreme right of his brigade, specifically Oates, to wheel left after crossing Plum Run and to advance toward the ravine between the Round Tops. Instead, he simply noted what ultimately happened on his extreme right—"In the meantime my brigade, on the right, had swept over the northern slope of Round Top, cleared it of the enemy, and then, making a partial change of front to the left, advanced upon Little Round Top." See Law, "The Struggle for 'Round Top,'" *Battles and Leaders*, 3: 324.

63. Law did divert the 44th and 48th Alabama regiments from the extreme right of his brigade toward Devil's Den specifically to address Smith's Battery. See Laney, "Wasted Gallantry," *The Gettysburg Magazine*, Issue 16, 37.

64. OR 27/2, 392; Clifford Dowdey, in his *Lee and His Men at Gettysburg* (p209–210) nearly hit the nail on the head as to what happened on the extreme right of Longstreet's attack. Dowdey, with a palpable hint of glee at the disregard for Longstreet's orders to abide by Lee's directive and attack up the Emmitsburg Road, wrote bluntly, "Evander Law...refused to allow the system of command to negate the course of military logic. In one of the least-mentioned aspects of the whole 'Longstreet drama,' Evander Law flatly disobeyed orders. He caused the second day of Gettysburg to be fought in defiance of Lee's battle order to which Longstreet gave stubborn obedience." Dowdey continued on in this vein, "Before the command of the division came to him, Law, on his own responsibility, sent his brigade straight toward the base of Little Round Top, in violation of the orders to move obliquely northward.... In a sense, the battle on the right became Law's battle for Little Round Top." Dowdey was correct that this subtopic has been one of the least highlighted (but most consequential) of all subtopics over the decades when it comes to analysis of the July 2 battle; however, the jury is still out as to whether this extreme rightward movement toward the Round Tops was solely precipitated by Law. The brigade-turned-division commander at Gettysburg certainly showed disobedience when he ordered Oates to advance toward the ravine between the Round Tops early in the attack; however, as noted earlier, other evidence suggests Hood talked of a "digression" away from the Emmitsburg Road before the assault began, perhaps even instigating the Round Tops' ravine order before his wounding. Meanwhile, Oates in his official report stated point-blank that he disregarded Law's order to wheel left after crossing Plum Run, instead wheeling right. Whoever is to blame, Dowdey was altogether correct when he declared that much of Hood's division fought on July 2 "in defiance of Lee's battle order." Only a few battle studies have drawn limited attention to Oates' disobedience of Law's initial "left-wheel" order specifically. For example, see Bradley M. Gottfried in his *The Maps of Gettysburg* (p. 146) and *Brigades of Gettysburg: The Union and Confederate Brigades at the Battle of Gettysburg* (p. 430–431); Pfanz, *Gettysburg: The Second Day*, 169, 217; Laney, "Wasted Gallantry," *The Gettysburg Magazine*, Issue 16, 37; and Gary P. Bruner, "Up Over Big Round Top: The Forgotten 47th Alabama," *The Gettysburg Magazine*, Issue 22 (2000), 15; Edwin Coddington, in his *The Gettysburg Campaign* (p. 392), highlighted Oates' disregard of Law's order,

but appears to have found the regimental commander's reasoning for ignoring them acceptable. Coddington's misunderstanding of the sequence of events may have led him to accept Oates' justification. He wrote, "Just before Oates reached the highest part of the hill [Big Round Top]," and then introduced Law's order, "when he received Law's order to left wheel with his regiment." It is clear in both Oates' official report and his lengthy postwar account (*The War Between the Union and the Confederacy*) that he received Law's order well before scaling Big Round Top. In his official report, Oates wrote he received the order "after crossing the [stone] fence" at the base of Big Round Top, while in his postwar account he claimed it was "as we were advancing" and before or while crossing Plum Run. The referenced stone fence and Plum Run are located nowhere near the "highest part" of Big Round Top. Additionally, Coddington framed Law's order as directing him "to join in the attack on Devil's Den," whereas Oates wrote in his report he was to "move in the direction of the heights upon my left," which was further clarified in his postwar account to mean "to hug the base of Great Round Top and go up the valley between the two mountains." Stephen Sears' work, *Gettysburg* (p. 271), does not mention Oates' disregard of Law's wheel left orders and quotes half of Law's full order. According to Oates, Law's full order was "hug the base of Great Round Top and go up the valley between the two mountains, until I found the left of the Union line, to turn it and do all the damage I could," whereas Sears represents the order as "to locate 'the left of the Union line, to turn it and do all the damage I could.'" Sears' work presents Oates' movement up Big Round Top as a matter of course and within the confines of his orders, when in fact it was not. With all of this to say, it is necessary to reiterate and stress that Law's order disregarded Longstreet and Lee's order to attack up the Emmitsburg Road (keeping in mind that Hood may have had influence on Law's order), and then Oates disregarded Law's order by wheeling right and continuing up Big Round Top. On one page of Allen Guelzo's *Gettysburg: The Last Invasion* (p. 265) the author describes regiments in Hood's division, specifically from Robertson's and Law's brigade, as "wobbl[ing] rightward," "wandering rightward," and "stumbl[ing] even farther rightward," but then provides little commentary on how or why these regiments moved rightward.

65. Carol Reardon and Tom Vossler, *A Field Guide to Gettysburg*, Second Edition, 196–197; Guelzo, *Gettysburg: The Last Invasion*, 265; Laney, "Wasted Gallantry," *The Gettysburg Magazine*, Issue 16, 34–35; Before being pushed back to Big Round Top, Stoughton's men were initially posted to the west of Plum Run between the Reverend Michael Bushman and John Slyder Farms, with their right flank posted near the Slyder Farm Lane. Law's skirmishers, made up of five companies from the 47th and 48th Alabama regiments, pushed Stoughton back toward Big Round Top. According to Oates' postwar account, these five companies then continued to drift right toward the southern face of Big Round Top and passed entirely around to the eastern side of the hill. See Oates, *The War Between the Union and the Confederacy*, 207–208n; Gary Bruner in his 2000 article, "Up Over Big Round Top" in *The Gettysburg Magazine* (Issue 22, p. 12), clarifies how Stoughton's eastward retreat unfolded, noting that five companies on his left fell back toward the stone wall near Big Round Top, while three companies on the right retreated toward Devil's Den.

66. Initially, Law's skirmishers, and then Oates' men pushed Stoughton's sharpshooters toward and up Big Round Top. Stoughton described how this action developed in his official report, written July 27, 1863: "I moved forward to a brook some 200 yards beyond a second cross-road running perpendicular to the Emmitsburg pike, and intersecting with it in front of Sugar Loaf hill [Little Round Top]....The enemy then advanced a line of battle covering our entire front and flank. While they were advancing, the Second Regiment did splendid execution, killing and wounding a great many. One regiment broke three times, and rallied, before it would advance. I held my position until their line of battle was within 100 yards of me and their skirmishers were pushing my right flank, when I ordered my men to fall back, firing as they retired. My left wing retreated-up the hill." See *OR* 27/1, 518–519; Stoughton wrote to Gettysburg historian John Bachelder in December 1881 with a keen memory as to the actions of his sharpshooters. Confirming the substance of his official report, Stoughton wrote, "My men were distributed in front of Round Top and Sugar Loaf [Little Round Top] by Companys [sic] placed on the higher points of ground, and pickets were sent out into the Emmitsburg Pike beyond which was a wheat field where the right of the Rebel Army formed.... We were driven from our lookout by the advance of the Rebel skirmishers; the line extending around the foot of Round Top Mountain, until the general attack was made when the right of my line swung back onto the Mountain among the Rocks." See David L. and Audrey J. Ladd, *The Bachelder Papers*, Vol. II, September 6, 1880, to April 12, 1886, 767; Oates described the action from his perspective in one of his postwar accounts, writing, "When crossing the little run [Plum Run] we received the first fire from the Federal infantry, posted behind a stone fence near the foot of Round Top mountain. Our line did not halt, but pressing for-ward drove our enemy from the fence and up the side of the mountain.... I continued to advance straight up the southern face of Round Top.... I pressed forward until I reached the top and the highest point on top of Round Top." See William C. Oates, "Gettysburg—The Battle on the Right," *SHSP* 6:174–175. Note that in this particular postwar account published in the *SHSP*, Oates did not draw attention to what he subtly included in his other postwar account, *The War Between the Union and the*

Confederacy, and overtly in his official report—namely that he ignored Law's alleged order to wheel left after crossing Plum Run; Oates also wrote a letter to John Bachelder in March 1876, where he again neglected to mention Law's alleged wheel left order and his disregard of that directive. See David L. and Audrey J. Ladd, *The Bachelder Papers*, Vol. I, January 5, 1863, to July 27, 1880, 464–465.

67. Oates, *The War Between the Union and the Confederacy*, 210–211; *OR* 27/2, 392; David L. and Audrey J. Ladd, *The Bachelder Papers*, Vol. I, January 5, 1863, to July 27, 1880, 465; Hessler and Isenberg, *Gettysburg's Peach Orchard*, 127; Pfanz, *Gettysburg: The Second Day*, 217; Tucker, *High Tide at Gettysburg*, 252–255, 265–267; Coddington, *The Gettysburg Campaign*, 402–403; Apparently, Oates always held onto the belief that Big Round Top was actually *the* key position, not Little Round Top, and blamed Longstreet for not recognizing this during the fight. Oates wrote in a March 1898 letter, "[Lt. Gen. James] Longstreet was responsible for the loss of the battle—that had he been in his proper position he could have won it by holding great Round Top & planting artillery on it." See Glenn W. LaFantasie, ed., "William C. Oates Remembers Little Round Top," *The Gettysburg Magazine*, Issue 21 (1999), 59.

68. Oates, "Gettysburg—The Battle on the Right," *SHSP* 6:175; In Evander Law's postwar account, he also drew attention to Longstreet being physically located with McLaws' division during his July 2 attack, and therefore concluded that the First Corps commander knew little about Hood's (Law's) attack through personal observation. Law wrote, "The meagerness of the details of the operations [of Hood's division] referred to may be accounted for by the fact that General Longstreet personally superintended the left of his line, consisting of McLaws' division of his own corps... and hence knew comparatively little from personal observation of the movements of Hood's division." See Law, "The Struggle for 'Round Top,'" *Battles and Leaders*, 3: 319; Likewise, in a March 1876 letter to John Bachelder, Joseph Kershaw expressed his understanding that Hood's division largely acted on its own on July 2, writing, "Hood's division passed altogether to the right and operated as I have always understood, independently against Round Top." Kershaw's statement about Hood's men passing "altogether to the right" further highlights that division's divergence from the Confederate High Command's guiding directive to attack up the Emmitsburg Road. See David L. and Audrey J. Ladd, *The Bachelder Papers*, Vol. I, January 5, 1863, to July 27, 1880, 454.

69. David L. and Audrey J. Ladd, *The Bachelder Papers*, Vol. I, January 5, 1863, to July 27, 1880, 449; *OR* 27/2: 405; Tucker, *High Tide at Gettysburg*, 264, 267; Coddington, *The Gettysburg Campaign*, 749; Garry E. Adelman, "Benning's Georgia Brigade at Gettysburg," *The Gettysburg Magazine*, Issue 18 (1998), 63. Here is a brief note on Benning: It was intended that his brigade support Law's brigade. However, as indicated in his official report, he discovered later that woods obscured his ability to see Law's men and had actually advanced in support of Robertson's brigade. Benning wrote, "Our own first line also became visible advancing about 400 yards in our front. The part of it in our front I took to be Law's brigade, and so I followed it. In truth, it was Robertson's, Law's being farther to the right. This I did not discover until late in the fight, a wood on the right concealing from me most of Law's brigade." See *OR* 27/2: 415.

70. This temporary halt of action, followed soon thereafter by support from McLaws' division, is confirmed in other Confederate participants' official battle reports. For example, Colonel William W. White, who took over command of George T. Anderson's brigade after Anderson's wounding, wrote in his official report, "The support not coming up in time and the enemy coming up on our left flank, Genl. Anderson changed the front of the left wing of the 7th Ga. Regt. (which occupied the extreme left of the brigade) but soon found they could not hold the enemy in check he then ordered the brigade to retire to the crest of the hill in the edge of the timber where the charge commenced. But a short time elapsed before McLaws division came up on our left, when Genrl. Anderson ordered another advance." See *OR* 27/2: 397; White was referring to Joseph Kershaw's 15th South Carolina regiment (McLaws' division), which came up on the left of Anderson's 9th Georgia before the second attack went forward. See Gottfried, *Brigades of Gettysburg*, 453.

71. Law, "The Struggle for 'Round Top,'" *Battles and Leaders*, 3: 324–325; Pfarr, *Longstreet at Gettysburg*, 102–103; It is worth mentioning that Law's testimony about speaking to Kershaw just before McLaws' division attacked is not corroborated in Kershaw's writings, namely his official report (*OR* 27/2: 367–368), *Battles and Leaders*, 3: 333–334 or in postwar letters (for instance: David L. and Audrey J. Ladd, *The Bachelder Papers*, Vol. I, January 5, 1863, to July 27, 1880, 452–458).

72. Daniel Laney, in his 1997 article, "Wasted Gallantry" for *The Gettysburg Magazine* (Issue 16, p. 39), stated appropriately, "As three of Law's Alabama regiments struck east and the other two passed in their rear and in the rear of the 4th and 5th Texas, Lee's plan of attack melted away." John Gibbon, Federal Second Corps division commander at Gettysburg, wrote about standard military practice for obeying orders when addressing the Meade-Sickles Controversy at Gettysburg; however, the rule would apply here too regarding what happened on the extreme right of Hood's front on July 2. Gibbons wrote, "In cases of this kind there is and can be but one rule in armies. If a soldier is ordered to go to a certain point on the field of battle, he goes there if he can. If he does not get orders to go there, he does not go, with the one single exception that overwhelming necessity requires him to make the move, *when he is so*

situated that he cannot solicit or receive the order of his commanding officer [emphasis added]." See Broadwater, *Gettysburg as the Generals Remembered It*, 89–90; James Longstreet, *From Manassas to Appomattox*, 370–371.

73. For additional details on why Lee requested Longstreet closely oversee McLaws' division at Gettysburg, see Pfarr, *Longstreet at Gettysburg*, 100.

74. In his essay on the Federal Third Corps at Gettysburg, historian William Glenn Robertson underscores that Sickles' "advance... threw the Confederate attackers off stride." Stephen Sears has perhaps sized up the scenario facing Longstreet on July 2 best when succinctly declaring, "Minute by minute the Confederate High Command was forced to revise its already altered attack plan." See Robertson, "Daniel E. Sickles and the Third Corps," 55; Sears, *Gettysburg*, 271.

75. Pfarr, *Longstreet at Gettysburg*, 102–105; *OR* 27/2: 367; David L. and Audrey J. Ladd, *The Bachelder Papers*, Vol. I, January 5, 1863, to July 27, 1880, 455.

76. It would probably be more accurate to say that Paul Semmes' brigade, ultimately advancing into battle on Kershaw's right, established a weightier connection with G.T. Anderson's left flank between 6:15 and 6:45 p.m. That said, the 15th South Carolina remained to the left of the 9th Georgia even throughout the entirety of John Caldwell's Wheatfield counterattack. See Gottfried, *The Maps of Gettysburg*, 170–179, and G.T. Anderson's December 1894 letter to John Bachelder in David L. and Audrey J. Ladd, *The Bachelder Papers*, Vol. III, April 12, 1886, to December 22, 1894, 1871. Anderson indicated "De Saussure's [*sic*] regiment from Kershaw was ordered on my left." Colonel William D. DeSaussure commanded the 15th South Carolina regiment.

77. This area of the Wheatfield Road was defended by the batteries of Ames, Thompson, Hart, Clark, Philipps, and Bigelow, along with the 2nd New Hampshire, 3rd Maine, 68th Pennsylvania, 141st Pennsylvania, and 3rd Michigan infantry regiments. See Gottfried, *The Maps of Gettysburg*, 186–187, and Hessler, *Sickles at Gettysburg*, 184, 195.

78. "Kershaw's Brigade at Gettysburg," *Battles and Leaders*, 3: 334–336; David L. and Audrey J. Ladd, *The Bachelder Papers*, Vol. I, January 5, 1863, to July 27, 1880, 455.

79. Yet another caveat is that before moving behind Humphrey's division, Caldwell was posted on Hancock's left flank. Caldwell's move off Cemetery Ridge further weakened Hancock's line, which nearly had drastic consequences for the Federals once Cadmus Wilcox's and David Lang's Confederate Third Corps brigades joined the attack to Barksdale's left. For additional details, see Hessler, *Sickles at Gettysburg*, 218, and Pfarr, *Longstreet at Gettysburg*, 104–107.

80. Sears, *Gettysburg*, 298; Coddington, *The Gettysburg Campaign*, 406–407; "Kershaw's Brigade at Gettysburg," *Battles and Leaders*, 3: 337; McLaws, "Gettysburg," *SHSP* 7: 74; James Hessler has pointed out three of the foremost factors that led to Barksdale's success against Sickles' line at the Peach Orchard, namely that Barksdale only needed to advance 600 yards to reach the Federal line; a sizable gap existed between the 68th and 114th Pennsylvania, which Barksdale exploited; and the four regiments to the left of those two regiments—the 2nd New Hampshire, 3rd Maine, 141st Pennsylvania, and 3rd Michigan—were all from different brigades (Burling, Ward, Graham, and De Trobriand). Having outlined these factors, Hessler has also drawn much attention to the significant casualties Barksdale sustained on July 2, particularly after his brigade achieved its breakthrough at the Peach Orchard. See Hessler and Isenberg, *Gettysburg's Peach Orchard*, 156–157, and Hessler's speech, "Gettysburg's Peach Orchard," August 8, 2019, U.S. Army Heritage and Education Center.

81. John Imhof, *Gettysburg Day Two: A Study in Maps*, 150, 153; Hessler, *Sickles at Gettysburg*, 200; Hessler and Isenberg, *Gettysburg's Peach Orchard*, 192.

82. James Longstreet, *From Manassas to Appomattox*, 372.

83. Ibid., 372; Pfanz, *Gettysburg: The Second Day*, 328–329; Coddington, *The Gettysburg Campaign*, 406; Gottfried, *The Maps of Gettysburg*, 176–181; James Longstreet, "Lee in Pennsylvania," *Annals of the War*, 424; Pfarr, *Longstreet at Gettysburg*, 105–112.

84. Jay Jorgensen, "Wofford Sweeps the Wheatfield," *The Gettysburg Magazine*, Issue 22 (2000), 37–41; Pfarr, *Longstreet at Gettysburg*, 103, 118–120; Gottfried, *Brigades of Gettysburg*, 420–421.

85. Hessler, *Sickles at Gettysburg*, 318, 321, 380; Sauers, *Gettysburg: The Meade-Sickles Controversy*, 71.

86. David L. and Audrey J. Ladd, *The Bachelder Papers*, Vol. I, January 5, 1863 to July 27, 1880, 100.

87. Hessler, *Sickles at Gettysburg*, 368, 374–375.

Essay 3

1. Jeffry D. Wert, *General James Longstreet: The Confederacy's Most Controversial Soldier*, 268–269; Robert K. Krick, "'If Longstreet Says So... It Is Most Likely Not True': James Longstreet and the Second Day at Gettysburg," in *The Second Day at Gettysburg: Essays on Confederate and Union Leadership*, ed. Gary W. Gallagher, 70.

2. John C. Oeffinger, ed., *A Soldier's General: The Civil War Letters of Major General Lafayette McLaws*, 197, Krick, "'If Longstreet Says So... It Is Most Likely Not True,'" 65; Cory M. Pfarr, *Longstreet at Gettysburg: A Critical Reassessment*, 95–100.

3. John C. Oeffinger, ed., *A Soldier's General: The Civil War Letters of Major General Lafayette McLaws*, 197; Lafayette McLaws, "Gettysburg," *Southern Historical Society Papers (SHSP)*, 7: 70, 76–77..

4. Gilbert Moxley Sorrel, *At the Right Hand of Longstreet: Recollections of a Confederate Staff Officer*, 168; McLaws, "Gettysburg," *SHSP* 7: 84.

5. David A. Powell, "A Reconnaissance Gone Awry: Capt. Samuel R. Johnston's Fateful Trip to Little Round Top," *The Gettysburg Magazine*, Issue 23 (2000), 88–90; Bill Hyde, "Did You Get There?: Capt. Samuel Johnston's Reconnaissance at Gettysburg," *The Gettysburg Magazine*, Issue 29 (2003), 90–93; Pfarr, *Longstreet at Gettysburg*, 58, 60, 64–65.

6. McLaws, "Gettysburg," *SHSP* 7: 68–69; John B. Hood, *Advance and Retreat*, 57.

7. McLaws, "Gettysburg," *SHSP* 7: 69.

8. For additional information on Johnston's additional reconnaissance activities following his early morning scouting mission, see Pfarr, *Longstreet at Gettysburg*, 73–74, 76–77.

9. McLaws, "Gettysburg," *SHSP* 7: 68, 76; Glenn Tucker, *Lee and Longstreet at Gettysburg*, 20; Pfarr, *Longstreet at Gettysburg*, 58–59, 66–67, 76.

10. Historians have regularly discounted the claim Lee ordered or expected Johnston to lead the First Corps marching column along a concealed route to its attack jump-off points—a claim clearly present in McLaws' postwar accounts. In contesting this claim, they almost always hang their hat on Johnston's postwar claim that he had "no idea that I had the confidence of the great Lee to such an extent that he would entrust me with the conduct of any army corps moving within two miles of the enemy's line." For whatever reason, less attention has been drawn to McLaws' thoughts, specifically, on this claim of Johnston's, which are captured in the margin of a document in McLaws' papers, called "Notes on Gettysburg," written by Johnston in the late 1880s. McLaws argued, "He [Johnston] seems not to realise [sic] that he was conducting my column, for he was the only one who was supposed to know or could know, the route to take. He denies that Gen. Lee or anyone else said anything to him about finding a route to go on ... which would be invisible to the enemy & yet when I was following the route *he must* have designated as the proper one he tells General Longstreet 'without being asked' that by this route my movements would be disclosed to the enemy.'" See Edwin B. Coddington, *The Gettysburg Campaign: A Study in Command*, 736n95. For additional commentary on this debate, see Pfarr, *Longstreet at Gettysburg*, 75–77.

11. McLaws, "Gettysburg," *SHSP* 7: 69; Tucker, *Lee and Longstreet at Gettysburg*, 31; Hyde, "Did You Get There?" 87; Pfarr, *Longstreet at Gettysburg*, 64–65, 77; James Longstreet, *From Manassas to Appomattox*, 363; *The War of the Rebellion: A Compilation of the Official Records of the Union and Confederate Armies*, 128 vols. (Washington D.C. 1880-1901), Series 1, Vol. 27, Pt. 2, 350; hereafter cited as *OR*. All references are to Series 1 unless otherwise noted. James A. Hessler, *Sickles at Gettysburg: The Controversial Civil War General Who Committed Murder, Abandoned Little Round Top, and Declared Himself the Hero of Gettysburg*, 110, 127.

12. Tucker, *Lee and Longstreet at Gettysburg*, 31–32.

13. Wert, *General James Longstreet*, 268–269, 279.

14. James M. McPherson, *Battle Cry of Freedom: The Civil War Era*, 657; Shelby Foote, *The Civil War, A Narrative: Fredericksburg to Meridian*, 498; Noah A. Trudeau, *Gettysburg: A Testing of Courage*, 312.

15. Glenn Tucker, *High Tide at Gettysburg*, 235–236.

16. McLaws, "Gettysburg," *SHSP* 7: 68–69; Stephen W. Sears, *Gettysburg*, 255.

17. Allen C. Guelzo, *Gettysburg: The Last Invasion*, 238.

18. Douglas Southall Freeman, *Lee's Lieutenants: A Study in Command*, One-Volume Abridgement, ed. Stephen W. Sears, 576–577.

19. *Ibid.*, 577; Clifford Dowdey, *Lee and His Men at Gettysburg: The Death of a Nation*, 187, 191.

20. Edwin B. Coddington, *The Gettysburg Campaign: A Study in Command*, 378.

21. Krick, "'If Longstreet Says So...It Is Most Likely Not True,'" 70–71.

22. Harry W. Pfanz, *Gettysburg: The Second Day*, 113, 118–119.

23. *OR* 27/2: 349.

24. It is worth noting that, in the postwar years, Johnston disputed Pendleton's official report claim that he accompanied the artillery chief on an early morning reconnaissance on July 2. Rather, Johnston claimed that the only time he reconnoitered with Pendleton was on the evening of July 1 (with Long and Walker). As recounted, in his official report, Pendleton did not name Johnston as among the party of officers who scouted with him on July 1. See Powell, "A Reconnaissance Gone Awry," 93; *OR* 27/2: 349.

25. *OR* 27/2: 349–351; Pfarr, *Longstreet at Gettysburg*, 74.

26. Letter from General A.L. Long, "Causes of Lee's Defeat at Gettysburg," *SHSP* 4: 66–67.

27. Edward Porter Alexander, *Fighting for the Confederacy: The Personal Recollections of General Edward Porter Alexander*, 235–236; Edward Porter Alexander, *Military Memoirs of a Confederate: A Critical Narrative*, 391; Edward Porter Alexander, "Letter from General E.P. Alexander," March 17, 1877, *SHSP* 4: 101.

28. John L. Black, *Crumbling Defenses or Memoirs and Reminiscences of John Logan Black, Colonel C.S.A.*, https://babel.hathitrust.org/cgi/pt?id=wu.89059412684 (accessed November 2020), 37–39; David L. and Audrey J. Ladd, *The Bachelder Papers*, Vol. II, September 6, 1880 to April 12, 1886, 1240–1241, 1269; Pfanz, *Gettysburg: The Second Day*, 116.

29. Wert, *General James Longstreet*, 268–269; Jeffry D. Wert, "No Fifteen Thousand Men Can Take That Position," *James Longstreet: The Man, the Soldier, the Controversy*, ed. R.L. Dinardo and Albert A. Nofi, 86–87.

30. McLaws, "Gettysburg," *SHSP* 7: 69.

31. In his postwar accounts, Alexander made no mention of speaking with Longstreet between the time of receiving his orders during the 9 a.m. hour and when the First Corps' divisions ultimately attacked in the late afternoon. Alexander did allege he saw Longstreet's marching column halted near Black Horse Tavern. For reasons unknown, it appears that while there, he never spoke to Longstreet or anyone else in authority. For a full analysis of Alexander's short (but often discussed) appearance at Black Horse Tavern, see Pfarr, *Longstreet at Gettysburg*, 80–83.

32. Tucker, *High Tide at Gettysburg*, 227; Tucker, *Lee and Longstreet at Gettysburg*, 46; Coddington, *The Gettysburg Campaign*, 372–375; Dowdey, *Lee and His Men at Gettysburg*, 181; Sears, *Gettysburg*, 254, 257; Guelzo, *Gettysburg: The Last Invasion*, 235–238; Pfanz, *Gettysburg: The Second Day*, 105–107, 116–117.

33. John C. Oeffinger, ed., *A Soldier's General: The Civil War Letters of Major General Lafayette McLaws*, 197; McLaws, "Gettysburg," *SHSP* 7: 78, 84.

Essay 4

1. See Cory M. Pfarr, *Longstreet at Gettysburg: A Critical Reassessment*, Chapter 9: "The First Corps March Conundrum," 75–83.

2. Ibid., 84.

3. Letter from James Longstreet to Harry Heth, February 14, 1897, *Southern Historical Society Papers*, 44: 246. Hereafter cited as *SHSP*.

4. Pfarr, *Longstreet at Gettysburg*, 73–78; *The War of the Rebellion: A Compilation of the Official Records of the Union and Confederate* Armies, 128 vols. (Washington, D.C. 1880–1901), Series 1, Vol. 27, Pt. 2, 358, 366–367; Hereafter cited as *OR*. All references are to Series 1 unless otherwise noted.; Gilbert Moxley Sorrel, *At the Right Hand of Longstreet: Recollections of a Confederate Staff Officer*, 168; Lafayette McLaws, "Gettysburg," *SHSP* 7:68; Evander Law, "The Struggle for 'Round Top,'" *Battles and Leaders*, 3:320; William C. Oates, "Gettysburg—The Battle on the Right," *SHSP* 6:173.

5. Pfarr, *Longstreet at Gettysburg*, 76–77; Glenn Tucker, *Lee and Longstreet at Gettysburg*, 20.

6. Characteristic of the claim that Lee was most worried about speed of movement on the morning of July 2 (as opposed to concealment) is Longstreet critic Robert Krick's contention, "The march surely would have taken considerable time under the best of circumstances. Inevitably such moves involved delays. Given the urgency of the situation, celerity (to use one of the favorite words of the sorely missed T.J. Jackson) clearly was in requisition. Longstreet ignored that patently obvious imperative from the outset." See Robert K. Krick, "'If Longstreet Says So…It Is Most Likely Not True': James Longstreet and the Second Day at Gettysburg," in *The Second Day at Gettysburg: Essays on Confederate and Union Leadership*, ed. Gary W. Gallagher, 70; McLaws, "Gettysburg," *SHSP* 7:69; Tucker, *Lee and Longstreet at Gettysburg*, 31; James A. Hessler and Britt C. Isenberg, *Gettysburg's Peach Orchard: Longstreet, Sickles, and the Bloody Fight for the "Commanding Ground" Along the Emmitsburg Road*, 65.

7. See Pfarr, *Longstreet at Gettysburg*, Chapter 9: "The First Corps March Conundrum," 75–83.

8. Ibid., 66–77; McLaws' postwar recollection was 1 p.m. Similarly, Joseph Kershaw, commanding McLaws' leading brigade, wrote that "we lay there waiting orders until noon, or an hour later." In an 1876 letter to Gettysburg historian John Bacheler, Kershaw claimed his brigade moved "about one and a half o'clock." For Kershaw's accounts, see Joseph Kershaw, "Kershaw's Brigade at Gettysburg," *Battles and Leaders*, 3:331 and David L. and Audrey J. Ladd, *The Bachelder Papers*, Vol. I, January 5, 1863, to July 27, 1880, 453.

9. McLaws, "Gettysburg," *SHSP* 7:68; *OR* 27/2: 608, 614.

10. Kershaw, "Kershaw's Brigade at Gettysburg," *Battles and Leaders*, 3:331; David L. and Audrey J. Ladd, *The Bachelder Papers*, Vol. I, January 5, 1863, to July 27, 1880, 453; James Longstreet, *From Manassas to Appomattox*, 366; James Longstreet, "Lee in Pennsylvania," *Annals of the War*, 423; Pfarr, *Longstreet at Gettysburg*, 77–79; Hessler and Isenberg, *Gettysburg's Peach Orchard*, 65–66; Karlton D. Smith, "'To Consider Every Contingency': Lt. Gen. James Longstreet, Capt. Samuel R. Johnston, and the factors that affected the reconnaissance and countermarch, July 2, 1863," http://npshistory.com/series/symposia/gettysburg_seminars/11/essay4.pdf, 11–12.

11. Pfarr, *Longstreet at Gettysburg*, 78–83.

12. Kershaw, "Kershaw's Brigade at Gettysburg," *Battles and Leaders*, 3:331; David L. and Audrey J. Ladd, *The Bachelder Papers*, Vol. I, January 5, 1863, to July 27, 1880, 454; *OR* 27/2: 366.

13. Krick, "'If Longstreet Says So…It Is Most Likely Not True,'" 72; Edward Porter Alexander, *Fighting for the Confederacy: The Personal Recollections of General Edward Porter Alexander*, 236. In a March 1877 letter to the Southern Historical Society—written 20 years before his *Fighting for the Confederacy*—Alexander similarly contended that when he arrived at the Black Horse Tavern scene, the head of Longstreet's column was "standing halted in the road where it was in sight of Round Top" and mentioned that once "they had halted, in finding themselves already exposed." See E.P. Alexander, "Letter from General E.P. Alexander, Late Chief of Artillery, First Corps, A.N.V.," in series "Causes of Lee's Defeat at Gettysburg," *SHSP* 4:101. Contrary to Alexander's 1877 letter and his *Fighting for the Confederacy*, he wrote more indistinctly and with less commitment in his 1907 book, *Military Memoirs of a Confederate*: "Riding back presently to learn the cause of their non-arrival, the head of the column was found halted, where its road became exposed to the Federal view, while messages were sent to Longstreet." See E.P. Alexander, *Military Memoirs of a Confederate*, 392.

14. Longstreet, "Lee in Pennsylvania," *Annals of the War*, 423; James Longstreet, "Lee's Right Wing at Gettysburg," *Battles and Leaders*, 3: 340; Longstreet, *From Manassas to Appomattox*, 365–367; Sorrel, *At the Right Hand of Longstreet*, 168.

15. OR 27/3: 488.

16. Kershaw, "Kershaw's Brigade at Gettysburg," *Battles and Leaders*, 3:331; McLaws, "Gettysburg," *SHSP* 7:69.

17. Sauers, *Gettysburg: The Meade-Sickles Controversy*, 33, 64; Hessler, *Sickles at Gettysburg*, 106, 109, 125–127.

18. Cadmus M. Wilcox, "General C.M. Wilcox on the Battle of Gettysburg," *SHSP* 6: 113–114.

19. Alexander, *Military Memoirs of a Confederate*, 392.

20. In their study on July 2, 1863, David L. Schultz and Scott L. Mingus, Sr., stated similarly, "Instead of facing about his entire division to avoid congestion, McLaws likely ordered Kershaw…." See David L. Schultz and Scott L. Mingus, Sr., *The Second Day at Gettysburg: The Attack and Defense of Cemetery Ridge, July 2, 1863*, 258.

21. Stephen Sears, *Gettysburg*, 259; Glenn Tucker, *High Tide at Gettysburg*, 234.

22. McLaws, "Gettysburg," *SHSP* 7:68, 71–72; John B. Hood, *Advance and Retreat*, 57.

23. William J. Hardee, *Rifle and Light Infantry Tactics for the Exercise and Manoeuvres [sic] of Troops When Acting as Light Infantry or Riflemen: Volume II*, 79–80; "Civil War Biography: William J. Hardee," American Battlefield Trust, https://www.battlefields.org/learn/biographies/william-j-hardee (accessed September 24, 2020).

24. Hardee, *Rifle and Light Infantry Tactics, Volume II*, 79–80.

25. McLaws, "Gettysburg," *SHSP* 7:69.

26. *Ibid.*; OR 27/2: 350; Smith, "To Consider Every Contingency," 13.

27. Kershaw, "Kershaw's Brigade at Gettysburg," *Battles and Leaders*, 3:332; David L. and Audrey J. Ladd, *The Bachelder Papers*, Vol. I, January 5, 1863, to July 27, 1880, 449; Smith, "To Consider Every Contingency," 13–14. It is worth mentioning here that the entirety of McLaws' division remained in the lead as the column set off down the "ravine road" (with Hood waiting to follow), save for Colonel Henry Cabell's artillery battalion (under McLaws), which got cut off at the Fairfield Road-Ravine Road crossroads and had to wait until Hood passed down Willoughby Run before rejoining McLaws' division. See Hessler and Isenberg, *Gettysburg's Peach Orchard*, 67, 67n8; Schultz and Mingus, Sr., *The Second Day at Gettysburg*, 255, 257, 259–260.

28. McLaws, "Gettysburg," *SHSP* 7:69; OR 27/2: 350, 367; David L. and Audrey J. Ladd, *The Bachelder Papers*, Vol. I, January 5, 1863, to July 27, 1880, 454; For reference, as far as distance covered during the entirety of the march—to include the march, countermarch, and resumed march—Gettysburg Licensed Battlefield Guides James A. Hessler and Britt C. Isenberg have estimated "the total actual march for Kershaw's head of column was about five and a quarter miles." Hessler and Isenberg further note that if the column had not countermarched, but instead elected to continue down Black Horse Tavern Road past the elevated point, "Kershaw's total marching distance would have been about two and three quarter miles." See Hessler and Isenberg, *Gettysburg's Peach Orchard*, 68, 68n10.

29. Longstreet, "Lee's Right Wing at Gettysburg," *Battles and Leaders*, 3:340; Longstreet, *From Manassas to Appomattox*, 366–367.

30. Longstreet, "Lee in Pennsylvania," *Annals of the War*, 423; Hood, *Advance and Retreat*, 57.

31. Wilcox, "General C.M. Wilcox on the Battle of Gettysburg," *SHSP* 6: 113–114; Sorrel, *At the Right Hand of Longstreet*, 168.

32. Edwin B. Coddington, *The Gettysburg Campaign: A Study in Command*, 379, 737n99.

33. Tucker, *High Tide at Gettysburg*, 235.

34. Douglas Southall Freeman, *Lee's Lieutenants: A Study in Command*, One-Volume Abridgement, ed. Stephen W. Sears, 578.

35. Shelby Foote, *The Civil War: A Narrative, Fredericksburg to Meridian*, 493.

36. Tucker's statement is sandwiched between his recounting of some postwar recollections from Evander Law and Joseph Kershaw. In endnotes eight and nine for that chapter, "The Story of the Missing Canteens," Tucker noted his use of *Battles and Leaders*, Volume III, pages 320 and 332 (corresponding with Law's and Kershaw's articles), but the details afforded by those officers confirm nothing about Hood passing in front of McLaws during the march. See, Tucker, *High Tide at Gettysburg*, 420n8–9.

37. Coddington, *The Gettysburg Campaign*, 380; Harry W. Pfanz, *Gettysburg: The Second Day*, 123.

38. Pfanz, *Gettysburg: The Second Day*, 122, 490n56.

39. Hood, *Advance and Retreat*, 57; Pfanz, *Gettysburg: The Second Day*, 122.

40. Law, "The Struggle for 'Round Top,'" *Battles and Leaders*, 3: 320; David L. and Audrey J. Ladd, *The Bachelder Papers*, Vol. I, January 5, 1863, to July 27, 1880, 454, 464; Oates, "Gettysburg—The Battle on the Right," *SHSP* 6:173; Kershaw, "Kershaw's Brigade at Gettysburg," *Battles and Leaders*, 3:332; McLaws, "Gettysburg," *SHSP* 7:70; OR 27/2: 358.

41. Coddington, *The Gettysburg Campaign*, 380, 737n104; Clifford Dowdey, *Lee & His Men at Gettysburg: The Death of a Nation*, 199; John C. Oeffinger, ed., *A Soldier's General: The Civil War Letters of Major General Lafayette McLaws*, 196; McLaws, "Gettysburg," *SHSP* 7:71–72.

42. In a September 12–13, 2020, conversation with historian Ed Lowe on Facebook Messenger about "double on the front," Ed forwarded me a response from military historian David Powell, who wrote in part, "'Doubling', in this context, probably means forming behind, in a support line." A response from Robert Carter, a Chickamauga

Battlefield tours guide, similarly held, "To me the order 'double on the front' would be given in extreme dire circumstances and would reinforce the division in front."

43. Longstreet, "Lee's Right Wing at Gettysburg," *Battles and Leaders*, 3:340; Longstreet, *From Manassas to Appomattox*, 366–367; McLaws, "Gettysburg," *SHSP* 7:69–72; John C. Oeffinger, ed., *A Soldier's General*, 196; *OR* 27/2: 367.

44. Longstreet, *From Manassas to Appomattox*, 366–367; McLaws, "Gettysburg," *SHSP* 7:70, 72; *OR* 27/2: 351.

Essay 5

1. Harry W. Pfanz, *Gettysburg: The Second Day*, 352–353; Carol Reardon and Tom Vossler, *A Field Guide to Gettysburg*, Second Edition, 363; Bradley M. Gottfried, *Brigades of Gettysburg: The Union and Confederate Brigades at the Battle of Gettysburg*, 574–576; "Richard Heron Anderson," Civil War Biography, https://www.battlefields.org/learn/biographies/richard-h-anderson; Chester G. Hearn, Rick Sapp, and Steven Smith, *Civil War Commanders: From Fort Sumter to Appomattox Court House*, 17; Douglas S. Freeman, *Lee's Lieutenants: A Study in Command*, One-Volume Abridgement, 37, 108, 135–136, 138, 283, 376, 400–401, 410, 503–504; 523–535; Lynda Lasswell Crist, Mary Deaton Dix, and Kenneth H. Williams, eds., *The Papers of Jefferson Davis*, Volume 8 (1862), 229–230; J. Rickard (February 10, 2007), Richard Heron Anderson, 1821–1879, http://www.historyofwar.org/articles/people_anderson_rh.html; Jeffry D. Wert, *General James Longstreet: The Confederacy's Most Controversial Solider, A Biography*, 28–31, 38–46.

2. For a detailed account of Anderson's division during the Gettysburg Campaign, see especially, Eric. A. Campbell, "'Sacrificed to the bad management of others': Richard H. Anderson's Division at the Battle of Gettysburg," *The Army of Northern Virginia in the Gettysburg Campaign*, http://npshistory.com/series/symposia/gettysburg_seminars/7/essay6.pdf. Also see Cory M. Pfarr, *Longstreet at Gettysburg: A Critical Reassessment*, 105–112; Stephen Sears, *Gettysburg*, 317–318; Pfanz, *Gettysburg: The Second Day*, 385–387; Allen C. Guelzo, *Gettysburg: The Last Invasion*, 332–334; William Woods Hassler, *A.P. Hill: Lee's Forgotten General*, 161–162; Gottfried, *Brigades of Gettysburg*, 574–603.

3. Just after leading the Florida Brigade at the Battle of Chancellorsville, Edward Perry contracted typhoid fever and missed the entire Gettysburg Campaign. Before temporarily taking over brigade command, David Lang had been the colonel of the 8th Florida regiment. See Gottfried, *Brigades of Gettysburg*, 584.

4. Pfarr, *Longstreet at Gettysburg*, 69, 73, 106.

5. *Ibid.*, 73; Campbell, "'Sacrificed to the bad management of others,'" 6–7.

6. For full coverage of this topic, see Pfarr, *Longstreet at Gettysburg*, chapters 6–13 (pp. 57–104).

7. *Ibid.*, 105–112; Bradley M. Gottfried, *The Maps of Gettysburg: An Atlas of the Gettysburg Campaign, June 3—July 13, 1863*, 204–211. Much has been made of the actions of Mahone's brigade in Gettysburg scholarship over the decades. One argument has been advanced by modern popular historian John Horn, who contends "a myth has developed that Mahone's brigade failed to move at all on the evening of July 2." In addressing this claim, I would posit that the allegation "Mahone's brigade failed to move" is less a myth and more a simple difference of historical focus. Most historians have understandably focused their attention on how Mahone's brigade failed to move during Wilcox's, Lang's, and Wright's attack (with limited help from Posey). In short, Mahone's brigade made no contribution to Anderson's main attack carried out roughly between 6 and 8:30 p.m., which is the crux of the matter, not that Mahone engaged in some movements after darkness set in. Horn himself has demonstrated his understanding of this distinction when he notes in his own writings, "The fact of the matter is that around 8:45 p.m., near dark, Mahone's brigade shifted to its right and advanced too late to help Wright's, Lang's, and Wilcox's brigades of Anderson's division seize Cemetery Ridge"; "Mahone's brigade moved too late to be of assistance"; "Though too late to assist the rest of their division"; and "Mahone *did* advance, though not in time to continue the en echelon attack." See John Horn, "The Myth that Mahone's Brigade Did Not Move on July 2, 1863," *Gettysburg Magazine*, Issue 65 (2021), 47, 51–52, 56. Academic historian Hampton Newsome has also recently drawn attention to this late movement by Mahone's brigade. He characterizes it as "Mahone's Night Attack, July 2, 1863," draws attention to "two accounts from veterans of William Mahone's brigade describing a night attack planned for July 2 against the Union center at Gettysburg," and asserts that "sometime after dark, Mahone's regiments gathered for a night assault." See Hampton Newsome, "Gettysburg—Mahone's Night Attack, July 2, 1863," December 18, 2017, https://hamptonnewsome.blogspot.com/2017/12/gettysburg-mahones-night-attack-july-2.html.

8. Glenn Tucker, *Lee and Longstreet at Gettysburg*, 220. In one of E.P. Alexander's postwar memoirs, *Military Memoirs of a Confederate*—published in 1906—Alexander claimed that soon after the battle, Anderson replied to a newspaper correspondent "P.W.A." and their accusations regarding the inactivity of some of his brigades during the fight. According to Alexander, Anderson stated "that he was under orders from Hill to hold two brigades in reserve"—presumably referring to Posey and Mahone. Anderson also argued in his response "that when Wilcox's call for help was received he was unable to find Hill and refer the matter to him." See Edward Porter Alexander, *Military Memoirs of a Confederate*, 401. Along with

the Mahone "night attack" argument, some historians have also focused much time and effort on the contention that A.P. Hill had allegedly ordered Anderson to keep Posey and Mahone in reserve and only issued peremptory orders for Wilcox, Lang, and Wright to attack. They most often draw from E.P. Alexander's 1906 commentary and a letter E.P. Alexander received from Hillary Herbert on August 18, 1903, to argue Posey and Mahone performed as they did on July 2 because Anderson was under orders from Hill to keep two brigades in reserve (Posey and Mahone) and that Anderson had trouble finding Hill during the fight to free the brigades from those orders. Yet, Anderson's own after-battle report contradicts his statement to newspaper correspondent "P.W.A." regarding reserve brigades. In his report, Anderson said nothing of an alleged order to keep two brigades in reserve; rather, he plainly states, "…and the line of battle was formed, with the brigades in the following order: Wilcox's, Perry's (commanded by Col. David Lang), Wright's, Posey's, and Mahone's…. And I was at the same time ordered to put the troops of my division into action by brigades as soon as those of General Longstreet's corps had progressed so far in their assault as to be connected with my right flank." Anderson named all five of his brigades, made reference to sending "the troops of my division into action by brigades," and never mentioned any order to hold certain brigades in reserve. Neither is there mention of this alleged order in Hill's, Posey's, nor Mahone's official reports. Other historians have also drawn into question the "reserve" assertion upon underscoring the location of Posey's and Mahone's brigades in the Confederate battle line. They were not located in the rear of Wilcox, Lang, or Wright to offer effective and timely reserve support, but instead, next to them, in position to continue the division's en echelon attack with Mahone acting as the connecting brigade with Pender's division. For differing views on this topic, see John Horn, "The Myth that Mahone's Brigade Did Not Move on July 2, 1863," *Gettysburg Magazine*, Issue 65, 47–57; Bradley M. Gottfried, "Mahone's Brigade: Insubordination or Miscommunication?" *The Gettysburg Magazine*, Issue 18 (1998), 67–76; and Campbell, "'Sacrificed to the bad management of others.'" For Hill's, Anderson's, Posey's, and Mahone's official reports, see *The War of the Rebellion: A Compilation of the Official Records of the Union and Confederate Armies*, 128 vols. (Washington, D.C., 1880–1901), Series 1, Vol. 27, Pt. 2, 608, 614, 621, 633–634. Hereafter cited as *OR*. All references are to Series 1 unless otherwise noted. Interestingly, in weighing the merit of Anderson's response to newspaper correspondent "P.W.A.," Park Ranger-Historian Eric Campbell bluntly concludes (on p. 30n99), "It appears that Anderson's version of both Mahone and Posey being 'reserves' was simply a cover story he created to shift the blame."

9. Eric A. Campbell, "So Much for Comrades in Arms," https://www.historynet.com/much-comrades-arms.htm.

10. Lt. Col. Arthur J.L. Fremantle, *Three Months in the Southern States: April—June 1863*, 259–260; Pfarr, *Longstreet at Gettysburg*, 106, 111–112; Campbell, "'Sacrificed to the bad management of others,'" 3–4.

11. James Longstreet, *From Manassas to Appomattox*, 365–367, 369, 408; Col. John L. Black of the 1st South Carolina Cavalry, according to a March 1886 letter to Gettysburg historian John Bachelder, was "turned over" to Longstreet on the morning of July 2 "to explore his ground[,] watch his flank[,] and do whatever came to hand." Black discussed many of Longstreet's alleged movements on July 2. Curiously, as it relates to the topic of this essay, was Black's claim that "Gen. Longstreet rode to the head of Wilcox's division [sic] as it moved. Genl. L. caused Wilcox to incline to the right as he was about to expose his line of march to the enemies [sic] observation." To my knowledge and based on my research, I know of no other account that suggests Longstreet rode at the head of Wilcox's brigade as it advanced. There is ample evidence Longstreet personally led Kershaw's and Wofford's brigades (of McLaws' division) into battle, but not Wilcox's Third Corps brigade. Perhaps writing 23 years after the battle, Black was confusing Wilcox for Wofford. See David L. and Audrey J. Ladd, *The Bachelder Papers*, Vol. II, September 6, 1880, to April 12, 1886, 1241.

12. James Longstreet, "Lee in Pennsylvania," *Annals of the War*, 424; James Longstreet, "Lee's Right Wing at Gettysburg," *Battles and Leaders*, 3:341.

13. *OR* 27/2: 358–359.

14. Clifford Dowdey, *Lee and His Men at Gettysburg: The Death of a Nation*, 193, 230; *OR* 27/2: 318; Harold M. Knudsen, e-mail messages to the author, April 29, May 1, 2022. Author and historian Harold M. Knudsen provided me with some interesting food for thought on Lee's use of the word "co-operate" in his July 2 orders to A.P. Hill, associating it with the modern military terminology of Operational Control (OPCON). Knudsen suggested, "To the trained military mind, it is clear Lee was attempting to ensure that, even with Pickett absent, Longstreet would retain full, three-division-strength with Hood's and McLaws' division, and one division from Hill's corps (Anderson). This is known in modern military terms as Operation Control (OPCON). By definition, this command relationship means the gaining unit, which in this case was Longstreet's corps, would have authority to assign tasks, designate an objective, and issue other related orders to accomplish the mission. Command is not the same as OPCON. Command is a formal status established by orders giving an officer a range of administrative and legal powers over the unit he commands. OPCON is a temporary relationship with another unit that only gives the gaining unit authority to issue orders for that particular mission.

This OPCON arrangement is probably what Lee wanted to happen with Anderson's division on July 2. Unfortunately, Lee's language was too imprecise to achieve the understanding that should have resulted in a more effective participation by Anderson. Lee's vague wording on the second day regarding Anderson's role was to 'co-operate' with Longstreet's corps. For a unit from one corps to 'co-operate' with another, it also must establish communications to receive adequate information about its status so it can then plan and execute the necessary support or co-operation. This can be done by sending over a liaison. However, in the case of a division allocated to 'co-operate' with another corps going into an attack, it will need direction from that corps' leadership. An in-person meeting between the division commander and the gaining corps commander is necessary. Ideally, Anderson should have reported to Longstreet to receive his mission orders for the day. This, of course, did not happen. Again, the future doctrines of military command relationships that would have remedied Lee's less-than-precise guidance to 'co-operate' did not exist during the Civil War. OPCON of Anderson's division by Longstreet that Lee hinted at was ultimately not realized and Longstreet's corps would remain at two-division strength for this attack."

15. Shelby Foote, *The Civil War: A Narrative, Fredericksburg to Meridian*, 510; Gilbert Moxley Sorrel, *At the Right Hand of Longstreet: Recollections of a Confederate Staff Officer*, 128.

16. Foote, *The Civil War: A Narrative, Fredericksburg to Meridian*, 510; OR 27/2: 608.

17. OR 27/2: 614, 618, 622–624, 631–632; Cadmus Wilcox wrote a lengthy and combative postwar article on his brigade's actions at Gettysburg in Volume 6 of the *Southern Historical Society Papers*. As in his official report, Wilcox mentioned nothing about Longstreet having any sort of command role over Anderson or any of his brigadiers on July 2. See Cadmus M. Wilcox, "General C. M. Wilcox on the battle of Gettysburg," *Southern Historical Society Papers*, 6: 97–124.

18. OR 27/2: 621–624, 633–634; Eric A. Campbell, "So Much for Comrades in Arms"; Pfanz, *Gettysburg: The Second Day*, 386–387, 544n128. According to a postwar account from E.P. Alexander, Anderson rather oddly claimed just after the battle that on one of those occasions when Wilcox asked him for support, "he [Anderson] was unable to find Hill and refer the matter to him." See Alexander, *Military Memoirs of a Confederate*, 401.

19. Sears, *Gettysburg*, 318; Pfarr, *Longstreet at Gettysburg*, 109; Campbell, "'Sacrificed to the bad management of others,'" 16.

20. Campbell, "'Sacrificed to the bad management of others,'" 7, 9.

21. Guelzo, *Gettysburg: The Last Invasion*, 237–238, 317; James L. Robertson Jr., *General A.P. Hill: The Story of a Confederate Warrior*, 216, 221–222.

22. Campbell, "So Much for Comrades in Arms"; Guelzo, *Gettysburg: The Last Invasion*, 334; Pfanz, *Gettysburg: The Second Day*, 387.

23. "Richard Heron Anderson," Civil War Biography, https://www.battlefields.org/learn/biographies/richard-h-anderson; Rickard, Richard Heron Anderson, 1821–1879, http://www.historyofwar.org/articles/people_anderson_rh.html; Joseph Cantey Elliott, *Lieutenant General Richard Heron Anderson: Lee's Noble Soldier*, 121; Freeman, *Lee's Lieutenants*, 666–668, 672, 796–797, 802. It is worth noting that Anderson's promotion to lieutenant general was never officially confirmed by the Confederate Congress.

Essay 6

1. Jim Betts, "The Widow Longstreet Will Battle This Out," *The Gainesville Times*, exact date unknown, The Longstreet Society Collection (hereafter cited as LSC), Piedmont Hotel, Gainesville, Georgia, accessed October 18, 2019.

2. Helen Dortch Longstreet, *In The Path of Lee's "Old Warhorse,"* Introduction by Clark Thornton (2009), 6–7; "Helen Dortch Longstreet papers," The Georgia Historical Society, http://ghs.galileo.usg.edu/ghs/view?docId=ead/MS%201341-ead.xml; Jennifer Kinniff (head of archives and special collections, Loyola Notre Dame Library), e-mail message to author, August 16, 2019.

3. "Veteran's Wife Fights Thief," *The Gainesville Times*, exact date unknown, LSC, accessed October 18, 2019.

4. "Brenau Woman of Distinction: Helen Dortch Longstreet," Brenau University pamphlet, LSC, accessed October 18, 2019; "Helen Dortch Longstreet Trail System: Tallulah Gorge State Park," exhibit at LSC, accessed October 18, 2019; Helen Dortch Longstreet, *In The Path of Lee's "Old Warhorse,"* Introduction by Clark Thornton (2009), 6–7; Betts, "The Widow Longstreet Will Battle This Out," *The Gainesville Times*; "Widow Will Oppose Tallmadge!" exact date unknown, LSC, accessed October 18, 2019.

5. Betts, "The Widow Longstreet Will Battle This Out," *The Gainesville Times*; "Helen Riveter," exhibit at LSC, accessed October 18, 2019; "Confederate General's Widow," page from an unknown magazine, exact date unknown, LSC, accessed October 18, 2019.

6. Helen Dortch Longstreet, *In The Path of Lee's "Old Warhorse,"* 53–56.

7. For full commentary on how the Lost Cause, anti-Longstreet group narrative of the postwar years extensively influenced most subsequent secondary source histories of Gettysburg, and particularly coverage of Longstreet's performance at the battle, see Cory M. Pfarr, *Longstreet at Gettysburg: A Critical Reassessment*; William Garrett Piston, *Lee's Tarnished Lieutenant: James Longstreet and His Place in Southern History*; R.L. Dinardo and Albert A. Nofi, eds., *James Longstreet: The Man, the Soldier, the Controversy*; Edward H. Bonekemper

III, "Did James Longstreet Lose the Battle of Gettysburg and Thus the War?" from his *The Myth of the Lost Cause: Why the South Fought the Civil War and Why the North Won*, 143–192; Thomas L. Connelly, *The Marble Man: Robert E. Lee and His Image in American Society*; and Thomas L. Connelly and Barbara L. Bellows, *God and General Longstreet: The Lost Cause and the Southern Mind*.

8. Helen Dortch Longstreet, *Lee and Longstreet at High Tide: Gettysburg in the Light of the Official Records*, 34.

9. For numerous examples showing how historians have typically mischaracterized James Longstreet's postwar writings, see Pfarr, *Longstreet at Gettysburg*, 17–18.

10. Helen Dortch Longstreet, *Lee and Longstreet at High Tide*, 7; Regarding Leslie J. Perry:—"Robert N. Scott compiled and edited v. 1–18, 1880–87, and also collected the greater part of the material for v. 19–36, 1887–91. After his death in 1887 the work was continued by Henry M. Lazelle, 1887–89, and by a board of publication, 1889–99, consisting of George B. Davis, 1889–97, Leslie J. Perry, 1889–99, Joseph W. Kirkley, 1889–99, and Fred C. Ainsworth, 1898–99; from 1889–1901 edited by Fred C. Ainsworth and Joseph W. Kirkley," as stated in *The War of the Rebellion: A Compilation of the Official Records of the Union and Confederate Armies*, 128 vols. (Washington D.C. 1880–1901), Hereafter cited as *OR*, https://books.google.com/books/about/The_War_of_the_Rebellion.html?id=vo8tAAAAIAAJ. All references are to Series 1 unless otherwise noted.

11. *The War of the Rebellion: A Compilation of the Official Records of the Union and Confederate Armies*, 128 vols. (Washington D.C. 1880–1901), Series 1, vol. 27, pt. 2, 493; Hereafter cited as *OR.*.

12. Pfarr, *Longstreet at Gettysburg*, 57, 172; Douglas Southall Freeman, *Lee: An Abridgment in One* Volume, ed. Richard Harwell, 328. This noteworthy example from Freeman's 1934 book reminds me of a good question I received after speaking at an event in support of my last book, *Longstreet at Gettysburg: A Critical Reassessment*, where the audience member was genuinely curious as to my thoughts on which historian I thought was most consequential in inculcating the lies and misrepresentations of Longstreet's Gettysburg performance for future historians and students of the war. I briefly considered replying with one or two modern historians; however, I almost immediately defaulted back to Freeman. Freeman won the Pulitzer Prize for his 1934 biography of Lee and then went on to write the equally well received *Lee's Lieutenants: A Study in Command* in 1942. Freeman was most certainly a talented researcher, writer, and historian, which made it that much more consequential and shocking that he completely bought into the postwar anti-Longstreet group's agenda-driven writings on the Longstreet-Gettysburg Controversy—especially in his earlier work. Because of his reputation as a discerning historian and his knack for careful research on many other Civil War generals and topics, he lent a gravity and authority to the charges against Longstreet's Gettysburg performance that has had far-reaching repercussions on future histories of the battle up to the present day. Freeman essentially cemented the Lost Cause interpretation of Longstreet's alleged actions at Gettysburg as the accepted narrative. Only a few book-length works published since the 1950s have sought to seriously challenge this pervasive narrative.

13. Helen Dortch Longstreet, *Lee and Longstreet at High Tide*, 9, 32-33.

14. *Ibid.*, 32; Richard D. Starnes, "Forever Faithful: The Southern Historical Society and the Confederate Historical Memory," *Southern Cultures* 2, no. 2 (Winter 1996): 177–178; Adam Wesley Dean, "Who Controls the Past Controls the Future," *Virginia Magazine of History & Biography* 117, no. 4 (September 2009): 319–355.

15. Helen Dortch Longstreet, *Lee and Longstreet at High Tide*, 36, 39. This argument has been most robustly advanced in a recent publication (2019) by James A. Hessler and Britt C. Isenberg, titled *Gettysburg's Peach Orchard: Longstreet, Sickles, and the Bloody Fight for the "Commanding Ground" Along the Emmitsburg Road*.

16. Helen Dortch Longstreet, *Lee and Longstreet at High Tide*, 118.

17. Glenn Tucker, *High Tide at Gettysburg: The Campaign in Pennsylvania*, 440.

18. Helen Dortch Longstreet, *Lee and Longstreet at High Tide*, 34–35.

19. Gordon was a later arrival to the anti-Longstreet group. His participation in the controversy did not begin in earnest until the mid-1880s when Gordon, a Democrat and anti-Reconstructionist, fully identified the Republican Longstreet as a political rival in northern Georgia. Gordon realized the likely political benefits he could accrue from his tenuous connection with Robert E. Lee during the war and from his active participation in the postwar Lost Cause hero worship of Lee and further denigration of Longstreet (especially as it related to his alleged failings at Gettysburg). Gordon went on to serve two terms in the United States Senate (1873–1880, 1891–1897) and a term as governor of Georgia (1886–1890). As Gordon transitioned out of his stint as governor, he also became the first commander-in-chief of the newly organized (1889) United Confederate Veterans (UCV) group, serving in that position until his death in 1903. A year later when Longstreet died in 1904, less than five percent of the then over 1,000 UCV chapters passed resolutions honoring Lee's "Old Warhorse." See William Garrett Piston, *Lee's Tarnished Lieutenant: James Longstreet and His Place in Southern History*, 141, 163, 169.

20. Piston, *Lee's Tarnished Lieutenant*, 168; John B. Gordon, *Reminiscences of the Civil War*, Memorial Edition, 160, 167–169.

21. Helen Dortch Longstreet, *Lee and Longstreet at High Tide*, 45.

22. Helen Dortch Longstreet, *Lee and Longstreet at High Tide*, 56; Piston, *Lee's Tarnished Lieutenant*, 130; Connelly, *The Marble Man*, 40-42; Jubal Early, *The Campaigns of Robert E. Lee, An Address Before Washington and Lee University, January 19, 1872*, http://leefamilyarchive.org/reference/addresses/early/index.html; Gordon, *Reminiscences of the Civil War*, 160.

23. Helen Dortch Longstreet, *Lee and Longstreet at High Tide*, 56-63.

24. *Ibid.*, 71-74.

25. *Ibid.*, 59-60, 67, 75-76.

26. *Ibid.*, 24, 44, 67; For information on the additional Confederate reconnaissance activities conducted prior to the First Corps march via postwar testimonies from Captain Johnston and Lafayette McLaws, see Pfarr, *Longstreet at Gettysburg*, 73-77; For more information on Longstreet's march and countermarch in general, see, chapter nine, "The First Corps March Conundrum" of Pfarr, *Longstreet at Gettysburg*, 75-83.

27. Helen Dortch Longstreet, *Lee and Longstreet at High Tide*, 21-22, 66-71; Pfarr, *Longstreet at Gettysburg*, 71-73.

28. Helen Dortch Longstreet, *Lee and Longstreet at High Tide*, 36-39.

29. For descriptions of how the anti-Longstreet group's allegations against Longstreet evolved in the postwar years, see Pfarr, *Longstreet at Gettysburg*, 9-11, 123; Piston, *Lee's Tarnished Lieutenant*, 117-120, 130-131; William Garrett Piston, "Marked in Bronze: James Longstreet and Southern History," in *James Longstreet: The Man, the Soldier, the Controversy*, R.L Dinardo and Albert A. Nofi, eds. (Da Capo Press, Inc., 1998), 202-216.

30. For examples of some historians' advancement of this argument, see Pfarr, *Longstreet at Gettysburg*, 123-127.

31. Helen Dortch Longstreet, *Lee and Longstreet at High Tide*, 46-47.

32. *Ibid.*, 54; Pfarr, *Longstreet at Gettysburg*, 131-135; Cory M. Pfarr, "James Longstreet and the Third Day: 'We Were Not Hunting for Any Fight,'" in *Gettysburg Magazine*, Issue 62 (January 2020), 4-8.

33. Helen Dortch Longstreet, *Lee and Longstreet at High Tide*, 46-47.

34. *Ibid.*, 23, 53-55.

35. *Ibid.*, 35; Gordon, *Reminiscences of the Civil War*, 160, 167-169. Putting Gordon aside for a moment, when it comes to this debate about Longstreet's alleged comportment at Gettysburg (typically characterized as "sulky"), Longstreet critics have generally always hung their hat on a postwar recollection from one of his former staff members, Gilbert Moxley Sorrel: "There was apparent apathy in his movements. They lacked the fire and point of his usual bearing on the battlefield." For a detailed analysis of this quote, see Pfarr, *Longstreet at Gettysburg*, 46-47, 62-63.

36. Pfarr, *Longstreet at Gettysburg*, 92-95; Helen Dortch Longstreet, *Lee and Longstreet at High Tide*, 39.

37. Helen Dortch Longstreet, *Lee and Longstreet at High Tide*, 63-64; Pfarr, *Longstreet at Gettysburg*, 101-104.

38. Helen Dortch Longstreet, *Lee and Longstreet at High Tide*, 70-71; *OR* 27/2: 318-319; Pfarr, *Longstreet at Gettysburg*, 105-117.

39. Ewell was born in the Georgetown neighborhood of Washington, D.C., but grew up near Manassas, Virginia, starting at age three.

40. Helen Dortch Longstreet, *Lee and Longstreet at High Tide*, 46-47, 54-55.

41. For details on these many accounts, see Pfarr, *Longstreet at Gettysburg*, 140-142.

42. E.P. Alexander, Longstreet's principal artillery officer at Gettysburg, incisively emphasized this point in one of his postwar memoirs: "Then, it must be remembered that the preparations for this charge were made deliberately, & under the observation of Gen. Lee himself, & of all his staff. From sunrise to 1:30 p.m. was nine hours, all devoted to this business, & within a few hundred acres of land. It seems to me impossible to believe that Gen. Lee did not know quite accurately the location of every brigade he had upon that battlefield, hours before the cannonade opened. Certainly he & his staff officers also were all about in my vicinity, during the morning." See E.P. Alexander, *Fighting for the Confederacy*, 280.

43. Helen Dortch Longstreet, *Lee and Longstreet at High Tide*, 55.

44. A few examples would be Daniel Harvey (D.H.) Hill (May 1863), John B. Magruder (July 1862), Theophilus H. Holmes (July 1862), Benjamin Huger (July 1862), and Jubal A. Early (March 1865).

45. Gordon, *Reminiscences of the Civil War*, 160.

46. Helen Dortch Longstreet, *Lee and Longstreet at High Tide*, 78-82; *OR* 52/2: 550; Thornton, *General James Longstreet: A Family Portrait*, 387-388; Piston, *Lee's Tarnished Lieutenant*, 100; Pfarr, *Longstreet at Gettysburg*, 175-176.

47. Pfarr, *Longstreet at Gettysburg*, 6-10; Jubal Early, *The Campaigns of Robert E. Lee, An Address Before Washington and Lee University, January 19, 1872*, http://leefamilyarchive.org/reference/addresses/early/index.html.

48. Helen Dortch Longstreet, *Lee and Longstreet at High Tide*, 33-34, 84.

49. *Ibid.* 34, 71, 77; Connelly, *The Marble Man*, 27.

50. Helen Dortch Longstreet, *Lee and Longstreet at High Tide*, 56; Jubal Early, *The Campaigns of Robert E. Lee, An Address Before Washington and Lee University, January 19, 1872*, http://leefamilyarchive.org/reference/addresses/early/index.html.

51. Pfarr, *Longstreet at Gettysburg*, 39, 44-45, 57-58, 129-130, 133-135; Helen Dortch Longstreet, *Lee and Longstreet at High Tide*, 47, 77.

52. Helen Dortch Longstreet, *Lee and Longstreet at High Tide*, 32. Characteristic of this naïveté and overconfidence regarding the degree to which future history would confide in the anti-Longstreet

group's narrative was James Longstreet's commentary in an April 1875 letter to William Pendleton: "School-boys may be misled by you, but even with them I fancy that only the most credulous may be temporarily misled. It is my opinion that your abuse, so far from impairing my interests or my reputation, will be more likely to enhance them in the estimation of honorable men." See Piston, *Lee's Tarnished Lieutenant*, 123–124.

53. Longstreet served as a U.S. marshal from 1881 to 1884, all under Republican Presidents Rutherford B. Hayes, James A. Garfield, and Chester A. Arthur. Longstreet was actually removed from this position by President Arthur in 1884 allegedly as a result of some fraud and corruption accusations leveled against Longstreet's deputies and his chief deputy, who happened to be his 36-year-old son, John Garland Longstreet. That said, it is more likely these allegations provided a more convenient excuse to relieve Longstreet than the real political differences separating the general and the president. Longstreet did not support Arthur's reelection bid and both men were in opposite camps of Republican thought with respect to how to proceed with Reconstruction in the post-war South. President Arthur went on to replace Longstreet with John E. Bryant, one of his most loyal supporters in Georgia. It is likely Longstreet would have soon been relieved from the position anyway, given that Grover Cleveland, a Democrat, was elected president in 1885. Additionally, not to give the reader the wrong impression of John Garland Longstreet, the general's oldest child, and his alleged involvement in this scandal—the accusations against him in particular were far from ever proven and General Longstreet always thought they were politically motivated. "Garley" was a courier for his father during the Civil War, a graduate of the Virginia Military Institute (class of 1869) and went on to become an accomplished architect, surveyor, and engineer. For more details, see Piston, *Lee's Tarnished Lieutenant*, 139–140, and Clark T. Thornton, *General James Longstreet: A Family Portrait*, 386–387.

54. Helen Dortch Longstreet, *In The Path of Lee's "Old Warhorse*," 51–53.

55. Ibid., 55.

56. Ibid., 57–58.

57. Helen Dortch Longstreet, *Lee and Longstreet at High Tide*, 128.

58. Longstreet served as U.S. commissioner of railroads from 1897 until his death in 1904, under Republican Presidents William McKinley and Theodore Roosevelt.

59. "Helen Dortch Longstreet papers," The Georgia Historical Society, http://ghs.galileo.usg.edu/ghs/view?docId=ead/MS%201341-ead.xml; "Longstreet's Widow Still Fights For His Recognition," *Savannah Evening Press*, March 30, 1940, LSC, accessed October 18, 2019. Christy's painting of Longstreet is currently on display in the museum at the Chickamauga Battlefield Visitor Center. For many years, a copy of the painting was located at the Gettysburg Battlefield—stored in the visitor center basement of all places—but has since been on indefinite loan to the Longstreet Society and displayed at its headquarters, the Piedmont Hotel, in Gainesville, Georgia.

60. Helen was an honorary guest at an elaborate and well-attended two-day ceremony (July 2–3, 1941) in Gettysburg to dedicate the site for the anticipated equestrian statue, which was to be placed in the field across from the State of Alabama Monument on the east side of South Confederate Avenue. See Sue Boardman, "Gettysburg Connections," *Civil War News*, 25th Annual Gettysburg Section, July 2019, 20–21. Serving as a visual representation of what was to come, a miniature bronze model of the statue was even created in 1940 by the artist and sculptor, Paul Manship. The model depicts Longstreet on his horse, Hero (actually "Haro"), arm outstretched with hat in hand, leading his men into battle. The statue would also sit on an ornate pedestal adorned with scenes of soldier life and banners reading "Pleasures of Camp Life," "Preparing Dinner," "The Folks at Home," and "The Visit Back Home"—collectively almost ancient Egyptian-looking in design as was characteristic of sculptor Paul Manship's archaic and classical style. See Paul Manship, *Study for Longstreet Memorial*, 1940, bronze, Smithsonian American Art Museum, Bequest of Paul Manship, 1966.47.11A, found in: https://americanart.si.edu/artwork/study-longstreet-memorial-15932 (accessed August 16, 2020). After the 1940s plan fell through, it was not until the 1990s that the idea to erect a Longstreet equestrian statue on the Gettysburg Battlefield was once again revived. Finally, in 1998, a statue of Longstreet by sculptor and artist Gary Casteel was placed and unveiled in Pitzer's Woods at a location just north of where Longstreet directed William Barksdale's brigade to advance against the Joseph Sherfy Peach Orchard on July 2.

61. "Longstreet's Widow Dies at Age of 99," newspaper unknown, May 1962 (exact date unknown), LSC, accessed October 18, 2019; Dan Paterson (James Longstreet's great-grandson), e-mail message to author, October 31, 2019.

62. Helen Dortch Longstreet, *Lee and Longstreet at High Tide*, 114–115, 125.

63. Pfarr, *Longstreet at Gettysburg*, 17–19.

64. Robert K. Krick, "'If Longstreet Says So…It Is Most Likely Not True': James Longstreet and the Second Day at Gettysburg," in *The Second Day at Gettysburg: Essays on Confederate and Union Leadership*, ed. Gary W. Gallagher, 57.

65. See Pfarr, *Longstreet at Gettysburg*, 18, 170–173, 177–183; 188–189*ch1n12*; Piston, *Lee's Tarnished Lieutenant*, chapters 7–10; Piston, "Marked in Bronze: James Longstreet and Southern History," 206–216.

66. Longstreet's non-Virginia status is an important segue into what became the general's larger issue of never really being able to associate himself with one specific state. As one might expect, state pride was a significant issue

for the South in the years leading up to the Civil War, throughout the conflict, and in the postwar decades that followed. Throughout the course of Longstreet's life, he accumulated not one or two, but at least five significant state affiliations. He was born in South Carolina, grew up in Georgia and Alabama, alternated living in New Orleans, Louisiana, and Lynchburg, Virginia (usually in the summer months), in the immediate postwar years, and then finally returned to Georgia in 1875.

67. Helen Dortch Longstreet, *Lee and Longstreet at High Tide*, 68, 90; Pfarr, *Longstreet at Gettysburg*, 180–183; Piston, *Lee's Tarnished Lieutenant*, 132.

68. Helen Dortch Longstreet, *Lee and Longstreet at High Tide*, 89–90.

Bibliography

Adelman, Garry E., "Benning's Georgia Brigade at Gettysburg," *The Gettysburg Magazine,* Issue 18 (1998).

Alexander, Edward Porter, *Fighting for the Confederacy: The Personal Recollections of General Edward Porter Alexander,* ed. Gary W. Gallagher (Chapel Hill: The University of North Carolina Press, 1989).

Alexander, Edward Porter, *Military Memoirs of a Confederate: A Critical Narrative* (New York: Charles Scribner's Sons, 1907).

Ambrose Ransom Wright, 1872 (image). [no date recorded on caption card] Photograph. Retrieved from the Library of Congress, https://www.loc.gov/item/2002712787/. (Accessed April 30, 2022).

Annals of the War, Originally published in the *Philadelphia Weekly Times,* republished (Edison, New Jersey: The Blue & Grey Press, 1996).

Archer, John M., *East Cemetery Hill at Gettysburg: "The Hour Was One of Horror,"* (Gettysburg, PA: Thomas Publications, 1997).

Battles and Leaders of the Civil War: The Tide Shifts, Volume III (New York: Castle Books).

Betts, Jim, "The Widow Longstreet Will Battle This Out," *The Gainesville Times* [exact date unknown] (Gainesville, Georgia: The Longstreet Society Collection, Piedmont Hotel).

Black, John L., *Crumbling Defenses or Memoirs and Reminiscences of John Logan Black, Colonel C.S.A.,* https://babel.hathitrust.org/cgi/pt?id=wu.89059412684.

Blue & Gray Magazine. Columbus, Ohio: Blue & Gray Enterprises, 1987, Vol. 5–6.

Boardman, Sue, "Gettysburg Connections," *Civil War News,* 25th Annual Gettysburg Section, July 2019.

Bonekemper III, Edward H., "Did James Longstreet Lose the Battle of Gettysburg and Thus the War?" in Bonekemper III, *The Myth of the Lost Cause: Why the South Fought the Civil War and Why the North Won* (Washington, D.C.: Regnery History, 2015).

"Brenau Woman of Distinction: Helen Dortch Longstreet" (Brenau University pamphlet). (Gainesville, Georgia: The Longstreet Society Collection, Piedmont Hotel).

Brig. Gen. A.L. Long, Va. (image). [no date recorded; between 1861 and 1865] Photograph. Retrieved from the Library of Congress, https://www.loc.gov/item/91793717/. (Accessed April 30, 2022).

Brig. Gen. William Tatum Wofford. (image; half-length portrait, facing right, in Confederate uniform), None. [no date recorded; between 1860 and 1880] Photograph. Retrieved from the Library of Congress, https://www.loc.gov/item/96524677/. (Accessed April 30, 2022).

Brinsfield, Jr., John Wesley, ed., *The Spirit Divided: Memoirs of Civil War Chaplains: The Confederacy* (Macon, Georgia: Mercer University Press, 2005).

Broadwater, Robert P., ed., *Gettysburg as the Generals Remembered It: Postwar Perspectives on Ten Commanders* (Jefferson, North Carolina, and London: McFarland & Co., Inc., Publishers, 2010).Brock, Robert Alonzo, ed., *Southern Historical Society Papers, Volume 4* (Richmond, Virginia: Virginia Historical Society, 1877).

Brock, Robert Alonzo, ed., *Southern Historical Society Papers, Volume 5* (Richmond, Virginia: Virginia Historical Society, 1878).

Brock, Robert Alonzo, ed., *Southern Historical Society Papers, Volume 6* (Richmond, Virginia: Virginia Historical Society, 1878).

Brock, Robert Alonzo, ed., *Southern Historical Society Papers, Volume 7* (Richmond, Virginia: Virginia Historical Society, 1879).

Brock, Robert Alonzo, ed., *Southern Historical Society Papers, Volume 23* (Richmond, Virginia: Virginia Historical Society, 1895).

Brock, Robert Alonzo, ed., *Southern Historical Society Papers, Volume 23* (Richmond, Virginia: Virginia Historical Society, 1910).

Bruner, Gary P., "Up Over Big Round Top: The Forgotten 47th Alabama," *The Gettysburg Magazine,* Issue 22 (2000).

Campbell, Eric. A., "'Sacrificed to the bad management of others': Richard H. Anderson's Division at the Battle of Gettysburg," The Army of Northern Virginia in the Gettysburg Campaign, http://npshistory.com/series/symposia/gettysburg_seminars/7/essay6.pdf.

Campbell, Eric A., "So Much for Comrades in Arms," https://www.historynet.com/much-comrades-arms.htm.

"Civil War Biography: Richard Heron Anderson,"

American Battlefield Trust, https://www.battlefields.org/learn/biographies/richard-h-anderson.

"Civil War Biography: William J. Hardee," American Battlefield Trust, https://www.battlefields.org/learn/biographies/william-j-hardee.

Coddington, Edwin B., *The Gettysburg Campaign: A Study in Command* (New York: Simon and Schuster, 1968).

"Confederate General's Widow" (page from an unknown magazine) Gainesville, Georgia: (The Longstreet Society Collection, Piedmont Hotel: exact date unknown).

Connelly, Thomas L., *The Marble Man: Robert E. Lee and His Image in American Society* (Baton Rouge: Louisiana State University Press, 1977).

Connelly, Thomas L., and Barbara L. Bellows, *God and General Longstreet: The Lost Cause and the Southern Mind* (Baton Rouge: Louisiana State University Press, 1982).

Crist, Lynda Lasswell, Mary Deaton Dix, and Kenneth H. Williams, eds., *The Papers of Jefferson Davis*, Volume 8 (1862) (Baton Rouge: Louisiana State University Press,, 1995).

Currier and Ives. *Death of General Robert E. Lee: At Lexington, Va., October 12th, aged, 62 years, 8 months and 6 days.* (image), 1870. Photograph. (New York: Currier and Ives). Retrieved from the Library of Congress, https://www.loc.gov/item/91480008/. (Accessed April 30, 2022).

Daniel Edgar Sickles, 1914. (image) [ca. 1902] Photograph. Retrieved from the Library of Congress, https://www.loc.gov/item/2003677327/. (Accessed April 30, 2022)

Davis, Jefferson, *The Rise and Fall of the Confederate Government*, Volume II (New York: D. Appleton and Company, 1881.)

Dean, Adam Wesley, "Who Controls the Past Controls the Future," *Virginia Magazine of History & Biography* 117, no. 4 (September 2009).

Dowdey, Clifford, *Lee and His Men at Gettysburg: The Death of a Nation* (Lincoln and London: University of Nebraska Press, 1958).

Early, Jubal, *The Campaigns of Robert E. Lee, An Address Before Washington and Lee University, January 19, 1872*, http://leefamilyarchive.org/reference/addresses/early/index.html.

Early, Jubal, *A Memoir of the Last Year of the War for Independence, in the Confederate States of America: Containing an Account of the Operations of His Commands in the Years 1864 and 1865* (Lynchburg, Virginia: Charles W. Button, 1867).

Eckenrode, Hamilton James, ed., *Southern Historical Society Papers*, Volume 44 (Richmond, Virginia: Westmoreland Club, June 1923).

Elliott, Joseph Cantey, *Lieutenant General Richard Heron Anderson: Lee's Noble Soldier* (Dayton, Ohio: Morningside House Inc., 1985).

Foote, Shelby, *The Civil War, A Narrative: Fredericksburg to Meridian* (New York: Random House, 1963).

Freeman, Douglas Southall, *Lee: An Abridgement in One Volume*, ed. Richard Harwell (New York: Touchstone, 1997).

Freeman, Douglas Southall, *Lee's Lieutenants: A Study in Command*, one-volume abridgement, ed. Stephen W. Sears (New York: Simon and Schuster, 1998).

Fremantle, Lt. Col. Arthur J.L., *Three Months in the Southern States: April—June 1863* (Lincoln and London: University of Nebraska Press, 1991).

"General Longstreet," New Orleans *Times-Democrat*, June 8, 1867, 4, https://www.newspapers.com/image/201847707/.

General Longstreet in 1901 (image). Retrieved from the Longstreet Society, Gainesville, Georgia.

Gordon, Hon. John B. of GA. (image), [no date recorded; between 1870 and 1880] Photograph. Retrieved from the Library of Congress, https://www.loc.gov/item/2017893292/. (Accessed April 30, 2022).

Gordon, John B., *Reminiscences of the Civil War* (New York: Charles Scribner's Sons, 1903).

Goree, Thomas J., *Longstreet's Aide: The Civil War Letters of Major Thomas J. Goree*, ed. Thomas W. Cutrer (Charlottesville and London: University Press of Virginia, 1995).

Gottfried, Bradley M., *Brigades of Gettysburg: The Union and Confederate Brigades at the Battle of Gettysburg* (Skyhorse Publishing, 2002, 2012.)

Gottfried, Bradley M., "Mahone's Brigade: Insubordination or Miscommunication?" *The Gettysburg Magazine*, Issue 18 (1998).

Gottfried, Bradley M., *The Maps of Gettysburg: An Atlas of the Gettysburg Campaign, June 3—July 13, 1863* (New York, and El Dorado Hills, California: Savas Beatie, 2013).

Gramm, Kent, "The Chances of War: Lee, Longstreet, Sickles, and the First Minnesota Volunteers," in *The Gettysburg Nobody Knows*, ed. Gabor S. Boritt (New York, Oxford: Oxford University Press, 1997).

Guelzo, Allen C., *Gettysburg: The Last Invasion* (New York: Alfred A. Knopf, 2013).

A Guide to the J. William Jones Papers, 1861–1892. Accession 21294. Personal papers collection, The Library of Virginia, Richmond, Virginia, https://ead.lib.virginia.edu/vivaxtf/view?docId=lva/vi01129.xml.

Hardee, William J., *Rifle and Light Infantry Tactics for the Exercise and Manoeuvres [sic] of Troops When Acting as Light Infantry or Riflemen, Volume II, School of the Battalion* (Philadelphia: Lippincott, Grambo & Company, 1855).

Haskew, Michael E., *Appomattox: The Last Days of Robert E. Lee's Army of Northern Virginia* (Minneapolis,: Zenith Press, 2015.)

Hassler, William Woods, *A.P. Hill: Lee's Forgotten General* (Chapel Hill: The University of North Carolina Press, 1957, 1962, 2000).

Hearn, Chester G., Rick Sapp, and Steven Smith, *Civil War Commanders: From Fort Sumter to Appomattox Court House* (New York: Metro Books, 2008).

"Helen Dortch Longstreet papers," The Georgia

Historical Society, http://ghs.galileo.usg.edu/ghs/view?docId=ead/MS%201341-ead.xml.

"Helen Dortch Longstreet Trail System: Tallulah Gorge State Park" (exhibit at The Longstreet Society Collection, Piedmont Hotel). Gainesville, Georgia.

"Helen Riveter" (exhibit at The Longstreet Society Collection, Piedmont Hotel), Gainesville, Georgia.

Hessler, James A., *Sickles at Gettysburg: The Controversial Civil War General Who Committed Murder, Abandoned Little Round Top, and Declared Himself the Hero of Gettysburg* (New York, and El Dorado Hills, California: Savas Beatie, 2009, 2015).

Hessler, James A., and Jack Drummond, "Sickles Returns," *The Gettysburg Magazine,* Issue 34 (2006).

Hessler, James A., and Britt C. Isenberg, *Gettysburg's Peach Orchard: Longstreet, Sickles, and the Bloody Fight for the "Commanding Ground" Along the Emmitsburg Road* (El Dorado Hills, California: Savas Beatie, 2019).

History in Full Color.com, *General James Longstreet* (image), https://images.historyinfullcolor.com/finished/h881A3AD0#h881a3ad0.

Hood, John B., *Advance and Retreat: Personal Experiences in the United States and Confederate States Armies* (Boston: Da Capo Press, 1993).

Horn, John, "The Myth that Mahone's Brigade Did Not Move on July 2, 1863," *Gettysburg Magazine,* Issue 65 (2021).

Hyde, Bill, "'Did You Get There?': Capt. Samuel Johnston's Reconnaissance at Gettysburg," *The Gettysburg Magazine,* Issue 29 (2003).

Hyde, Bill, *The Union Generals Speak: The Meade Hearings on the Battle of Gettysburg* (Baton Rouge: Louisiana State University Press, 2003).

Imhof, John, *Gettysburg Day Two: A Study in Maps* (Moraga, California: Baumgratz Publishing, Inc., 2019).

James Longstreet and Helen Dortch Longstreet (image). [no date recorded] Retrieved from the Longstreet Society, Gainesville, Georgia.

Jorgensen, Jay, "Wofford Sweeps the Wheatfield," *The Gettysburg Magazine,* Issue 22 (2000).

Jubal Anderson Early (image; bust, facing left, in civilian clothes). [no date recorded; between 1870 and 1893] Photograph. Retrieved from the Library of Congress, https://www.loc.gov/item/2005692152/. (Accessed April 30, 2022).

Krick, Robert K., "'If Longstreet Says So … It Is Most Likely Not True': James Longstreet and the Second Day at Gettysburg," in *The Second Day at Gettysburg: Essays on Confederate and Union Leadership,* ed. Gary W. Gallagher (Kent, Ohio, and London, England: The Kent State University Press, 1993).

Ladd, David L, and Audrey J., eds., *The Bachelder Papers,* Vol. I, January 5, 1863, to July 27, 1880 (Dayton, Ohio: Morningside House Inc., 1994).

Ladd, David L., and Audrey J., eds., *The Bachelder Papers,* Vol. II, September 6, 1880, to April 12, 1886 (Dayton, Ohio: Morningside House Inc., 1994).

Ladd, David L., and Audrey J., eds., *The Bachelder Papers,* Vol. III, April 12, 1886, to December 22, 1894 (Dayton, Ohio: Morningside House Inc., 1995).

LaFantasie, Glenn W., ed., "William C. Oates Remembers Little Round Top," *The Gettysburg Magazine,* Issue 21 (1999).

Laney, Daniel M., "Wasted Gallantry: Hood's Texas Brigade at Gettysburg," *The Gettysburg Magazine,* Issue 16 (1997).

Lee, Robert E., *The Recollections and Letters of General Robert E. Lee (*New York: Konecky and Konecky, 1992).

Lee, Susan Pendleton, *Memoirs of William Nelson Pendleton, D.D.* (Philadelphia: J.B. Lippincott Company, 1893).

Longstreet, Helen D., *In The Path of Lee's "Old Warhorse,"* (Atlanta: A.B. Caldwell Publishing Co., 1917).

Longstreet, Helen D., *Lee and Longstreet at High Tide: Gettysburg in the Light of the Official Records* (Gainesville, Georgia: published by the author, 1904).

Longstreet, James, *From Manassas to Appomattox,* (J.B. Lippincott Company, 1895; republished Boston: Da Capo Press Inc., 1992).

"Longstreet's Widow Dies at Age of 99" (newspaper unknown). [May 1962, approximate date; exact date unknown].The Longstreet Society Collection, Piedmont Hotel, Gainesville, Georgia.

"Longstreet's Widow Still Fights For His Recognition," *Savannah Evening Press,* March 30, 1940, The Longstreet Society Collection, Piedmont Hotel, Gainesville, Georgia.

Manship, Paul, *Study for Longstreet Memorial,* 1940, bronze, Smithsonian American Art Museum, Bequest of Paul Manship, 1966.47.11A. Retrieved from https://americanart.si.edu/artwork/study-longstreet-memorial-15932.

McCabe, Jr., James D., *Life and Campaigns of General Robert E. Lee* (Atlanta, Georgia: National Publishing Company, 1870).

McLaws, Lafayette, "The Federal Disaster on the Left," *Philadelphia Weekly Press,* August 4, 1886.

McPherson, James M., *Battle Cry of Freedom: The Civil War Era* (New York: Ballantine Books, 1988).

Meier, Kathryn Shively, "Jubal A. Early: Model Civil War Sufferer," *J19: The Journal of Nineteenth-Century Americanists,* Volume 4, Number 1 (Spring 2016).

"Monument to the 3rd Brigade, 2nd Division, 3rd Corps at Gettysburg," Gettysburg National Military Park.

Gen. John B. Hood, C.S.A (image). [no date recorded] Retrieved from https://catalog.archives.gov/id/529378 (Accessed April 30, 2022).

Lt. Gen. Ambrose P. Hill(image; bust-length) [no date recorded]. Retrieved from https://catalog.archives.gov/id/530490 (Accessed April 30, 2022).

New Orleans Times, June 8, 1867, https://the reconstructionera.com/gen-longstreets-infamous-letter-on-joining-the-republicans-betraying-the-confederates-1867/.

Newsome, Hampton, "Gettysburg—Mahone's Night Attack, July 2, 1863." December 18, 2017, https://hamptonnewsome.blogspot.com/2017/12/gettysburg-mahones-night-attack-july-2.html.

Oates, William C., *The War Between the Union and the Confederacy and its Lost Opportunities with a History of the 15th Alabama Regiment and the Forty-Eight Battles in Which it was Engaged* (New York, and Washington, D.C.: Neale Publishing Company, 1905).

Oeffinger, John C., ed., *A Soldier's General: The Civil War Letters of Major General Lafayette McLaws* (Chapel Hill, and London: The University of North Carolina Press, 2002).

Pfanz, Harry W., *Gettysburg: Culp's Hill and Cemetery Hill* (Chapel Hill, and London: The University of North Carolina Press, 1993).

Pfanz, Harry W., *Gettysburg: The Second Day* (Chapel Hill, and London: The University of North Carolina Press, 1987).

Pfarr, Cory M., "James Longstreet and the Third Day: 'We Were Not Hunting for Any Fight,'" *Gettysburg Magazine,* Issue 62 (January 2020).

Pfarr, Cory M. (interview), "Longstreet at Gettysburg," Pennsylvania Cable Network, PA Books, April 3, 2019.

Pfarr, Cory M., *Longstreet at Gettysburg: A Critical Reassessment* (Jefferson, North Carolina, McFarland, 2019).

Pfarr, Cory M. (interview), "Reassessing James Longstreet at Gettysburg with Cory Pfarr," Keith Harris, The Rogue Historian Podcast, November 6, 2019.

Piston, William Garrett, *Lee's Tarnished Lieutenant: James Longstreet and His Place in Southern History* (, and London: The University of Georgia Press, 1987).

Piston, William Garrett, "Marked in Bronze: James Longstreet and Southern History," in *James Longstreet: The Man, the Soldier, the Controversy,* R.L. Dinardo and Albert A. Nofi, eds. (Boston: Da Capo Press Inc., 1998).

Portrait of Maj. Gen. Cadmus M. Wilcox, officer of the Confederate Army (image). [no date given; between 1860 and 1865] Photograph. Retrieved from the Library of Congress, https://www.loc.gov/item/2018666552/ (Accessed April 30, 2022).

Powell, David A., "Advance to Disaster: Sickles, Longstreet, and July 2nd, 1863," *The Gettysburg Magazine,* Issue 28 (2003).

Powell, David A., "A Reconnaissance Gone Awry: Capt. Samuel R. Johnston's Fateful Trip to Little Round Top," *The Gettysburg Magazine,* Issue 23 (2000).

Power, J. Tracy, "Jubal A. Early (1816–1894)," *Encyclopedia Virginia,* https://www.encyclopediavirginia.org/Early_Jubal_A_1816-1894.

Raver, K. Paul, "Deception and the Citizen-General: The Sickles Faction at Gettysburg," *The Gettysburg Magazine,* Issue 31 (2004).

Reardon, Carol, *The Gettysburg Campaign: June-July 1863,* The U.S. Army Campaigns of the Civil War, Center of Military History (U.S. Army: Washington, D.C., 2013).

Reardon, Carol, and Tom Vossler, *A Field Guide to Gettysburg,* Second Edition (Chapel Hill: The University of North Carolina Press, 2017).

"A Reconstructed Rebel," *Chicago Tribune,* June 10, 1867, 2, https://www.newspapers.com/image/465983800/.

Reuben Lindsay Walker, 1890. (image). [no date recorded on caption card] Photograph. Retrieved from the Library of Congress, https://www.loc.gov/item/2002712779/ (Accessed April 30, 2022).

Rickard, J. (February 10, 2007), Richard Heron Anderson, 1821–1879 (February 10, 2007), http://www.historyofwar.org/articles/people_anderson_rh.html.

Robertson, William Glenn, "Daniel E. Sickles and the Third Corps," in *The Second Day at Gettysburg: Essays on Confederate and Union Leadership,* Gary W. Gallagher, ed. (Kent, Ohio, and London, England: The Kent State University Press, 1993).

Robertson, Jr., James I., *General A.P. Hill: The Story of a Confederate Warrior* (New York: Vintage Books, 1987).

Ross, Fitzgerald, *A Visit to the Cities and Camps of the Confederate States* (Edinburgh and London: William Blackwood and Sons, 1865).

Sauers, Richard A., *Gettysburg: The Meade-Sickles Controversy* (Washington, D.C.: Potomac Books, Inc., 2003).

Scheibert, Captain Justus, *Seven Months in the Rebel States During the North American War, 1863,* W. Stanley Hoole, ed. (Tuscaloosa: The University of Alabama Press, 2009).

Schultz, David L., and Scott L. Mingus, Sr., *The Second Day at Gettysburg: The Attack and Defense of Cemetery Ridge, July 2, 1863* (El Dorado Hills, California: Savas Beatie, 2015, 2016).

Scott, Robert Nicholson, ed., *The War of the Rebellion: A Compilation of the Official Records of the Union and Confederate Armies,* 128 vols. (Washington, D.C. 1880–1901), Series 1, Vol. 27, Pt. 1.

Scott, Robert Nicholson, ed., *The War of the Rebellion: A Compilation of the Official Records of the Union and Confederate Armies,* 128 vols. (Washington, D.C. 1880–1901), Series 1, Vol. 27, Pt. 2.

Scott, Robert Nicholson, ed., *The War of the Rebellion: A Compilation of the Official Records of the Union and Confederate Armies,* 128 vols. (Washington, D.C. 1880–1901), Series 1, Vol. 27, Pt. 3.

Sears, Stephen W., *Gettysburg* (Boston, New York: Houghton Mifflin Company, 2003).

Smith, Karlton D., "'To Consider Every Contingency': Lt. Gen. James Longstreet, Capt. Samuel R. Johnston, and the Factors that Affected the Reconnaissance and Countermarch, July 2,

1863," http://npshistory.com/series/symposia/gettysburg_seminars/11/essay4.pdf.

Sorrel, Gilbert Moxley, *At the Right Hand of Longstreet: Recollections of a Confederate Staff Officer* (Lincoln and London: University of Nebraska Press, 1999).

Starnes, Richard D., "Forever Faithful: The Southern Historical Society and the Confederate Historical Memory," *Southern Cultures* 2, no. 2 (Winter 1996).

Swinton, William, *Campaigns of the Army of the Potomac: A Critical History of Operations in Virginia, Maryland and Pennsylvania, from the Commencement to the Close of the War, 1861-1865* (New York: Charles Scribner's Sons, 1882).

Thornton, Clark T., *General James Longstreet: A Family Portrait* (Scotts Valley, California: CreateSpace Independent Publishing Platform, 2011).

Trudeau, Noah A., *Gettysburg: A Testing of Courage* (New York: HarperCollins, 2002).

Tucker, Glenn, *High Tide at Gettysburg: The Campaign in Pennsylvania* (Gettysburg, Pennsylvania: Stan Clark Military Books, 1958, reprint 1995).

Tucker, Glenn, *Lee and Longstreet at Gettysburg* (Dayton, Ohio: Morningside Bookshop, 1982).

Tucker, Glenn, "Longstreet: Culprit or Scapegoat?" *Civil War Times Illustrated*, Volume 1, 1962-1963.

"Veteran's Wife Fights Thief," *The Gainesville Times* (Gainesville, Georgia: The Longstreet Society Collection, Piedmont Hotel, exact date unknown).

Wakelyn, Jon L., *Biographical Dictionary of the Confederacy* (Santa Barbara, California: Greenwood Press, 1977).

Wert, Jeffry D., *General James Longstreet: The Confederacy's Most Controversial Soldier* (New York: Touchstone, 1993).

Wert, Jeffry D., "No Fifteen Thousand Men Can Take That Position," in *James Longstreet: The Man, the Soldier, the Controversy*, R.L. Dinardo and Albert A. Nofi, eds. (Boston: Da Capo Press Inc., 1998).

"Widow Will Oppose Tallmadge!" (The Longstreet Society Collection, Piedmont Hotel, Gainesville, Georgia: exact date unknown).

Wikimedia Commons, *Bust Portrait of William Nelson Pendleton* (image), https://commons.wikimedia.org/wiki/File:Bust_portrait_of_William_Nelson_Pendleton.png#/media/File:Bust_portrait_of_William_Nelson_Pendleton.png (Accessed April 30, 2022).

Wikimedia Commons, *Gen. Evander Law and staff, circa 1862* (image), https://commons.wikimedia.org/wiki/File:Gen._Evander_Law_and_staff,_circa_1862.jpg#/media/File:Gen._Evander_Law_and_staff,_circa_1862.jpg (Accessed April 30, 2022).

Wikimedia Commons, *John William Jones DD* (image), https://commons.wikimedia.org/wiki/File:John_William_Jones_DD.jpg#/media/File:John_William_Jones_DD.jpg. (Accessed April 30, 2022).

Wikimedia Commons, *Lafayette McLaws, seated* (image), https://commons.wikimedia.org/wiki/File:Lafayette_McLaws,_seated.jpg#/media/File:Lafayette_McLaws,_seated.jpg (Accessed April 30, 2022).

Wikimedia Commons, *Lieutenant General Richard Heron Anderson* (image), https://commons.wikimedia.org/wiki/File:Lieutenant_General_Richard_Heron_Anderson.jpg#/media/File:Lieutenant_General_Richard_Heron_Anderson.jpg (Accessed April 30, 2022).

Wikimedia Commons, *Portrait of William C. Oates* (image), https://commons.wikimedia.org/wiki/File:Portrait_of_William_C._Oates.jpg#/media/File:Portrait_of_William_C._Oates.jpg (Accessed April 30, 2022).

William J. Hardee, Lieut. General (image). [no date; between 1861 and 1865, printed later] Photograph. Retrieved from the Library of Congress, https://www.loc.gov/item/00652519/ (Accessed April 30, 2022).

Williams, David S., "J. William Jones (1836-1909)," *New Georgia Encyclopedia*, https://www.georgiaencyclopedia.org/articles/history-archaeology/j-william-jones-1836-1909.

Wright, Catherine M., "Lee Chapel," *Encyclopedia Virginia*, https://www.encyclopediavirginia.org/Lee_Chapel.

Index

Numbers in **_bold italics_** indicate pages with illustrations

Adam Butt Farm (and Schoolhouse) **_87_**, 98–**_99_**, 110
Alexander, Edward Porter (E.P.) 11, 20–21, 71, 78, 117, 143, 192e6n42; on controversy over R.H. Anderson's July 2 attack 188–189e5n8, 190e5n18; on effect of extension of Federal line on July 2 to Devil's Den 44, 46; on effect of Federal's July 2 reinforcement of Union left 34, 47–48; on Ewell's July 2 shortcomings 33; July 2 reconnaissance activities 83–**_87_**, 88–91, 174e1n22; on Longstreet's July 2 march and countermarch 102–103, 106, 186e3n31, 186e4n13; on Sickles' move 41, 178e2n42
altering of primary sources 6, 79–80, 93
Anderson, George T. (G.T.) 49, **_53_**, **_56_**–57, **_62_**, 111, 183e2n70, 184e2n76
Anderson, Richard H. 3, **_35_**, **_45_**, 47, 58, 60, **_99_**, 105, 117, **_124_**, 128–131, 138, 152–153, 174e1n22, 188e5n2, 188e5n7, 189–190e5n14, 190e5n17; controversy over partial support to Longstreet's July 2 attack 33, 61–62, 125–127, 132–137, 158, 188–189e5n8, 190e5n18; military career in leadup to Gettysburg 121–**_122_**, 123; orders to support July 2 attack 98, 129–130; post-Gettysburg career 137, 190e5n23
Appomattox 21–22, 137, 159–161, 171, 174e1n23
"armchair general" (mode of argument) 5, 63, 67, 77–78, 82, 92, **_95_**, 106–108, 114, 118
Association of the Army of Northern Virginia 24
Ayres, Romeyn 60–**_62_**

Bachelder, John 18, 55, 86, 96, 98, **_111_**, 115, 174e1n19, 178e2n36, 180e2n59, 182–183e2n66, 183e2n68, 189e5n11

Barksdale, William 48, 55–**_56_**, 57, **_58–59_**, 60–**_62_**, 63, **_124_**–125, 158, 179e2n47, 184e2n79, 193e6n60; his brigade's July 2 performance 48, 60, 184e2n80
Benning, Henry 46, 49, 52–**_53_**, **_62_**, 111, 180e2n59, 181e2n61, 183e2n69
Berdan, Hiram 83, 86
Biesecker's Woods **_35_**, **_53_**, 83, 116
Big Round Top (Round Top) **_35–36_**, **_43_**, **_45_**, 49–**_53_**, 54–55, 65, 83, **_87_**, **_99_**, 158, 181e2n61, 182e2n64, 182e2n65, 182e2n66, 183e2n67
Bigelow, John 48, 184e2n77
Birney, David B. **_35_**, **_56_**, 64–65, **_124_**, 175e2n8, 176e2n9, 177e2n28, 178e2n43
Black, John L. 71, 86–**_87_**, 88–91, 189e5n11
Black Horse Tavern 73, 78, 86–**_87_**, 98–**_99_**, **_100–101_**, 102–107, 112–113, 118–119, 151, 186e4n31, 187e4n28
Bliss Farm **_56_**, **_124_**, 126
Bream's Hill **_87_**, **_99–102_**
Buford, John 30, 75, 86
Bulger, Michael 53
Burling, George 176e2n9, 177e2n27, 177e2n28, 184e2n80
Bushman Farm **_35_**, **_53_**, 55, **_99_**, 182e2n65

Caldwell, John C. **_35_**, **_56_**, 60–61, 184e2n76, 184e2n79
Cemetery Hill 18, 37, **_43_**, **_45_**, 49, 65, 80–81, 85, **_87_**–88, 90, **_99_**, 103, 154, 174e1n19, 174e1n20; as main objective of Longstreet's July 2 attack 38–40, 42, 63, 98, 152–153
Cemetery Ridge 2, 12, 18, 29, 31, 34, 37–38, 40–**_43_**, **_45_**, 48, **_56_**, 60–65, 84, **_87_**, **_99_**, 103, **_126_**, 175e2n6, 175e2n8, 176e2n9, 176e2n12, 178e2n31, 178–179e2n43, 179e2n44, 181e2n61, 184e2n79, 188e5n7
Chancellorsville, battle of 9, 71, 123, 131, 178e2n42, 188e5n3

Clarke, John J. 71–73, 86–**_87_**, 88, 90–91
Coddington, Edwin 49, 79, 81–82, 90–91, 113–116, 147, 182e2n64
Codori Farm **_35_**, **_43_**, **_45_**, **_56_**, **_87_**, **_99_**, **_124_**–125
Copse of Trees **_35_**, **_56_**, **_124–126_**
Comte de Paris 8, 15
Culp's Hill 18–19, 30, **_43_**, **_45_**, **_87_**, **_99_**, 103, 180e2n54

Davis, Jefferson 14, 23, 108, 162
De Trobriand, Philippe R. **_35_**, 61, 176e2n9, 177e2n27, 184e2n80
Devil's Den **_35–36_**, 42–**_43_**, **_45_**, 52–**_53_**, 60–**_62_**, 69, **_87_**, 92, **_99_**, 166, 177e2n28, 181e2n61, 181e2n63, 182e2n64, 182e2n65; as initial location of Federal main line's extreme left during July 2 attack and its effects 44, 47, 49–50, 65, 178e2n43, 179e2n47
Dowdey, Clifford 79–81, 90–91, 115, 129–131, 135, 146, 181e2n64

Early, Jubal 24, **_45_**, **_99_**, 141, 143; anti-Longstreet group member 1, 3, 8, 13, **_21_**, 28, 161; Gettysburg performance 18–19, **_20_**; immediate postwar actions 19–20; relief from command 19, 21, 174e1n21; "Sunrise Attack" theory proponent 149, 163
East Cemetery Hill 19–**_20_**
Emmitsburg Road Ridge 44, 107
Ewell, Richard 8, 16, 39, **_43_**, **_45_**, 76–77, 80–82, 88, 98, 123, 143, 150, 152, 154, 178e2n43, 192e6n39; July 2 orders 18, 32–33, 158; lack of support to Longstreet's July 2 attack 19, 32–33, 158; Lee's plan to move his corps to the Confederate right 18, 151, 180e2n56

Fairfax, John W. 149, 157–158
Fairfield Road **_43_**, **_45_**, 83,

86–87, 99, 100, *102*, 103, *110*–111, 187e4n27
Foote, Shelby 78–79, 113–114, 130–132, 135
Freeman, Douglas Southall 79–81, 113–114, 144, 181e2n61, 191e6n12
Fremantle, Arthur J. L. 44, 126–127
From Manassas to Appomattox (Longstreet's memoirs) 11, 31–33, 36–37, 53, 75, 98, 111, 127–128, 137, 140–142, 149, 164–165, 170–171
"future history" (historians' treatment of Longstreet's Gettysburg performance) 5, 17, 164, 191e6n12, 192–193e6n52

Geary, John 29, 175e2n8
Gibbon, John 35, *56*, *124*–125, 176e2n12, 183e2n72
Gordon, John B. 7, 19, 145, *147*, 174e1n20, 174e1n21, 192e6n35; anti-Longstreet group member 22, 191e6n19; *Reminiscences of the Civil War* 143, 146–150, 152–163, 168
Graham, Charles 35, *56*, 61, *124*, 184e2n80
Gramm, Kent 179e2n44
Greene, George 33, 180e2n54
Guelzo, Allen 79–80, 91, 135–136, 147, 176e2n12, 182e2n64

Hall, Norman 48, *56*, *124*–125
Hall, Samuel E., Dr. (residence) *87*, 98–*99*, 103
Hancock, Winfield Scott 30, 37, *45*, *56*, 60, *99*, *124*, 176e2n12, 177e2n13, 184e2n79
Hardee, William 94, 108–*109*, 119
Harrow, William 48, *56*, *124*
Herr's Ridge Road 98, 103, 110
Herr's Tavern *87*, 98–*99*, 103, 105
Hessler, James 1–4, 30, 175e2n8, 177e2n14, 177e2n17, 178e2n31, 184e2n80, 187e4n28, 191e6n15
Heth, Harry 95, 125, 148
Hill, Ambrose Power (A.P.) 40, *43*, *45*, 61, 71, 85, *99*, 105, 121, 123, *124*–125, *130*, 135, 137–138, 161; July 2 orders 33, 131, 189e5n14; lack of support to Longstreet's July 2 attack 32–33, 131–132, 158, 188–189e5n8
hindsight (mode of argument) 66–67, 78–80, 88, 92, 107–108, 114, 179e2n44
Hood, John Bell 3, 32, 38–40, 42–*43*, *45*, 47–48, *50*, 57, 66, 72, 76, 82, 89, 94, 96–*99*, 103, 106–*110*, 117–121, 123, 125, 128, 131, 148–149, 152, 154–158, 163, 178e2n36, 179e2n47, 180e2n56, 180e2n59, 187e4n27, 189e5n14; allegations he moved in front of McLaws during Longstreet's July 2 march 111–116, 119,

187e4n36; "digression" during initial stages of July 2 attack 49–51, *53*, 65, 181–182e2n64, 183e2n68, 183e2n72; misleading assertions on Hood's July 2 orders 49–50, 180–181e2n61; thinning of his division during July 2 attack 34, 36, 44–46, 65; wounding 49, 52, *55*, 178e2n29
Horsey, Fred 71, 86–*87*, 88, 90–91
Houck's Ridge 30, 34, *35*–*36*, 41–42, 44, 46–47, 49, 52–*53*, *56*, 61, *62*–*63*, 65, *124*, 176e2n12, 177e2n13, 180e2n59
Humphreys, Andrew *35*, *56*, 60, 65, *124*–125, 176e2n9, 177e2n27, 177e2n28, 184e2n79
Hunt, Henry 29, 176e2n12, 177e2n13, 178e2n31

Jackson, Thomas "Stonewall" 9, 23, 123, 161, 170, 186e4n6
Johnston, Samuel 83, 86–*87*, 102–104, 174e1n22, 185e3n24, 192e6n26; background 71; concealed route reconnaissance 73–82, *87*, 93, 96–97, 151, 185e3n8; conducting Longstreet's initial march 97–99, 185e3n10; early morning reconnaissance 42, 71–73, *87*, 88, 90–91
Joint Congressional Committee on the Conduct of the War 29, 175e2n5, 175e2n8
Jones, John William 2, 7–*8*, 9–15, 18, 22–26, 149, 161

Kershaw, Joseph 34, 52–*53*, 115, 158, 179e2n47, 183e2n68, 183e2n70, 183e2n71, 184e2n76, 187e4n28, 189e5n11; his brigade's July 2 attack 55–*56*, 57, *58*–*59*, 60, *62*–*63*; initial July 2 orders 116–117, 119; recollections of Longstreet's July 2 march and countermarch 96, 98, 101, 103–105, 111–112, 118–119, 186e4n8, 187e4n36
Klingle Farm *35*, *56*, *58*–*59*, 84, *87*, *99*, *124*
Krick, Robert 68, 82, 102–103, 168–170, 186e4n6

Ladies' Lee Monument Association 24
Lang, David 48, *56*, 62, 98, *124*–125, 132–134, 136, 155, 158, 184e2n79, 188e5n3, 188–189e5n7
Law, Evander 36, 39, 42, 46, 49, *51*, 52–53, 76–81, 81–82, 88, 93, 96, 98, 111, 115, 118–119, 152, 155, 157, 178e2n29, 178e2n36, 180e2n56, 180–181e2n61, 181e2n63, 182e2n65, 182–183e2n66, 183e2n68, 183e2n69, 183e2n71, 183e2n72, 187e4n36; his brigade's rightward shift during July 2 attack 46–47,

49–50, 53, *54*–*55*, 61, 63, 65, 180e2n59, 181–182e2n64; his Round Tops' "valley" orders for Oates 50–51, *53*, *181e2n62*, 181–182e2n64
Lee, Fitzhugh 8, 16, 18, 23–24, 42, 143, 145, 157
"Lee in Pennsylvania" (Longstreet postwar article) 13, 15, 32, 103, 105, 112, 152
"Lee intended" (mode of argument) 14, 152, 171
Lee-Longstreet relationship 160–161
Lee Memorial Association 22, 24
"Lee Memorial Volume" project 23–24
Lee Monument Association 24
Lee worship (postwar) 7, 9, 22–*25*, 26, 141–142, 144, 162–163
"Lee's Right Wing at Gettysburg" (Longstreet postwar article) 15, 103, 111, 128, 170
Little Round Top 2, 27, 29–30, 34–*35*, *36*, 37–40, 42–*43*, *45*, 46–47, 49–51, *53*, *62*, *63*, 64–65, 71, *87*–88, *99*, 146, 148, 157, 175e2n7, 175e2n8, 176e2n9, 176e2n12, 177e2n28, 178e2n38, 178e2n43, 179e2n44, 180e2n57, 181e2n62, 181e2n64, 182e2n66, 183e2n67; Federal signal station on and its effect 73, 85, 89, 96, *99*, 102–105, 107, 113, 118, 151; "the gorge at" 60–62, 63; misleading assertions concerning 38–39, 49–50, 152–153, 180–181e2n61
Long, Armistead Lindsay (A.L.) 14, 71, *81*, 83–85, *87*, 89–90, 149, 185e3n24
Longstreet, Helen 64, 168–171, 193e6n60; brief biography 139–141; early advocate Peach Orchard was first objective of Longstreet's July 2 attack 152–153; *Lee and Longstreet at High Tide* 3, 5, 28, 141–164, 167–168, 171; relationship with James Longstreet 140–141, 164–*167*
Longstreet-Lee relationship *see* Lee-Longstreet relationship

Mahone, William 62, 98, *124*–128, 132–136, 158; "night attack" argument 188e5n7; "reserve brigade" argument 188–189e5n8
Mark Forney Farm *87*, 98–*99*, 110
Marshall, Charles 14, 23–24, 149, 151
Marshall, J. Wilson 71, 86–*87*, 88, 90–91
McCabe, James, Jr. 12
McGilvery, Freeman 48
McLaws, Lafayette 3, 32, 34–*35*, 37–38, 41–*43*, 44–*45*, 46–48, 52–*53*, 55–*56*, 57, *58*–*59*, 60–*62*,

Index

66, **68**, 71–80, 82, 89–91, 94, 111–121, 123–**124**, 125, 128–129, 131–133, 137, 148–149, 151, 154–156, 158, 178e2n36, 179e2n45, 179e2n47, 180e2n56, 180e2n59, 180e2n61, 183e2n68, 183e2n70, 183e2n71, 184e2n73, 189e5n11, 189e5n14; during Longstreet's July 2 march and countermarch 96–**99**, **100–102**, 103–**110**, 111, 119, 185e3n10, 186e4n8, 187e4n20, 187e4n27, 187e4n36; on Johnston's concealed route reconaissance 73–82, 96–97, 118, 151, 192e6n26; July 2 "force of circumstances" 92–93; morning of July 2 meeting with Lee and Longstreet 40–42, 72–73, 79–80, 96, 107; post-battle letter to wife 67–70, 91; thoughts on Sickles' move 37–38, 46, 179e2n50
McPherson, James M. 78–79, 180e2n61
Meade, George G. 12, 37, 41, 178e2n33, 179e2n44, 183e2n72; predominant focus on Federal right in leadup to Longstreet's July 2 attack 104–105, 176e2n10; shifting Federal troops during Longstreet's July 2 attack 32–33, 47, 60, 65; and Sickles Controversy 29–30, 175e2n5, 175e2n8, 176e2n10, 176e2n11, 176e2n12, 177e2n14, 177e2n17, 177e2n23, 180e2n54
Millerstown Road **58–59**, 84, 111–112, 114
"The Mistakes of Gettysburg" (Longstreet postwar article) 15, 34
Montcure, Thomas Jefferson 72–74, 79

Oates, William **52**, 96, 115, 119; on Big Round Top as the key position 51, 183e2n67; disregard of orders during July 2 attack 50–53, 65, 181e2n62, 181–182e2n64, 182e2n65, 182–183e2n66
Old Mill Road 98, 103, 110

Peach Orchard 29–32, 34–**35**, 36–39, 41–**43**, 44–**45**, 47–49, 55–**56**, 57, **59**, 60–61, 63–64, 69–70, 83, 86–**87**, **99**, 103, 107, 115, 175e2n7, 176–177e2n13, 177e2n14, 177e2n17, 177e2n27, 177e2n28, 178e2n43, 179e2n44, 184e2n80, 193e6n60; as first objective of Longstreet's July 2 attack 38, 41, 48, 53, 146, 152–153, 191e6n15
Pender, William Dorsey **99**, 125–126, 132, 148, 154–156, 189e5n8
Pendleton, William **14**, 110–111, 117, 171, 174e1n23; anti-Longstreet group member 1, 13, 24, 28, 141, 145–146, 161, 163, 193e6n52; Gettysburg performance 20–21; July 2 reconnaissance efforts 71, 75–76, 83–**87**, 88–91, 93, 185e3n24; postwar devotion to Lee 22–24; "Sunrise Attack" theory proponent 13–16, 22, 24, 143, 149–153, 163, 168, 174e1n22
Perry, Edward 62, 125, 128, 133, 155, 158, 188e5n3, 189e5n8
Perry, Leslie J. 142, 147, 149, 163, 170, 191e6n10
Pitzer's Schoolhouse 39, 65, **87**, **99**, 107, 110–111, 115–117, 119, 125
Pitzer's Woods 30, **35**, **58**, 82–84, 86, 116, 125, 193e6n60
Pfanz, Harry 42, 48, 79, 82, 86, 91, 114–115
Pickett, George 21, 46, 61, 81–82, 123, 135–137, 148, 154–156, 159, 189e5n14; absence from Longstreet's July 2 attack and its effect 37–38, 72–73, 77, 125, 152, 180e2n53, 180e2n56
Pickett-Pettigrew-Trimble Charge 9, 18, 20, 46, 155, 158
Plum Run Valley 49, 177e2n28, 180e2n60
Posey, Carnot 62, 98, **124**–128, 132–136, 158, 188e5n7; "reserve brigade" argument 188–189e5n8

Ramseur, Stephen 174e1n20
Reardon, Carol 181e2n61
Red Oak Lane 98, 110
Robertson, Jerome 42, 49, 52–**53**, 180e2n59, 180e2n61, 182e2n64, 183e2n69
Robertson, William Glenn 179e2n44, 184e2n74
Rodes, Robert **99**, 174e1n20
Rose Woods **35–36**, **53**, 55, **56–57**, 60, **62**, **124**
Ross, Fitzgerald 41

Sauers, Richard 176e2n9, 177e2n17
Scheibert, Justus 44
Sears, Stephen 79–80, 91, 106, 147, 180e2n61, 182e2n64, 184e2n74
2nd U.S. Sharpshooters **35**, 51–**53**, **54**, 63, 65
Sedgwick, John 33, **45**, **62**, 123; and the Federal Sixth Corps 64, 104, 156, 176e2n11
Semmes, Paul **53**, 56–57, **58–59**, 60, **62–63**, 184e2n76
Shannon, S.D. 134
Sickles, Daniel 2, 4, **31**, 32–**35**, 36–**45**, 46–49, 57, 60–61, 63–65, 75, 77, **99**, 104, 152, 178e2n33, 178e2n42, 179e2n50, 180e2n61, 181e2n61, 184e2n80; controversy surrounding his Gettysburg performance 2, 29–31, 63–64, 175e2n5, 175e2n6, 175e2n8, 176e2n9, 176e2n10, 176e2n12, 176–177e2n13, 177e2n14, 177e2n16, 177e2n17, 183e2n72; his July 2 move's effect on Longstreet's attack 2, 40–65, 69–70, 92, 178e2n31, 178–179e2n43, 179e2n44, 180e2n57, 184e2n74; Longstreet's thoughts on Sickles' July 2 move 30–38, 64; postwar relationship with Longstreet 2, 27–**31**
Slocum, Henry 27, **45**, **99**, 104–105, 176e2n10
Slyder Farm (and Lane) **35–36**, **53–54**, 182e2n65
Smith, James E. (battery) 34, **36**, 50, **53**, 181e2n63
Smith, James Power 143
Smith, William P. 71, 75, **87**, 174e1n22
Sorrel, Gilbert Moxley 11, 70, 96, 103, 113, 131, 192e6n35
Southern Historical Society (& *Papers*) 2, 4, 7–8, 15–16, 23, 96, 145, 149, 182e2n66, 186e4n12, 190e5n17
Spangler's Woods **58**, 85
Stony Hill **35**, **53**, **56**, 60, **62**, **124**, 177e2n28
Stoughton, Homer 51, 182e2n65, 182e2n66
Stuart, James Ewell Brown (J.E.B.) 19, 71, 77–78, 143, 161, 180e2n56
"Sunrise Attack" theory 2, 13–14, 22, 24, 29, 143–144, 149–150, 153, 163, 168
Sweitzer, Jacob 61
Swinton, William 2, 9–13, 15–18, 25–26, 161
Sykes, George **45**, 60–**62**, **99**; and the Federal Fifth Corps 33, 44, 63–64, 104, 176e2n10, 179e2n44

tactical suggestions (Longstreet to Lee) 8, 11–13, 77–78, 138, 163–164
Taylor, Walter 8, 14, 24, 143, 149
Tilton, William 61
Tremain, Henry E. 60, 175e2n6, 175e2n8
Trostle Farm (and Woods) **56**, **59**, **62–63**, **87**, **99**, **124**, 177e2n28
Trudeau, Noah 78, 147
Tucker, Glenn 48, 90–91, 106, 113–114, 146–147, 175e2n4, 178e2n43, 179e2n44, 187e4n36; on Johnston's concealed route reconaissance 76, 78–79

United Confederate Veterans 23, 191e6n19

Venable, Charles 14, 32, 74, 149, 151
Vincent, Strong 47, **53**
Virginia Division 24

Walker, R. Lindsay 71, 83–**84**, 85, **87**, 91, 151, 185e3n24
Ward, John Henry Hobart 34–

35, *36*, 49, *53*, 61, 177*e*2*n*27, 177*e*2*n*28, 184*e*2*n*80
Warfield Ridge 32, *55*, 70, 81, 85–86, 98, 107, 110, 115, 119, 156
Warren, Gouverneur K. 30
Webb, Alexander *56*, *124*–125
Weikert's Woods *59*, *63*
Wentz Farm *35*, *56*, 84, *124*
Wert, Jeffry 76–77, 79, 88–89, 181*e*2*n*61
Wheatfield *35*, *43*, *45*, *53*, 55–*56*, 60, *62*–*63*, *87*, *99*, *124*, 177*e*2*n*28, 184*e*2*n*76
Wheatfield Road 46, 48–49, *56*–57, 60, *62*–*63*, 65, *124*, 179*e*2*n*47, 184*e*2*n*77
Wilcox, Cadmus 30, 48, *56*, *58*, 62, 71, 83–84, 86–*87*, 90, 98, 105–106, *124*–125, 128, 132–*133*, 155, 158, 185*e*2*n*79, 188*e*5*n*7, 188–189*e*5*n*8, 189*e*5*n*11, 190*e*5*n*17, 190*e*5*n*18; anti-Longstreet group member 15–16, 105; thoughts on R.H. Anderson's July 2 performance 134–135
Willard, George 48, *56*, *124*
Williams, Seth 176*e*2*n*11
Willoughby Run *43*, *45*, 83, *87*, 90, *99*, 103, 107, *110*, 111–*112*, 114, 119, 187*e*4*n*27
Wofford, William 55–*56*, 57, *58*–*59*, *61*, 158, 189*e*5*n*11; line of attack during Longstreet's July 2 assault 60–61, *62*, 63
Wright, Ambrose *56*, 62, 98, *127*–128, 132–134, 158, 188*e*5*n*7, 189*e*5*n*8; his brigade's July 2 attack *124*–*126*, 127; thoughts on R.H. Anderson's July 2 performance 134, 136–137

Youngblood, William 17